Russian Industrialists in an Era of Revolution

Russian Industrialists in an Era of Revolution

The Association of Industry and Trade, 1906–1917

Ruth AmEnde Roosa

Edited by
Thomas C. Owen

M.E. Sharpe
Armonk, New York
London, England

Library of Congress Cataloging-in-Publication Data

Roosa, Ruth A. (AmEnde)
Russian industrialists in an era of revolution: The Association of Industry and Trade, 1906–1917 / by Ruth AmEnde Roosa: edited with a foreword by Thomas C. Owen
p. cm.
Includes bibliographical references and index.
ISBN 0-7656-0154-0 (alk. paper)
1. Russia—Economic conditions—1861–1917. 2. Russia—Economic policy. 3. Industries—Russia. 4. Sovi͡et s''i͡ezdov predstavitelei̐ promyshlennosti i torgovli (Petrograd, R.S.F.S.R.) 5. Capitalists and financiers—Russia. I. Owen, Thomas C. II. Title.
HC334.5.R62 1997
338.0947—dc21 97-8403
CIP
Printed in the United States of America

The paper used in this publication meets the minimum requirements of American National Standard for Information Sciences—Permanence of Paper for Printed Library Materials, ANSI Z 39.48-1984.

∞

BM (c) 10 9 8 7 6 5 4 3 2 1

Contents

Editor's Foreword

Until recently, the autocratic tradition in Russia and the Soviet Union appeared to foreclose any movement toward liberal democracy, free markets, and the rule of law. The title of Alan Ball's fine study, Russia's Last Capitalists (1987), made this assumption explicit. The New Economic Policy, 1921-28, represented the Soviet government's final accommodation with the free market. Even under perestroika, which began in 1985, the Soviet leadership sought to maintain the main features of the economic system that had emerged from the great debate over economic policy in the mid-1920s: five-year plans, the emphasis on military production, strict limits on private entrepreneurship, the preference for large units of production, and paternalistic control over working conditions.

In the wake of the collapse of the Soviet Union, evolution toward capitalism on the western model appears possible. Boris Yeltsin, the first democratically elected leader in Russian history, committed his government to the introduction of capitalist institutions. Although some Americans in the early 1990s looked hopefully toward a glorious future for Russian capitalism in the aftermath of centuries of bureaucratic tyranny, economic history suggested that it might be unwise to abandon the notion of institutional continuity. Indeed, the removal of Egor Gaidar, Yeltsin's most reformist policy maker, after less than a year in office, and the erratic course of economic reform in the past several years serve to remind us that many of the same geographical, ethnic, and cultural patterns that underlay the tsarist autocracy and made Marxism-Leninism possible in Russia from 1917 to the end of the 1980s persist today. Despite its rich endowment of natural resources, the victory of liberal democracy, corporate capitalism, and the rule of law is by no means assured, and Russia remains a huge country at the periphery of the European cultural and economic system.

Economic historians have sought to make sense of the great paradox of the Russian economy on the eve of World War I: the contrast between impressive rates of growth, in absolute terms, of such indicators as iron and coal production, length of the rail network, and grain exports, and stubbornly low per-capita indices for precisely these same indicators in comparison to those of European countries on the eve of World War I.[1] What Valentine Bill called "the forgotten class" in 1959 has finally attracted the attention of social historians.[2] Several representative institutions of business interests, known in the United States as "trade associations," have been the subject of books, articles, and dissertations that attempted to explain the structural weaknesses of Russian capitalism.[3]

All in all, however, our understanding of capitalist institutions and their leaders remains rudimentary, especially in comparison with other aspects of Russian history. The multiple biographies of radical thinkers of the mid-nineteenth century, like Nikolai G. Chernyshevskii and Petr N. Tkachev, whose main significance lay in their elaboration of ideas eventually utilized by Lenin, testify to the high level of scholarship, in both qualitative and quantitative terms, in Russian intellectual history. Recent studies of the history of late imperial Russia have illuminated aspects of the great drama of economic and social change, particularly the cultural traditions that imparted to the revolution of 1917 its peculiarly chaotic and brutal character. Labor history has revealed the great variety of subgroups within the factory work force under the last tsar, the different economic and political aspirations of these groups, and the complexity of their interactions with radical political parties. Likewise, peasant life has received attention from scholars sensitive to variations according to region, ethnicity, and gender. The political activities of the landed gentry have interested researchers intent on explaining the influence of a declining social class in the era of industrialization.

In contrast, the careers of the most influential spokesmen for Russian capitalism in the early twentieth century, such as Nikolai S. Avdakov, Vladislav V. Zhukovskii (Władysław Żukowski), and Adolf A. Volskii (Wolski), are familiar only to a handful of specialists. No one has explained which features of the late imperial economy represented successful transplantations of essentially European institutions to Russian soil and which demonstrated the persistence of unique traditions into the twentieth century. Any comprehensive analysis of Russian capitalism in the immediate future must proceed from an understanding of the functioning of capitalist institutions in the late Russian Empire. Given the enormous political and military implications of this issue, the essence of

Russian capitalism--past, present, and future--therefore constitutes an intellectual puzzle of immense complexity and significance.

Some recent studies have delineated the outlines of Russian capitalism under Gorbachev and Yeltsin, but these works make little or no reference to historical context. To the historian, the new institutions have both a familiar and an ominous appearance. Under the last emperor, Russian capitalist institutions--corporations, stock exchanges, and trade associations--remained weakly developed, geographically concentrated in a handful of large cities, essentially foreign in terms of their legal stature and the ethnicity of their personnel, and resented by major groups in Russian society, from peasants and workers to nationalistic journalists, bureaucrats, and anti-Semites. Such generalizations apply to Russian capitalism now.

Fortunately, we now have a major scholarly analysis of the most important business organization in imperial Russia: the Association of Industry and Trade. Ruth AmEnde Roosa, a student of Geroid T. Robinson at Columbia University, completed her doctoral dissertation on this association in 1967. In the past three decades, she published a variety of pioneering articles on the Association. All recent histories of the Russian Revolution that raised the issue of the political activities of businessmen in the great upheaval have relied on Ruth Roosa's articles on the economic program of the Association and its stand on the labor question. Several other scholars have occasionally investigated aspects of the Association's activities, but no comprehensive study has yet appeared. Carl Goldberg's dissertation, completed in 1974, remains unpublished, and the manuscript of a monograph written by one of the Association's staff members has apparently disappeared.[4]

Ruth Roosa's book on the Association has all the characteristics of a solid case study. It focuses on a single organization, the nerve center of Russian capitalism in the dozen years between the revolutions of 1905 and 1917. The product of many years' work in libraries in New York, Washington, London, Helsinki, Leningrad, and Moscow, it draws also on the author's meetings and discussions with former representatives of Russian business who left the country after the revolution and with colleagues in the United States, Europe, and the Soviet Union. The book examines in exhaustive detail the most weighty policy issues that faced Russian businessmen and bureaucrats in this crucial period. It is based primarily on the voluminous publications of the Association, including its newspaper and the proceedings of its congresses. It presents a new interpretation of the classic dilemmas of economic backwardness that received theoretical formulations by Marxist and liberal economists of the late imperial period, by Soviet historians, and by the American economic historians Alexander Gerschenkron and Theodore H. Von Laue. The book's uniqueness lies in the ways that it examines entrepreneurial activity and economic development in a crucial period not otherwise covered in detail from primary sources. The Russian archivist Yuri Afanasiev, rector of the Russian archives school, when asked what archives would be most important for new research in understanding Russian history today, referred to two periods--the Petrine and the prerevolutionary years covered by this account, 1906-17.

As the author admits, the records of the Association, held in the Central State Historical Archive of the USSR (fond 32), were not yet open to foreigners when she carried out her research in Leningrad. Thus, many aspects of the internal functioning of the Association, including policy disputes among its leaders, remain unclear. She also points out that the cogency of the Association's economic program has yet to be tested against economic realities, whether by econometric models or by other methods. Some readers may wish to see fewer paraphrases of the Association's published statements and more analysis of the views of bureaucrats, politicians, labor leaders, and spokesmen of agrarian interests in the great debate on economic policy in the late imperial period. These weaknesses, in my opinion, do not detract from the importance of the book. As an unprecedented description and analysis of the economic program of the Association of Industry and Trade, it provides a firm basis for understanding the uniqueness of Russian capitalism, past and present.

The contemporary relevance of her findings is striking, despite the many changes that have occurred in Russian cultural and economic life under Soviet rule, including, on the positive side, improvements in education and, on the negative side, the suppression of entrepreneurship, political freedom, and cultural diversity as well as the creation of ecological disasters. What Ruth Roosa identifies as the peculiarly Russian "dilemmas of backwardness" on the eve of the Bolshevik Revolution remain acute in the 1990s. Even as the Association denounced "state socialism"--the activities of massive state-owned enterprises that hindered private initiative--it depended on the tsarist bureaucracy for various kinds of economic support, ranging from import tariffs, improvements in the transportation network, and commercial credit, with which to meet the economic threat from foreign business interests, particularly those based in Germany. As managers of corporations, cartels, and trade associations, Russian capitalists sought to introduce European economic institutions into a largely agrarian society, but in so doing they inevitably stimulated the resentment of workers, peasants, journalists, and bureaucrats who regarded capitalism itself as an alien force. Russian capitalists strove to improve the living standards of the masses in hopes of creating a strong domestic demand for the products of their factories, but the perceived need for high rates of industrial investment and profit inevitably undermined the purchasing power of the poor in the short run.

Having presented papers with Ruth on several scholarly panels at conventions of the American Association for the Advancement of Slavic Studies and elsewhere, I can attest to the encouragement that she showed to her fellow historians. She generously shared with all interested scholars her incomparable knowledge of the Association and inspired others by her example of diligent scholarship in a poorly developed field of historical study. When illness left her unable to undertake further revision, Ruth's daughter and son-in-law, Meredith and Karl F. Inderfurth, requested my assistance in preparing the manuscript for publication. Ruth left this work essentially complete on her death in 1993. Professor Harley D. Balzer of Georgetown University, an historian of Russian and Soviet technology and the engineering profession, and Dr. John P. Hardt, a senior expert on the Russian economy at the Library of Congress, gave useful advice. Aleksandr A. Fursenko and Boris V. Ananich, two historians at the Institute of Russian History in St. Petersburg who had encouraged Ruth's work over the decades, provided essential information on many obscure individuals named in the text. Sarah Case, a graduate student in Russian at American University referred to me by Professor Balzer, examined publications of the Association at the Library of Congress to clear up some final editorial details.

My work on Ruth's manuscript was limited to essentially editorial tasks, primarily the reduction of the text to about half its original size and the standardization of the names of commercial-industrial organizations in the Russian Empire. With the aid of Boris Ananich and Aleksandr Fursenko, I supplied full first names of individuals whenever possible. A few references to sources were made more precise than in the author's text. For the benefit of readers who might wish to investigate the subject further, I amplified the notes by citing recent scholarship on the history of Russian capitalism without, however, modifying the text. Appendix IV contains Ruth's discussion of the main sources for the study of the Association, plus some concluding remarks of my own on recent and particularly obscure sources. The Bibliography contains all sources cited in the notes as well as Ruth's list of publications of the Association, the most extensive in the secondary literature. The original manuscript is on file with the Harriman Institute in Columbia University. Except for occasional transitional sentences added in the editorial process, the structure, logic, and prose style remain those of the author. Dates are given according to the Julian (Old-Style) calendar, and transliteration from the Cyrillic alphabet follows the system of the Library of Congress, except that proper names lack soft signs (Kharkov, Lure, Nobel, Volskii, and Vorobiev vice Khar'kov, Lur'e, Nobel', Vol'skii, and Vorob'ev).

Fortunately, Ruth's meticulous research and careful composition of the manuscript permitted me to carry out these tasks with ease. As a historian of Russian capitalism who has long respected and admired the work of Ruth Roosa, I am delighted that her groundbreaking analysis of the Association of Industry and Trade is now available to all who seek to understand this important subject. Russia's past and possible future come alive in these pages.

Thomas C. Owen
Louisiana State University
Baton Rouge

1

The Russian Business Community

The Crisis of 1905

Although the relationship between industry's representatives and monopolistic organizations remains a subject for historical investigation, its relations, economic and political, with the world of officialdom, both before and after 1905, have prompted intense, protracted, and inconclusive debate among historians. Much prerevolutionary Marxist, especially Menshevik, writing stressed the success of organized trade and industry in influencing official economic (and occasionally political) policies. In contrast, western historical scholarship has generally emphasized the dependence, economic as well as political, of Russian business circles on the government and the predominant importance of governmental initiative and direction in the economic development of the Empire. Between these extremes, Soviet historians have steered an uncertain course.[1] The same conditions that permitted a wide range of governmental intervention in the affairs of business also gave to the business leadership of prerevolutionary Russia broad opportunities for influencing governmental action.[2]

Inconclusive though the evidence may be concerning the success of the business community in influencing the economic policies of the Empire, there can be no question of the closeness of the organizational relationship between the government and organized industry before 1905. None of the representative organizations operated free of some degree of official supervision and control. Chartered by the government, they all were required to satisfy official requests for information concerning their particular branches of industry. Their elections of officers were subject to governmental confirmation. Advance approval was required for the agendas of their congresses, and they were obliged to include in them any subject that the government wished to have considered. The congresses (and often the meetings of their executive councils and their numerous specialized committees) customarily included prominent government officials among their participants, at least one of whom usually bore an official responsibility for influencing the proceedings.[3]

Counterbalancing, to some extent, these restrictions and obligations was the government's recognition of the various organizations as the legitimate representatives of their particular branches of industry within the geographic areas encompassed by them. These organizations enjoyed the right to address petitions to government officials, and the government consulted with them on all issues involving their economic interests, inviting both written statements of opinion on specific questions and their participation through their chosen delegates in official conferences and committees. Prior to 1905, such contacts were most commonly channeled through the Ministry of Finance, although consultation with other official agencies was not unusual. These relationships had their origins in the 1870s and 1880s, but it was during Sergei Iu. Witte's tenure as minister of finance (1892-1903) that the government most actively encouraged the organization of business interests for representational purposes and developed its own use of them as consultants.[4] As early as 1896, a member of the council of the ministry of finance declared to the Commercial-Industrial Congress at Nizhnii Novgorod that "the ministry has always listened attentively to the voice of the industrialists and the merchants."[5] Yet, seven years later, despite the noteworthy progress that had been made in the organization of industry and trade, Witte, addressing a conference of representatives of exchange committees, found it advisable to exhort the country's businessmen to unite in permanent organizations for the advancement of their own interests. Offering assurances of a sympathetic governmental reception for their efforts, he admonished them:

> Try to see each other as often as possible, to meet, to confer about your needs. If you explain your needs to the government in a thorough and convincing way, you will more quickly obtain their satisfaction. Have your own press organs for the elucidation of your interests and rights. . . . Try to influence public opinion. . . . Most important of all, for you, is the possibility of publicly explaining your views; and you will acquire this only by having your own organization. Organize, therefore, in order that you may meet periodically at general and regional congresses, in order that you may possess your own permanent bureaus or other unifying institutions.[6]

Thus, well before 1905, at a time when the organizing efforts of most elements in Russian society encountered suspicion and even repression by a distrustful government, clear channels of communication had been firmly established between that government's principal agency in economic affairs, the Ministry of Finance, and the representatives of organized industry and trade. Through a steady flow of petitions and a continuing round of consultations, Russia's businessmen had won acceptance by a generally sympathetic government of their right to be informed and to have their opinions considered in the determination of official economic policies.

Yet, beneath an apparently harmonious exterior there was growing turmoil within the business community. The Revolution of 1905 found it unprepared to participate in the momentous events of that year. Intellectually and politically, the businessmen remained immature. Immersed in the details of their own immediate economic concerns and unburdened, for the most part, by political interests or convictions, they appeared to lack any broad understanding of their long-run economic interests, particularly as they related to the fundamental political issues that confronted the Empire.[7] Nevertheless, the signs of a rising sense of an identity of interests among the more alert leaders in the business world were unmistakable. Underlying this emerging self-consciousness was a growing dissatisfaction both with the substance of official economic policies and with the quality of their own relationship with the government.

The departure of Count Witte from the Ministry of Finance in 1903, had, despite the general acceptability of his successor, Vladimir N. Kokovtsov, deprived the business community of the strongest and most enthusiastic protector it had ever known within the government. Even before Witte's departure, moreover, the protection of the ministry had, in the absence of a unified governmental policy, offered no security against unfriendly intervention in industrial and commercial affairs by the agrarian-oriented Ministry of Internal Affairs and other unsympathetic agencies. Both before and after 1903, a number of provocative incidents served as recurrent reminders to businessmen of their essential helplessness in the face of an arbitrary and often capricious bureaucracy.[8] Within this context, the constant tutelage to which private enterprise was subject, even by relatively friendly governmental organs--a condition deeply rooted in the archaic legislation that deprived Russian businessmen of the legal rights and freedoms commonly enjoyed by their confreres in the West--now gave rise to a new and deeper restiveness. Against this background, both the effectiveness of the existing forms of industrial and commercial organization and the usefulness of the traditional system of consultation between organized industry and the government on questions of economic policy began to be seriously questioned by business leaders. It is true that in 1905 the conservative Nikolai S. Avdakov asserted that in his experience "no one has ever constrained us in anything; on the contrary we have always enjoyed broad scope."[9] One of his colleagues echoed his assurances before the thirtieth congress of the Association of Southern Coal and Steel Producers in 1906.

> Having participated for almost thirty years in the congresses, I am accustomed to observing how our representatives in the highest governmental spheres, being always well informed about matters, were always able in good time to forestall various occurrences and unexpected decrees with respect to our industry.[10]

Avdakov's assertion, which has been widely quoted, loses much of its force, however, when considered in context. In fact, it was issued as a rebuttal to a proposal of a liberally inclined bureaucrat and industrialist, Vladimir I. Kovalevskii, that the largely government-dominated associations be replaced by new organizations free of official controls. Furthermore, Avdakov stressed the benefits to industry of the "semi-governmental" character of its existing institutions. "The entire difficulty," he observed, "consists in the fact that you proceed from the future, which is still unknown to us, and I from experience."[11] Only a few months later, moreover, representatives of some twenty-two business organizations complained that "thus far all questions concerning industry and trade have been discussed and decided in the ministries, without the participation of persons and enterprises interested in them, and on only a few questions has the government convened congresses."[12] Shortly afterward, Adolf A. Volskii, a business leader long associated with the powerful Consultative Board of Iron Producers, told one of industry's organizing congresses that "the most vital questions for industry and trade have been decided, and continue to be decided, in our governmental institutions almost without any influence on the part of Russian industry and trade."[13]

Signs of disillusionment with the governments' conduct of economic affairs had begun to appear within the business community even before Witte's departure. He had failed to solve the fundamental problems of the financing of industrial expansion and of marketing industry's products.[14] As the Association's journal, Industry and Trade, subsequently noted, in both his political ideas and in his promotion of the cause of "state socialism" (that is, in his advancement of the entrepreneurial role of the state in industry and, especially, in the railroads), Witte had remained "separated from the commercial-industrial milieu."[15]

General economic conditions also contributed heavily to the businessmen's growing awareness of the extent to which conditions embedded in Russia's way of life and in the traditions and policies of its government hampered industrial growth and prosperity. The economic crisis that began in 1899 proved severe, and the signs of recovery that first appeared in 1904 were soon dissipated by the difficult and costly war with Japan. During the five-year depression that preceded the revolution, the potentially disastrous consequences of the government's lack of a systematic economic policy became manifest. The government's proclaimed devotion to national economic development and its satisfaction of various demands of business circles for subsidies, contracts, and tariff protection could not substitute for a positive program designed to foster industrial expansion and commercial stability. Despite the government's faithfulness in consulting businessmen with respect to economic policy, consultation all too often found little reflection in the official practices that ensued.

Still more disquieting, perhaps, were the government's efforts to bolster its own financial position and that of the weakened landed gentry by implementing tax and credit policies that drained capital away from industry. Industrial and commercial enterprise was already taxed more heavily than land, but a direct tax on business was instituted and soon afterward increased. In general, the government's tax policies, which placed a disproportionately heavy burden on the unpropertied classes, served further to constrict the purchasing power of an already pitifully impoverished home market, the value of which as a base for industrial development was now, under the impact of depression, becoming belatedly evident to Russia's businessmen. Although industry had admittedly benefited from a generally high protective tariff, the industrialists became restive under the trade agreements that Russia had concluded with Germany, Russia's principal trading partner, in 1894 and in 1904. With considerable justification, the industrialists considered the tariff treaties a patent sacrificing of the interests of industry to those of agriculture.

Above all, the dependence of the entire economy on a capricious harvest and on the will of a powerful and arbitrary government made for instability in economic life. Intensifying the cumulative effect of these unfavorable conditions was industry's heavy dependence on foreign capital, which, when confronted with the unhopeful prospects of pre-1905 Russia, showed an alarming inclination to withdraw in search of more auspicious fields of investment. Clearly, without a more congenial environment, Russian industry would fail to attract and hold the lifeblood of its own existence and further growth.[16]

Early in the twentieth century, a new source of irritation arose out of the growing restiveness of industrial labor. Already accustomed to looking with jealous eyes on the favored position enjoyed in official circles by their agrarian rivals, the industrialists now viewed with consternation the government's efforts to pacify disaffected workers by enacting labor and factory legislation[17] and by grouping them into state-supported unions that championed their economic grievances against their employers. Ironically, it was the bitterness engendered by the government's sponsorship for the Zubatov system (albeit in the face of the employers' own resistance to nearly all concessions)[18] that served, more than any other single factor, to crystallize the industrialists' realization that nothing less than broadly conceived political reforms could remove the underlying causes of this growing economic discontent.

In the upheaval of 1905, all these causes of discontent came into focus for the first time. If Russia's industrialists entered the revolutionary era still only vaguely cognizant of their own political and economic "credo,"[19] they nevertheless keenly felt their grievances. Increasingly restive under the restraints of their environment and imbued with a growing awareness of their dignity and worth as a class, they had been rapidly approaching a turning point in their relations with the government. The events of "Bloody Sunday" on January 9, 1905 precipitated a crisis in these relations and forced Russia's business leadership, for the first time, to examine seriously its own intrinsic interests and aspirations. At a time when all other groups in Russian society were resorting to direct action in defense of their own interests, the businessmen would have been extraordinarily apathetic had they not begun to think of doing likewise.

In March 1905, the liberal textile manufacturers of Moscow, led by Savva T. Morozov, convened a congress of some thirty-two industrialists from the industrial regions except that of Lodz, to discuss the labor question.[20] From an organizational point of view, the March Congress produced no concrete results, but it set in motion the sequence of events that ended with the establishment of the Association of Industry and Trade some seventeen months later. The congress's decision to create a permanent organization of united industry was unanimously adopted, and a "statute on general congresses of representatives of industry," drawn up by a commission led by the liberal Ural metal producer Vladimir I. Kovalevskii and forwarded to the Ministry of Finance for approval, served as tangible evidence of industry's first halting step toward unity. The powers of the new organization, the membership of which was to consist of existing business organizations, were to have been modest indeed, being limited to the right to petition the government on industry's interests; to maintain relations with other organizations; to organize courses of lectures, exhibitions, laboratories, and so forth; to gather statistical information; to issue periodical publications; and to own property. However, the Kovalevskii project hinted at higher ambitions. It took for its model the German Handelstag, or congress of chambers of commerce, which had first met in Heidelberg in 1861. A law of 1897, much admired by Russian businessmen, mandated that the Handelstag consider all bills concerning German industry, trade, or transport prior to their introduction into the Reichstag; nor could the German government conclude any trade agreement without having first consulted with that body.[21] In the years that followed, the German practice remained the ideal of the Russian industrialists.

Despite the differences that continued to divide the industrialists, their growing determination to extract political reforms from the government and their common opposition to the economic demands of labor steadily pushed them toward a growing measure of cooperation among themselves. This trend was evident both in the appearance, beginning in the spring of 1905, of a number of new employers' organizations, generally patterned after the Petersburg Society of Mill and Factory Owners, and in the resistance with which the industrialists responded to the government's effort, through a commission chaired by Minister of Finance Kokovtsov, to introduce modest reforms in factory and social legislation.[22] Their insistence that any discussion of economic concessions to labor must await the implementation of the political reforms promised in the Rescript of February 18 and the convening of a representative assembly clearly served a dual purpose.

Evidently, one political question had assumed primary importance in the industrialists' eyes during the short period since January: industry's representation in the promised elected assembly. At the end of May, acting on rumors that an electoral law unfavorable to industry would soon be published, the Organizational Commission of the March Congress addressed a memorandum to Kokovtsov (whom it described as "the sole expressor of our needs and defender of our interests" within the government), declaring industry's intention to petition for a change in the projected law and enclosing a draft of a memorandum to be submitted to a forthcoming second congress of industrial representatives.[23] Under the proposed law, the memorandum protested, industry's delegates would enter the State Duma (the lower house of the legislative assembly) "only by accident; industry as such will not be represented at all." Asserting that the "the interests of industry would be better represented even under a system of universal, equal suffrage," it recommended adoption of the Austrian system of representation according to estates, and, in the absence of suitable institutions in Russia, the election of industry's representatives by the existing "advisory" organizations.[24]

Despite their refusal to grant economic concessions to the workers, the industrialists consistently adhered to their established position in support of political rights for labor. Pointing out that "the organized and politically conscious class of factory and mine workers"[25] would be completely without representation under the proposed law, the memorandum recommended that a special workers' curia be created in order to assure their presence in the new State Duma. Early in June, a conference of industrialists from all parts of the Empire met again in Moscow under the auspices of the Moscow Exchange Society to petition the Emperor

> that industry be guaranteed proper representation in the State Duma by means of the direct election of representatives from the most important districts and branches of industry, which election with respect to industrialists could be carried out by the existing advisory institutions for industry.[26]

Clearly, however, the industrialists' eagerness to obtain political representation expressed their predominant concern with economic issues. Both the May memorandum and the June petition stressed the urgent need, in their view, for the future State Duma (lower house of the legislative assembly) to undertake a program of national economic reform and development. "One of the main tasks of the State Duma," the memorandum declared, "will be the creation of a correct economic policy, the carrying out of broad economic reforms, directed toward the development of the productive forces of the country and toward efficiency in the organization of popular work."[27] The economy, it further asserted, must be directed toward radical renovation and intensified growth, leading to an increase in the productivity of labor and in the well-being of the population at large. Such a program must rest on a carefully conceived economic policy, harmonizing the disparate needs and interests of all branches of economic life. It could neither be elaborated nor put into practice without the participation of the industrialists in the Duma, because the knowledge and power of the business community were indispensable to its success. The industrialists, the memorandum rather defensively added, were poor neither in spirit nor in wisdom; nor were they limited by a narrow class point of view. On the contrary, they were fully capable of a "profound understanding of their social [sotsial'nyi] role," and "worthy to discuss all questions from the point of view of the state's interests."[28]

As midsummer approached, the political movement of the industrialists reached its peak, spurred on by military defeat, deepening economic depression, the swelling force of revolution, and the government's reluctance to put its halfhearted promises of February into effect. Yet, despite their cooperation for the purpose of assuring industry's representation in a future State Duma, the industrialists remained divided over the question of the powers to be attributed to the new organ. From mid-May onward, the Petersburg industrialists and an influential minority of their Moscow colleagues insisted that the Duma must possess full legislative powers. In taking this position, they found themselves not only in close sympathy with the zemstvo liberals, but also increasingly at odds with older, predominantly mercantile, elements in the business leadership itself. Early in June, the conservative majority of the Moscow Exchange Society, headed by the veteran president of its Committee, Nikolai A. Naidenov, voted in favor of a consultative Duma only.[29] As a result of the growing split within the Society on this issue, leadership among the industrialists of the Empire began to shift away from the Moscow textile manufacturers who controlled the Moscow Exchange Committee to the iron and steel industry, represented by the Petersburg-based Consultative Board of Iron Producers.

Despite these difficulties, the Moscow Exchange Committee joined with the Petersburg industrialists late in June in convening a second Empire-wide congress of business leaders for the primary purpose of creating a political party that would represent and defend their interests in connection with the convening of the Bulygin Duma. The initiative in calling the congress lay with the heavy industry of Petersburg, particularly Magnus F. Norpe, chairman of the Consultative Board of Iron Producers, and Adolf A. Volskii, the board's principal "organization man." Together, these two men were largely responsible for the liberal political program that was submitted to the congress.[30] The date of the congress, July 4-6, was timed to overlap with the first Zemstvo-City Congress, scheduled for July 6, in the hope that cooperation could be established between the two groups. More broadly representative than the March congress, that of July brought together fifty-two delegates representing twenty-three organizations from all parts of the Empire. Slightly more than half of the delegates represented industrial organizations rather than exchange committees.[31]

The effort to enter actively into political affairs soon foundered, however, on the differences that divided the businessmen, particularly on the issue of the powers that the forthcoming State Duma should enjoy. Far from creating a political party to represent united industry and trade, the July Congress became the occasion for an open break between the more conservative, old-fashioned, and predominantly commercial elements in Moscow, who regarded a consultative Duma as the only feasible possibility "in view of the present development of the people,"[32] and the more liberal, Europeanized and predominantly industrial and banking majority, who sought nothing less than a Duma with full legislative powers. Prompted by the conservative minority, which held formal control of the Moscow Exchange Committee, the government threatened to close the proceedings if political issues were not abjured. Rejecting such a restriction as impractical, "since the further economic development of the country is impossible without the establishment of order in political life,"[33] twenty-two of the twenty-three attending organizations, led by the Moscow liberals, soon to be known as "the young party of the Moscow Exchange Society," transferred the meetings to the spacious home of the millionaire Pavel P. Riabushinskii. There, recognizing the inexpedience of any attempt to create a political party of the commercial-industrial class at that time, the congress elected a Bureau, composed of eighty-two leaders in industry and banking and headed by Norpe, to institute a permanent Empire-wide organization of large-scale industry and trade for the general defense of common economic interests. Months later, this Bureau produced a draft charter for a Union of Commercial-Industrial Enterprises of the Russian Empire.[34]

Despite their recognition of the hopelessness of establishing a viable political party, the liberal industrialists continued to attribute central importance to the attainment of political reforms. By a majority of sixteen institutions, the now illegal congress adopted a political program almost indistinguishable from that of the Zemstvo-City Congress.[35] In addition to calling for the usual civil liberties, equality of all before the law, and legal protection for property rights, the program recommended a bicameral legislature, each chamber of which should have the right of legislative initiative, "the right of control over the actions of the government in the field of administration and finance, [and] the right to have ministers who are responsible before the chambers."[36] Although this statement left the composition of the upper house unspecified, it stipulated that the lower house (the State Duma) should be elected by universal manhood suffrage and a secret ballot, in two stages.[37] Declaring the necessity of political reform for the sake of "the correct development of Russian industry," the industrialists further announced their intention of taking an active part in any future national election "in the hope that the deputies elected to the State Duma will concern themselves with the most rapid reorganization of the popular representation in accordance with the principles proposed above."[38] Finally, the industrialists called for freedom in the organization of labor unions and other professional organizations, for the establishment of special courts to mediate disputes between labor and management, for the liquidation of the peasant commune, and for a measure of local autonomy in outlying parts of the Empire.[39]

Although a few of the more radical Moscow industrialists began to toy with thoughts of boycotting the government and even of inciting the workers against it if the Bulygin Duma should prove to have only consultative powers,[40] the vast majority opted for more moderate methods of protest. When the Bulygin Manifesto of August 6 announced only a consultative role for the State Duma and an extremely undemocratic electoral system, the blow was softened by assurances of representation for the commercial-industrial class. Surprisingly, perhaps, it produced no notable crisis in business circles.[41]

During the two months that elapsed between Bulygin's announcement and the October Manifesto--a time of generally rising revolutionary tempers throughout the Empire--the industrialists seem to have focused mainly on the place of their own class in the new, emerging order. In part, this reflected their continuing preoccupation with the attainment of strong representation for the industry in the Duma; but it also found expression in new efforts to define the economic and social program, for which political reform was valued mainly as an indispensable means. The most noteworthy step in this direction, no doubt, consisted in a report prepared for the Consultative Board of Iron Producers by Volskii. Apart from the substance of its economic and financial proposals (to be considered later), the report broke new ground in attempting to arouse the businessmen to an awareness of their own "mission" within the state. Not only, it asserted, did the Empire face the danger of economic, financial and political catastrophe at home; disaster threatened in the international arena as well. To the bitterness of defeat at the hands of Japan was added the even more dangerous threat of "Germany at the Urals in the near future."[42] In this time of national crisis, Volskii declared, the country must recognize that only industrialization offered hope of restoring the Empire's stability and power. Yet what of the industrialists themselves, who dominated the "third estate . . . that everywhere in the world has been the sole agent of real economic progress?"[43] In Russia they remained numerically insignificant, almost universally disliked, and discouragingly apathetic. "The very word 'industrialist' has somehow become synonymous with the words 'swindler,' 'bloodsucker,' 'exploiter,' and other, no less flattering, names." Far from rising to meet the challenge of the times, however, industrialists "have been silent, they are silent, and, apparently, they intend to remain doggedly silent, as if affirming the justice of our gracious public opinion."[44]

Volskii's bitterness was equalled only by his sarcasm:

> We are living through a period when every thoughtful man must understand and, so far as is possible, act upon the principle: caveant consules ne res publica quid detrimenti sapiat! [Let the consuls take care that the republic suffer no injury!] The most recent history of cultured countries testifies that the role of Roman consuls is now being fulfilled (for better or for worse--that is another question) by the bourgeois (commercial-industrial) class of the population. And in our country? This class does not even know whether it should be addressed as "my dear fellow" or as "master"?![45]

Clearly, the time had not yet come when the industrialists would spontaneously proclaim themselves the class destined "by history" to shape the future of Russia. But Volskii, no industrialist himself but a mining engineer and the "organization man" par excellence of nascent big business, already beckoned them in that direction.

The industrialists' earlier hope of coordinating political activities with the zemstvo-city movement foundered on the socio-economic issues that divided them. No further effort toward cooperation occurred after September, when a Zemstvo Congress adopted a program advocating an eight-hour workday in industry and the expropriation of state and possibly private lands in order to increase peasant holdings. The political outlook of the more liberal industrialists remained close to that of the zemstvo men, however. The Petersburg Society of Mill and Factory Owners, the "young men" of Moscow, and Vladislav V. Zhukovskii, speaking for Polish heavy industry, all protested the exclusion of the workers from the right to vote under the Bulygin Manifesto.[46]

Moreover, both during the general strike that preceded the publication of the October Manifesto and immediately afterward, the industrialists maintained pressure on the government for liberal reform. Some individual employers provided financial assistance to the striking workers;[47] and on October 14, three days before the issuance of the Manifesto, the moderate Moscow industrialists, now in control of the Exchange Committee under the leadership of Grigorii A. Krestovnikov, who had replaced Naidenov as president,[48] warned that any resort to force to break the strike would not only "endanger the lives of our workers, the majority of whom are not given to violence," but would so arouse them as to create "a calamity difficult to repair." Insisting still that the workers' movement remained "much more political than economic in character," the industrialists declared pacification to be impossible without immediate reforms satisfying "the strivings of the overwhelming majority of society toward the reconstruction of our life on principles fully protecting us against the possibility of a return to the old forms that have brought Russia to its present extreme catastrophe." Such reforms must include the conversion of the State Duma into a fully legislative organ "and the radical revision of the law on elections, which is now founded on the completely false principle of a property qualification and the complete exclusion of the entire class of the factory population from the vote." A compromise underlay the new unity within the Moscow Exchange Society, however. The Moscow men declared themselves

> definitely against the introduction at the present time of elections based on a universal, secret and direct ballot, recognizing that such a procedure can be acceptable only in a politically mature state and not in Russia, where the preponderant majority of the population is illiterate and completely foreign to political life.[49]

The publication of the Manifesto of October 17 marked the beginning of the final phase of the political movement of the industrialists during the 1905 Revolution. Although it would seem not to have precipitated the abrupt shift from revolution to reaction that has often been depicted,[50] the promise of concessions that it held forth did greatly moderate the oppositional temper of the industrialists and provided the foundation for a more conciliatory attitude toward the government.

Yet the Manifesto was by no means greeted with unanimous approval. On the day of the Manifesto's appearance, Volskii, speaking in the name of the Bureau of the July Congress, expressed doubts that the country could be pacified even by the convening of a fully legislative State Duma and declared the existence of an essential community of interests between the industrialists and the striking workers.[51] In a statement issued shortly after the publication of the October Manifesto, the iron producers, while declaring themselves to be "far from supporters of the right of universal suffrage in theory," nevertheless, in deference to the contributions of labor and the intelligentsia to the revolutionary movement, petitioned the government to proclaim at once "the participation in the State Duma of the representatives of all the people, elected by universal suffrage." Welcoming the Manifesto, the iron producers could not refrain from expressing blunt skepticism of the government's good intentions. They warned Witte, now chairman of the Council of Ministers, "directly and frankly that between words and deeds there is a tremendous difference. We must directly declare: Russia believes only in facts; her blood and her poverty do not yet permit her to believe in words."[52] Denouncing the reactionary "black hundreds," they further demanded the abolition of the "exceptional rules" that had been instituted for security purposes, and the complete amnesty of all persons arrested for political reasons.[53]

After the beginning of November, harassed by labor's growing violence and by its increasing emphasis on economic grievances, the industrialists gradually ceased to champion the political and civil rights of the workers. Alarmed still further by the Kronstadt mutiny and by the spread of revolutionary disturbances in Poland and elsewhere on the periphery of the Empire, they turned, hesitantly but in mounting desperation, to the government for the maintenance of law and order. In December, the Moscow uprising completed the process. Amid strikes and lockouts, industrialists all over Russia appealed to the government for the suppression of disorder by military action.

Yet the industrialists' retreat was neither complete nor unanimous. As late as the end of November, the Petersburg Exchange Committee warned that "when the position becomes unbearable . . . the bourgeoisie will go to the proletariat and stand under the red banner."[54] Some industrialists began to display a new appreciation of the need to assuage at least a few of the workers' grievances. The Moscow Exchange Society, for example, not only requested that forceful suppression be combined with measures to improve the economic security and living conditions of the workers but offered, if the government were financially unable to provide assistance, to accept a temporary increase in the business tax during 1906 for that purpose.[55] Late in the year, industry still expressed distrust and disgruntlement at the government's slowness in implementing the October Manifesto. Witte's additional concessions in December--virtually universal suffrage and representation of group (including commercial and industrial) interests in a reformed State Council, or upper legislative chamber--only partly allayed the businessmen's dissatisfaction. On December 29, thirteen industrial organizations joined in protesting against the provision whereby their estate (soslovie) representatives in the State Council would be elected by such older and less active institutions as the committees of trade and manufacturing, rather than by the newer and more vigorous industrial associations.[56]

The elections to the first State Duma foreclosed all political action by industrialists in the legislature because of their insignificant numbers.[57] However, they by no means abandoned their fundamental objective: to exert influence on official economic policy. Except for a few outstanding individuals, most notably Pavel P. Riabushinskii and the deceased Savva T. Morozov, the industrialists had always regarded politics more a means to an economic end than a goal in itself. They readily shifted to other methods of action when they saw the impracticability of the electoral procedure.[58] Alternative means were ready at hand in industry's representative organizations, the number of which had increased substantially during the last months of 1905 and throughout 1906. Not only syndicates and "employers' unions" (the latter designed to counter the growing strength of organized labor), but new advisory associations arose to represent industries and areas that had thus far been without organization. More important, industry's new and more effective effort toward unification in a single Empire-wide organization for the defense of purely economic interests had paralleled its political campaign.

Even before their political defeat became fully manifest, the industrialists were preparing a return to the older, time-tested methods of influencing official action through their representative organizations. Whether this constituted the unqualified reversion to the ways of the past and an abandonment of liberal political principles, as has often been alleged,[59] may, however, be questioned. While the industrialists made their peace with an unsatisfactory government for the sake of law and order and returned to the old pattern of consultations and petitions within the bureaucracy after 1905, they did so from a new position of organizational strength. Moreover, they now grasped the opportunity to make their weight felt as a pressure group, operating in the lobbies and to some extent within the chambers of a national legislature.

The experiences of the year of crisis had sharpened the industrialists' thinking on economic and social problems, broadened their outlook, and made them, if not wiser, certainly better equipped intellectually to challenge the bureaucracy and the public at large in defense of their own interests. As for the political liberalism of the industrialists, it was, perhaps, not so much abandoned in favor of a more conservative outlook as laid aside, a temporarily useless tool. Years later, when bureaucratic procedures again failed to satisfy the industrialists' economic demands and when national crisis again confronted the homeland, the old political tool would be rediscovered. Dulled with disuse, and wielded by hesitant and unaccustomed hands, it would again prove tragically incapable of resolving the great challenges facing Russian society.

The Founding of the Association of Industry and Trade

The collapse of industry's political aspirations in the late spring of 1906 lent new impetus to its leaders' simultaneous efforts to create a representative organization on an Empire-wide basis for the pursuit of exclusively economic objectives. Against industry's established background of participation, however tangentially, in the formation of official economic policies, the experiment with political action was soon to appear--and, indeed, were so described by many who had been its most active proponents--as an ill-considered aberration, conclusively demonstrating the superiority of older procedures. Moreover, despite industry's flirtation with politics and the partial breakdown in communication with governmental departments that preceded and attended it,[60] Russia's industrial leadership had never abandoned its tortuous quest for a permanent, national organization that could promote its common interests.

After the Congress of July 1905, the Consultative Board of Iron Producers became not only the founder of the most liberal of industry's political parties but also the most active sponsor of industrial unification. Both these efforts were channeled through the Bureau that was appointed in July under the chairmanship of Magnus F. Norpe. In addition to Norpe, the energetic drive behind the Bureau's work centered in two outstanding leaders, Adolf A. Volskii, the director of the permanent secretariat of the Consultative Board, and Vladislav V. Zhukovskii, chairman of the Polish Coal and Iron Association. Engineers and administrators, they both had long experience in industrial organizations. Along with Nikolai S. Avdakov, who shared their common professional background (although not their relatively liberal outlook), these men were destined, to an extent far exceeding any other individuals, to shape the policies and guide the activities of the future Association of Industry and Trade.

Although the Bureau of the July Congress strove primarily to create a political party, it never lost sight of industry's need for a unified representative organization, and as the prospect of success in its first objective dwindled, its attention focused increasingly on the second goal. In November 1905, it drafted a charter for a proposed Union of Commercial-Industrial Enterprises of the Russian Empire (Soiuz torgovo-promyshlennykh predpriiatii Rossiiskoi imperii). This effort was unrelated to the All-Russian Commercial-Industrial Union, which made its appearance almost simultaneously, but the two organizations shared similar organizational structures and a common interest in increasing industry's share in the formation of governmental economic policies.

Support for the movement gathered rapidly, and by November its adherents numbered about a hundred of the Empire's most prominent businessmen, including not only a central core of large-scale industrialists but also leaders in trade, banking, insurance, and railroads.[61] Undoubtedly, the avowedly nonpolitical character of the proposed organization helped to overcome both the suspicions of the government and the political differences that divided the business community. The leaders drew encouragement from the success of the exchange societies in attaining the Empire-wide unification of commercial interests earlier in the year in the Association of Trade and Agriculture.[62] The institution of a new Ministry of Trade and Industry late in October provided a new and important stimulus to industry's organizing efforts. The creation of a governmental department exclusively concerned with industry and trade made the prospect for influencing official economic policies through bureaucratic channels more promising than ever before. Finally, the formation of the elected national legislature and the emergence of public opinion as a force to be reckoned with in national affairs held out the promise of new and perhaps equally effective means for making industry's voice heard and respected in influential quarters.

In January and April 1906, two congresses met in St. Petersburg for the purpose of founding a Russian industrial association. At the first of these gatherings, the Union of Commercial-Industrial Enterprises held its first and only congress. Attended by 127 persons, it heard several reports. In the most noteworthy of these, Volskii emphasized the failure of organized industry and trade, both then and in the past, to win governmental support for its interests;[63] the virtual certainty that industry and trade would be weakly represented in both the State Duma and State Council; and the necessity of maximizing influence on the Duma and other governmental and public institutions by applying the principle of "strength through unity." The congress reaffirmed the earlier decision to avoid political issues. It also stressed the need to promote the organization of those branches of industry and trade that remained unorganized.

The discussion centered, however, on the draft charter drawn up by the Bureau of the July Congress. Some speakers expressed dissatisfaction with the allegedly undue complexity and unwieldiness of the proposed organization and, especially, with the centralization of power in the Bureau of its executive Council.[64] As a result, the congress elected a new Bureau, representing forty organizations of industry and trade,[65] again chaired by Norpe. It was charged with revising the charter in accordance with the principles of the autonomy of member organizations within the new organization and a minimum of centralization and of "bureaucratic" authority in the executive organ, which should, however, be endowed with limited "plenary powers" for independent action between meetings of the congresses. The report also instructed the Bureau to call a congress of the new organization in April, before the convening of the First State Duma.[66]

Addressing the first meeting of the Organizational Bureau, which convened on February 1, 1906 in the building of the Consultative Board of Iron Producers, Norpe had stressed the difficulty of unifying Russian industry and trade. Conflicting economic interests divided the business community, and geographic, ethnic and social differences were compounded by the vast size of the country, inadequate transportation facilities, and the tensions of the current moment. The dimensions of the problem, without parallel in other countries, reduced the extent to which reliance could be placed on foreign models. Nevertheless, Norpe considered unity on the basis of common interests both a practical possibility and a vital necessity, inasmuch as an agrarian-dominated

> State Duma will hardly react with any particular sympathy to trade and industry, since our landed people are too little acquainted with its real needs, and our public is rarely aware of the tremendous importance of trade and industry in the state economy.[67]

In subsequent meetings, the Bureau reaffirmed the strictly nonpolitical character of the emerging organization and decided to adopt as its structural basis the draft charter for General Congresses of Representatives of Industry, drawn up in Moscow during April 1905. Hence the main work of the Organizational Bureau consisted in revising that charter for submission to the forthcoming second congress.

The April Congress, after an initial social gathering in a St. Petersburg restaurant, brought together 138 businessmen, of whom 61 represented 28 local and specialized organizations.[68] The proceedings focused almost entirely on a detailed consideration, revision, and approval of the draft charter submitted by the Organizational Bureau.[69] In addition, the congress approved a modest ("niggardly," in the view of one prominent member)[70] provisional budget of 100,000 rubles for the first year of the Association's activity.[71]

Finally, the congress elected a Provisional Council of 36 members, with Emanuil L. Nobel as chairman, which bore responsibility for the final editing of the charter, the division of the members of the new organization into classes for purposes of voting and dues collection, the collection of dues, and preparation of a general congress. The Council included mostly representatives of large-scale industry, especially the metal-working, petroleum, and sugar-refining industries and the industry of Moscow, Petersburg, Warsaw, and the Urals. It included delegates from the Russian Insurance Association, the association of privately owned railroads, and six exchange committees.[72] Six of its members held seats in the newly reorganized State Council as delegates from industry and trade: Vasilii I. Timiriazev, Grigorii A. Krestovnikov, Konstantin A. Iasiuninskii, Stanislav M. Rotvand, Pavel O. Gukasov, and Stanislav P. Glezmer. Having thus acquitted themselves, "the members of the congress," according to a contemporary newspaper account, "departed, it was generally agreed, with profound confidence in the brilliant future of the powerful new union that has been called forth to raise the trade and industry of the motherland to their proper height."[73]

After the April Congress, the remaining formalities connected with the legal establishment of the new organization proceeded with what for Russia was unusual despatch. The charter, submitted to the government in May, received approval by the Council of Ministers on July 18 and by the Emperor on August 24. The opening of the First Regular Congress in St. Petersburg on October 12 marked the formal commencement of the Association's activity.

Yet despite this orderly succession of events, the path trod by the Provisional Council during the months between April and October was not always smooth. Public expressions of optimism notwithstanding, the end of the April Congress had left the future of the new organization in doubt. As one of the vice-chairmen of the newly elected Provisional Council, Ignatii I. Iasiukovich, observed, although the Congress had seemed more successful than anticipated, the proof of its success depended on the readiness of existing representative institutions to assume membership in it and to support it financially. Whether such support would actually be forthcoming on the scale needed to enable the Association to carry out its ambitious program was, moreover, questionable. Iasiukovich admitted that a significant measure of opposition to the Association existed among the local and specialized organizations of industry, which feared that it would deprive them of their own raison d'être. He cautiously expressed the hope that this resistance would prove ephemeral.[74]

Iasiukovich's guarded optimism proved to be justified. In August another vice-chairman, Nikolai A. Belotsvetov, noted that a majority of the largest industrial organizations had already declared their intention to join the Association and that some very large enterprises were preparing to accept the consultative (or advisory) membership for which they were eligible. Belotsvetov declared that the Association's finances would be "completely solid," enabling it to develop its activities to the full without delay. Its funds thus assured, the Provisional Council was energetically preparing the way for the commencement of the Association's activity.

> We are taking spacious quarters in the center of town; we are furnishing them, organizing the office and a reference library; we are considering candidates for the carrying out of the intellectual work of the Association; we are attracting new members; we are drawing up lists of those foreign organizations with which we intend to establish permanent working business relationships. About September 15, when a majority of our commercial-industrial leaders return to business after the summer vacation, we shall begin the work of the Provisional Council at full steam in order to convene in October the first regular Congress for the purpose of resolving the many questions that life has already, long since, placed urgently before us. By this time we probably shall have succeeded in completely setting up our information division, to which we attach very great importance.

To this glowing account the vice-chairman attached only one qualification. Noting the shortage of capable and well-educated professional and clerical workers in Russia, he admitted that "the productivity of the Association will depend on the extent to which it is able to attract a worthy executive personnel."[75]

Yet resistance to the new organization evidently still survived within the business world. In contrast with the earlier months of the year, this resistance was no longer located within industry itself. The smaller industrial organizations, their fears partly assuaged by assurances that their autonomy would be respected, hastened to join as founding members. Rather, the predominantly commercial interests in the business community now showed their reluctance to participate. In September, the Petersburg Exchange Committee explained its refusal, and the refusal of a "significant number" of other exchange committees, to join the Association. Bluntly, it cited the work of the Provisional Council and the agenda of the First Regular Congress in support of its contention that "the projected organization has had as its aim not so much to serve the interests of trade as of industry." Moreover, under the charter of the Association, delegates from both commercial and industrial organizations would participate with equal rights in decisions affecting trade alone. "In the opinion of the exchange committee, the resolution of questions affecting trade must first of all be entrusted to trade itself, with industry participating only in connection with questions that concern the latter as well; questions concerning industry should be arranged in the same way."[76] In addition, the Petersburg Committee objected to "the extreme inequality in the representation of commercial-industrial organizations"[77] in the Association, which depended on the amount of dues voluntarily paid, and to the provision whereby individual enterprises were given only a consultative voice in its affairs. No doubt the hostility that had long divided the business communities of St. Petersburg and Moscow was a major, if unspoken, reason for the disaffection of the Petersburg Committee.

A second dispute arose just before the October Congress: whether syndicates should be admitted to full (deistvitel'nyi) membership in the Association. Although a substantial minority held that, as organizations directly engaged in business activities, they were barred from full membership by the charter, a majority of the Provisional Council voted on October 2 to admit the syndicate Prodameta on an equal basis with representative organizations. A week later, the six members of the Provisional Council who were also members of the State Council resigned on the grounds of conflicting obligations and also "because of organizational considerations." Their opposition to the Council's action proved effective, for the First Congress reversed the decision and relegated syndicates to consultative (soveshchatel'nyi) membership in the Association.[78]

The success of the Provisional Council in overcoming the numerous problems confronting it owed much to the firm and consistent support that it received from the most influential groupings of industrialists, notably the manufacturers of iron, petroleum, and sugar and the Moscow Exchange Committee. The new Association also benefited from the encouragement and active assistance of the government itself. The unusual dispatch (viewed in the light of normal Russian procedures) with which the charter was granted indicated the official approval that the organization enjoyed from the beginning. The government's speedy confirmation of the charter, lending substance to the Provisional Council's slogan of "Strength through Unity," probably helped to dispel early doubts and opposition within the ranks of industry itself.[79]

Confidence in a broadly sympathetic and cooperative relationship with the government in the future underlay Iasiukovich's rather ambiguous assertion in April that "if the Association had existed even half a year ago, many questions would stand entirely differently from the way they stand now. To the quiet voice of the institution behind which stand billions, the government would have listened very attentively."[80] The founders' hopes of a close working relationship between the emerging Association and the government were also reflected in a report by Volskii to the Provisional Council, outlining a program of work for the Association. Having listed the principal economic issues likely to come before the new legislature, he pointed out:

> On all such questions Russian industry and trade must, in the interest of their own self-preservation, not only express their own broadly based views but also be able to implant those views in those institutions and groups on which will depend the carrying into effect of those or other laws and measures. Precisely here lies the whole essence of the work and the whole meaning of the Empire-wide Association of Industry and Trade.[81]

Apparently, industrialists based their confident view of their future role on the willingness of the government, during the summer and early autumn of 1906, to draw representatives of the future Association into its own councils. Questions discussed ranged from the technical problems considered in the interdepartmental commission on the traffic capacity of the railroads to such broadly significant issues as the reorganization of the Ministry of Foreign Affairs and the revision of the Provisional Rules of March 4.[82]

Both the respect that the government accorded to the young Association and the latter's own emerging conception of its relationship with the government were well illustrated by the favorable outcome of one potentially divisive issue. The industrialists had from the beginning shown a marked interest in the forms of industrial representation prevailing in Germany. The January congress had heard a detailed report on the German Handelstag, an organization for the "official" representation of industry and trade which, by law, enjoyed the privilege of considering and commenting upon legislation affecting its interests in advance of its submission to the legislature. Clearly, the industrialists hoped that their new organization would fill a comparable role as a Vorparlament or a "pre-duma" in Russia. Noting that "to introduce all disputes into the State Duma can hardly be considered feasible," Norpe had concluded that "it is necessary to create an institution in which it would be possible to debate and prepare in a preliminary fashion all questions that are to be introduced into the Duma, and to discuss objections to proposals harmful for industry and trade."[83] Meanwhile, the new Ministry of Trade and Industry had been preparing its own proposal, formally announced early in 1906, for the creation throughout the Empire of local chambers of commerce, which would constitute the base of a new system, clearly modeled upon the Handelstag, of official representation of commercial and industrial interests. In March, the Organizing Bureau, obviously emulating the Handelstag, with which the proposed Association was now frequently compared in the press,[84] successfully induced the ministry to submit the project to it for comment before introducing it into the State Duma. Thus, even before the First Regular Congress of the Association, in October 1906, the imperial government began the practice, faithfully maintained in later years, of soliciting the Association's views at an early stage in the preparation of all legislation affecting industry and trade.

Despite this favorable development, however, the Ministry's project for a Russian Handelstag aroused the virtually unanimous opposition of the exchange societies, which feared both a diminution of their own influence and a democratization of the representation of the business community at the expense of large-scale enterprise.[85] At the April Congress, they proposed petitioning the government to drop its project for its alleged competition with the new Association.[86] After the proposal was rejected, Iasiukovich hastened to reassure the Ministry of Trade and Industry that its impression that the Congress had "reacted negatively" to its project constituted "a small misunderstanding." In a statement that was no doubt as carefully worded as it was logically disconcerting, he proffered industry's support for the government's project, while simultaneously suggesting that the Association itself represented, in fact, the fulfillment of the official objective.

> The Association, from the very beginning, has set itself the aim of assisting the most rapid rise of chambers of commerce and industry, on the pattern of the German chambers, and the establishment of a Handelstag. Thus we not only do not have the slightest basis for opposing the ministry's project; on the contrary, we directly promote it, working in one and the same direction and creating the same organs that are referred to in the ministerial project. I am convinced that the Ministry must, in this respect, sympathize in every way with our enterprise.[87]

The government's subsequent deletion of the term "Empire-wide" (obshcheimperskii) from the name of the Association in the course of approving its charter may have signified a desire to differentiate the new organization from its own proposed "official" system of business representation.[88] In any case, the ministry seems not to have pressed its project further at that time. At the First Regular Congress, an official from the Ministry of Finance, present as a specially invited guest in recognition of his contribution to the founding of the Association, significantly hailed the occasion as marking, at last, the appearance of "a Russian Handelstag."[89]

For its part, the Association adopted a notably conciliatory approach toward those issues that were potentially productive of friction with official Russia. The question of the chambers of commerce was but one example. Far more difficult was the question of labor. The January Congress had expressed sharp opposition to the Kokovtsov Commission's proposals, first advanced in 1905 and still supported by the government, for a reduction in the maximum workday. As the conflict between labor and management grew in intensity during the early months of 1906, the Provisional Council devoted much of its attention to a consideration of means of resisting labor's demands for shorter hours, higher wages, and a share in decisions affecting employment, as well as to measures for combatting strikes and other acts of violence. These remained, however, "private" discussions. The Council cautiously refrained from placing the labor question on the agenda of the First Congress, considering that the currently "excited atmosphere" made this undesirable.[90]

Both to appease the government and to minimize conflict within the organization, the Provisional Council repeatedly stressed the nonpolitical character of the new Association. Indeed, the Provisional Fundamental Rules of the Empire, issued by the government on March 4,[91] forbade any linking of "representational" with political activities. The Council's determination to avoid all political issues undoubtedly reflected as well the diversity of political outlooks within the Association's membership and its own lack of confidence as it looked forward to the convening of Russia's new legislature. The fragile hope with which the industrialists looked to the new assembly had been undermined by their recognition that its predominantly agrarian membership would reflect popular distrust of the business community. In a pamphlet published in February 1906, the Association clearly expressed the fears of the industrialists:

> It is hardly possible to hope that the Duma will treat industry and trade sympathetically, that the questions of labor and of tariff policy will not be resolved to their injury, and that taxes will be justly distributed among all classes of the population and will not weigh almost exclusively on industrialists and merchants, since our agricultural elements are very little acquainted with the actual importance of industry and trade. Our public is almost unaware of the enormous role that these activities play in the national economy and regards industrialists and traders as a parasitical, moneyed class that can bear the burdens of taxation without particular difficulty.[92]

The failure of the business community's electoral campaign, continuing political divisions among the industrialists themselves, and the preoccupation of the First State Duma with issues far removed from industry and trade served only to strengthen the industrialists' conviction that the best hope for influencing both the legislature and the executive agencies of the government lay in building up a strong, united organization along strictly nonpolitical lines. Business leaders did not abandon the hope of ultimately influencing the legislature from within, although this hope at the moment rested almost entirely on the twelve official representatives of industry and trade who sat in the State Council. The possibility, however remote, of a more favorable orientation toward industry within the Duma at some time in the future always persisted.[93] To this hope the Association continued to cling, with varying degrees of sanguineness, in the years that followed. Meanwhile, industry's prospects for influencing official economic policies depended mainly on the building up of a harmonious and fruitful relationship with the executive branch of the government.

For the First Regular Congress, the Provisional Council prepared a heavy agenda, with reports on such diverse topics as the labor question, railroad construction and freight capacity, the taxation of business incomes and of electric power, inspection of steam boilers, and the institution of a fortnightly journal by the Association. Only three days before the Congress convened, however, it was announced that its activities would be limited largely to the formalities of an opening convention.[94] Accordingly, the three days of meetings, on October 12-14 in St. Petersburg, assumed the air of a gala celebration in honor of the new Association. Lending both brilliance and reassurance to the occasion was the presence of highly placed government officials, including the ministers of finance, communication, and trade and industry, each of whom wished the new organization success and assured the gathering of the willingness of his department to assist it in carrying out its appointed tasks. The minister of trade and industry went even further in declaring that the Association's effort to unify the commercial-industrial class before the government and other public institutions "has an undoubted right to count on the government's support."[95]

After a welcoming speech by Emanuil L. Nobel in his capacity as chairman of the Provisional Council (and a representative of both the Baku Petroleum Association and the Petersburg Society of Mill and Factory Owners), the Congress elected Grigorii A. Krestovnikov, president of the Moscow Exchange Society, to serve as chairman. Nikolai S. Avdakov, representing the Association of Southern Coal and Steel Producers, was elected vice-chairman.[96] The remainder of the first day was given over to additional welcoming speeches, which expatiated in grandiose, if not always precise, terms, on the tasks confronting the new organization. Minister of Finance Kokovtsov struck a patriotic note:

> Especially at the present time, after a disastrous war and a period of national calamities, Russia must settle down and secure for itself the position that our country is entitled to occupy among the nations--a position worthy of its natural resources and the qualities of its people. In this sphere of activity the new institution must take a leading part.[97]

The addresses of Nobel, Krestovnikov, and Avdakov reiterated the theme of industry's "state importance" and the necessity, in the words of Nobel, to "root in the consciousness of society the fact that the interests of industry and trade have important state significance and that the well-being of the people and the prosperity and power of the country are inconceivable without the broad development of industry and trade." The Association, he declared, must "conquer for itself the serious role of an experienced and objective consultant and expert in all those cases where the government and legislator stand in need of assistance."[98]

The leadership's underlying concern with the organization's potential role as a "pre-parliament" was even more evident in Avdakov's blunt assertion that "the awakening of political consciousness has called to life a large number of political parties and unions, but among these varied voices the voice of industry and trade has not been heard. Now this silence has ended: industry and trade have spoken."[99] Both Avdakov and Krestovnikov warned, however, that the Association must take its stand on the firm ground of "state interests," renouncing all partisanship, whether inspired by politics or by the special interests of particular branches of economic life.[100] Similarly, nearly every speaker stressed the need for industry to resolve the labor question and to recognize the essential unity of interest between industry and agriculture.

The only issues that received detailed consideration at the Congress concerned organizational procedures. The budget for 1907 proved to be a subject of divided opinion. In attempting to resolve the difference between the revenue of 66,000 rubles anticipated from members' dues and the estimated 128,000 needed to fulfill the ambitious program that had been proposed by the Provisional Council, the Congress approved only the lower figure. However, it also took under advisement the views of those delegates who upheld the necessity of instituting the Association's work immediately despite inadequate finances, "on a broad basis in accordance with the tremendous scale of the tasks to be fulfilled and the urgency of the many questions that stand in need of resolution."[101]

Having decided fundamental issues of finance and membership, the Congress proceeded to elect its delegates to the new permanent executive

Council, with a Presidium made up of Vasilii I. Timiriazev as chairman and Avdakov, Nobel, and Iasiukovich as vice-chairmen.[102] The election of Privy Councilor Timiriazev, a prominent figure in both the business and the official world, symbolized industry's hopes for a cooperative relationship with governmental authorities.[103] Reinforcing this impression was the appointment of Avdakov as one of the vice-chairmen. Although an active participant in industry's efforts to organize on an Empire-wide basis early in 1905, he had remained conspicuously aloof from the political movement that followed. One of industry's most experienced representatives in the official bureaucracy, he was well known for his conservatism as industry's leading "petitioner" and for the favorable light in which he had viewed governmental attitudes toward industry in the past.[104]

Finally, the Congress declared the headquarters of the new Association to be in St. Petersburg, although congresses might also be held in Moscow or other cities, at the discretion of the preceding congress. It also announced that it had taken "spacious quarters" at No. 100 on the Nevskii Prospekt. The substantial building at "Nevskii sto" remained its home until its demise at the beginning of 1918. (Its facilities included a large auditorium. The building still stands, although the offices have been converted to living quarters and the auditorium into a cinema.)

The Congress also voted to convene a special congress early in January 1907 in St. Petersburg to consider the most urgent problems confronting industry, namely, those of labor, the taxation of business (on both of these issues the Government was preparing bills for introduction into the Duma) and the inadequacy of Russia's railroads. Less immediately pressing questions, including agrarian reform, were postponed until the next regular congress at an unspecified time.[105]

On the afternoon of October 14, 1906, the Congress declared itself closed. It did not disband, however, but continued in "private session," from which all outsiders were barred, during that evening and all of the following day. Those meetings evidently considered Russia's critical oil shortage in preparation for the Association's participation in an official conference on this subject called by the minister of trade and industry.[106] Thus, the Association's First Regular Congress marked also a notable step toward the fulfillment of its founders' ambition that it should function as a Vorparlament in the German tradition, forging the united voice with which industry would speak as a participant in the formulation of official economic policies.[107]

The Growth of the Association: Unity and Conflict

Addressing the January Congress in 1906, Volskii had emphasized the importance of the principle of "strength through unity" and the need to create "a dense network" of commercial-industrial organizations that would cover Russia's entire non-agricultural economy.[108] In the years that followed, the Association assisted the rise of new representative organizations, although its efforts were often a source of acrimony in its uncertain relationship with the government.

The available information concerning the results of industry's organizing activity during the inter-revolutionary period remains, however, fragmentary and often inconsistent.[109] According to a Soviet study, some 101 stock and commodity exchanges existed in Russia in 1915-16, of which 45 had arisen after 1906; there were also forty "congress"-type associations of national importance, twelve representative "societies," and six specialized chambers of commerce devoted to the promotion of exports. The great majority of the organizations in these last three categories were of post-1905 vintage.[110] Thus, well before the outbreak of the First World War, nearly all important branches of Russian industry and trade possessed their own representative organizations. Despite many differences in function and in organizational structure, they represented large-scale capital. Almost without exception, the determining voice lay with a handful of the largest enterprises within a given industry.[111]

As might be expected marked progress occurred in those areas that had been least organized before 1905, namely, the various machine and metal working industries (although it was not until 1916 that a national or "All-Russian" association of this industry was founded), transportation, construction, and light industry. Industries that acquired organization for representational purposes between 1905 and 1917 included agricultural tools and machinery, locomotives and railroad car building, shipbuilding, chemicals, glass, leather and furs, printing, fishing, various food and confectionery industries, brewing and distilling, and inland shipping on the Volga and Black Sea. Numerous industries, and especially the metal, lumber, and flour milling industries, maintained regional and local organizations as well as national federations. By 1914 the textile industry had also achieved a substantial measure of organization in the Russian Society of Linen Manufacturers (1906), a Russian Society of Woolen Manufacturers (1910), and societies of cotton textile manufacturers in Moscow and Lodz (1913), the latter serving both as representative organs and as export syndicates.

Still lagging was the world of finance, although associations of accident and fire insurance companies made their appearance; an Association of Provincial Commercial Banks was formed in 1915; and in 1916 a reorganization of the hitherto inactive Russian Banking Association seemed to promise a more influential role for banks. Advances also occurred in the establishment of nonspecialized local and regional organizations. Various "employers' unions," patterned in whole or in part after the Petersburg Society of Mill and Factory Owners, made their appearance. Of these, the most noteworthy were the Central Society of Manufacturers, established in 1905 under the chairmanship of Sergei I. Chetverikov; the Moscow Society of Manufacturers, headed by Iulii P. Guzhon (Jules Goujon); the Odessa Industrial Society (later, the Odessa Society of Manufacturers), 1908; the Society of Polish Manufacturers, 1909; and the South Russian Association of Industry and Trade, 1911. In August 1917 the employers' groups were united in a Russian Union of Manufacturers' Societies.

Almost without exception, Russia's new industrial organizations helped to swell the membership rolls of the Association of Industry and Trade, to expand its financial resources and, no doubt, to increase the authority with which it was able to speak in the name of "united industry." According to its charter, the Association operated under the direction of the Ministry of Trade and Industry

> for the purpose of the examination and discussion of questions concerning the general needs of industry and trade, for the elaboration of measures directed toward their advancement, and, equally, for the unification of the representation of the common interests of industry and trade.[112]

More specifically, the declared objectives of the Association were: to unify the representation of industry and trade before governmental and "public" institutions; to promote the further organization of industry and trade; to assist in "regularizing" relations between capital and labor; to organize "competitions, exhibitions, experimental stations, laboratories, museums, schools, courses for workers," and other measures serving the technological advancement of production and the education of the population in the needs and importance of industry and trade; and to issue periodical organs and to collect and publish statistical data and other information concerning industry and trade and the issues confronting them. With the exception of the fourth, which was given little implementation, the charter's statement of aims provides a fair summary of the actual work of the Association. (See Appendix I.)

The charter of the Association not only limited its membership to large-scale enterprises but also concentrated power and responsibility in the hands of a small group of leaders at the top. Because membership in the Council became to some extent self-perpetuating, the same individuals appeared on its rolls year after year. One of the Council's duties was to prepare lists of candidates for election to its own membership by the Congresses. Those lists appear to have been approved more or less automatically. In addition, the members of the Association displayed a marked tendency to reappoint the same persons as their delegates to the Council. Within the congresses themselves, the concentration of influence remained strong because votes were weighted according to the size of the members and because certain prominent individuals often represented several organizations simultaneously. The charter permitted this practice, subject only to the stipulation that one person could represent no more than three full members or cast no more than ten votes. (See Appendix II for additional discussion of the Association's structure.)

No history of the Association of Industry and Trade would be complete without some attempt to assess the organization's claim to represent "united industry." Closely interrelated with this broad question are the subsidiary issues of the role of the professional staff--the so-called "third element"--in the determination of its policies and the extent to which conflict existed within the Association beneath an external appearance of harmony.

Some historians and contemporary observers of the Russian business community interpreted its public activities as primarily the work not of the businessmen themselves but of their professional staffs. The most vigorous exponent of this view, the Menshevik historian Gushka, maintained that the veritable "army of the intelligentsia" that served organized industry consisted not only of its professional and clerical employees but also included, in some cases, the persons who fulfilled "the most responsible, highest functions, occupying the posts of directors of affairs and even of chairmen of Councils or Committees" and the editors of periodicals.[113] Among the latter organizations he included the Association of Industry and Trade.[114]

Both the question of the role of the "third element" and the issue of the unity and representativeness of the Association of Industry and Trade came to the fore at the Fourth Congress in a report presented by a delegate from Odessa, S. I. Sokolovskii. In his report, which was received by the congress without comment, Sokolovskii contended that Russia's business organizations as a whole lacked vitality and the Association itself did not represent local interests.[115] Despite the impressive number of the country's business organizations, they failed, in his judgment, to represent their membership and therefore could not fulfill their class mission in the modernization and development of the Russian state.

The root of the difficulty allegedly lay in the domination of the business groups by their "organization men." Among the latter Sokolovskii included not only employees but the top leadership as well.

> The same persons appear as leaders in the various institutions of the commercial-industrial class--in the Council of our Association, in the Council of the Association of Trade and Agriculture, in the Petersburg and Moscow Exchange Committees and other organizations of the capital. . . . Old, respected names, it is true, but names, not organizations and not even their substitutes. Who directs these organizations? It would be hypocrisy or self-deception to say that councils, boards of directors, committees, and similar elected representatives of industry and trade . . . direct the Russian commercial-industrial organizations. That would be a bitter untruth. The Russian commercial-industrial organizations, with few exceptions, are governed by a bureaucracy: secretaries, directors of affairs, administrators, and such. This is the third element of our commercial-industrial institutions, and it not only holds in its hands all our commercial-industrial life; it speaks for it. And where the director of its affairs is a talented man with a spark of public fire, the organization comes alive; where this is not the case, the organization vegetates, or expires completely, existing only on paper. . . . The third element in industry and trade has to do with the few persons who compose the Committee; it has no connection with the commercial-industrial population or even with the members who themselves make up the society, since those members are, in part, only counted and even pay their membership dues with reluctance.

Asserting that "the Russian public commercial-industrial organizations do not satisfy even their own most elementary objectives, that of representation before governmental institutions," he concluded:

> In order to represent, it is necessary to know and demand; and in order to demand it is necessary to be strong, that is, to feel in oneself the beat of the pulse of millions, to be confident of their support. This role not a single public institution of the commercial-industrial world in Russia can assume; not even the Association of all commercial-industrial organizations of Russia could take it upon itself, because the authority of those representatives would not issue from those depths where the real right to act and to decide lies hidden.[116]

The validity of Sokolovskii's position insofar as it applies to the Association is difficult to assess, for the evidence is incomplete and contradictory. Certainly, the leadership of the Council and the Committee of the Association remained remarkably stable and numerically limited. Indeed, it is probably no exaggeration to say that most of the initiative and responsible direction displayed within the organization was attributable to the three men who largely shaped its history: Avdakov, Zhukovskii, and Volskii. Any history of the Association would be incomplete without some attention to their individual backgrounds and interests.

More than with any other single person, the Association was identified with Nikolai Stepanovich Avdakov, chairman of its Council from early in 1907 until his death in September 1915. Educated as a mining engineer, Avdakov spent a long career, from the time he left school in 1878 until 1907, in the coal and iron mining industry of the South of Russia, which he served first as an employee and later, from 1900 to 1906, as chairman of the Association of Southern Coal and Steel Producers. He was also a principal founder of the Kharkov Coal and Iron Exchange. It was after resigning his chairmanship of the Association of Southern Coal and Steel Producers in order to become its representative in St. Petersburg that he earned his credentials as one of the "founding fathers" of the Association of Industry and Trade. Simultaneously, he became chairman of the coal syndicate, Produgol. In the following years, while serving as chairman of the new Association, he developed ever more diverse interests. He served as a director of a shipping company and of the Northern Donets Railroad as well as chairman of the board of the Lena Gold Mining Company. While continuing his close associations with the Kharkov Exchange, Produgol, and the Southern Association, he took an active part in Prodameta and assumed the chairmanship of the Consultative Board of Gold and Platinum Producers. Avdakov also served as a member of the Council of the Ministry of Trade and Industry and represented mining interests in the official councils on railroads, freight rates, and mining affairs. Finally, he represented industry and trade in the State Council beginning in 1906. On his death, Industry and Trade (Promyshlennost' i torgovlia) spoke of him as "king of the iron and steel industry" and the spirit behind the syndicates Produgol and Prodameta, through whose hands "passed millions" of rubles.[117]

Yet, despite his lifelong devotion to business interests and the power that he wielded within the business community, Avdakov was regarded by his associates less as a fellow businessman than as an administrator and technician. Indeed, Avdakov would appear to have been Russia's "organization man" par excellence. The son of an army doctor, he had no family roots in industry and trade. Throughout his business career, he maintained his own professional interests, contributing frequently to engineering and mining publications. Essentially, he was a conservative and colorless bureaucrat. Politically, he remained an Octobrist. He inclined toward timidity in his relations with the government and was widely known, and often condemned, as industry's principal "petitioner." Nevertheless, the Association undoubtedly owed much to his initiative and, especially, to his organizing and mediating abilities. His death left a gap that no one could fill.[118]

Vladislav Vladislavovich Zhukovskii (in Polish: Władysław Żukowski), who succeeded Avdakov as chairman of the Council in September 1915, directed the Association during the eleven months that remained until his own premature death in August 1916. It was presumably his Polish nationality that had prevented his appointment as chairman before 1915. He had been active in the Association since its founding, however, and from 1911 until his death, his was probably the most vigorous influence within the organization. In addition, following Volskii's resignation early in 1911, he bore primary responsibility for supervising the work of the secretariat within the Committee and Presidium of the Council.

Superficially, Zhukovskii's background resembled that of Avdakov. He, too, was less a businessman than a member of industry's technical and administrative elite. Like Avdakov, he had received training as an engineer, and his roots lay in the Polish mining and metallurgical industry. Later, his interests also became more diversified, as he became active, particularly, in the insurance business of St. Petersburg. Although Zhukovskii lacked the economic power of Avdakov, he demonstrated a broader political outlook. A patriotic Pole who believed that Poland's cause required a close association with a prosperous, liberal, and Europeanized Russia, he served actively in the Second and Third State Dumas, where, according to Pares, he was "the best critic" of the government's budget.[119] His influence in the Duma owed much to his position as chairman of the Commercial-Industrial Group of Members of the Duma and State Council.

Zhukovskii impressed his colleagues as "a very cultured man,"[120] widely read and well informed on economic conditions and economic thought in the West. His knowledge and interest enriched his contributions to the work of the Association, particularly the efforts to draw up a plan for Russia's economic development; to organize systematic statistical records with a view to regulating the business cycle; to implement legal (and, presumably, political) reform in Russia as a precondition of national economic growth; and to draw businessmen into contact with academic circles and into direct participation in the work of the legislature. The eulogies that followed Zhukovskii's death expressed a warmth of feeling and a sense of loss that had not attended Avdakov's death a year earlier. In the words of an anonymous member of the Association's staff, "not a single serious undertaking, not a single commission or meeting of any real importance" had occurred within the organization during the past five or six years without his presence as chairman or as an "indispensable" member.[121] Even more important, according to Baron G. Kh. Maidel, was Zhukovskii's prominent role as a source of ideas and initiative within the Council "from the very moment of the rise of the new organ of united industry."

> Every social class must have its spiritual leaders, i.e. people who can disassociate themselves from everyday affairs and look into the future, viewing the importance of their work in the perspective of the national interest as a whole. . . . Among such leaders, the future historian of Russia will doubtless count Vladislav Vladislavovich Zhukovskii.[122]

More difficult to characterize, both as an individual and as a leader of the Association, was Adolf Adolfovich Volskii (in Polish: Wolski). Like Avdakov and Zhukovskii, he was trained as an engineer; and, like Zhukovskii, he was Polish. Until 1906, when he assumed direction of the Association's secretariat, he had headed the staff of the Consultative Bureau of Iron Producers. He played an active part in the founding of the Association. As director of the secretariat and editor of Industry and Trade until early 1911, he provided much of the initiative behind the organization's work, particularly in assessing the causes of Russia's economic backwardness and in emphasizing the need to draw up a program for national economic development. Although he held a position in the Association below that of Avdakov and Zhukovskii, he appeared a far stronger and more colorful personality than either of them. Energetic, aggressive, ebullient, he displayed a vitriolic temper. His caustic and highly colloquial commentaries on irksome episodes in Russian business life occasionally enlivened the pages of Industry and Trade.[123] His turbulent presence left an indelible mark on the early history of the Association.

Although, as we have seen, the leadership within the Association remained highly concentrated, it did not operate in a vacuum. Representatives of member organizations participated in its work on a broad basis, and, in the last analysis, exercised very real control. At the congresses, moreover, differences of opinion among the delegates, and even among delegates representing the same organization, occurred as a normal part of the debates. For example, the convening of the Association's only Special Congress in November 1911 resulted directly from the inability of the Fifth Regular Congress to reach agreement on policies to be advocated with respect to the operation of Russia's railroads.[124] Nor were divisions within the Association limited to friendly differences of opinion. Indeed, it would have been surprising if conflicts in economic interest within its membership had not posed a continuing problem for its leadership. Such conflicts were, in fact, numerous. In some cases--as for example in the rivalry between coal and oil interests, between coal and iron producers, between the latter and the manufacturers of finished metals and machines, and between machinery producers and the textile interests--conflict appeared endemic and irreconcilable.

Differences among geographic regions led to numerous clashes, as Sokolovskii's report testified. Not the least of these was the continuing rivalry between Moscow and Petersburg, which, as we have seen, had erupted during the very founding of the Association. Despite the prominent role played by the delegates from Moscow at the congresses and on the Council,[125] its representation on the Committee and the Presidium of the Council remained weak. Indeed, from 1908 onward Moscow was represented on the Committee only tenuously by one delegate (Genrikh G. Vissendorf) from the provincial textile center of Ivanovo-Voznesensk. In 1910, the old capital acquired its own delegate on the Presidium in the person of Nikolai A. Iasiuninskii, but after his death in September 1912, Moscow again remained without representation at the center of the Association's leadership. In contrast, Petersburg always enjoyed a strong presence.[126]

Although the Association therefore seemed to be primarily a Petersburg organization, there is reason to believe that the situation was in part, at least, of Moscow's own making. Secure in their position as the acknowledged leaders of the Russian merchant estate, the Moscow industrialists perhaps did not aspire to an active role in the Association.[127] Moreover, the evidence of Petersburg's domination of the Association is not entirely convincing. The Petersburg Exchange Society never joined, and although the powerful Petersburg Society of Mill and Factory Owners was well represented on the Committee and the Presidium,[128] its views did not always prevail.[129] In fact, it often acted as a competitor of the Association.[130]

Certainly much hostility existed between the two capitals, and occasionally it flared out of control. Such an instance occurred at the Seventh Congress, when, in a bitter exchange, Pavel P. Riabushinskii, according to one delegate, virtually accused the Council of seeking to impose the hegemony of Petersburg over the rest of the country.[131] Significantly, however, the dispute resulted from Moscow's desire to remain apart from a national organization that the Association wished to create for the centralized handling of industry's uncollected debts. A year later, on the occasion of the seventy-fifth anniversary of the Moscow Exchange, the Council's carefully worded greetings hailed the Exchange Society as "the glorious leader of the all-Russian merchants" and acknowledged its great influence in commercial-industrial circles even when other business organizations had not always agreed with its position.[132]

Throughout its twelve-year history, conflict and disunity within the Association undoubtedly remained a constant problem for the Council. In the spring of 1908 it declared "itself the true representative of the all-Russian interests of industry and trade" but admitted that its task lay in "the examination of separate, not infrequently conflicting, interests and their reduction to a common denominator."[133] In fact, the Association's effort to reconcile conflicting interests and to present a picture of a truly "united industry" to the world may well account, in part at least, for the difficulty of defining the actual center of power within the organization. The Council's role, moreover, was by no means limited to that of a passive mediator, for it clearly strove to educate and guide the many elements among its membership that had not yet achieved an understanding of the needs of a modern industrial economy.

Yet the leadership of the Association itself could not remain immune to criticism from its membership. During the early years, much of this criticism centered on the controversial figure of Volskii, the editor of Industry and Trade. Rumblings of discontent first became public at the Third Congress, which nevertheless voted to continue the journal on its established basis.[134] At the Fourth Congress, the debate became more heated as a result of a recommendation by the Audit Commission that the Council supervise closely both the content of the journal's leading articles and the conduct of its financial affairs. Nikolai F. fon-Ditmar, chairman of the Association of Southern Coal and Steel Producers, insisted that the lead articles "must express the opinion of all industry and trade; they must be such that all branches of industry and trade can take on themselves responsibility for these articles." Avdakov stated that the Committee of the Council had repeatedly considered reducing the scope of the journal or halting its publication altogether, steps to which he was strongly opposed. Citing the attention with which Industry and Trade was read in "governmental spheres," in "broad public circles," and by "many members of the Legislative Institutions," he maintained that the struggle with the many prejudices from which industry and trade suffered "is possible only through the mediation of a serious organ that objectively illuminates all the varied aspects of the economic position of the country." Volskii satisfied fon-Ditmar by agreeing with the need for such a review and explaining that the lead articles in fact received the approval of the Committee of the Council. Another speaker went still further, however, in demanding that the journal print only articles "that, without exception, interest all industry and trade."[135]

In the end, the Congress voted unanimously to continue Industry and Trade with no change in either its scope or its policies. The issue remained unresolved, however. In December 1909, the Council instructed the Committee to establish a special commission to study the financial problems of the journal. This step led ultimately to the formation in September 1910 of an Editorial Commission under the Committee for the purpose of supervising lead articles. The Commission included Avdakov, Zhukovskii, Guzhon, Iasiukovich, and Nikolai N. Iznar, but not Volskii.[136]

The question of Industry and Trade did not, however, tell the whole story of the Council's difficulties with Volskii. During the early summer of 1908, the press reported rumors of an extraordinary audit of the Council's finances and of the impending departure of Volskii in connection with it, rumors that were firmly refuted in an article unmistakably written by Volskii himself.[137] At the end of the year, a serious dispute erupted between Volskii and the Council over the propriety of introducing a change in the journal of one of its meetings. Volskii refused to make the change that the Council requested and submitted his resignation. The Council yielded.[138] Both the Third and Fourth Congresses adopted positions in sharp disagreement with those advocated by Volskii. At the Fourth Congress, especially, Volskii's defense of the policy of Minister of Finance and Chairman of the Council of Ministers Kokovtsov on the question of state loans to industry aroused the outspoken dissent of Krestovnikov, Guzhon, Zhukovskii, and others.[139]

Under these circumstances, Volskii's resignation, and the Council's acceptance of it on February 1, 1911, both as editor of Industry and Trade and as director of the Secretariat, surprised no one. Baron G. Kh. Maidel succeeded him as director. Ippolit B. Glivits (in Polish: Hypolit Gliwic), formerly assistant editor and chief of the secretariat's Commercial-Industrial section, became editor. On January 1, 1913, Baron Maidel assumed the editorship and retained both posts until the end of April

1917, when E. L. Liubovich, chief of the Council's legal section, succeeded him. However, Volskii's successors exercised neither his independent initiative in directing the work of the organization's staff nor his influence over its journal. After his departure, the dominant voice in the determination of the policies of Industry and Trade lay not with its editor but with the Editorial Commission of the Council.[140]

Other conflicts shook the Association during its early and middle years. It is significant, for example, that Krestovnikov took his chairmanship of the Fourth Congress as an opportunity to try to "answer the question whether there are visible results of the work of our Organization," a question that he answered strongly in the affirmative, finding the most tangible evidence of the Association's work in a greater understanding and respect for industry and its needs among the public at large.[141] The Fourth Congress, it may be recalled, listened in silence to the critical observations of the delegate from Odessa, but it also approved measures "for enlivening its relations with the provinces."[142] By doing so, the Congress sought to allay the discontent of those members who clearly resented the strong direction at the center of the organization.

The last months of 1910 and the first months of 1911 witnessed a major crisis in the affairs of the Association. Mysterious circumstances surrounded the postponement of the Fifth Congress, originally scheduled to meet in the autumn of 1910. (See Appendix III.) When the Congress finally convened in the spring of 1911, not only had Volskii's resignation occurred but the agenda lacked an ambitious report, prepared by the secretariat under his direction and approved by the Council, on ways and means of promoting national economic development.

The year 1910, in addition to being the only year between 1906 and 1915 when a congress failed to meet, witnessed an unusual dullness and restraint in the work of the Council and its journal. In part this may be explained by the transition in Russia's economic development that occurred in 1910. The prolonged economic depression had ended at last, but the problems attendant on a rapidly expanding economy had not yet appeared. Nor had mounting international tensions yet entered the critical stage. Hence the Association faced fewer pressing problems than there had been before or there would be soon again.

In any event, the Fifth Congress marked the end of a period of transition, and perhaps of turmoil, in the affairs of the Association. Krestovnikov, rather than Avdakov (as was usual), presented the Council's report on its work to the Congress. He pointed out rather enigmatically that

> if there were some organizations belonging to the Association that did not agree with certain of the Council's decisions, then nevertheless there was no disagreement in principle on the general, correct direction in which the work of the Council and its individual members was proceeding.[143]

During the Congress, the theme of unity appeared again and again. "And from that moment when we shall have succeeded in uniting ourselves," Zhukovskii stated in his report on the legislature, "we shall with justification also speak out and strive for the gradual elaboration of a state program from our commercial-industrial point of view as the synthesis of our practical interests and our ideological [ideinyi] outlook."[144]

Even more suggestive than the proceedings of the Congress itself, perhaps, were the words of the lead article in Industry and Trade immediately before the Congress convened:

> The past five-year period was a period of incredible work. All members of our organization, all who took part in its work, have had to work like fiends, intensively, under strain, in haste. We hardly succeeded in coping with one question when another, just as important, just as complex, just as impatient of delay, gathered head and demanded to be resolved. . . . The results of this enormous work are not always perceptible, not always tangible. Our point of view is far from having always triumphed. But if at the present time the public opinion of the country is somewhat more attentive to the needs of industry, if it is possible to see even the smallest particle of the influence of our organization, then we can consider ourselves compensated a hundredfold for all our work.

The journal made it clear that the perceptible change in the Association's work was not accidental.

> Our Association arose in a period of unprecedented public creative activity. The general tempo of life forced us to work with feverish intensity. At the present time, a period of quiet has begun. Our organization, perhaps, will not in the period ahead have many occasions for coming forward clearly and effectively; but all the firmer, all the more solid, must be our every word. All the more solidarity must underlie our every appearance. In some quarters there is talk about the thinness of the program of the Fifth Congress. But in fact the practice of former congresses has taught us to restrict ourselves to a small number of thoroughly studied and investigated questions, and in this sense to narrow as far as possible the agendas of the Congresses. From general questions we are passing to concrete, specific questions of business, so that when there is need we can return, well armed, to general questions.[145]

In fact, the Congress's agenda contained only two items: railroads and zemstvo taxation of business enterprise. Its failure to reach agreement on either of these questions necessitated the convening of the Special Congress in the autumn.

The withdrawal of the Association from its former concern with the broad issues confronting the economy was short-lived. Its return to an even more vigorous outlook by the end of 1911 no doubt reflected the rise of Zhukovskii to a position of leadership within the organization. Not only did the Council now reveal a new and growing concern with events in the legislature and with political affairs generally; it also devoted itself with renewed energy to the task, begun under Volskii's prodding, of developing a program of economic development.

The Association received a rare tribute from David Lloyd George on the occasion of a visit by a British Parliamentary delegation early in 1912.

> You have created [in Russia] what we have not yet been able to create in England. . . . We do not have such a general organization that unites all and which considers all questions, as your Association does, not from the point of view of one or another branch of industry, but from the point of view of the interests of the whole, from the point of view of the state and the national welfare.[146]

Nevertheless, the last two and one-half years before the war witnessed increased tension and turmoil in the Association. Reference has already been made to the bitter exchange between the leadership of the Council and the Moscow delegation at the Seventh Congress. The effect of renewed prosperity--goods shortages and rising prices--greatly intensified the economic rivalries among the industrialists. Especially troublesome became the question of tariff protection for goods that were expensive or in short supply. The distinguished chairman of the joint commission of the Association and of the Association of Trade and Agriculture, Vasilii I. Timiriazev, pleaded before the Eighth Congress for support and assistance in "helping the Commission become a true central organ of industry" in carrying out its task.[147]

Not only internal divisions but also mounting international tensions and the Association's growing embroilment, on both economic and political issues, with the government and with the public at large contributed to the burgeoning sense of crisis that dominated its outlook by the spring of 1914. In the press and within official circles as well, the Association became the target of diverse attacks. Some charged that it represented only the selfish and narrowly conceived interests of "united industry" against those of the country as a whole. Others alleged that it was inadequately organized to serve as a genuine and effective agent of the industrial community, whose interests it habitually subordinated to its overriding concern with broad, national issues, with promoting or retarding (as the case might be) the growth of the national economy.[148]

2

The Industrialists Look to Russia's Future

"Whither Russia?": Industry's Goals

Emerging out of one revolution and destined to meet its end in a second and far more decisive upheaval, the Association of Industry and Trade faced not only the insistent demands of the present but also the potentially explosive needs of Russia's future. In the relative tranquillity that settled for a brief period over Russian life in the wake of the first revolution, the industrialists' urgent and continuing preoccupation with the question of the Empire's future course stood out, although, to be sure, the same preoccupation characterized most of the more thoughtful and articulate organizations and individuals in Russia at the time. To what long-range goals did the Association aspire?

Although the Association began its career at a time when the Russian economy was still sunk in the depression that had begun at the turn of the century and which had been further aggravated by the political and social upheaval of 1905, the new organization looked to Russia's more distant future with confidence. Grounded in an almost mystical faith in Russia's destiny to join the ranks of powerful industrialized nations, its optimism survived undiminished, despite manifold discouragements, until nearly the end of the prewar period. Yet the industrialists saw the gulf that separated backward Russia from the "cultured" countries of the West. In accepting the challenge to overcome this gulf, they displayed not only determination but an enthusiasm that was evidently born, in some degree at least, of the very events that had given rise to their organization. Russia, they believed, had arrived at a fundamental turning point in its history, in which the recent reforms in political life must be buttressed by equally far-reaching changes in economic affairs.

During the months before the First Congress in October 1906, frequent references in the public statements of the organization's leaders to the need for a "radical renovation" of national life and to the "intense work" that lay ahead bore witness that the business community was fully aroused to the challenge of its own era. For example, they justified in these terms the decision of the All-Russian Commercial-Industrial Union to abandon its unsuccessful effort to form a political party and to unite with the emerging Association:

> It should not be forgotten that in the very immediate future there must take place among us a colossal amount of work on the economic and financial reconstruction of the country; and on the correct outcome of this work will depend the entire well-being of our motherland. It is necessary, therefore, that the commercial-industrial class be imbued with all the importance of the historic moment through which it is living.[1]

The grandeur of Russia and the prosperity of its people appeared as the acme of the Association's aspirations, but the realization of these goals depended on Russia's attaining a level of economic, and particularly industrial, development comparable to that of the most advanced countries of the West. By its own account, the promotion of national economic growth always remained the Association's prime raison d'être and the object of its most solicitous concern. It reinforced this position both by its unremitting consciousness of Russia's backwardness and by its faith in the bright future that ultimately awaited Russian industry. "Its prospects are vast," Industry and Trade assured its readers, "for Russia, by its natural resources and population, is a country of unlimited economic potentialities."[2] Admittedly, these happy prospects lay far in the future. As the Council observed in a formal address to the minister of trade and industry shortly before the war:

> Russian industry and trade, despite their comparative youth, occupy an honorable place among the industries of the other countries of the world. But, in order to stand in one of the first places, appropriate to its natural resources and its population, a long course of development still faces it.[3]

As early as the spring of 1906, one of the Association's "founding fathers," Konstantin A. Iasiuninskii, gave its viewpoint succinct expression when he called on Russia's new legislature to accept two "basic principles" guiding its work:

> that industry is a branch of popular work without which cultural progress is inconceivable in the country, without which the attainment of the ideal of the economic independence of the state in international relations is incon-

> ceivable at any time, even in the distant future; and that the interests of industry are interests of state importance.[4]

Similarly, the chairman of the Provisional Council, Emanuil L. Nobel, told the First Congress that "the interests of industry and trade have important state significance and that the well-being of the people and the prosperity and power of the country are inconceivable without the broad development of industry and trade."[5]

Throughout the peacetime years, the Association continued to propound the "state importance" of industry and trade and its own conviction (in words borrowed from Finance Minister Kokovtsov's address to the Fourth Congress) that "the development of industry and trade is a necessary condition of the life of the country."[6] In subsequent years, both Kokovtsov's words and the Fourth Congress's own resolution were quoted and requoted in the Association's publications, and no congress passed into history without reasserting the "state importance" of industry and trade. At the Fifth Congress, for example, Avdakov declared:

> Actually, industry and trade are subjects of high importance in all cultured countries, and they occupy a respected place in every cultured country. Industry and trade are the movers of culture and progress; industry and trade give wages to the population, assist the accumulation of capital, and, at the same time, promote the development of all the productive forces in Russia.[7]

The organization insisted that economic questions, and particularly the advancement of national economic development, be given high priority among the many urgent problems that confronted the government.[8] In mid-1909, the election of delegates from industry and trade to the State Council provided an occasion for the Association to assert its belief that "obviously, economic questions must stand on the first place in connection with the regeneration of Russia."[9] At the Fourth Congress a few months later, this position became the dominant theme. In a formal resolution, the Congress asserted

> that the time has come when the development of the economic forces of the country must be placed at the base of state policy, on the first plane of importance; that the adoption of all measures for the most rapid strengthening of industrial activity is necessary in the interest of reinforcing those foundations on which the well-being of the country and of the state finances rests.[10]

The Special Congress of 1911 added its conviction that "now, more than ever, the development of industrial and commercial activity in the country must constitute the most important task of state activity,.[11] Somewhat later, the appointment of Kokovtsov as chairman of the Council of Ministers and of Petr L. Bark as deputy minister of trade and industry provided additional occasions for emphasizing the "primary importance of economic interests" in governmental affairs.[12] The same theme dominated the Sixth Congress. The Council emphasized that the "correct" development of industry and trade "constitutes the most important task of the present day."[13] Avdakov welcomed Kokovtsov to the gathering with this admonition:

> It is not necessary to persuade you of the fact that when this development is given first priority and proper importance is attached to it, the country will grow stronger and the well-being of the masses of the people will rise, and that in direct relationship with the economic development of the country lies its political power. . . . I permit myself to say that at the present time Russia needs energetic work more than ever, and Russia needs it more than any other country.[14]

Although 1909 marked the end of Russia's prolonged depression and the beginning of a period of economic growth and prosperity rivaling that of the 1890s, the Association's insistence on the necessity of a concerted drive for national economic development not only continued but intensified. In part, the organization expressed anxiety concerning the rate of the economy's progress in response to widespread criticism directed at industry because of its failure to meet promptly and completely all the rapidly burgeoning demand for its products. More fundamentally, its concern reflected its mounting apprehension over Russia's security in a crisis-ridden world and its ever-present fear that the economic "boom" would be followed by a "bust," as had occurred at the end of the nineties.

The Association also feared that industry would be unable to satisfy the heavy demands made upon it as a result of the further implementation of the Stolypin agrarian reforms. Industry and Trade quoted approvingly from the journal of the Association of Southern Coal and Steel Producers:

> The grandiose process of the liberation of agricultural work, until now hampered in its development by the primitive form of communal life, will undoubtedly have as its result an increase in the productivity of agriculture and the proletarianization of a significant part of the masses--more grain and more working hands. And this surplus of grain and people must be absorbed, first of all, by our industry.

Asserting that the government's economic policy contained no "reflection of this colossal process of the radical reconstruction of our economic life of the people," the article declared:

> The economic and political conjuncture at the present time is such that it is already impossible to continue to live as God intends; it is necessary to place a conscious, definite aim before our internal policy, and this basic aim, this basic task can be only one: THE INDUSTRIALIZATION OF RUSSIA. All measures of the government, all efforts of the leaders of our policy must be directed toward our industry's attaining a powerful development, for only on a firm economic basis are both external greatness and the cultural flourishing of the people possible.[15]

During the last months before the war, however, the Association emphasized the danger that Russia's lagging industrial growth posed not only to its position as a great power but to its very independence as a nation. Noting that advances in military techniques had greatly changed the methods of warfare, Industry and Trade stressed the need for highly developed and technically advanced industry to "keep pace with the seemingly headlong mad competition of the great powers in the manufacture of war equipment."[16] Avdakov warned the State Council:

> states are measured not only by the strength of their war fleet and their weapons of war, but also by their economic power. Therefore for us also, in order to catch up with and, if not to catch up with, then only to draw near to [the countries of the West], it is necessary to develop our economic well-being, to concern ourselves about the material sufficiency of our population.[17]

Behind the Association's growing apprehension during the immediately prewar months lay its mounting disillusionment with the government's desire or intention, despite frequent verbal reassurances, actively to assist industrial development[18] and its own discouragement with the slow pace of Russia's industrial progress in the face of increasingly ominous international conditions. As early as the spring of 1912, Avdakov told the Sixth Congress: "All that which has been done for the success of industry and trade is only the beginning of the vast work that confronts us for the sake of Russia's economic development."[19] A year later, in a speech that was warmly commended by the Association, the prominent Moscow textile industrialist and financier, Aleksandr I. Konovalov, warned the State Duma: "We are still exceedingly far from a real regeneration of our productive forces; we are still exceedingly far from the beginning of a rise and strengthening of the well-being of our national economy."[20] Shortly afterward, Avdakov, addressing the State Council on the state of the Empire's economic progress, declared scornfully: "We are only beginning to develop ourselves in all this, and already we are calling these steps, praise God, our economic boom."[21]

As Russia stood on the verge of disaster in July 1914, the Association's alarm at the inadequacy of the country's economic progress and its warnings of the dire consequences to be expected from current official economic policies dominated its published work. In two speeches before the State Council, Avdakov stressed Russia's "dangerous economic dependence."[22] "Russia," he pointed out, was "still far from an economic flowering and must take extraordinary measures to develop internal production."

> Our present economic growth must be welcomed because it is the beginning of an economic expansion that must in the future be developed an infinite number of times beyond that which now exists. Only under such conditions shall we be freed from our economic dependence on foreign states; only under such conditions shall we develop the productive forces of the country; only under such conditions shall we respond to the call from the height of the throne for the development of internal forces.[23]

In its dawning realization that no economic improvement could be hoped for until official policies had changed, the Association hovered between resignation and near despair. "We shall have to mark time," Industry and Trade advised its readers, "until the contradiction between reality and what the government itself recognizes in principle as necessary is removed."[24] Two weeks later, however, its patience appeared to be at an end. "It is obvious," the journal declared in its last issue before hostilities began, "that the current state of affairs cannot be endured."[25]

Although the cause of Slavic "brotherhood" exerted an attraction for the industrialists immediately after 1905, the still stronger pull of Russian nationalism was apparent not only in their later reactions to issues in foreign policy but also in their response to the problems of Russia's domestic economic development. Hostile to Slavophile doctrines of Russia's "uniqueness," especially the desirability of basing the country's economic and social structure on agriculture rather than on industry, the Association looked to the industrialized and "cultured" countries of the West both as the measure of Russia's backwardness and as the model after which the motherland should fashion itself in the future. Even before the founding of the Association, Volskii had foreshadowed its Westernism.

> Before us lies the time when we must also cast away the ridiculous Slavophile preaching of Russian uniqueness and when in industrial life we must follow the English motto and remember that "if knowledge is not power, it shows the way to power." . . . It is now time for us to view our private problems and narrow questions within the framework of the entirety of Russian and international life. It is time to understand, if only through the bitter experience of the Russo-Japanese War, that, by retreating into his own unique and self-sufficient cell, the Russian citizen in general, and the Russian industrialist in particular, is outwitting no one and will have to yield his place to peoples and elements better adapted to the contemporary struggle for existence.[26]

Typical of the Association's more mature view was Industry and Trade's assertion that Russia must follow the general European path.

> Having before us the vast experience of cultured countries, we must follow their example, adapting to local conditions, painstakingly studying them, and striving not only for the maintenance of that which we already possess, but also for the conquest of new paths. The raising of the production of the country and, together with that, of popular well-being--that is the goal.[27]

Early in 1912, in a mood of unwonted optimism, the journal wrote:

> Now it is recognized not only that Russia is following in the footsteps of the western European countries, which have far outdistanced it, but that its industrialization is necessary, that it is important even for the progress of our extremely backward, primitive, agriculture. In it lies its salvation.[28]

In an address before the State Council less than a year before the outbreak of war, Avdakov offered perhaps the most definitive, as well as the most thoughtful, statement of the Association's Westernism.

> Ordinarily we compare Russia in all questions with the western European states. In these questions, that is, in economic questions, it is possible to compare us with western European states only in the sense of where we should go and how we should develop ourselves. The western European states have long since passed through the period of their initial economic rise. They have long since passed through the period when they had to be concerned about various aspects of their own national economy: the development of railroads, waterways and paved roads, the defense of private initiative, and others. They have ascertained their own wealth and they know what they possess; they have applied labor, knowledge, technique, and measures that have brought their material well-being up to the maximum limits. Industry and trade in the western European states are so immeasur-

ably above ours that we need only look and follow after them.[29]

On the very eve of hostilities, the Association once more declared its rejection of Slavophile thinking:

> It is possible, certainly, to dream about realizing the utopia of a purely agricultural state, which pays for foreign products with the products of its own soil. But even the not entirely satisfactory harvest of the current year reminds us of the flimsiness of such a foundation for the national wealth and the state finances of the country. The realization of such a utopia would require, along with the rejection of industrial development, the rejection of the role of a great power.[30]

The Association's Westernism did not signify, however, an unquestioning acceptance of all western economic policies. While urging its listeners to hark to the example of the West, the organization also observed, in a major report of the Council to the Seventh Congress, that "bookish formulas, worked out by Western science, are hardly applicable in their entirety to Russia."[31] In fact, the Association frequently pointed out instances in which western conditions differed fundamentally from those prevailing in Russia. In such cases, western policies had no relevance. For example, in connection with its effort to minimize any conflict between industry and agriculture--an effort that was manifestly necessary, if only in order to disarm agrarian opposition to industrialization--the Association insisted that "the sharp opposing of agricultural and commercial-industrial interests does not at all correspond to Russian reality but represents an unsuccessful borrowing from western European practice."[32] Although England's highly developed industrial economy was broadly admired, its policy of free trade in international commerce remained anathema to the Association. Similarly, the United States' protective tariff and its achievements in the construction of railroads won praise, but the "trust-busting" activities of American presidents, from Theodore Roosevelt through Woodrow Wilson, excited nothing but horror.

England, the United States, and Germany all, in varying aspects of their economic policies, offered lessons useful for Russia, but it was Germany, above all, to which the industrialists looked for guidance. Ironically, Germany, as the principal threat to Russia's "independence" and thus the object of their most profound fear and hostility, also remained the object of their deepest admiration as a formerly backward country that had raised itself by intelligence, determination, and hard work to a foremost place among the great powers. In its more candid moments, the Association also recognized similarities between the German and Russian political systems, with all that was implied respecting the conditions under which businessmen worked. This gave to the German example a more practical appeal than any that western liberalism could muster. Thus, the various aspects of what the Association described as its economic "credo" included some that had clear counterparts in Western liberal thought. Others, more numerous, resembled German practice, and a few, deeply rooted in the Russian experience, found no real parallel anywhere in the West.

Incomplete as this Westernism was, it unquestionably buttressed the fundamental optimism of the Association's outlook with a strong faith in the inevitability of industrialization, a faith evidently rooted in an almost Marxist belief in a deterministic pattern of economic development common to all countries. Thus, Industry and Trade respectfully quoted A. A. Kotliarevskii, a member of the State Duma, who upheld, in terms that obviously struck a sympathetic chord, the impossibility "of skipping a whole series of steps in the historical staircase, which inexorable, objective necessity forces human society to tread."[33] Whether this outlook reflected an indirect and unconscious influence of Marxist thought on Russian industrialists, the lingering impact of outmoded concepts of natural law, or merely a blind faith in their own future defies any precise answer. In any case, both their Westernism and their optimism flowed from their belief that, in approaching its predestined task of industrialization, Russia not only followed in the footsteps of more advanced countries but remained solidly in the mainstream of the course that all countries must eventually follow.

Their belief in the necessity and inevitability of economic growth notwithstanding, the industrialists held eclectic attitudes toward economic doctrines. Indeed, the businessmen, priding themselves on being "practical men" of affairs, had little use for the theoretical economics of the academician, whether western or Russian. Thus, the Association found itself in frequent and open conflict with "the professors who represent economic science." The fact that the professors were generally liberally inclined only deepened the gulf between them. As Baron Maidel once wrote, their views are "diametrically opposed to ours not only in the solution of problems but in their very formulation."[34]

Yet the Association could not remain indifferent to the views of professional economists and occasionally cited their words, either in approbation or in condemnation. Although it showed no dogmatic attachment to any one school of economic thought, it found its closest affinity in the neomercantilist doctrine of Friedrich List and his Russian disciple, Dmitrii I. Mendeleev. Describing List as "the famous German patriot, economist, and nationalist, in the best sense of the word," Industry and Trade quoted with admiration his words on the necessity of national economic development:

> A nation that possesses a large territory, is supplied with varied resources, is significantly populated, and combines agriculture, manufacture, navigation, foreign, and domestic trade, is much more civilized, more developed in a political respect, and more powerful than a people that is only agricultural. . . . Therefore, a nation that attaches any value to its independence and self-preservation is obliged to employ all efforts in order to raise itself from a lower to a higher level of civilization in the interests of the most rapid creation, within its territorial limits, of agriculture, manufacturing, navigation, and trade.[35]

Toward the end of the prewar period, especially, the Association reiterated Mendeleev's statement that "the development of the complex industrial life that has already been initiated elsewhere represents the only path to the completion of the synthesis of Russia as one of the biggest world units."[36] Even more than in its emphasis on the desirability of industrial development, the importance that neomercantilism attached to the maintenance of a favorable balance of trade and international payments and to a policy of tariff protection as the most effective means to that end won the enthusiastic endorsement of the Association. Yet, while valuing gold as a basis for greater international economic strength and an assured means of payment in international exchange (and while urging increased utilization of Russia's natural reserves of this metal), the Association did not follow the neomercantilist purists who saw in specie the ultimate measure of a nation's wealth.

It was with respect to Adam Smith and the classical economists of the Manchester School that the eclecticism of the Association's economic "philosophy" became most starkly apparent. On the one hand, in assessing Russia's problems, it readily accepted the classical formulation of the factors of production. Noting Russia's wealth in labor and natural resources, for example, the organization stressed the country's more urgent needs for capital and for markets as the keys to national economic growth. In its relative indifference to gold for its own sake and in its emphasis on socially productive labor as the primary source of national wealth, the Association may have revealed an unconscious (and certainly an unacknowledged) debt to Ricardo.

> We hope that our society will at last be permeated with an awareness that

> . . . all industry, from the turning of the virgin soil for sowing to the manufacturing of clocks and astronomical instruments, is essentially one uninterrupted whole--the application of human labor, mental and physical, to the making of objects of consumption. The former view, that the land is the source of all goods . . . must be replaced by an understanding that the source of all values is human labor and, in fact, the labor of creative thought, which points out the methods of applying physical labor. Since the wealth of the state, that is, the economic well-being of its citizens, depends exclusively on the sum of labor productively expended, the organizing of labor must, in all its aspects, find as broad application as possible in every field of economic activity.[37]

The Association's defense of the labor theory of value, albeit modified to emphasize the contribution of entrepreneurial talent, ironically drew it perilously close to Marxian dogma. In a seeming approximation to the well-known Soviet formula that "He who does not work shall not eat," the organization earnestly declared its belief that "among us the time is not far distant when work [trud] will become the cult it ought to be, when that solid rule that only he who works and produces has the right to consume will become universal property."[38] In keeping with this conviction, the Association declared that a successful program of national economic expansion must be founded upon an increase in the intensity and productivity of labor. This increase must in turn arise, in part at least, out of a spontaneous upsurge in popular enthusiasm for work as a value in itself.[39] It further followed, as the Association never tired of emphasizing, that in Russia the demands of consumption must await the prior fulfillment of the demands of production. Thus, that "bright and happy future" for the masses of the population to which the organization aspired remained a remote goal, attainable only as the ultimate reward, to be reaped perhaps by an unknown generation, of hard work and austerity.

The Association's approach to questions of the organization of society revealed most clearly its ambivalence toward classical liberal economics. Derisively denouncing the views of Adam Smith on the desirability of free international trade, the industrialists could also respectfully cite him, and declare themselves liberals, in extolling the virtues of a governmental policy of laissez-faire toward industry and in support of their own campaign against Russian "state socialism."[40] Conversely, toward Smith's recommendations for governmental restraint of industrial monopoly they showed no sympathy; and against the liberal values of economic individualism and free competition the Association raised the banners of organization and "cooperation." In contrast, the French economist, Charles Gide, who advocated the cooperative movement, received the Association's acclamation as "one of the wisest and finest economists in the world at the present time."[41]

Within Russia, Dmitrii I. Mendeleev remained the object of the Association's its most respectful admiration, both in his emphasis on the necessity of industrial development and in his views on foreign trade and tariff protection. Among Russia's economic statesmen, the solidly conservative ministers of finance, Ivan A. Vyshnegradskii and Kokovtsov, undoubtedly ranked highest in its esteem. Toward the more colorful Count Witte, an early advocate of organization among businessmen for "representative purposes" and an occasional participant in the congresses of the Association, the industrialists expressed a curious compound of respect and disapprobation. Witte's currency reforms; his commitment to a policy of industrialization, systematically implemented; his role in the completion of the Trans-Siberian Railroad; and his contribution to railroad construction generally inspired admiration. However, his political conservatism appeared distasteful, and certain of his economic policies, particularly his insistence on a mixed system of state and private ownership of railroads, led the Association to condemn him as the "father" of Russian "state socialism."[42]

The ambivalence of the industrialists' Westernism should not seem surprising. Neither the need to overcome economic backwardness nor the dependence of industry and trade on an autocratic state that dominated much of the economy was totally without precedent in western experience, particularly in the recent history of the German Empire. Yet the magnitude of these conditions in Russia presented its businessmen with problems for which solutions remained untested and untried in the early twentieth century. Under these circumstances, it is appropriate to ask what kind of economic order might have emerged in Russia if its businessmen had enjoyed the opportunity to shape it to their own liking. The question can be answered only hypothetically, for in fact they did not address it specifically. Yet it seems clear that the West European values of individualism and free competition in the marketplace would have found little place in an economy reconstructed under their aegis.

The industrialists, as creatures of their cultural environment, embraced the traditional Russian principle of the organization of economic classes for the defense and "representation" of their own interests vis-a-vis the government, opposing group interests, and the public at large. This principle, in the Association's outlook, would provide the basis both for harmonious relations and for an orderly and systematic participation of diverse economic interests in the formation of governmental policies if expanded to include elements that were thus far only partially organized, particularly agrarian interests, industrial labor, and the consuming public. Despite its frequently proclaimed hostility to the prevailing system of "state socialism," the Association would, it seems, have moved only a relatively short distance toward the freer economy of Western Europe and America. In many respects, it sought to construct an economic system along syndicalist lines, albeit modified by guarantees of freedom for private property, entrepreneurial initiative, and the rule of law in economic relations.

The Business Class and Russia's Future

Behind the Association's continuing preoccupation with the future of Russia, and notwithstanding its reluctance to embrace the cause of political reform, lay, as we have seen, a keen awareness of the revolutionary potential of its own times. From the beginning, moreover, and with increasing clarity as the years passed, the Association equated the prospects for a favorable resolution of Russia's problems with the rise of the commercial-industrial class to a position of influence in national affairs.

However impressive the evidence of the Association's preoccupation with the development of Russia's backward national economy, the sincerity of its professions did not go unchallenged. Among its critics, Marxists occupied a prominent place, but they were not alone in their skepticism. The liberal intelligentsia and, most conspicuously, the agrarian conservatives also expressed their mistrust of the Association's intentions. All these groups evidently shared a profound suspicion that the organization's true objectives lay less in the advancement of the national welfare than in the promotion of the narrow interests of the business class. Moreover, while leftist radicals stressed the Association's hostility toward labor and social welfare legislation, and the liberals condemned its political inaction, both groups lent their support to the conservative contention that the industrialists, far from seeking to promote national economic development, actually endeavored, through monopolistic organizations, to restrain expansion in order to maximize profits. Thus The Odessa News (Odesskie novosti) complained late in 1911 that "under current conditions of production and sale, the big industrialists are interested least of all in the development of trade and industry, They are concerned, on the contrary, with achieving a standstill in the growth of the productive forces of the country."[43] Following the Sixth Congress, in 1912, Industry and Trade observed that

> the press continues . . . to say that the industrialists do not understand the tasks of economic development, that they hamper this development and place obstacles in the way of the development of the productive forces in the name of their egotistic interests.[44]

This thesis, forcefully expounded by the Association's conservative critics, found vigorous expression in the work of Soviet historians. For example, Livshin wrote:

> Concealing its true purposes, hiding them behind sonorous phases, the monopolistic bourgeoisie tried to present this program as a program for the development of the productive forces of the country. Prominent representatives of the financial oligarchy (N. S. Avdakov, V. V. Zhukovskii, G. A. Krestovnikov, and others) demagogically upbraided tsarism for its lack of any definite "constructive" program, spoke about the crying economic backwardness of the country, declaimed on behalf of "culture," for "a powerful development of the productive forces," for the attainment of "a balance between economic weakness and political power." But they remained silent about the real, basic causes of Russia's economic backwardness. . . . Representing its economic program as a program for the development of productive forces, the monopolistic bourgeoisie tried to leave unchanged the general economic condition of the development of the country [and] to adapt the prevailing economic conditions to its own rapacious interests. The main purpose of this program consisted in guaranteeing to capitalistic monopolies the highest possible level of profits. The ideology of the financial oligarchy was openly and cynically made clear by the prominent [business leader] A. A. Volskii: "The industrialists have one program--the ruble."[45]

In Livshin's view, not only did the Association's impact on the Russian economy entirely contradict its announced goals; the Association bore a major responsibility for the cataclysm that ultimately engulfed the Empire.

> Extreme egoism and self-seeking, plundering, a complete disregard for the basic and urgent interests of the people, a reactionary and counter-revolutionary outlook, developed to the nth degree, distinguished the Russian monopolistic bourgeoisie. Its policy of opposing the interests of the people hampered the economic development of the country, weakened Russia's position in the world capitalist system, and threatened the loss of national self-sufficiency and independence. Drawn into an alliance with tsarism and the landowners . . . , the monopolistic bourgeoisie led the country into an impasse and pushed it to the threshold of economic catastrophe.[46]

These commentaries raise far too many complex questions to be illuminated by the limited evidence contained in the Association's own publications. Certainly, the organization's proclaimed goals were not always consistently supported by its specific recommendations. Its emphasis on the need to raise the living standards of the population contrasted oddly, for example, with its stand on taxation policy and with its insistence on the necessity of giving priority to the interests of the producer over those of the consumer. Likewise, the contrast between the importance that the Association attributed to the labor question and the absence of any clear exposition of its views on this subject suggested a decided ambivalence in its position. Its vigorous sponsorship of syndicates and other monopolistic combinations, its fears of overproduction, and its concern for order and stability in economic relationships appeared inconsistent with a genuine interest in expanding output, despite other evidence of the organization's continuing preoccupation with the need to advance national economic growth.

Most questionable of all, perhaps, was the Association's unequivocal stand with respect to entrepreneurial profits. In its opinion, the profits of Russian industry lagged far behind those of European enterprise and remained inadequate to its own needs for capital expansion.[47] At the same time, however, it candidly considered high profits a sine qua non of industrial progress, without which national economic development and hence national prosperity and power would remain empty goals.

The fact that the Association sought reductions in taxation and costs of transportation as well as a broad variety of other measures designed to reduce entrepreneurial expenses and maintain high price levels was not surprising. What else could be expected of an organization dedicated to advancing the interests of an admittedly profit-hungry industry? More disconcerting, however, was the unabashed zeal with which the Association upheld industry's quest for profits not only as a necessary part of its program for industrial expansion but also as an inherent, and essentially admirable, feature of the businessman's outlook. According to the Association's pragmatic "credo," charity and capital were "incompatible things,"[48] and the former was only a deplorable form of human frailty. Industry and Trade wrote:

> Our contemporary press has begun to understand that industry and trade exist not only for the sake of the earnings of the capitalists but are also not without usefulness for the toiling population and, hence, for the state as a whole. At the same time, our press still fails to comprehend that industry is not an almshouse and that charity, in accordance with the very nature of

> the human enterprising spirit, is not natural to it. Consequently, it appears to our periodical press that industrialists fail to raise wages and reduce working time solely because of the hard-heartedness of the domestic entrepreneur and his striving for fabulous profits. . . . Our press, undoubtedly, will come ultimately to understand that entrepreneurial profit is a sacred right and a cultural obligation of capital; and that the life-giving power of capital consists, in fact, in its lack of the principles of charity, which corrupt the human spirit.[49]

Defending the "civilizing" role of foreign capital in Russia, the journal declared:

> Let the foreign capitalist be greedy and rapacious; let him be endowed with no altruistic goals; let his only purpose be to extract as large a profit as possible from the funds expended. Let all this be true, for he is only a capitalist and he does not pretend to the calling of a philanthropist. But such is the nature of capital itself that, forever alien to every philanthropy, it is, apart from everything and in spite of everything, the life-giving principle that creates the well-being of the country.[50]

The western concept of coupling profits and business philanthropy evidently still eluded the Association. Its primitively acquisitive contempt for charity (although hardly borne out in the practice of many of Russia's leading industrialists) comported ill with industry's self-appointed role as the architect of a "bright and happy" future for the Russian homeland.

Implicit in the Association's insistence on the "state importance" of industry and its own "state point of view" was its unqualified confidence in the inherent ability of men of business not only to judge what was best for Russia but also to provide practical leadership necessary for the implementation of their program. Far transcending a simple belief in the competence of the commercial and industrial middle class in economic affairs, this confidence stemmed from a profound and almost messianic faith in the historic destiny of its own class to become the architect of Russia's future.

As in many other respects, Volskii became one of the earliest and most articulate exponents of this philosophy. In 1905, he propounded the view that Russian businessmen must lead the effort to carry through the timely program of national economic development that alone could save Russia from the mounting danger of German domination.[51] The first years of the Association clearly did nothing either to change Volskii's convictions or to ease his misgivings. In mid-1909, he asserted that national "regeneration" must, as a matter of historical necessity, rest with the industrial-commercial class.

> If Russia is really to be regenerated and grow strong, this will occur only through the efforts of its most efficient class, which in Russia, as everywhere in the world, is made up of the promoters of industry and trade. History, obviously, is giving it the word. Whether it will prove sufficiently weighty is the question that our public men from the industrial and commercial world must ponder.[52]

Volskii's was not, however, the only voice urging Russia seemingly reluctant businessmen to a greater awareness of their historically ordained mission. Late in 1908, Aleksandr I. Konovalov, the prominent Moscow industrialist, financier, Duma member, and member of the Association's Council, took the occasion of the fiftieth anniversary of his family enterprises to declare, in an address that was warmly applauded by Industry and Trade:

> The period through which our country is now living is extremely serious. The requirements of economic reality, the growing needs of the economic life of a great country are powerfully coming into their own. A tremendous upsurge of strength and energy on the part of all elements of the population is necessary for the enormous work that lies ahead. And on us, as the representatives of industry, lies also a moral obligation to take an ardent part in the task of organizing the economic growth of the country on firm principles.[53]

A year later, the question of the national role of organized industry came to the fore even more emphatically in S. I. Sokolovskii's report to the Fourth Congress. Although he criticized the policies of the Association, he appealed to the commercial-industrial class to awake and realize its mission: the advancement of the country's life as a nation. Stressing "the important role of the commercial-industrial class, its responsibility for all that which has been accomplished thus far, and for that which is being prepared in the future by the almost irresistible course of our domestic economic process," Sokolovskii propounded its obligation, as a class uniquely qualified for the task, to devote itself to improving the economic "health" of Russia, "to recognize its own rights and duties, and to approach its objectives not blindly but consciously, with weapon in hand, as an organized class."

> I maintain that at the present historic moment the interest of the entire state, its progress, and its greatness, demand this because the commercial-industrial class is the only class in Russia which, in the current confusion of

ideas, aspirations, demands, and conflicts with opposing interests, retains a healthy mind and unshaken memories. It, more than all others, is interested in the prosperity of the backward element of the population and, by virtue of its own practice, its own occupation, and its own psychology, is better adapted than others to the systematic construction that Russia, languishing in its own helplessness, so desperately requires.

Sokolovskii's concluding words eloquently appealed to the business class to rise to the challenge that lay before it:

In the tremendous expanse of distances, in the races and dialects that toiling Russia embraces, the authentic voice of our awakening class has not once been heard. History awaits this beginning as a stage in the progress of the entire country, as the commencement of its economic and political regeneration. Let us contribute our own bit to the common treasure-house of the efforts of the masses; let us make it possible for our own class to become strong and to fulfill its duty to the country.

Only through more effective organization, both in representative institutions and in a new political "party of national regeneration," could the businessmen emerge at last in the form of "a class movement" able to fulfill its destiny.[54]

Although the Congress heard Sokolovskii's plea without comment, his speech perhaps prompted Krestovnikov, as chairman, to welcome the gathering with assurances respecting both the achievements of the Association itself and the progress that had been made in the great work of national reconstruction. The normally restrained Avdakov, in bidding the Congress farewell, added his own weighty voice to the appeal for greater class consciousness and unity. The essence of industry's "mission" consisted, he declared, in bringing about the greater tranquillity, prosperity, and glory of Russia, as well as in the elevation of industry and trade to "that honorable place in the condition of Russian life that these branches of popular work enjoy in all the cultured countries of the world." Although he admitted that "in this respect we are significantly behind western Europe," Avdakov concluded with cautious optimism:

But insofar as the industrialists themselves recognize their cultural mission in the state and insofar as the representatives of industry work boldly and firmly, through the unification of all their forces, in the direction of a rise in popular welfare, it is possible to assert that the importance of industry as a big, public, cultural force will soon receive universal recognition. Our Association is doing much toward this end.[55]

Appeals for greater class consciousness and unity were neither new nor unusual in the history of the Association. Indeed, they were the very seedbed of its origins and the essence of its declared purpose. However, these objectives assumed an added urgency during the last three years before the outbreak of the World War. Industry's mission, moreover, took on an aura of destiny that seemed almost mystical in its determinism. Industrialization appeared as inevitable as it was necessary, and who but the owners and operators of industrial enterprise could be the preordained agents of its realization? Viewing the "correctly understood" interests of the state and of the commercial-industrial class as but opposite sides of the same coin, and considering the "salvation" of the former to rest in the hands of the latter, the Association increasingly chafed under the many constraints--economic, legal, social, and political--that daily limited the business class's conduct of its affairs. Thus the growing antagonism between the government and organized industry that marked the final prewar years gave added zest to industry's assertions of its national mission. At the same time, however, conflicts mounted within its own midst. Hence, the Association's ever more frequent appeals to its membership to rise to an awareness of its destiny as a class were increasingly coupled with urgent exhortations to greater class unity.

It was, therefore, no accident that the issues raised at the Fourth Congress should have reappeared in even sharper relief at the Fifth. One prominent participant declared the need, by raising the "productive forces" of the country, to raise simultaneously the "authority" of the commercial-industrial class, so that "industry will become a real social force, which at the present time it is not."[56] Avdakov, for his part, reiterated the lesson of the preceding congress, emphasizing in his welcoming address that only through more effective organization "can we actually place our industry and trade in that place of honor where they find themselves in all the states and cultured countries of Western Europe."[57]

By far the most eloquent voice at the congress, however, belonged to the Association's rising star, Zhukovskii. In the first of a series of annual reports on the work of the legislature, he sought to instill in the industrialists both a new appreciation for the importance of ideas in national life and a recognition and acceptance of their own "social obligation" to concern themselves with the "general condition" of the country.

> We are practical men; we are men who wish to do our own business, seeing in it great importance for the state and for the people. In addition to our

practical work we not only can, we not only should, we are obligated to think about the general condition of the country. It is our duty to manifest a definite conscious attitude of our own toward national tasks; we ourselves must strive to be, in part, the brain of the country; we cannot reject work in the field of ideas. For the inheritance that one generation transmits to another consists not only of material goods but also of certain moral principles and ideological directions [ideinykh ukazanii]. The wealth of a people lies not only in land, not only in factories, not only in money, but, mainly, perhaps, in certain moral principles and philosophical [ideinykh] endowments. And here, is this connection, it is necessary that the commercial-industrial class should display its own work, its own thought, and its own consciousness. And from that moment when we shall have succeeded in uniting ourselves, we shall rightly also speak out and strive for the gradual elaboration of a state program from our commercial-industrial point of view, as the synthesis of our practical interests and our ideological outlook.[58]

The Fifth Congress constituted only the opening round in what was to become a veritable crescendo of complaints and exhortations. By 1914, the twin questions of the destiny of Russia and of its commercial-industrial class colored the Association's outlook on all the lesser issues that confronted it. At the Sixth Congress, Zhukovskii concluded his second report on the legislature--issued this time in the name of the Council--with a quotation from his resounding appeal of the previous year.[59] The preceding year had witnessed a potentially momentous reappraisal of the ways in which industry's quest for self-realization might best be advanced. Shortly before the election of the Fourth State Duma, in 1912, the Association had turned clearly, if still with many qualifications, in the direction of political action. Vigorously reaffirming the business community's dedication to "a representative, constitutional system" as one that was inextricably interwoven with the destiny of its own class,[60] and also attributing Russian's lack of a national economic program to the "indifference and ignorance" of the Third Duma, the Council called upon the industrialists to forsake their narrow preoccupation with business affairs and to assume a new and livelier role in national life.

Recognition of the necessity of the representative system, on the one hand, and a conviction of the unsuccessful activity of the Third State Duma, on the other, oblige us not only to criticize but also to strive to take part in legislative work. The interests of trade and industry require an attentive and competent attitude toward them. These interests are too important for us to be able to remain on the sidelines in elections that will determine the

> composition of the legislature. But, apart from practical matters, considerations of state policy become obligatory in the present epoch of social and economic reconstruction. Business people must break away from their counters, offices, and workshops, for the country needs them in the state arena.[61]

To the charges of the "extreme right-wing paper," The Moscow News (Moskovskie vedomosti), that "the industrialists have united and are calling representatives of the commercial-industrial class into the State Duma in the name of their class interests," Industry and Trade replied:

> With all the strength of conviction we can only fervently protest against such a perversion of the tasks of the representatives of the commercial-industrial class in the State Duma. We hope that in the Fourth Duma the commercial-industrial class will more loudly raise its voice because, as the Chairman of the Council of Ministers said in his Moscow speech, "the interests of the commercial-industrial class always coincide with that direction which assures a healthy life for the state--the direction of healthy work and construction."[62]

Behind the Association's unwonted incursion into politics lay both a keen discontent with restrictive conditions and growing concern over the intraclass disunity that posed perhaps an even more serious obstacle to the business class's fulfillment of its "destiny." One of the firmest expressions of this concern was to be found in the following example of prerevolutionary "self-criticism" by a prominent member of the Council:

> If, at the present time, the commercial-industrial class does not play the role that it should play in the country in connection with a correct economic development, this is not because various laws prevent it but because the commercial-industrial class is still insufficiently stable, does not pour out its interests broadly enough, and has rallied together inadequately for this defense; therefore those laws emerge that at the present time regulate our country. When the commercial-industrial class joins together, grasps its own common interests, and operates more consistently, then, quite naturally, a different situation will emerge and we shall have that toward which we have striven, creating our own legislature.[63]

Despite the manifold problems confronting industry, the Association retained a hopeful view of the future. One of its founders, for example, assured the congress "that at the present time we are entering a period that can be said to be a bright star for that class of which all of us present are representatives."

For us (it will not be immodest to say), the cultured upper levels of the commercial-industrial class who are present here . . . , fate, it seems, is beginning to favor this class . . . . The basic slogan of the country is coming to be the development of the productive forces of the country. . . . The nation is taking as its starting point the task that is also the task of the commercial-industrial class. . . .[64]

More judiciously, Industry and Trade observed:

With confidence in the future, with understanding of the importance of the task we have assumed, in full awareness that "at the present time to the representatives of industry and trade . . . there truly belongs the resolution of tasks of tremendous national importance" [quoted from Kokovtsov's address to the congress], we have begun our work of strengthening healthy economic principles in our country; and we shall continue it in the hope that the time is not far distant when the representatives of our public opinion, who have so recently looked on industry and trade from the point of view of consumers' interests, will understand that the only saving point of view for Russia is the point of view of the producer, and will go hand in hand with us.[65]

Only a few months after the Sixth Congress, industry's growing class consciousness and anxiety for the future again found expression at the festivities held in honor of the hundredth anniversary of the Konovalov textile firm. The high point consisted in a banquet attended by some 600 persons and accompanied, as reported in Industry and Trade, by "many speeches." Avdakov greeted Aleksandr I. Konovalov on behalf of the Association in the name of "united industry," but the need to reinforce class unity dominated the statements of the industrial leaders. Konovalov called upon "the commercial-industrial class" to unite for the defense not only of its own interests but of the "rights of the Russian citizen as well":

Through the fulfillment of the duties imposed at the present time on the independent merchant class [kupecheskii klass] by history itself, it must obtain public recognition of its preeminent role in the destinies of the country, since in the success of its toiling and public work lies, in fact, the guarantee of a future powerful, rich, and free Russia.[66]

These thoughts were vigorously seconded by Konovalov's Moscow colleague, Pavel P. Riabushinskii, who emphasized even more than Konovalov the destiny of the business class as the force fated to guide the course of Russia's future. Criticizing those businessmen who sought enhancement of their status outside the limits of their own class, he challenged the traditional claim of the gentry to social preeminence.

> The gradually growing internal self-consciousness of the merchant estate [kupechestvo] is creating a definite force and is capable of directing Russia along the correct path. . . . The gentry is weakened, is losing its land, although it still strongly clings to its rights, even enrolling some of us in its depleted ranks. . . . We are free people, obligated only to our own forces, to our own selves; for us there is no place in the ranks of the gentry. Fate itself promises the merchant estate the preeminent role in the future. . . . Therefore the growth of internal self-consciousness is important; it is necessary to understand its calling, its mission. We shall continue unceasingly to work for the creation of the material and moral power of the merchant estate, securing thereby the necessity for society to reckon with its wishes, which have but one objective: to direct Russia along the path of wealth, glory, and happiness.[67]

Even Industry and Trade, in its own commentary on the jubilee, while cautiously avoiding any discussion of the "socio-political questions that were touched on," also emphasized the role of the business class as the predestined successor of a declining landed aristocracy:

> We must, however, echo the justice of the idea expressed by the above-mentioned speakers concerning the integral connection between the broad development of industry and the successes of the civil order [grazhdanstvennost']. With respect to the words about the right of the industrial and the business class generally to a preeminent place in the destinies of the country, we can cite the universal historical fact that the preeminent role in the life of a state belongs, in fact, to the nobility, but only until the end of the period of conquest, until the establishment of the stable frontiers of the state. And then this role has gradually, in a natural way, shifted to the representatives of the creative forces of the country, to the men who secure for it both consolidated economic power and civic prosperity.[68]

If little place thus remained for an outmoded nobility in Russia's future, the potential contributions of the intelligentsia also appeared doubtful.

> If the intelligentsia seriously thinks about "the regeneration of Russia," about its own work for the benefit of this regeneration, if it cherishes any proud dreams with respect to Russia, it must overcome its pettiness and lack of spirit. For it must be remembered that the solidarity of the "captains" of commercial-industrial development gives to the latter strength and breadth of outlook against which the members of our intelligentsia offer nothing. The wedding of Russia to the new forms of economic life, the awakening of

backward localities and branches of work from the sleep of ages, this also constitutes the authentic "construction of life" long sought by the intelligentsia, which, like every creative work, does not need further justification.[69]

The exhortations of industry's leaders would seem to have met with little practical response, however. At the Seventh Congress, in May 1913, Zhukovskii found it necessary to repeat his familiar lecture on the obligation of businessmen to express their own views on the broad issues confronting the Empire.[70] Fortuitously, perhaps, the "sharp, insulting words" recently addressed to the representatives of industry by the notorious reactionary, Nikolai E. Markov II, in the State Duma provided Zhukovskii with a further opportunity to assert the dignity of the business class. Although he welcomed, as evidence of "the self-consciousness of the commercial-industrial class," the proposal of a member of the Duma that the Congress seek permission from the minister of trade and industry to reply to Markov in defense of commercial-industrial organizations, Zhukovskii nevertheless rejected the suggestion as unnecessary,

for the time has come to an end when trade and industry only sued for favors; it is time for them to raise their heads and look at everyone as equals. The rule of serfdom and of the nobility has ended; it is now time for work; it is now time for individual merits, not heredity pretensions. But I think that there is no need for our Association to turn to the minister of trade and industry with a request for defense. Mister Markov did not hurt the dignity of the commercial-industrial class, for he stands too far away for this. We can look down at him from above; we can look down from the height of those services that the exchange committees and our organizations have, in spite of everything, given to the motherland.[71]

In the press commentary on the Seventh Congress, charges of ineffectualness, vacuousness, and colorlessness mingled strangely with a recognition, sometimes by organs normally unsympathetic to business interests, of the public-spirited approach of "united" industry and trade and the rising self-consciousness of the business class. For example, The Voice of Moscow (Golos Moskvy) characterized by Industry and Trade as the voice of the Duma's agrarian majority, asserted that the recent congress had added "nothing to the authority of the Association as an organization," but acknowledged that

united trade and industry cannot but acquaint broad strata of society with their own needs and hopes, being accustomed to believe that at the base of these wishes there lie not the selfish interests of the group but the same

> interests of state policy that guide other groups as well, when they come forward with statements concerning their own needs.

Generously, the paper concluded that the Association "has been able to base itself on this, the only correct, level; it has always tried to illuminate questions of commercial-industrial life, not separating the needs of trade and industry from general needs of the common people." Even The Russian Word (Russkoe slovo), which Industry and Trade regarded as consistently hostile, commented almost benevolently on the growing class consciousness of Russia's businessmen:

> The regular congress of industrialists revealed, without any doubt, the rise of self-consciousness in the commercial-industrial milieu. However one may react in matters of substance to the demands and wishes of our industrialists, it is impossible not to note the progressive-cultural importance of this fact in the historical moment through which we are living.[72]

The trend in the press, however, remained far from favorable to organized industry. The Eighth Congress, where the business community's messianic class consciousness appeared even more boldly than it had been at the Seventh, inspired uncompromisingly hostile commentary in the right-wing papers. The nationalistic Voice of Russia (Golos Rusi) accused the "big industrialists" of "anti-state desires" and strivings. The semi-official New Times (Novoe vremia) declared:

> Our huge country hardly enters into the Congress's sphere of vision. The industrialists are interested in preserving the privileged position of a hothouse plant, which the government is under obligation to tend. In order that the industrial class may rightfully play a prominent role in the economic policy of the country, it is necessary that the opinions expressed by it should conform to the broad needs of the population. Until then, the many "resolutions" passed by the industrialists represent only the desires of a limited number of commercial magnates.

Such comments sparked replies by newspapers sympathetic with industry, in opposition to the alleged conservative effort in The Petersburg Courier (Peterburgskii kur'er), for example, "to convert the assembly of the biggest industrialists into an agitational assembly of selfish persons who are pursuing only their narrow class interests." For its part, The Russian News (Russkie vedomosti) praised the Eighth Congress for having, unlike the nobility, defended broader interests than those of its own class:

> The congress of representatives of big industry could not pass resolutions permeated with an agrarian or a proletarian point of view. But every organization composed of elements forming a part of the state organism that are viable and not dying out can rise to a point of view that reflects the interests of the entire state and can formulate one of those ideas that, in one form or another, constitute, at a given moment, the property of society as a whole. The congress of representatives of the united nobility has, obviously, not been capable of this. But the congress of representatives of industry and trade has been able to do it, and it has done it now.[73]

Despite these widely divergent opinions, Industry and Trade found in them reassurance as to public recognition both of the importance of the Association and of the business community's growing self-awareness as a class.

> The newspapers, from the extreme right to the extreme left, those of the capital and provincial papers, attach to the Congress the importance of a big public event. The cause of such interest in the activities of the Congress was not the substance of the individual reports but the general shift, made clear at its meetings, in the temper of commercial-industrial circles toward greater self-determination.[74]

The businessmen's burgeoning class consciousness during the final months of peace reflected the mounting animosity that marked the Association's relations with the government, the growing danger of war, and, perhaps in less degree, conflicts between management and labor. On the very eve of the war, Industry and Trade charged that the government's policies in fact belied its declared aim of promoting economic growth. "Tragedy" had befallen contemporary Russia because, despite new principles, "noisily recognized, . . . life has not only failed to go forward; it has actually gone backward; it has become worse than it was before 1905."[75]

It was symptomatic both of the depth of the business leaders' despair and of their enhanced awareness of the "destiny" of their own class, as one ordained by "history" to be the salvation of its country, that they should have turned at this crucial point from their customary "practical" approach to Russia's problems toward an unprecedented searching for an explanation of the country's difficulties. In this rare moment of insight, those difficulties appeared rooted in the circumstances of Russia's past, which had prevented the country from following the pattern of Western development, and which, in consequence, had prevented the commercial-industrial class from fulfilling its historic mission.

> We keenly feel the inadequacy and comparative weakness in Russia of the middle class, which arose organically in the West, the growth and development of which comprise the external and cultural history of Western Europe during the past century. We cannot dwell for long on the reasons why Russia has not shared the general evolution of other countries: the responsibility for that lies in the isolation from the whole world in which Russia lived for so long. The belated development of railroads among us suddenly pushed a country with a natural economy into the whirlpool of a commercial economy. . . . The main point is that the inexorable requirements of life prevented the consolidation of the new social stratum that should have been the agent of the future development of the country. . . . The current state of affairs cannot be endured.[76]

The Association's despondency appeared to some extent premature, for ahead still lay three years of intense and effective activity. Yet, seen in the broader sweep of events, these words resounded prophetically. In equating the weakness of the Empire with the failure of its own class to become a significant force in national life, the Association had not only seized upon a crucial feature of Russia's historical development as a nation but had also written a fitting epitaph for the class in the name of which it spoke.

Toward a Program of National Economic Development

Far more difficult than the definition of future objectives was the complex problem of determining the methods by which economic growth might best be achieved. Lacking any direct knowledge of the problem of modernizing underdeveloped countries and with little more than Russia's own limited experience and the example of Germany (and possibly of Japan) as a guide, the industrialists nevertheless turned to their chosen task with exuberant confidence. Whether this confidence was born of ignorance or of insight, whether Russia's business leaders in fact had a valuable contribution to make to their country's future, can be decided only after a careful study of the specific proposals that they advanced.

Remarking upon the "deep rift between idea and economic reality" that prevailed among Russia's nineteenth century intellectuals, Alexander Gerschenkron observed that "the road of Russian economic development was rarely illuminated by the strong brilliance of prevision and prescience."[77] This judgment might also apply to the industrialists who proclaimed themselves the predestined architects of economic progress in the twentieth century. In fact, the idea that Russia's development should come about as the product of a rational, systematic "plan" did not originate with the Association of Industry and Trade, although it was probably Russia's most vigorous champion of economic "planning" (planomernost') between 1906 and 1917. Recognition of the need for a concerted program of measures to develop the economic potential of the Empire had lain at the heart of the policies championed by Witte during his tenure as minister of finance.[78] Unquestionably, the debacles of the Russo-Japanese War and the Revolution of 1905 stimulated reflection on the part of both the government and the articulate public concerning the means of overcoming the Empire's weakness and instability. These events also gave strong encouragement to those incipient inclinations toward a systematic development of the country's national economic potential.

The years between 1905 and the outbreak of the World War saw numerous attempts, both within the government and outside it, to encourage a systematic approach to economic growth. Within governmental ministries, for example, tentative "plans" were under consideration for the construction of roads and ports, for the improvement of harbors and internal waterways, and for the development of irrigation and cotton cultivation in Turkestan. These remained isolated and narrowly conceived projects, however, because they lacked the approval of the Emperor.[79] The Russian government, because of its predominant role in industrial and commercial affairs, has appeared to some historians to have introduced a measure of systematic direction into the economy that predisposed the country toward the ultimate acceptance of economic planning. Other historians have taken a contrary view, considering official economic policies haphazard in their conception and even injurious in their effect upon industry.[80] Needless to say, the absence of a consensus in the historical literature concerning the role of the government in the economy of the Empire greatly increases the difficulty of assessing the criticism that the Association directed toward it.

Outside official circles, the desirability of Russia's having an economic program was also widely recognized. Such recognition, moreover, was not limited to professional economists, among whom the need to introduce an element of rationality into the course of the country's development was common currency. Even the organized nobility, which held an agrarian point of view and hardly inclined toward rapid industrialization, showed a remarkable readiness to accord a respectful hearing to serious proposals for systematic development.[81] However, the Association remained dissatisfied with the public's limited understanding of the need for a rational approach to Russia's problems.

The industrialists' stress on economic planning in fact antedated the founding of the Association itself. In June 1905, future leaders of the Association, meeting in Moscow, dispatched a telegram to the minister of finance asserting the necessity of directing "the complex problems of the national economy . . . onto the path of radical renovation and intense activity." It also emphasized that

> the broad, fruitful, and stable development of the productivity of labor and the well-being of the population can result only from a planned, strictly thought out economic policy, harmonized with the needs and interests of all branches of the economic activity of the people.[82]

The year 1905 saw the publication of a second edition of Volskii's report to the Consultative Board of Iron Producers, analyzing the problems confronting Russia, postulating rapid industrialization as the key to both economic and political salvation, and offering specific recommendations to stimulate economic expansion.[83]

The broad outlines of the Association's economic program emerged during its formative years, until the end of 1909. The year and a half that followed, however, witnessed the organization's withdrawal into a relatively dull preoccupation with details of Russia's current economic needs. Perhaps this change reflected a new complacency induced by the prosperity that swept over the economy and by a premature inclination to assume that the necessity for a deliberate and systematic development of Russia's economic potential had at last won general acceptance by the public and the government. Perhaps a recognition of the difficulty of the task at hand contributed to the shift in emphasis. Disturbances in the organization's internal affairs just prior to Volskii's resignation may have played a part in the change in the Association's work. All this remains obscure. In any case, despite the outward dullness of the Association's work during this interval, the interest of its leadership in drawing up a program for Russia's further economic development survived unimpaired. In fact, the Secretariat at that time produced a comprehensive program for submission to the Fifth Congress. (Its failure to appear on the agenda when the much-delayed congress finally convened was unexplained.)

In contrast, the last three years before the outbreak of the World War marked a new period of vigorous work. Far from inducing complacency, the prosperity of those final years of peace intensified the Association's awareness of the instability of the Russian economy. To the satisfactions of prosperity were added new problems, ironically resulting both from industry's inability to supply the burgeoning demand for some products and from its mounting apprehension lest the day suddenly arrive when the market might once again prove incapable of absorbing its growing output. These conditions contributed not only to the embroilment with the government that clouded the last prewar years but also the renascent vigor of its interest in the elaboration of an economic program.

When the war broke out, this effort still had produced little more than a collection of loosely related parts. At long last, despite the disruption caused by the war, the Council presented to the Ninth Congress in May 1915 its substantial report, On Measures for the Development of the Productive Forces of Russia.[84] If its comprehension of economic planning remained rudimentary, it should be remembered that the organization was sailing a difficult course on uncharted seas. Moreover, many of its recommendations, both substantive and methodological, foreshadowed aspects of the first two Soviet five-year plans. While any direct connection between its work and that of its Soviet successors remains speculative, the resemblances testify, at the very least, to the existence of similar economic problems despite political changes. Lenin, as his frequent and caustic commentaries reveal, read the Association's publications closely. Although his uniformly hostile comments focused on the organization's role as the defender of the financial interests of its membership, they implied a familiarity with its broader goals. In view of the Marxist-Leninist thesis that a proletarian dictatorship, especially in a backward country, must borrow from capitalism methods that might be useful in constructing socialism, it seems reasonable to assume that the Association's work held a new and different interest for the Soviet leadership after 1917. In their concern with a common problem and in the similarity of some of their responses to it, Russia's prerevolutionary industrialists and the Soviet planners, knowingly or not, forged one of the strongest links in the chain of continuity that bound the old with the new Russia.

During 1908 and 1909, the Association also began to elaborate a methodology of planning, particularly in connection with proposals for drawing up programs for the development of particular branches of the economy. The various "industry" plans under consideration took the form of "five-year plans," although occasionally plans of ten, fifteen and even twenty years' duration were suggested. If these proposals foreshadowed later Soviet practice, the same may also be said of the Association's belief that an economic program should consist of two complementary and broadly parallel parts, namely, an industrial-commercial plan and a financial plan.

That a true economic program should incorporate the qualities of comprehensiveness, coordination, and a definition of priorities among the country's many competing needs also received recognition, if only incompletely and tangentially. In the debate at the Third Congress on Volskii's report, for example, one delegate pointed out that

> this report is far from exhausting the entirety of questions which must interest Russian industry. Moreover, the report contains no definition of particular questions according to their importance; and therefore at the given moment the Congress has at its disposition only the materials for working out a commercial-industrial policy, but it does not have at its disposition a systematic program. . . .[85]

Although the Association did not coordinate its many recommendations for the advancement of particular branches of economic life, the need for such coordination was clearly recognized. Toward the end of 1908, Industry and Trade observed:

> We are trying, in a series of articles, to show that only through the harmonious development of all the productive forces of the country, both agricultural and industrial, will Russia be brought out of the unfortunate impasse in which it finds itself in the present state of its immaturity.[86]

It remained for Krestovnikov to emphasize the importance of a precise definition of priorities. He also placed the task of drawing up a comprehensive economic program in a clearer perspective than had thus far been done. The brief period between the State Council's "economic day" and the convening of the Fourth Congress in November 1909 witnessed a noteworthy maturing of Krestovnikov's own understanding of the problem. In his criticism of Volskii's report, he pointed out that

> the drawing up of an economic program . . . consists not only in enumerating desirable measures but also in indicating their relative importance and the order of their fulfillment. Such a task is beyond the strength of the Association. It requires the work of all governmental institutions and many years' time. The task of the Association, the task of an organization representing industry and trade, is only to point out the general direction of economic and financial policy and to assist in the elaboration of its individual parts as they are advanced.[87]

If, as seems likely, Krestovnikov's position had the effect of discouraging the Association's own work toward the composition of a program, it also broke new ground in its recognition of the magnitude of the task that lay ahead and in its clear delineation of the functions of the government and of organized industry.

Understandably, the size and diversity of Russia's needs created crucial problems of determining priorities. Although the Association repeatedly pointed out the country's most urgent needs during 1908 and 1909 in the light of its developmental aspirations, its efforts were so generally lacking in consistency as almost to defy orderly analysis.

Generalization is difficult, and perhaps even misleading, under these conditions. Nevertheless, the problem of financing economic expansion apparently occupied first place in the judgment of the Association's leaders. Avdakov and Zhukovskii, especially, expressed the view that without increased supplies of capital and ready credit, Russia could not overcome its current state of backwardness. Zhukovskii's broad view emerged with particular clarity in the debate on Volskii's report to the Third Congress:

> The normal development of the national economy requires, above all, according to the formula of classical political economy, natural resources, in which Russia is rich; the working capacity of the population, which also no one denies; and finally, capital, of which there is none, and which, willy-nilly, must be obtained, because only this third factor, in the presence of the other two, will permit productive, organized work to be developed and Russia to be transformed from the country of consumers, which it has thus far been, into a country of producers.[88]

Rivaling the financial problem in importance was the need to improve the efficiency of agriculture in order to minimize the instability of an economy dominated by the uncertainties of the harvest. Also, an increase in well-being of the peasantry would expand the domestic market for industry's products. In a report to the Commercial-Industrial Group of the Members of the State Council and the State Duma on Russia's needs for its economic development, which served as the basis for detailed discussions by the group during the winter and early spring of 1909, Zhukovskii placed nearly equal emphasis on the problems of capital supply and the domestic market.

The Association also called for a larger measure of freedom for industry from governmental tutelage, a reduction in the bureaucracy's freedom to intervene in business affairs, and a greater respect for "legality" in economic life. The Third and Fourth Congresses stressed that industrialists themselves must manifest a higher degree of entrepreneurial initiative and "self-help" than before.[89] In this respect, the Association's position contrasted oddly both with its unremitting emphasis on the need for governmental leadership and with the importance that it attached to the broad development of cooperation in its diverse forms throughout the economy, including, in the Association's view, not only cooperatives of various types but also industrial syndicates and labor unions.

More specifically, the Association stressed the importance of the development of transportation and communication facilities, especially railroads; tariff protection for industry; and the development of markets abroad. Universal education and the advancement of "culture in the broadest sense" also appeared, at various times, on the list of vital ingredients of Russia's economic modernization.[90] In one of its early, and relatively rare, attempts to assess Russia's most urgent needs, Industry and Trade wrote:

> From whatever point one approaches the financial position of Russia, one always arrives at one and the same conclusion, repeated many times already in the pages of our journal: only the development of the productive forces of the country, the encouragement of trade and industry (in the first instance, the rational development of the railroad system in accordance with a plan), together with the encouragement of scientific agriculture and a rise in the general culture of the population, can save Russia and bring the country out of its horrible backwardness onto the road to prosperity.[91]

In its first hesitant steps toward the formulation of a program, the Association emphasized the need not only to expand the base of the industrial economy but also to increase its productivity. Means to this end received relatively little consideration, however. Also ignored was the connection between economic needs and the political system of the Empire. The Association raised this vital issue tangentially, in connection with industry's desire to see greater respect accorded to the place of law in economic affairs. The chairman of the Duma's Finance Commission, discussing Volskii's report, called

> attention to the absence of any connection between the possibility of realizing, and even of composing, an economic and financial program and the forms of the political system of the country. And yet this connection is very deep and real. For the development of public organizations, for their planned, fruitful activity, a representative system is necessary before anything else.[92]

Thus, by the end of 1909, the Association had shown its commitment to a systematic program of national economic development and had advanced its understanding of the Empire's diverse and competing economic needs, but its comprehension of what was involved in formulating a program remained rudimentary indeed. Obviously, both a clearer understanding of planning procedures and a keener evaluation of the country's substantive needs were required if the Association's high ambitions were to be transformed into practical achievement.

The period from the beginning of 1910 until mid-1911 constituted, as we have seen, one of transition in the affairs of the Association. This change affected its work with respect to an economic program for Russia. The confidence with which the organization had previously approached the broad problems of Russia's future no longer seemed appropriate. The easy superficiality of the first years gave way to a new appreciation of the need to lay a solid groundwork, "thoroughly investigated and studied in detail," so that, as Industry and Trade declared on the eve of the Fifth Congress, "when there is need we can return well-armed to general questions."[93]

To an even greater extent than in previous years, the Association held the government responsible for both the creation and the implementation of an economic program, and it often reproached officials for their failure to fulfill that responsibility. Most frequently, it criticized the condition of state finances. Although Volskii's defense of Kokovtsov's policy of frugality in his conduct of his fiscal duties had attracted heated criticism at the Fourth Congress, no doubt because frugality had been coupled with a reluctance to award large, long-term loans to industry, the Association now emerged as the Minister's steadfast admirer, enthusiastically applauding his unprecedented success in 1910 in balancing the government's budget. Nevertheless, the organization also warned that the newly attained balance could not long endure without the support of a healthy and well-developed economy, and that, to that end, a systematic approach was essential. As Industry and Trade wrote: "Now is the time to take upon ourselves the solution of the next tasks confronting the sagacious minister: it is time to draw up a financial and economic plan in order to place a firm foundation under state finances for the next decade as well." The "Explanatory Note" to the budget for 1911, the journal complained, consisted only of "the most generalized principles, after which, obviously, a business-like financial and economic plan must follow."[94] Six months later, in the spring of 1911, Industry and Trade hailed Russia's second deficit-free budget "with a feeling of profound satisfaction," but it also reiterated "the necessity of creating a financial and economic plan for the next decade, . . . a project on which our organization has been insisting since the day of its origin."[95]

As in the past, the Association continued to look hopefully to the legislature for some initiative in the composition of a program. The tenor of its commentary remained discouraged, however. The State Council had done nothing except advance "to a very simple formula: 'the removal of the obstacles that weigh upon industry and trade and the creation of favorable conditions for the successful development of these branches of the national economy.'"[96] Even more disappointing was the work of the Third State Duma.

> We do not see in it any plan marked out in advance, any program. It is equally possible to say that the Duma has done a great deal in the field of economic problems and that it has done nothing. Everything that is done is done as if by accident, incidentally. No one can suspect us of having a prejudiced attitude toward the State Duma; on the contrary, we have noted, and we continue to note, with profound satisfaction all the steps taken by the Duma for the purpose of putting our state finances in order and for the correct solution of a number of very important economic questions. We fully recognize also that the State Duma, by the very fact of its existence, establishes a certain control over the activity of the Government, constitutes in itself a "landlady's eye." All this is indubitable, and its importance should not be deprecated. Yet we cannot fail to observe that the State Duma, despite its three years of existence, has still not developed, or at least has not manifested, any kind of plan, in the broad sense of this word, in the field of financial and economic planning.[97]

Although the Association did not lose sight of its basic objective during this intermediate period, it made only meager progress toward the formulation of an economic program of its own. In fact, the organization's only significant step in that direction was to be found in the Council's abortive report of 1910. Emphasizing both the need to stimulate economic growth and to overcome the instability of the industrial economy, it offered several long-range recommendations: the rapid introduction of universal education and occupational training, "assistance to popular self-help through the cultivation of trade unions and cooperatives," the improvement of agricultural techniques, and the development of small-scale industry. Short-run proposals included the attraction of capital into industry, transportation, and local governmental enterprise; the development of municipal improvements and local credit facilities; the removal of governmental restraints on private enterprise; a more orderly issuance of treasury orders and contracts; changes in railroad freight rates and the customs tariff in order to promote economic growth; railroad construction and measures to increase the operating efficiency of existing lines; the development of a merchant marine; and "a more correct and intensive exploitation of Russia's state forests."[98]

The Fifth Congress, which met in March 1911, marked the climax of the Association's period of tentative "withdrawal" from an active part in producing a comprehensive program, but it also saw the first indication that the period was approaching its end. Zhukovskii's report, the first of a series on the work of the Duma and State Council, heralded the change.

> Gentlemen, there is nothing easier, and nothing more difficult, than to write a program. Simply to proceed from a lack of knowledge of the subject, in accordance with a well-known pattern, is not difficult; a different matter is the synthesis of an idea that has been developed analytically for a very long time, molding itself into concrete, definite shape, encompassing in brief form the entire essence of the subject.

At the same time, however, Zhukovskii protested against the narrowness of the Association's own work. In a thinly veiled allusion to the disunity that had hampered its effectiveness in recent months, he called upon the industrialists to free themselves from their limited outlook and to create a "state program" that would stand as testimony to the patriotism and enlightenment of their class: "a synthesis of our practical interests and our ideological point of view."[99] Unfamiliar as these words must have sounded to industry's delegates, they were to be heard again and again as Zhukovskii rose, during the following years, to become their acknowledged leader.

During the last three years before the war, the Association continued to stress the importance of agriculture and governmental purchasing policies as sources of economic instability. Concerning the former, Industry and Trade wrote:

> A healthy state organism cannot develop correctly on such an unsteady foundation as a harvest which, with our low level of agricultural techniques, makes incredible jumps; it cannot progress while having in its budget such a permanent item of expense as famine relief to the population. A more solicitous attitude toward the bread-providing land and an improvement in the methods of its cultivation constitute the most urgent tasks of our time; and about this there is no dispute.[100]

In addition, the Association attributed to the government primary responsibility for precipitating the shortages in basic commodities that crippled heavy industry. Having withheld orders and contracts for many years, the government, it charged, had suddenly confronted industry with enormous and urgent orders far exceeding its productive capacity. Government orders arrived without a plan, "by jumps and starts,"[101] thereby aggravating the natural fluctuations of the business cycle. The Association's complaint contained virtually Keynesian overtones:

> At those moments when the popular market has presented no demand, or a weak, stationary demand, Treasury demand has also been absent. No one has thought, during times that were difficult for the national economy, that it would be possible to construct roads, to build freight cars and locomotives as stock in reserve; no one has wished to think ahead about this. But when popular demand has grown stronger, when popular life has imposed very heavy demands on industry, then there has also appeared a much strengthened and very intense Treasury demand.[102]

The government's direct participation in economic affairs as an entrepreneur caused it to react with great sensitivity to market conditions. The large amount of arbitrary personal discretion enjoyed by individual officials also tended to ruin "the laws of supply and demand."[103]

While continuing to emphasize the role of a primitive agriculture and an uncertain governmental demand in contributing to instability in the Russian economy, the Association placed increasing emphasis, during the last years before the war, on the independent part played by the mysterious ebb and flow of the business cycle. No doubt this new emphasis mirrored, in large measure, the rising influence within the Association of Zhukovskii, perhaps the best informed and the most "western" in outlook of the organization's leaders. Under his direction, the secretariat began to undertake statistical and other studies of the fluctuations of the business cycle in Russia and in other countries as well.

The result was apparent in the growing sophistication of the Association's outlook. Earlier, it had tended to attribute cyclical fluctuations in economic conditions mainly to the forces of nature itself. Late in 1911, for example, in an exchange with Professor Mikhail I. Tugan-Baranovskii, who considered the Russian business cycle to be largely dependent on world economic conditions, Baron Maidel insisted on the independent impact of the harvest in determining both the course of the Russian economy and Russia's commercial and financial relationship with the outside world. Fluctuations in the balance of payments, he said, "depend on the harvest, and indisputably, the improvement of agriculture, which is inconceivable without the simultaneous development of industry, is the basic task of our economic future."[104] Shortly before the war, however, Maidel himself pointed out that "to the extent that individual countries, and Russia in particular, possess a developed industry, the general industrial crises experienced by the world economy extend to them also."[105]

The Association also insisted that only a concerted program of industrial expansion and economic modernization could provide the stability that was essential for sustained economic growth. Underlying this position were industry's fears, notwithstanding goods shortages and the Association's denials of any interest in restraining the current industrial expansion, that the domestic market might prove unequal to industry's growing productive capacity. By the Association's own admission, heavy industry dreaded a repetition of the events of the turn of the century, when the industrial "boom" of the nineties had ended abruptly in a prolonged depression.

The failure of mass purchasing power to keep pace with the general economic expansion kept light industry, and particularly the cotton-textile industry, from sharing fully in the current prosperity. Finally, ominous reports circulated of a possible downward turn in economic conditions in the West. Conscious of the power of the business cycle in the Russian economy and its inter-relationship with conditions abroad, the Association recognized that a crisis in other countries might soon infect Russia as well. Thus, on the eve of the war, the need to minimize instability rivalled the desire to maximize economic expansion as a motive behind the Association's insistence on Russia's need for an economic program.

Although the Association's interest in introducing a greater measure of stability into Russian economic life lent ammunition to many critics who charged it with deliberately restraining the rate of current industrial expansion, the organization looked to the future with an increasingly vigorous emphasis on the need to promote national economic development. Indeed, nothing in the Association's published statements suggests, in its long-range outlook at least, any contradiction between stabilization and continued economic growth.

Now, however, the Association placed heavy emphasis on the role of economic planning in reducing the instability that constituted a major obstacle to industrial development. Planning, the organization insisted, must also include a conscious effort to modify, if not to control altogether, the cyclical fluctuations of economic life as well as to foster economic growth. Against Professor Tugan-Baranovskii's allegedly "fatalistic" view of the business cycle as an uncontrollable natural force to be accepted with resignation, the Association propounded a proto-Keynesian hypothesis: "there exists . . . a whole series of conditions in real life by which the impact of crisis may be eased and in some cases caused to pass entirely unnoticed."[106]

Considering control of the business cycle to be a practical possibility, the Council under Zhukovskii's leadership seemed, on the eve of the war, to be departing from some of its earlier policies in its effort to carry this view into action. True, the importance that it attributed to backward agriculture as a source of general instability and lagging growth remained undiminished, and agrarian development continued to occupy a prime place among its recommendations. Ironically, however, in view of its increasing difficulties and disillusionment with the government, not to mention its own heated campaign against the evils of "state socialism," the Association ascribed to the government a far more influential role in the mechanics of planning than had been the case in earlier years. Previously, it had called upon the government to reduce one element of uncertainty confronting the entrepreneur by introducing a more orderly spacing of its orders and contracts over a period of years in accordance with a program worked out and published in advance. Now, however, it demanded that the flow of orders be regulated in order to alleviate and forestall economic crisis. "It is possible," Zhukovskii told the Eighth Congress, "to regulate Treasury demand so that it will serve not as an echo, but as a corrective and complement to popular demand."[107] Almost simultaneously, Baron Maidel urged the Treasury to assume responsibility for the regulation of market conditions. "A definite regulation of orders, a definite economic plan, is necessary, without which we shall always fall into periods either of a scarcity of goods on the market or of sharp overproduction."[108]

The rational exercise of its role as the principal consumer of industry's products did not, however, exhaust the methods by which the government could assist in stabilizing market conditions. In its capacity as an entrepreneur, the state should mobilize its tremendous financial resources to that same end. At the Eighth Congress, Zhukovskii observed that "in general, the pulse of the Treasury economy has slavishly followed the pulse of the national economy instead of being its regulator."

> This role of regulator could be assumed in Russia by the Treasury, the biggest owner in the world of subsoil and landed surface, the biggest lumber industrialist, the greatest owner of railroads, and the biggest purchaser, in this connection, of equipment and of objects of direct consumption. In this connection also, free cash gives the Treasury tremendous freedom of action in deciding when the Treasury could serve as the most powerful regulator of demand and consumption, and consequently, the regulator of the entire economic turnover. A striving toward such regulatory activity has not, thus far, been manifested in the Russian Treasury in sufficient degree.[109]

The Association continued to believe that primary responsibility in carrying out the government's regulatory functions should be shared with delegates from organized public interests. Thus, the Council called for the establishment of a central governmental organ in which representatives of the public would participate. This agency would initiate and coordinate official economic policies, direct them toward the stabilization of market conditions, and introduce a measure of "consciousness" into economic life.

> The government, for the correct fulfillment of its economic role, must possess a great knowledge and a great awareness of all aspects of the national economy. The government must have an organ that is capable continually to collect and analyze all the data of current economic life, deducing from this analysis practical proposals for legislation and for the executive activity of the departments. Such proposals [ukazaniia] should unify the economic policy of the departments, adapting it to the general tasks of the national economy and to requirements of the moment. The creation of such an organ under the Council of Ministers, with the participation of representatives of the Legislature, of men of learning, and of practitioners of business affairs, is a correct measure that can not only introduce some order into the rather chaotic field of the Treasury economy but also, in time, exert an enormous and useful influence on the whole economic life of the country in the sense of giving it greater stability and consciousness, necessary conditions of economic progress.[110]

In advocating that the government assume the role of "regulator" in the economy, the Association attached great importance to its having a reliable body of factual information with which to work. Zhukovskii pointed out to the Eighth Congress that the proposed "organ"

> would be obliged to issue its own survey of the state of the Russian economy once a year, on October 20, when the legislature convenes. Those surveys would serve as a kind of standard, a kind of regulator of the haphazard economic measures and economic improvisations, that in our country each department creates to suit itself. This would provide an objective view that would give the government a basis for introducing a certain planned activity into Russian business life.[111]

In this connection, the Council sought, unsuccessfully, to obtain improvements in the range and quality of official statistics.[112] In addition, as we have seen, the Council undertook to prepare its own statistical data, pointing out as early as the Fourth Congress the importance of reliable information both as a "firm support" in difficult times and an effective means of forestalling "undesirable phenomena" in times that were normal.[113]

A Special Commission established in cooperation with the editors of the Ministry of Finance's Herald of Finance (Vestnik finansov) and chaired by Zhukovskii undertook a study of the indications of approaching economic crises and possible measures for their prevention.[114] In mid-1913, a member of the Council's staff observed that while the formal "science" of economics remained mired in fruitless disputes about terminology and generalities, "being converted more and more into a collection of disputed opinions about things that are completely indisputable and entirely real," "practical men" had been making great progress in organizing the continuing observation of economic life for the purpose of predicting economic crisis.[115] Baron Maidel reiterated this attitude of pragmatism a year later.

> Whatever has been said by theorists, by representatives of learning, in practice the course of life is not to be explained either in a "liberal economic policy" or in a theory of industrial crises. Theory illuminates the phenomena of life and gives clues to the elucidation and resolution of practical questions; but to solve the problems that reality poses in accordance with economic theories, without calculating the real, mutual relationship of forces and conditions--such a path the representatives of industry cannot take.[116]

Although the Association accorded to the central government the main responsibility for the direction of economic affairs, it also argued that in certain cases the power of decision should be entrusted to local authorities and interests, as those best informed of local needs and most directly affected by what might be done. Particularly important was local participation in the composition of plans for the development of inland waterways, seaports, and roads. In connection with the plan for road construction elaborated by the ministry of transport, for example, the Council urged that zemstvo authorities draw up local road-building programs with the assistance of representatives from local industry, trade, and other interests.[117]

Moreover, although Zhukovskii endorsed a more active governmental role in introducing "a certain development in accordance with a plan" into its economic activities, he reaffirmed the Association's commitment to a system of private enterprise as the most productive and the one most suited to Russia's needs.[118] However, the Association's demand for Treasury regulation of market conditions, in conjunction, especially, with its vigorous and simultaneous campaign for a reduction in official intervention in economic affairs, caused some puzzlement outside the organization, if not within it. Replying to the protestations of Professor Mikhail I. Fridman concerning "the manifest illogic" of the Association's position, Baron Maidel offered an explanation rooted in the "practical" outlook of the businessmen:

> It is not the representatives of industry and trade who are illogical, but Russian life, which is not set within the limits obligingly pointed out by messieurs the professors. Our position is completely clear; we stand for a "liberal economic policy" [i.e. one based on private enterprise]. But practical men must take into consideration the situation that exists at the present time. Two-thirds of the rail network is in the hands of the Treasury. The Treasury is the biggest owner of forests, the sole owner of oil lands, the complete master of the economically tremendous liquor monopoly, and the sole large-scale purchaser for the needs of military defense and port construction. . . . Only theorists, for whom ideas based in principle are important but for whom the reality in which industry must live and work is not important, can fail to reckon with these conditions or to take into account the present role of the Treasury in the commercial-industrial turnover of the country.[119]

Private enterprise, of course, had an important role in introducing a greater stability into economic affairs. To what extent this direct role--as contrasted with industry's indirect role as an adviser in ministerial conferences--was to be played in partnership with, or independently of, the government remained unclear, however. The instrument of industry's action was to be the government's least favorite institution, the industrial syndicate. Baron Maidel, for one, defended the syndicates.

> For the purpose of combating economic crisis, the industrial life of Europe and the United States of North America has promoted the organization of capital in the form of syndicates, cartels, trusts, and so forth. Russian industrialists have also arrived at this stage in events. Organized capital struggles with crisis by means of a whole series of measures, the most important of which is the regulation [normirovka] of production. In fact, the last crisis abroad, in 1907-1908, was significantly eased through the influence of syndicates.[120]

Indeed, the Association considered the syndicate to be its primary agency for stimulating orderly economic growth. While rejecting charges that syndicates had deliberately restricted output, the Association acknowledged that the organization of production "on principles of precise, advance calculation" must "set its own limits" in accordance with the needs of the market as determined by statistical studies and the receipt of orders.[121] This appeared consistent with a policy of promoting national economic development. As Zhukovskii told the Seventh Congress:

> Certainly the most interesting country for us with respect to syndicates is Germany, both because its political system is more like that of the Russian state and because of its history. Only forty years ago, Germany was an agricultural country; and now, in a conscious way--and in this lies the distinction between German economic history and that of other countries--in a conscious and planned way it has created an industry for itself and has become a highly industrialized country. Whether it has done this well or not is another question, but the fact remains that Germany has followed the course that we wish to follow, that is, consciously to create in Russia a big, healthy industry. In other countries this process has taken place spontaneously under a certain confluence of natural conditions. In Germany it has had the character of expedient action.[122]

The possibility or desirability of improving the efficiency and profitability of Russia's major industries through technological improvements played a relatively small part in the Association's plans. Evidently, the technological level of the metallurgical and cotton textile industries, in particular, gave it little cause for concern.[123] Because the inefficiency of the workers appeared to be the primary obstacle to a growth in the productiveness of industrial output in those industries, the Association stressed the need to increase the productivity of labor. As early as the spring of 1908, Krestovnikov had expressed the organization's outlook in an address to the Minister of Trade and Industry:

> Is it not clear . . . that the road through which our state can emerge from its present disorder, I say, the salvation of Russia, lies in raising the well-being of the masses of the people as rapidly as possible? This is possible only by raising the intensiveness and productivity of the people's labor.[124]

To this end, the Association advocated the introduction of universal education and occupational training. "The top priority task of our time," the Eighth Congress declared, "is the broadest possible development of professional education for the purpose of raising the technical qualifications of the Russian worker."[125] In addition, an intensification of effort on the part of the workers themselves was essential. "Work alone," it was asserted, "can create popular well-being, and only it can bring tranquillity and prosperity to our native land."[126] The Association looked forward to the rise of a new "cult of labor" among the people, a kindling of mass enthusiasm for work such as the Russian people had never known and such as was later, under far different auspices, to be exemplified by the Stakhanovites of the 1930s. Here again, ironically, the industrialists in tsarist Russia anticipated their Soviet successors.

3

Promoting Economic Development: The Dilemmas of Backwardness

Financing Industrialization

More than any other single factor, capital constituted the sine qua non of national economic development. The dearth of capital therefore posed the greatest single material obstacle to Russia's further economic progress. "Our enrichment," Industry and Trade declared in its first issue, "is possible only if capital comes to us, is applied to our labor, and opens up an outlet for our natural wealth."[1] Hence the quest for capital, primarily long-term investment capital, preoccupied the Association in its efforts to devise an economic program for Russia.

Russia's poverty and its relative lack of substantial financial reserves, moreover, necessitated turning to other countries for much of the financing of economic growth. The condition of world money markets remained a constant concern of the organization during the prewar years. For the most part, however, the supply of foreign capital for investment appeared to represent less of a problem than the task of inducing it to seek investment in Russia, rather than in such rival underdeveloped regions as Latin America. The Association also noted the reluctance of Russian capitalists themselves to invest their funds in domestic industry.

Whatever the source of the capital, however, and whatever the channels through which it reached industry--direct investment, governmental borrowing, or banking intermediaries--the success of industry's effort depended mainly on governmental policies, above all the maintenance of the country's fiscal and monetary standing in the eyes both of the world and of its own subjects. High profits and attractive conditions generally within industry itself also owed much to official actions. Consequently, the Association focused on questions of state fiscal, monetary, and industrial policy as well as on the related issue of entrepreneurial profits. Indeed, hardly a single aspect of Russia's broad economic problem escaped scrutiny by the Association in its examination of the financial needs of industry.

In advocating the large-scale importation of foreign capital, the Association encountered widespread public opposition to what was regarded as foreign penetration or subversion of national economic, and, ultimately political, life. This opposition included the left wing of Russian politics, in both the Marxist and its Narodnik aspects, but the loudest objections came from the opposite end of the spectrum: extreme conservatives and nationalists suspicious of industrialism, who often inclined toward some variant of Slavophile thinking. In addition, influential liberals who ignored the logical connection between political liberalism and national economic development shared the "free-trade" viewpoints of the agrarians.[2]

By mid-1910, suspicion of foreign capital reached such proportions that Industry and Trade noted the beginning of a "campaign" in the press against "the so-called predominance of foreign capital in Russia." Despite the fact that only a year before "all of Russia" had applauded a declaration by the minister of trade and industry before the State Duma on the importance of foreign capital to the nation's development, the press now was filled with allegations of "foreign shackles" on national independence and "powerful and rapacious international capital openly attempting the bloodless conquest of Russia."[3] Various "false patriots," "nativist [samobytnye] economists," and others with a "folk handicraft [kustar] mentality," the journal charged, defended only the needs of "the notorious nonproductive consumer" and preferred to see Russia import foreign goods rather than adopt the means of advancing domestic production. "They are against foreign capital but, simultaneously declaiming for the reduction or abolition of customs duties, they are for the foreign product. If this is patriotism, then where is the logic in it?"[4]

The Association argued that, on the contrary, imported capital offered the only hope of attaining true independence. Citing the example of the United States, where the "flowering of industry" had occurred thanks to massive infusions of borrowed money,[5] it argued that only a similarly induced industrialization could free Russia from its financial and commercial dependence on other countries. "Thus foreign capital, by leading us out of the condition of being tributaries of foreign industry, in the end will make possible the rise of national capital. More than that, it will convert us gradually from importers into exporters." Foreign domination need not follow in the wake of foreign investment, for Russia, despite all its difficulties, was already too advanced, culturally and technologically.

> Only in hopelessly backward countries with an ignorant, stupid, and inert population is foreign capital accompanied by its own administrators, technicians, and workers. Despite all its economic backwardness, Russia is on such a cultural level that it is impossible to speak about importing foreign knowledge, foreign initiative, or energy to us. The enterprises established among us using imported capital are administered best and most profitably with the help of local forces, and this circumstance is already well understood by foreign capitalists.[6]

Further to allay Russian fears, Industry and Trade pointed repeatedly to the example of the southern metallurgical industry, which had grown up almost entirely on the basis of imported capital. Efficient and progressive enterprise there promoted both the economic and social advancement of the country and its people. This industry had not only set high standards of technological and productive achievement but had pioneered the building of railroads and towns, the establishment of schools and hospitals, and the granting of medical aid, insurance, and other benefits to its employees, not to mention the payment of "hundreds of millions" of rubles in salaries and dividends to Russian nationals.[7] Even if the foreign capitalist insisted on extraordinary rewards for his services, a major part of his proceeds must remain in Russia and contribute to its prosperity.

Despite the exhortations of the Association and repeated assurances of the ministries of finance and trade and industry, hostility toward foreign capital seemed to find increasing support within high governmental circles.[8] The semi-official newspaper New Times, for example, repeatedly inveighed against the flow of Russian gold to other countries in the form of dividends on invested capital. The burgeoning spirit of nationalism, moreover, reflected mounting tensions in international affairs and, above all, a growing fear of German intentions toward Russia.[9] It fed fears of foreign capital among middle-of-the-road intellectuals as well. Even the industrialists expressed a fear of foreign competition on home soil.[10] Finally, the government and the press blamed the machinations of foreign-dominated syndicates for the prewar shortages of basic commodities. The Association charged that foreign capital was made the scapegoat for domestic difficulties over which it had no control.

> Against the participation of foreigners in the quickening of our natural riches a campaign is being mounted that is as violent as it is unreasonable.

> On this issue prejudices, fictions, and authentic facts have been interwoven into a dense network out of which every individual can pull, according to his own judgment, whatever he needs at a given moment for the sake of argumentation.[11]

During the last six months before the outbreak of World War I, the controversy over the dangers of foreign "predominance" in the Russian economy raged with particular bitterness. Increasingly, the fear of foreign capitalists tended to crystallize into a general hostility toward all foreigners--a fear reflected in the appearance of a variety of proposals for the "nationalization" of various aspects of the economy, that is, for the establishment of complete Russian ownership and control and the elimination of all foreign influences.[12] Thus, New Times seized the occasion of Petr L. Bark's appointment as minister of finance early in 1914 to demand "radical reforms" in the country's entire financial and economic policy, including the "nationalization" of state credit, the freeing of the grain trade from the control of so-called "foreign parasites," the utilization in "a fully national sense" of the stocks of Russian gold held by bankers in other countries, and measures to combat the alleged "seizure of all the natural resources of the country by foreigners" through the development of truly "national" (i.e. Russian-owned) enterprises.[13]

Against these manifestations of "militant nationalism," the Association reiterated all its old arguments, pointing out not only the contributions of foreign capital to national economic growth and prosperity but also the fact that in the natural course of events foreign-owned shares in Russian enterprises must be, and in fact already were, being transferred to Russian ownership.[14]

Yet, despite its generally disdainful attitude toward the outcries of "false patriots," Industry and Trade itself proved susceptible to the trend of the times. Increasingly, it couched its defense of foreign capital and of foreign influences in apologetic terms. It referred to them as necessary evils rather than as factors desirable in their own right. Reliance on domestic capital appeared preferable, and only its failure to flow into industry in the needed quantities made foreign investments necessary. "No doubt," Industry and Trade observed, "it would be better if Russia could manage with her own resources. But what is to be done if our capital is not great and is growing very slowly?"[15] Russia's choice, it was emphasized, lay between an unpleasant, but temporary, reliance on imported capital and a permanent dependence on other countries for imported manufactures. True national independence could be attained only through industrialization.[16]

More troublesome was the question of Russia's dependence on other countries for technical advancement and on imported technicians, skilled workers, and managerial talent, but here, too, the Association adopted an optimistic tone.

> One of the reasons for the dissatisfaction of our public opinion with foreign capitalists is their drawing of engineers and skilled workmen from their native lands. According to data collected by the Ministry of Finance in 1903, 12.7 percent of the skilled workmen and directors of industrial enterprises in the Empire were foreign subjects. Needless to say, this is unpleasant and seemingly unjust. But this phenomenon, without doubt, is transitory. There was a time when engineers, skilled workmen, machinists were hired from abroad for the construction and operation of our railroads. Who thinks about this now? The same absolute predominance of foreigners was once observed in the textile and sugar industries. As foreigners acquire confidence in the knowledge and training of our technicians, the latter, being better acquainted with local peculiarities, will, on the indispensable condition of their having a knowledge of foreign languages, have more and more opportunities to squeeze out their foreign rivals.[17]

Admittedly, branches of German firms in Russia dominated such militarily sensitive industries as chemicals, electrical engineering, and machine production. Designed both to obviate the handicap under which Germany competed with France, Belgium, and England because of its relative lack of capital for export, and to surmount the obstacles to the exploitation of the market that were posed by the Russian protective tariff, those enterprises brought large numbers of technicians and workers, but little capital, into Russia. Notwithstanding its frequently proclaimed fears of German economic and military predominance, the Association defended the German branch firms for the technical benefits that they brought to Russia. Even the Germans, Industry and Trade assured its readers, would eventually be displaced by Russians.

> The ideal aim--the gradual transition of foreign enterprises into ownership by the citizens of the given country--can be attained, if it is feasible, with greater effort in the case of the branches than in the case of other enterprises. We must reconcile ourselves to this. The fact that in general such a transition is accomplished little by little should not be doubted. . . . Let Russia be developed and grow rich, and it will be possible little by little to buy out domestic enterprises from the control of foreigners. "At higher prices," people object in reply. Certainly. But this is the premium to foreign capital, to the pioneer, for risk or for technical improvement. The dream of doing without foreign capital altogether is obviously utopian.[18]

Why did Russia fail to attract investments on the scale that was needed, despite the apparent abundance of capital in the money markets of the West and even, in more limited degree, within Russia itself? In its search for an answer, the Association considered a wide variety of possibilities.

Above all, it blamed the very backwardness and instability of Russian life. "Foreign capitalists," a member of the Council's staff declared, "have no confidence that sums borrowed will receive productive application and will not be wasted."[19] Russia still lacked "conscious planning" for national economic development, which was essential to inspire confidence in the country's future. "An unstable country with no economic program," Industry and Trade observed: "is not one to which a sensible capitalist can cheaply loan money." Only a "financial, economic, and general political program" could, in its view, make Russia worthy of credit.[20]

> The essence of the problem . . . does not lie in the skill of this or that individual standing at the head of our Ministry of Finance. Not the inadequacy of financial genius but the absence of a clear and definite economic policy constitutes the stumbling block that obstructs the inflow of the foreign capital, which is essential for the fertilization of our natural wealth. So long as the course of this policy is not firmly adopted and precisely defined, foreign capitalists will have no assurance as to the fate of their capital.[21]

Russia's handicap transcended economics, however. Its backwardness in the most common amenities of civilization tended to discourage investment. Its largest cities commonly lacked paved roads, sewers, water systems, lighting, slaughterhouses, and "all that without which life would be unthinkable in even the small towns of the West."[22] The prevailing climate of public and official opinion, particularly the atmosphere of suspicion and hostility toward business enterprise in general and foreign capital in particular, also posed obstacles. Lamenting the tendency of international capital to flow freely into Africa, Asia, Australia, and America but only slowly into Russia, Industry and Trade pointed also to bureaucratic procrastination, ineptitude, and dishonesty.

> Capital avoids Russia not only because it has no confidence in a cessation of the policy of adventures and unpromising experiments of every kind, but also because a primordial and universal hostility toward capital is predominant among us. Both the bureaucrat [chinovnik] and the ordinary citizen in Russia, each in his own way, jibes at capital. To the good offices of the

> first there is attributable clerical red tape and circular interdepartmental irresponsibility. The second . . . only further strengthens our bureaucrat in his credo, "if you are fat, thank God for it" [a reference to the bribery of officials by businessmen, an indispensable step in the process of obtaining government contracts and other administrative rulings], to the point where the capitalist is ruined.[23]

Among the specific deterrents to foreign investment, low industrial profits occupied the primary place in the Association's view.

> It seems self-evident that capital is guided not by idealistic but by mercantile motives, and that it goes where it can count on the greatest interest. Individual human beings can be guided by other motives as well: by patriotism, ambition, love of one's neighbor, and so forth. But what is needed is not individuals but the efforts of a multitude of individuals and enormous amounts of capital. Aside from high profits, there is no way of creating the needed cadres of workers and of attracting large amounts of capital. Yet the entirely natural striving of the industrialists to extract from his enterprise the greatest possible profit meets with condemnation both among the public and in the press. . . . The more profitable industry is, the better; the greater the profits, the more rapidly they attract new capital, and the more rapidly they enrich the country.[24]

Particularly during the earlier years, the state of entrepreneurial profits attracted the Association's concern. At the Second Congress, for example, the Council reported that Russian industry and trade had been generally unprofitable ever since 1899, that even their basic capital was deteriorating. The value of industry and trade was not only declining but heading toward "complete ruin."[25] Throughout 1908 and 1909, the Association strove to deny widespread allegations of high profits in industry, to emphasize the importance of low profits as an obstacle to the importation of foreign capital and the accumulation of domestic capital, and to assert the necessity of raising profits as an essential first step toward the further development of Russia's "productive forces." Unfortunately, industrialists seeking capital had to compete not only with the more profitable industries of other countries but even with the Russian government itself because interest rates on government bonds and average dividends paid by officially guaranteed investments substantially exceeded the average dividends offered by joint-stock enterprise.[26]

As depression yielded to prosperity, the Association became, for a time, less concerned with publicizing industry's allegedly inadequate profits and increasingly defended it against mounting charges of profiteering and excessive profits on the part of both native "monopolists" and foreign capitalists. Yet the old lament, of the difficulty of competing with other, "exotic," countries in attracting foreign capital (as well as with industrialized Germany),[27] persisted. The last two or three years before the war witnessed renewed efforts to demonstrate the inadequacy of industrial profits in Russia and its deleterious impact on foreign investment. Early in 1912, the Council published the results of an elaborate study on the profitability of Russian joint-stock enterprises during the period 1901-9. The average dividend of 4 percent paid by accountable enterprises fell "significantly below the discount rate even on first-class bills of exchange."[28]

In the spring of 1912, industrial profits suddenly became an acute issue. During a debate in the State Council on a bill to create health insurance for workers, Count Witte took exception to the Association's contention that low profits hampered investment in industry. On the contrary, he charged, capital was in fact flowing into Russian industry, and "the assertion of the organ of united industry, Industry and Trade, about the higher profitability of German commercial-industrial enterprise is 'financial heresy.'" Needless to say, this accusation by one of such stature as Witte, who, Industry and Trade plaintively observed, had always in the past objectively assessed the position of Russian industry, disappointed the Association. Deprecating Witte's charges as a reflection of his forced removal from practical affairs and as an ill-considered move tending to "strengthen the mistaken views that are so firmly established in the educated part of society regarding the position of our industry,"[29] Baron Maidel insisted that the higher dividends allegedly paid in Germany had produced a more rapid flow of capital into German, than into Russian, industry. In Russia, moreover, capital went primarily into banks or speculative purchases on the exchanges rather than into long-term industrial investments.[30]

Although low industrial profits admittedly reflected the high costs of production and marketing in Russia, as compared with western countries, this disadvantage stemmed also from factors beyond industry's direct control. These included general economic conditions, such as geographic handicaps and the predominantly agricultural character of the Russian economy, as well as an uncertain and inefficient labor force, burdensome taxation, high railroad freight rates, and other governmental policies inimical to industry. In its zeal to ferret out the sources of industry's difficulties, the Association attacked such seemingly sacrosanct capitalist principles as the "middleman's profit" and free competition.

In assessing the broad range of unfavorable conditions--political, social, and economic--that confronted industry, the Association shifted its emphasis with changing times and conditions. During the early years, it attached much weight to the poverty of the peasant masses and their limited purchasing capacity. As Adolf A. Volskii asserted in his report to the Third Congress, "The weak consuming capacity of the population of the Russian Empire and the progressive decline in the economic well-being of the country are reflected in the most grievous way in the profitability of Russian joint-stock enterprises."[31] Apart from its more or less direct impact on profits, moreover, the limited capacity of the domestic market caused foreign investors to view with skepticism the potential of Russian industry for further expansion. "Russia's domestic market for the products of factory and mining industry is extremely dismal," Volskii told the Fourth Congress, "and, in any case, does not contain any elements encouraging for the investment of capital in Russian industry."[32]

Although high production costs exacerbated industry's difficulties in attracting capital,[33] only rarely did those costs submit to entrepreneurial manipulation. To the extent that free competition appeared to elevate both production and marketing costs, the Association sought its neutralization through the formation of syndicates and other monopolistic arrangements. To overcome the disadvantages of small size, it encouraged the growth of large, joint-stock enterprises at the expense of small producers. As we have seen, however, the Association paid little attention to the need to increase industry's own productivity through technological improvements and the rationalization of output.

In contrast, it attributed a major share of responsibility for industry's allegedly low profits to the government. The disproportionately heavy tax burden on industrial enterprise constituted a principal cause of industry's inability to attract the capital that it so desperately needed. (Taxation was one of the Association's major grievances against the government and it absorbed, probably, a greater share of its attention than any other specific issue.) The backwardness of Russia's political and legal system and the ineptitude of its government also provided explanations for industry's difficulties. One member of the Council's staff wrote:

> Actually, western European capital works with great difficulty in our country. Guilty in this respect are both the pseudopatriotic wails about the seizure of Russia by foreigners and our procedures, which make it possible for any parasite to attach himself to any business and, not infrequently, to bleed it to death.[34]

Over this inhospitable foundation, moreover, towered the inefficiency and hostility of Russia's powerful bureaucracy. Endless red tape, procrastination ("circular interdepartmental irresponsibility"), dishonesty, constant "tutelage," and arbitrary interference in the affairs of private enterprise created an atmosphere of harassment and uncertainty that reduced profits and frightened away the would-be investor. Thus, the reluctance of English capital to seek investment in Russian railroads stemmed from "the peculiar conditions prevailing here," in contrast with those that confronted the English businessman at home.

> The Englishman, through his character and his tradition, strives for freedom, unconstrained by unnatural restrictions of any kind on the development of business enterprises. When in Russia, therefore, in connection with the authorization and implementation of railroad concessions, individual ministries begin to introduce requirements that not only have nothing to do with the rational development of the enterprise but even deliberately make it difficult, the Englishman understandably refuses to invest his capital in such an enterprise. The Englishman would never agree to let a person appointed by the ministries direct his affairs, as, for example, is the case with our railroad companies. Such a procedure is, for him, inadmissible. All that Russia needs for the attraction of foreign capital into railroad construction is greater freedom for the owner of industry and the subordination of all other interests to the economic interests of the country and of the population, which is thirsting for an opportunity to live and to earn a living.[35]

The issue of governmental restrictions and bureaucratic interference in the affairs of private enterprise occupied an increasingly prominent place among the "obstacles" to the importation of capital.[36] The Association commented toward the end of 1910 with growing bitterness:

> Surveying calmly the entire expanse of Russian economic life, we can find reasons for the grievous fears of free capital only in that political oppression and that merciless persecution to which every manifestation of independent activity [samodeiatel'nost'] and every sign of initiative is subjected in our country. This destructive work is carried out equally well by our government and by the periodical press along the entire spectrum of its party colors. Their common ideology is: let no one earn anything. In the name of this dreadful principle, let everything perish, both popular welfare and international prestige, provided only that no one earns anything. In the name of this principle, our ministries do not hesitate to violate the clearest laws; they completely forget about their natural role, exhaust by unbearable red tape, and everywhere lay their heavy hand of sepulchral stillness.[37]

A year later, the organization welcomed Vladimir N. Kokovtsov's appointment as prime minister. The former minister of finance, it was noted, had recently advocated a reduction in governmental restrictions on industry and had also acknowledged that "a protective attitude toward foreign capital is necessary; Russia, without foreign capital, is not in a position to live and develop."[38]

The new optimism faded quickly, however. Increasingly, the Association blamed governmental hostility rather than intrinsic economic conditions for industry's difficulty in attracting capital. To the organization's long-standing and increasingly outspoken complaints of official restrictions on entrepreneurial freedom and arbitrary bureaucratic interference in business affairs there were now added fears of the new tendency of the government to expand its role as a direct competitor of private enterprise in the ownership and operation of industrial and commercial affairs. "State socialism" became a major grievance as never before. Industry and Trade wrote:

> The further expansion of the treasury economy, with the gathering together not only of operating but also of basic capital out of tax sources, obviously can only hamper the inflow of foreign capital that is necessary. It threatens the complete disorganization of the national economy in the future.[39]

With growing urgency the Association called on the government to remove the "fetters" that restrained industrial initiative and discouraged foreign investment. "The presence of administrative discretion, the absence of a firm foundation of legality, is, in our profound conviction," Baron Maidel wrote, "one of the main obstacles not only to the inflow of capital into industry but also to a correct development of existing enterprises." Charging the government with a "persistent failure to fulfill the law," he quoted a recent statement by Count Witte in support of the Association's contention that even domestic capital feared to go into industry:

> A no less important condition favoring the accumulation of capital than the presence of natural resources is the legal order, the degree of legality in a given country, which makes confidence in the future secure. Without firm confidence in the security of one's own person and property, without a clear idea of one's right of ownership and of the sure defense of this right by law against infringement of any kind, there can be no talk about striving for savings and still less about the confident investment of what has been saved from one's own or another's production. Every striving toward the investment of one's savings in enterprises of any kind, in the absence of

> confidence in the security of property, with a concept of ownership weakly developed in the country, is paralyzed by the fear of losing one's investment, at best, and is limited by the hoarding, by the hiding, of specie and precious stones, that is, by the accumulation of dead capital.

For his part, Baron Maidel commented darkly:

> In the presence of known surpluses of money, free funds go to the exchange, to the on-call game, as was the case here, for example, after the harvests of 1909 and 1910. Only into industry does money flow extremely unwillingly in our country.[40]

As the end of the prewar period drew near, new regulations that hampered the formation of joint-stock companies by restricting their right to own land and limiting the participation of Jewish and other non-Russian businessmen in industry, contributed heavily to the rising tide of the Association's discontent. Toward the end of 1913, Industry and Trade lamented that, once again, official indifference and hostility had let slip a favorable opportunity for the attraction of foreign capital.

> Under the present direction of internal policy, it is not only impossible to think about the creation of especially attractive conditions for foreign capital, but there are even grounds for fearing that various restrictive experiments, involving the limitation of joint-stock companies in the ownership of land, are to be put into effect. Under such conditions there can be no talk of a significant inflow of foreign capital.[41]

Increasingly, although still cautiously, the organization tinged its protests with the suggestion that the source of industry's difficulties lay deeply rooted in the policies of an outmoded government. Addressing the State Duma, Aleksandr I. Konovalov pointed bluntly to the need for "the rapid renovation of our state and public life" in the interest of speeding the flow of capital into Russia and promoting economic development generally.[42]

A thorough reform of the Empire's banking system seemed to offer the best means of channeling domestic and foreign capital into industry. The Association blamed the shortage of both of direct investment and of long-term credit on the subordination of Russia's two principal types of banks--the joint-stock commercial banks and the state savings banks--to the overriding purpose of supporting the financial structure of the state. Banks possessed the legal right to make industrial loans, but this right was in practice nullified by the government's requirement, designed to assure a permanent market for its own paper, that their reserve capital be invested in state paper only. Hence, "every kopek of the people's money is driven into state credits,"[43] to be channeled, in turn, into the Gentry and Peasant Land Banks and consumed in salvaging the interests of agriculture.[44] Whatever free capital the banks retained was hardly available either for such illiquid operations as investment in industry or for long-term loans. It tended instead to go either into short-term credits or into speculative transactions on the stock exchange. Although the total amount of capital involved remained small in per-capita terms, in absolute terms it was substantial. If productively invested, it could have been of great help in promoting national economic development.

The Association also advocated reforms in the relationship between lending banks and indebted industry. Soviet writers contended that large banks, which were themselves enthralled by foreign capital, controlled prerevolutionary Russian industry. The organization's published commentary on this question suggests that it favored some controls over the investment of banking in industry. Particularly revealing is the Association's admiration of German banks for bringing about rapid economic expansion:

> Without the help of the banks, German industry never could have attained such a rapid development and such a luxuriant flowering. The banks widely and boldly protected the German merchant wherever he worked, on both sides of the ocean; they assisted German ships in penetrating all the ports of the world; they forced the all-powerful London market to honor their domestic currency on its transoceanic acceptances and to reckon with it. The German banks supported and continue to support, by all methods, the political and economic undertakings of their government (in Africa, Asia, Turkey, and Russia), and in this they are rightly regarded not only as the vanguard of domestic industry but also as the bearers of German political and economic influence in all corners of the earth.[45]

The fact that German banks not only financed new and existing industrial enterprises but also took part in their management through representatives on their boards of directors appeared to offer distinct financial advantages to industry, especially since it raised the confidence of other investors in the stability of both industry and the banks. Moreover, "organic ties" united not only German banks and industry but also groups of banks organized for the purposes of pooling information on economic and financial conditions and conducting common policies. This cooperative relationship enabled German banks to participate effectively in promoting industrial expansion and to provide needed support for industry in difficult times. In Russia, however, banks had been unable to unite "even in the simplest matters." The Association advocated the organization of industry through groups of joint-stock commercial banks, functioning, presumably, as holding companies, to facilitate both the financing of industry and the organized sale of its products.[46]

As prosperity succeeded depression in Russia, the Association's dissatisfaction with the functioning of the banking system increased. Despite an "unprecedented" flow of money into banks, especially into the state savings banks, and the reinforcement of these funds by increased credits from the State Bank, the participation of the banks in the financing of industrial growth grew at a discouragingly low rate.[47] As before, most of the funds at the banks' disposal continued to flow mainly into government securities, the remainder being reserved for speculative maneuvers on the stock exchange and, increasingly, for short-term credits to industry. Industrial expansion depended largely on profits "ploughed back" into the individual enterprise.[48] Evidently the investment of domestic capital in industry through the medium of the banking system was hampered by the same "obstacles" that discouraged the flow of foreign capital into Russia. Cautiously, Industry and Trade observed:

> In Russia the long unseen moment of an abundance of money has arrived, unaccompanied by the issuance of new values; therefore it is possible that the banks, sooner or later, will undertake the financing of industry, provided the difficulties that have hampered the opening of new enterprises in our country are removed.[49]

Industry's most pressing need on the eve of the war, however, was for long-term credit. As before, the Association stressed the disorganization and inadequacy of the banking system, favored an increased concentration of bank ownership, and advised greater cooperation among banks in deciding basic questions of banking practice. In addition, the Association expressed concern over the increasingly inflationary situation that confronted the country as a result of the fact that an abundance of free capital shunned long-term investment in industry in favor of short-term investment. The economy operated too much on short-term credit and not enough on basic capital. The potential dangers included a distressing increase in bank failures and unfulfilled payment obligations for orders contracted on credit from manufacturers. Although the Association called loudly for the establishment of stricter standards of commercial law to prevent dishonest practices by unscrupulous merchants,[50] its reluctance to accept the imposition of tighter legal restrictions on banking operations seemed to contradict in some measure its proclaimed fears of an overexpansion in credit.[51] Its fears of an inflationary overexpansion in short-term credit were also rendered questionable by occasional articles in Industry and Trade alleging industry's need for additional amounts of such credit[52] and, even more inconsistently, by its mounting complaints of a currency shortage and appeals for a relaxation of the regulations restricting the State Bank's authority to issue paper currency.[53]

The Association also showed much interest in promoting the expansion of the Empire's small credit institutions, particularly cooperatives. The Third and Fourth Congresses and numerous articles in Industry and Trade strongly recommended the replacement of Russia's existing institutions for the provision of credit to favored estates: the gentry and peasantry. Instead, a network of credit cooperatives should issue small loans for fairly extended periods of time to agriculture and small-scale industry regardless of the social status of the borrower.[54] The Association also hailed as a major step toward the full utilization of popular savings by peasant agriculture and legislation in 1910 providing for the utilization of part of the funds deposited in savings banks to finance small credit institutions. In this connection, the Association stressed the need for the adequate development of small-scale credit. "Material help on the part of the state is an unavoidable and urgent necessity."[55]

During the immediate prewar years, the Association also expressed a growing concern with the need to make credit available to local governmental institutions in the zemstvos and cities. It supported a movement within the Ministry of Finance for the institution of a system of credit for zemstvo and municipal banks. In addition, the Association called for the establishment of a special Empire-wide bank for the provision of credit to municipalities.[56] The organization sought not so much to increase the financial resources available to industry as to assist the financing of railroad construction and such local public-works projects as the building of roads and bridges, hospitals, sewage and drainage networks, housing, and public water systems. As Industry and Trade wrote:

> Domestic industry and trade are interested in the most vital way in the very rapid organization of municipal credit. Only through the flow of money into railroad construction and municipal enterprises is it possible to expect that enlivening of domestic industry for which we cannot wait another ten years.[57]

The financing of needed municipal improvements by borrowing would shift the burden of payment onto succeeding generations, which, presumably, would be better able to assume it than was Russia's presently impoverished population.

Whether local credit belonged primarily in governmental or in private hands seemed, however, to be a subject of some confusion. On the national level, the Association clearly insisted that any future bank of municipal credit be a private, joint-stock institution. Thus it took strong exception to the effort of the Ministry of Internal Affairs to establish such a bank under its own control and to the tendency of other ministries and governmental agencies to establish their own departmental banks for the provision of credit within their own spheres of activity.

> The concept of treasury banks under individual ministries is obviously unacceptable. In any case, financial policy must be unified in one and the same center. Otherwise the country would risk finding itself in an extremely bad financial position one fine day, and we would be deprived even of the weak confidence that foreign capital has in us.[58]

State-owned banks, it was asserted, could not maintain the kind of close supervision over their creditors that the weak financial position of municipal and zemstvo institutions required.

On the other hand, city and zemstvo banks escaped the Association's general disapproval of governmental ownership. Thus the Association advocated the extension of the law of June 21, 1910, which provided for the use of part of the funds of state savings banks to support small credit institutions, to give increased aid to such banks as well as to private and cooperative savings and loan and other credit associations.[59] It also applauded the removal, early in 1912, of many restrictions on the activities of the municipal banks and the awarding to them of the right to conduct commercial credit operations.[60] It insisted, moreover, that privately organized local credit institutions remain under the authorization and control of the government in St. Petersburg.

The Association clearly recognized the urgency of expanding the financial resources at the disposal of industry. This, it understood, was crucial to any program for national economic development. As to the sources of these funds, the Association's position appeared unambiguous. Added capital in substantial quantities must come mainly from other countries, richer and more developed than Russia itself. Yet foreign capital, despite its apparent abundance in world money markets, failed to seek investment in Russian industry on the scale that was needed. To the industrialists' chagrin, it preferred the more exotic countries of Latin America and the East. Even domestic capital, which was accumulating on an encouraging scale, rejected the opportunity for investment in the Empire's own industry.

What was to be done? Here the Association failed to give clear answers. Although governmental policies undoubtedly bore a large share of the responsibility for Russian industry's unattractiveness to capital, the industrialists, in their reluctance to recognize industry's own obligation to increase productivity through improved techniques and managerial methods, could not escape blame. Equally vague were recommendations that the Association offered to resolve the basic question of the government's proper role in the financing of industrial expansion. Clearly, it recognized that the state must assist in obtaining the needed capital. But to what extent should governmental assistance imply a measure of governmental direction and control over economic life? And how should this direction be exercised? How could a financial plan be reconciled with entrepreneurial freedom from harassing governmental controls--a major cause, in its view, of industry's failure thus far to obtain the capital that it needed? No doubt it is too much to expect that the Association could have provided clear answers to these questions. In fairness, it must be acknowledged that the same questions continued, later in the century, to preoccupy those who would plan for the advancement of many "underdeveloped" societies and, in the 1990s, Russia itself.

Living Standards and the Domestic Market

One of the consequences of the industrial crisis at the turn of the century was to persuade Russian industrialists of the dangers inherent in excessive dependence on governmental demand. Under the continuing impact of the prolonged depression, the Association looked with new interest to the popular market as a stabilizing force in economic life.[61] As government orders dwindled, Russian industry faced the problem of survival in its most acute form. While calling for a renewal of governmental demand, limitations on imports, and the development of exports in order to alleviate the dangers of "overproduction," the Association recognized the poverty of the great masses of the population as "the main obstacle to the industrial development of our country."[62]

This new interest in increasing the purchasing power of the masses of the people underlay the Association's urgent concern with the development of agricultural productivity. As Grigorii A. Krestovnikov pointed out shortly before the First Regular Congress, "If nine-tenths of the whole population of Russia is engaged in agriculture, then it is natural that the well-being of domestic industry is entirely determined by the extent of the well-being of the agricultural population."[63] Nearly every succeeding Congress reiterated this idea. The Third Congress, for example, stressed

> the necessity of taking measures for the development of the agricultural life of the country, since only with an increase in the purchasing power of the peasantry, which constitutes the main group of consumers of the products of industry and trade, is the broad progress of these branches of national work possible, in accordance with a plan.[64]

If the Association looked to an expanded domestic market as a potential support for an expanding industry in the future, however, it viewed the present capacity of that market with gloom. In 1908, the Council estimated the average per-capita income in Russia at 74 rubles, as contrasted with 184 in Germany and 364 in the United States.[65] The following year, Stanislav M. Rotvand maintained not only that the proper figure was 58 rubles, but also that per-capita income had actually declined by five rubles during the past decade. "The country," he informed the Fourth Congress, "is not only living in great poverty, but is being reduced to pauperism."[66]

Volskii agreed that the domestic market for the products of Russian industry remained bleak.[67] At the end of 1908, he argued that, because of the inadequacy of the domestic market, Russia must "export or die."

> The frontiers of the Empire have already become too narrow for Russian factory work. The products of our factories and mills do not find the scope that is necessary on the domestic market. Our industry has already outgrown the needs of our poor agricultural society. The consuming capacity of the Russian subject has declined, rather than grown, during the past eight years.[68]

No doubt it was Volskii, the spokesman for the metal-working industry, who was mainly responsible for the Association's assertion that "the idea of building up our metallurgical industry on the basis of the horseshoes, axles, forged wheels, plows, and iron roofs needed by the Russian peasant will not appeal to practical people."[69]

Although Liashchenko and others correctly concluded that the industrialists' discouragement with opportunities in the domestic market led them, as early as 1908, to "return to the old system of a government market, state orders, subsidies, and protectionism,"[70] the Association's faith in the domestic market as a foundation for industrial expansion in the future remained undiminished. In an editorial note on the work of the State Council, for example, Industry and Trade declared with satisfaction that "awareness is steadily growing of the necessity of giving first priority to the question of the development of the productive forces of Russia and the improvement of the material position of the population."[71] At the Fourth Congress, the Council once again stressed the need to raise the level of popular welfare.[72]

The return of prosperity prompted the organization to complain of the failure of demand to keep pace with the growth in industrial output. As early as the spring of 1910, Industry and Trade declared:

> The capacity of our domestic market is not only lagging far behind the corresponding size of the markets of all the leading countries of the world, but is showing almost no signs of growth. Certain very important indices even show alarming signs of decline.

Per-capita consumption of such basic commodities as pig iron and cotton had declined since 1899, and

> even the past harvest, unprecedented in size . . . has had a favorable effect only on the condition of the State Treasury and has had almost no influence on the growth of internal demand. Meanwhile, our factory and mining industry has already outstripped domestic demand by a wide margin in certain fields, and before many enterprises there is arising the menacing specter of the question: "to be, or not to be."[73]

By 1911, prosperity had radically changed the condition of the market. The demand for coal, oil, and metal products had already exceeded existing capacity. Far from complaining of inadequate markets for their goods, those industries, supported by the Association, marshalled their forces to resist charges of the deliberate restraint of output. The textile and other consumer-goods industries, which depended more on popular than industrial and state demand, faced a quite different problem, however. In those areas, the industrialists continued to complain of lagging domestic demand and the inability of the domestic market to absorb the growing output of cotton cloth and similar products. Early in 1912, Industry and Trade pointed out that demand for textiles at the Nizhnii Novgorod Fair, which constituted the best index of rural prosperity, had actually declined substantially and that, the general prosperity notwithstanding, the Moscow textile industry remained in a state of depression.[74]

During the last two years before the war, opinions differed as to whether conditions were becoming worse or improving slightly. Against the optimistic position maintained by the government, the Association nevertheless took a strong stand,[75] and in mid-1913 their differences reached a climax in a noteworthy "debate" between Finance Minister Kokovtsov and Aleksandr I. Konovalov, who spoke for the cotton-textile industry in the State Duma. Attacking the finance minister's optimistic outlook in the explanatory note to the state budget for 1914, Konovalov asserted that the cotton-textile industry had for two years suffered a depression caused by declining sales, and that, although the growth of the industry since 1900 had been slower than the growth in population, it was nevertheless unable to dispose of all its output on the domestic market. Statistical data on per-capita consumption, he declared, "testify to only one thing: the extraordinary sickness of our internal market, its extraordinary weakness, and the extraordinary poverty of the masses of the Russian population." Against Kokovtsov's insistence that "the growth of the state budget is an index of the steadily growing well-being of the broad masses of the population," Konovalov argued that Russia's balanced budget reflected rather the poverty of an exploited and overtaxed people. The government must recognize, he concluded, that popular welfare was of primary importance, as

> all the successes of our national economy, as long as they are not based on a foundation of the growing well-being of the broad masses of the people, are not durable and cannot serve as a firm support for the further economic flowering of our native land.[76]

Other voices within the Association expressed a somewhat more cheerful view, however. In the spring of 1912, Krestovnikov cautiously told the Moscow Exchange Committee that an increase in the well-being of the masses of the people, although perhaps of only temporary duration, had contributed substantially to the general prosperity.[77] In the autumn Industry and Trade observed that two good harvests in succession had contributed materially to the prosperity of the textile and leather industries.[78] Commenting on the state budget for 1914, the journal noted "some growth in the purchasing power of the population" but concluded with a reminder of Russia's backwardness and a warning that the duration of the current wave of prosperity was unpredictable.[79] In May 1914, the Council also pointed to an increase in popular purchasing power as one significant index of expanding productivity.[80]

The Association's emphasis on the importance of popular well-being as an essential foundation for industrial growth and prosperity and for the strength and power of the Empire as well was but one side of the coin, however. On the opposite side, the organization unequivocally and dogmatically propounded its belief in the absolute priority that must, in all economic policy, be accorded the interests of the producer over those of the consumer whenever the two conflicted. In expounding this basic "credo," the Association advanced an austere program of "heavy industry first," which later became the watchword of Soviet economic planning. As early as 1908, Industry and Trade contended that

> it is necessary to be a producer first, and only then will it be possible to become a consumer. . . . Thus, as long as we remain a country of consumers, as long as national work in all fields of productive activity does not rise to the proper level of development, . . . the specter of popular hunger and state ruin will stand perpetually before us; our credit will remain marvelously pathetic and the danger of collapse will ceaselessly threaten our gold currency. Our economic improvement coincides with the interests of producers, and not of consumers. The sooner this unvarnished truth is comprehended, the better.[81]

The Association constantly lamented that industry suffered from a blindly hostile bias in favor of consumers' interests not only in the agrarian-oriented official world but also in the State Duma and society at large; "among us, everywhere the ideology of the consumer rules everything." Industry and Trade observed sadly: "Time is the best and only means of transforming the citizen-consumer into a citizen-producer. Apart from patience, nothing remains as consolation."[82]

The outlook could not have been so dismal as these words suggested, for only two weeks later the journal, in its first leading article for 1910, restated its "credo" in terms more uncompromising and more optimistic than ever: "We believe that the lament in defense of the consumer is rapidly becoming something antediluvian and that, instead, the interests of the producer will take first place in the minds of our publicists."[83] Several months later, the journal expressed even greater optimism:

> The clear truth is rapidly becoming obvious even to the blind, we hope, that before becoming a consumer it is necessary to be a producer, that the consumer who produces nothing is a parasite, and that the interests of the producer must therefore be satisfied before the interests of the consumer.[84]

More than a year later, it asserted that "the cult of the consumer must, finally, fall, and the interests of the producer must take their proper place."[85]

Events failed to bear out these hopes, however. Toward the end of 1911, a member of the Council's staff complained once more that "in our country the consumer is always right and the producer is always guilty."[86] The last years before the war, moreover, brought no satisfaction to the Association in its quest for priority for producers' interests. Early in 1912, attacking the alleged bias of the legislature in favor of consumers, it observed caustically that before the creation of the State Duma, when

> all public currents could appear among us only in literature, a slogan that places the interests of the consumer above everything else could be tolerated. . . . An irresponsible public opinion could permit itself the luxury of beautiful but unattainable utopias, since they remained only on paper.[87]

It expressed its

> hope that the time is not far distant when the representatives of our public opinion, who still so recently looked on industry and trade exclusively from the point of view of consumers' interests, will understand that the only saving point of view for Russia is the point of view of the producer and will go hand in hand with us.[88]

At the Sixth Congress, the Council declared that "for a country that lives mainly by work and not by accumulated wealth, for a country that exists by the turnover of a given year, for such a country the consumers' point of view is completely one-sided."[89] Shortly before the war, Industry and Trade again revealed a penchant for turning a Marxist phrase to its own purpose, declaring its opposition to what it described as "the consumers' ideal of 'to each according to his needs.'"[90]

Addressing the Seventh Congress, Zhukovskii once more identified the interests of the producer with those of the nation at large:

> I cannot recognize a dictatorship on behalf of consumers' demands and on behalf of judgments being made about all economic issues from this point of view. The interests of production, the interests of work, the interests of the national economy are much broader than the interests of the consumers--this is the first point.

Replying to the charges of "socialism" that had been raised against him as a result of his defense of the regulatory role of syndicates, he endorsed the socialist position on the priority of production over consumption and the irrelevance of that position to the interests of consumers:

> For the consumer, it is almost a matter of indifference whether production is state or private. They have produced, and he consumes. . . . We stand first of all for the point of view of the producer, and not of the consumer. We consider that the interests of the consumer cannot fail to be taken into account because the producer produces for the consumer. Therefore it is impossible to think that the consumer can be violated, destroyed, or exploited, for with that all consumption would end; but there is no doubt that our point of departure is that of the producer and not of the consumer, for whom the origin of a given product is a matter of indifference.[91]

It seems likely that the principle of "consumers' choice" would have played no larger role in an economy dominated by Russia's prewar industrialists than it did in that of the Soviets.

Although the Association's belief in the ultimate importance of the consumers' market to industrial development was clear in principle and unshaken despite the slow growth of popular demand, its increasingly skeptical assessment of the importance of that market in the immediate future caused it to assert, with growing urgency, the need to develop both foreign markets and alternative sources of domestic demand, within the government and within industry itself. Thus, along with its unrelenting demands for increased tariff protection, the Association insistently called for a more solicitous attitude toward private enterprise on the part of the government in the awarding of its orders and contracts. In particular, it sought to divert such purchases away from other countries and, as far as possible, away from government-owned enterprises in Russia.

The Association's hopes for an expanding domestic market did not rest solely with the government, however, or even with such large-scale consumers as the railroads. Increasingly, it looked to industry itself for a market. Industrial demand, it recognized, would be self-generating.

> The more developed the economic life of any country is, the more enterprises arise that do not have as their purpose the satisfaction of direct consumption, the closer becomes the cooperation of different branches of work in the manufacture of any one object of consumption, and the more complex is the path from the extraction of the raw material to the direct consumption of any article. In a word, with the growth of economic life production for further industrial processing, for industrial consumption, is increased. . . . The expansion and refining of demand, the increase in the price of raw materials, the shortages in the latter, the competition of substitutes--these are the stimuli for the progress of technique in this area, where everything is constantly in flux, where yesterday's objects of exclusively direct consumption are today fully established as objects of industrial consumption.[92]

Not only large industry, but also, as we have seen, small and middle-sized industry were expected to play important roles in this respect. On one occasion, at least, Industry and Trade seemed inclined to turn its back entirely on the peasant consumer in favor of a more stable industrial demand emanating from small-scale industry:

> In our country, which is still taking its first steps in its industrial development, interests of all kinds, including big industry, require that there should at last be created a serious, genuine consumer; not that consumer whose purchasing capacity is closely connected with the shifting fate of the harvest and in the last analysis is dependent on purely elemental accidents; not that apocryphal consumer, the favorite of our press, whose main virtue and service consist in the fact that he produces only that which he consumes; but a consumer who himself produces something. Such, and only such, a consumer gives industry a firm confidence in tomorrow.[93]

Organized small and middle-sized industry must, it was further suggested, play an essential role in fashioning the products of heavy industry into consumers' goods and in organizing sales and the development of new markets. Pointing to the example of Belgium in organizing its small and middle-sized bourgeoisie, the author concluded:

> And profiting from it, and also standing between large local industry and large trade on the one hand and the class of consumers on the other, closely acquainted with the frequently changing tastes and needs of the latter, these classes are the best and finest instruments for the expansion of the internal market and the conquest of external markets for the big industry of Belgium. So also, it is certain, will our middle and small bourgeoisie serve our Russian economy when it is organized in accordance with the example of Belgium and of Western Europe generally.[94]

Disappointed in its earlier hopes that a rise in popular purchasing power would provide a solid foundation for a new industrial expansion, the Association seemed to abandon its former view of the relationship between industry and the popular market. Industrial growth, it maintained during the last months before the war, must itself provide the foundation for an improvement in popular well-being--a change that must, in turn, stimulate further industrial progress.

Noting, for example, the failure of efforts to increase peasant consumption of iron by extending the use of iron roofing, Industry and Trade suggested that a growth in the popular market might result from industrial expansion.

> Therefore, however beneficial the raising of the peasant economy and the improvements in the well-being of the village population might seem to be for the development of iron consumption, the solution to the problem of increasing the per-capita consumption of iron in Russia lies in the expansion of industrial consumption (not at all of railroad consumption only, although the railroads are also still inadequate in our country). Broad prospects for metallurgy will also be opened up with the further growth of towns that lies ahead of us and the satisfaction of their most urgent needs with respect to public welfare. The absence or inadequacy in our towns of water mains, sewage disposal, and lighting is too generally known to dwell on at length. In a word, the further industrialization of the country, the raising of the peasant economy, that is, in other words, the growth of the productive forces and the general cultural development of the country--this is the direction in which we must work in order to approximate not Spain but the United States of North America in the amount of per-capita consumption.[95]

In the Association's new outlook, industry and trade appeared as veritable "creative forces, giving rise to popular well-being and, therefore, to a balanced budget."[96] The course was neither direct nor simple, however, for it required nothing less than the modernization of the national economy in all its aspects.

> Let us note above all that our low standards of per-capita consumption reflect our cultural backwardness; the high figures of per-capita consumption in the advanced European countries have always included unspecified amounts of industrial consumption of given products, which are naturally much greater in industrially developed countries. With the greater development of urban life, the greater density of the railroad networks in Western Europe, and most importantly, their more even distribution throughout those countries, consumption, which does not know our peculiar obstacles, cannot fail to be expressed in larger figures. Three paths lead to the raising of the per-capita standard in Russia: first, the growth of industrial consumption, that is, the development of industry; second, the further growth of towns and settlements of an urban type; and third, an increase in the productivity of peasant labor.[97]

Nothing, perhaps, better illustrated the organization's focus on economic issues than the fact that it was almost exclusively for the purpose of promoting national economic growth that a rise in the level of popular well-being was included among its most urgently proclaimed objectives. If the Association showed a commendable perspicacity in recognizing the connection between improved living standards for the masses of the people and national economic growth, it also pioneered in facing the bewildering problems of method that inescapably followed from this recognition. Although the difficult cycle of means and ends that confronts all underdeveloped countries seeking rapid modernization appears clear today, many decades later, world experience could provide scant assistance to Russia's prerevolutionary industrialists in their efforts to grapple with a complex task that was relatively new and of limited interest outside their own country.

In the Association's view, the dilemma of means was clear. On the one hand, a rapid increase in popular purchasing power could serve as a stimulant to industrial expansion. Such an increase could be achieved only by paying higher wages to industrial workers, by assuring the peasants higher prices for their produce, and by reducing the crippling burden of taxation on the masses of Russia's impoverished people. These measures, clearly, could be carried through only at the expense of the immediate financial interests of industrial enterprise itself. Yet industry could support such a program, the Association pointed out, only by substantial increases in its own productivity. These increases, in turn, could be achieved only as a result of improved conditions of production and higher entrepreneurial profits, which must, finally, rest on a foundation that would include, among other factors, enlarged markets for industry's output. The very measures required for an expansion of the domestic market were to a large extent attainable only through its prior development.

Torn between industry's conflicting needs for an expanded popular market on the one hand and for larger profits and massive capital formation on the other, the Association regarded the problem of the domestic market with ambivalence. Despite the importance that it consistently attached, in principle, to poverty as an obstacle to industrial progress, the organization unequivocally sided with the immediate interests of the entrepreneur when obliged to choose between them and those of the consuming public. In this respect, the link between the industrialists and their Soviet successors was unmistakable. Yet, despite the priority that the Association accorded to the interests of the producer over those of the consumer, it also held out the hope that such a choice might not be necessary. The very process of industrial development, by balancing increases in demand and in productive capacity as the need arose, might itself provide a solution to the dilemma. Again, the Association seemed to anticipate Keynesian precepts in arguing that poverty, a cause of industrial backwardness, could finally be eliminated only through industrialization.

Disputing an assertion in the press that "the growth of the productive forces, the rise of commercial-industrial life as such is far from being identical with the growth of the well-being of the broad masses of the population," Industry and Trade boldly replied: "It is possible and necessary to assert exactly the opposite: 'the growth of the productive forces of the country' in fact leads in the end to the growth 'of the well-being of the broad masses of the population'."[98]

Caught between its recognition of the importance of a mass consumers' market for industrial growth and economic modernization on the one hand and its conviction of the necessity of giving prior attention to industry's more immediate needs for profits and capital accumulation on the other, the Association tried to resolve the dilemma by assigning to popular demand a role that was at once derivative and yet essential in the process of national economic expansion. Whether this solution represented realism or mere rationalization on its part remained open to debate.

Russia in the World Economy: Protecting Nascent Industry

Questions of foreign trade and the overall balance of payments occupied a place of central importance in the Association's economic program. Its emphasis on the need for economic growth and for large-scale imports of foreign capital to promote that growth compounded the problem of foreign indebtedness. Russia's well-established favorable balance of trade, by which the Empire had maintained its precarious credit in the face of an unfavorable balance of payments, was currently declining, even as payments abroad on the foreign debt rose steadily.[99] Confronted with the need to increase the Empire's supplies of foreign exchange in order to meet payments on the current and future debt, and opposed in principle to the export of gold except in dire emergency, the Association focused its attention on the balance of trade.[100]

As international tensions mounted, a substantial measure of national economic self-sufficiency became an increasingly important objective, both as a means of assuring national independence against the threat posed by more advanced and commercially aggressive powers--notably Germany--and as a military necessity in the event of war. Disclaiming any interest in economic autarky for its own sake, the Association nevertheless upheld economic self-sufficiency as a prerequisite for the creation of a powerful and truly independent Russia. Moreover, if a reduction in imports of goods and an increased importation of capital represented necessary steps along the hard road to genuine economic and political independence, their place in the attainment of military security was indispensable. Pointing out that sea communications--Russia's only means of obtaining military supplies from her allies in the West--would inevitably be severed in a war with the Central Powers, Industry and Trade argued: "The first rule of a well-organized military program must be the manufacture of all necessary equipment and all military supplies in one's own country. Only by such a strategy can a country avoid becoming the plaything of various accidents and petty incidents."[101] Moreover, the economy must also be capable of supplying everything needed by the civilian population in the event of war. Thus, while resolutely resisting the clamor of the country's "false patriots" against the dangers of domination by foreign capital, the Association stressed the perils of foreign commercial predominance and the necessity of a strong industry, founded on a dual policy of official protectionism and capital imports, as the only possible foundation for the maintenance of both economic and political independence.

The task of minimizing imports and maximizing exports involved great difficulties, for it went to the very heart of Russia's economic problem. Only a radical transformation in the pattern of the Empire's foreign trade could convert Russia from a "backward" country, almost wholly dependent on imported manufactures and on the relatively unrewarding exportation of grain and other relatively inexpensive and bulky unprocessed commodities, into a "cultured" country, less dependent on external sources of supply and able to sell its own processed and manufactured goods in the markets of the world. Russia's heavy reliance on grain as the primary component in its favorable balance of trade already exceeded, it was recognized, what was desirable, with prevailing agricultural techniques, from the point of view of the nutritive requirements of the Russian people themselves. Moreover, this hard-earned asset, founded as it was on a capricious harvest, also constituted a major cause of the Empire's inability to support a favorable balance of trade of the magnitude needed, the main source of the perilous instability of that balance, and a stubborn obstacle to any substantial improvement in it. The Association recognized that agriculture must continue for many years to be Russia's primary source of exports. With a view to maximizing its value, it advocated a variety of measures designed to increase the productivity of agriculture, to improve the quality of its product, and to raise the proportion of processed commodities in the export total. But from a long-range point of view, industrialization offered the only viable solution to Russia's financial and commercial problem. The Association's entire strategy for national economic development would promote the attainment of a firmly favorable balance of trade.

Although Russia's prolonged economic depression, which gave

urgency to the industrialists' demands for increased protection of domestic industry, finally gave way in 1909 to a new period of prosperity, the Association's concern for the reduction of imports continued to grow. Increasingly conscious of Russia's weakness and fearful of Germany's eastern ambitions, the industrialists, to a greater extent than ever before, upheld national self-sufficiency as a primary goal of state policy. Because Russia possessed "all the prerequisites" for becoming "a completely self-sufficient state," they insisted on reducing imports to an absolute minimum, eliminating all goods for which productive capacity existed, or could be developed, within the Empire.[102] To this end, the Association emphasized the need not only for the protection of existing industry against foreign competition but also the necessity of building up additional industries in order to make possible sharp reductions in imports in the future.

> It is necessary to make state assistance to native businessmen more systematic than hitherto; and for this purpose it is necessary to petition the Ministry of Trade and Industry to work out, with the participation of representatives of industry, trade, and agriculture, measures for initiating and developing the production and extraction of those goods which are now imported from abroad but for the production of which the economic conditions are available in our native land.[103]

Economic, financial, and diplomatic problems during the last two and one-half years before the war enhanced the importance of foreign trade both as a current issue and as an essential part of any broad program for national economic development. Ironically, Russia's long-awaited prosperity brought with it the very antithesis of the commercial independence that the Association had urgently sought. Imports rose sharply in the face of a rapidly increasing demand for industrial products that far exceeded the capacity of Russian industry to supply. The fact that the increase in imports consisted mainly of manufactures and industrial raw materials--notably coal, pig iron, and machinery--appeared to industrialists as confirmation of Russia's backwardness, of her "colonial" position as an exporter mainly of agricultural products and raw materials and an importer primarily of finished goods. Recognizing, but heavily discounting, the more hopeful significance of the increase in imports as a natural, and probably unavoidable, consequence of the heightened demand that attended a period of rapid economic growth, the Association stressed its unfavorable impact on the balance of trade. Compounding the problem were poor harvests and declining agricultural surpluses, which led to reduced exports in 1912 and 1913.[104]

As a result of this unfortunate combination of circumstances, an adverse balance of trade threatened to become a reality in 1913 and the first half of 1914. By the early summer of 1914, both a drainage of gold abroad and a decline in the exchange value of the ruble suggested that the Association's worst fears were about to be realized. These developments might well constrict the flow of capital from abroad, thereby dashing all hopes for any large-scale industrial expansion. Moreover, as if Russia's broad economic position were not sufficiently troublesome, the increasing importance of Germany as both the principal source of Russia's imports and the main market for its exports, together with the prospect of renegotiating the unfavorable trade agreement with Germany in 1917, seemed to raise ever higher the dread specter of Russia's economic, and perhaps political, "enslavement" by its ambitious and more advanced neighbor. With this danger urgently in mind, the Association undertook once again, early in 1914, to elaborate a plan for the development of those branches of industry in which imports were particularly threatening. "The ever-increasing importation into Russia of foreign manufactures, mainly from Germany, forces us," it observed, "to consider the question of measures for the development of individual branches of production for the purpose of successful competition with foreign output."[105]

Thus, the final peacetime months were marked by a mounting sense of impending crisis within the Association. This ominous presentiment pervaded Russian society, but there was little agreement as to either its cause or its cure, so that the last months before the war passed in a welter of recriminatory charges and countercharges. Many prominent figures, both in the government and outside, bitterly criticized the industrialists, holding them mainly accountable for the worsening balance of trade. Industry had allegedly precipitated the increase in imports, either through its lack of enterprise in expanding domestic output or by a willful restriction of production designed to maintain domestic prices at their customary high level. The Association's denial of these charges and its efforts to elicit from the government an assurance of vigorous action to arrest the decline in the balance of trade met, however, with a cold response from the government. When a special delegation from the Council, acting on instructions from the Eighth Congress, visited the Chairman of the Council of Ministers and the minister of trade and industry in June 1914 in order to emphasize (along with certain other subjects of concern) the dangers inherent in Russia's rapidly worsening commercial and financial position, it was received with a conspicuous and insulting indifference that aroused widespread comment in the press. The crisis, evidently, lay not only in the field of foreign trade but also in the embittered relations between the government and the business community.

Intensifying the impact of this official rebuff was the fact that it came as a climax to a long history in which the organization had looked mainly to the government as the only source of possible action in reducing imports. Although the Association occasionally conceded that industrial self-help, directed toward reducing production costs, might reduce the need for purchases in other countries, such admissions occurred rarely and were usually coupled with qualifications stressing the concurrent and urgent need for official assistance. In 1911, for example, Nikolai S. Avdakov cautiously declared:

> A considerable part of this importation can be squeezed out through our private initiative, but the removal of a significant part of it nevertheless depends on governmental measures. It should be pointed out that those branches of industry that, properly speaking, can reduce imports only by means of reducing the cost of their products can, nevertheless, hardly achieve this in view of the different conditions of work in Russia and in the countries of Western Europe.[106]

The Association based its program to reduce imports on three primary measures: the reduction of railroad and shipping freight rates; the encouragement of domestic purchases by government and industry; and high tariffs. As early as 1907, the Council described as "a matter of state importance of the first degree" the Association's effort to obtain a reduction in the freight rate charged by the railroads on the shipment of Donets coal to the Baltic district in order to enable it to displace the English coal that was in general use in that area.[107] Instead of charging what the traffic would bear, the Russian railroads should, the Association insisted, keep rates at a minimum in order to counteract both the disadvantages resulting from the great distances to be traversed in Russia and the impact of the preferential railroad rates employed by Germany to facilitate its conquest of the Russian market. Railroad rates should, moreover, be closely coordinated with customs duties in order to strengthen the internal market and to promote the flow of exports to other countries. The organization tirelessly reiterated its philosophy over the years, as in Industry and Trade in the spring of 1914:

> But from the point of view of [the railroads'] direct influence on the development of the productive forces of the nation, there can be only one view: if they do not assist this economic development and only extract gains and profits from the transport of goods, they are not fulfilling their purpose. With respect to foreign trade, the role of the railroads must be outlined with

> perfect clarity: they must aid in the conquest of foreign markets, and they must create the most favorable conditions for competition on the domestic market for domestically produced goods with products of foreign origin.[108]

The Association also campaigned for a reduction in relatively large orders that were annually placed both by the government and by private purchasers with firms in other countries for industrial products which, it contended, either were produced or could be produced in Russia. In its effort to obtain the diversion of these orders to native producers, the "passion for things foreign" that, in its view, characterized both the Russian government and the Russian public. During the earlier years, such orders deprived the country's depressed industry of much-needed work and its people of employment, and in the later, more prosperous times, the practice posed financial and military dangers to the state itself. Purchasing abroad inhibited the growth of Russia's own armaments industry and made the armed forces dependent on foreign sources of supply for munitions and repair parts. Likewise, the dependence of the Baltic fleet on English coal threatened national security and hampered the conduct of the Empire's diplomacy. As the single largest purchaser of industrial products, both abroad and at home, the government attracted most of the organization's criticism, but private industry and the privately-owned railroads also received blame for their part in undermining the Empire's favorable balance of trade.[109]

In its prolonged efforts to divert orders from foreign to Russian producers, the Association challenged the validity of the arguments most often marshalled in defense of the practice, namely that the quality of the foreign product was superior, that its price was lower, and that orders and contracts were filled more promptly and reliably in other countries. Against the first point, the Association refused to recognize a difference in quality sufficient to explain discrimination against domestic industry. While tending to acknowledge, at least implicitly, the justice of the charge concerning the dilatory fulfillment of orders by Russian producers, the Association attributed this fault largely to the government's failure to space its orders regularly over a period of years and to apprise industry of its long-term plans. As it was, industry must endure long lean years with relatively few orders, only to be inundated with demands beyond its ability to fulfill on short notice.[110]

As for prices, the Association conceded that foreign products often were cheaper than their Russian equivalents, but it saw in higher Russian prices a reflection of the generally unfavorable economic conditions at home and the discriminatory and burdensome requirements imposed on

Russian, as distinct from foreign, contractors by governmental agencies. In order to equalize the conditions under which domestic and foreign firms competed in the auctions for government contracts, the Association demanded an end to the special obligations imposed on Russian producers. These included the requirement that domestic producers place a deposit with the government as security for the fulfillment of the order according to the contract--a requirement often deliberately designed, it was charged, when combined with a contract impossible of precise fulfillment, to defraud the helpless producer of his money. The government often refused to grant advance payments to native firms, such as were commonly made to foreign contractors, and paid Russian producers only over a protracted period of time. Russian industry's limited resources and credit capacity made all these requirements almost insuperable handicaps in its rivalry with foreign producers for government contracts.[111]

In any event, it maintained, the price differential should be overlooked in view of the long-range benefits to be derived from patronizing native industry. Moreover, a collapse of Russian industry for lack of orders would inevitably be followed by a sharp rise in the cost of imported goods. Foreign producers, united in monopolistic organizations, would, the Association warned, take advantage of Russia's inability to meet its needs by dumping goods of shoddy quality at exorbitant prices on the Russian market. Russia must realize that "the striving to purchase where it is cheaper is not always a sign of economic wisdom."[112]

Volskii attacked the profound and unreasoning preference of Russians generally, both officials and private individuals, for goods of alien origin:

> Russian society views its own affairs, including the products of domestic industry, with a surprising kind of mistrust and even contempt. Of two objects that are completely identical in price and quality, our society prefers the one that carries a foreign label. . . . Obviously, it is necessary systematically to influence our public opinion with the aim of developing in the population a healthy and patriotic attitude toward native work.[113]

To this end, Volskii proposed the institution of a "League for the Defense of Domestic Industry" to instill in consumers the urgency of the need to "buy Russian." Enlarging on this theme, <u>Industry and Trade</u> condemned not only the lack of patriotic concern for the national welfare reflected in the Russian's unthinking adulation of all things foreign but also the alleged and closely related national disinclination toward work of any kind. At the root of the difficulty lay the familiar "cult of the consumer." Deeply rooted in the national character as this ailment was, the journal found no reason to hope for an early cure.

> We have already repeatedly written about the Russian passion for everything foreign. To cure this defect is not at all easy, for among us the ideology of the consumer is everywhere, and in everything, dominant. We must reeducate ourselves in the spirit of work enterprise and self-help. Only then will everyone among us understand that it is necessary to be a producer before having the right to become a consumer. Under prevailing conditions, the Russian subject will still, for a long time, continue to send his money abroad, not suspecting that he is doing any harm either to the country or to himself. It will be a long time still before we have a patriotism that is not noisy, not emotional, and not measured in rubles, but is healthy, calm, systematic, and powerful.[114]

In the Association's view, all branches of the government, central and local, including the Ministry of Trade and Industry itself, displayed a compulsive predilection for the products of foreign manufacture. The ministries of war and navy appeared to be the most flagrant offenders. During the early years, the Association's vigorous protests against the expenditure of governmental funds for foreign goods seemed to meet with some limited success. Early in 1909, remarking on the government's recent decision to forego the purchase of warships abroad in favor of the domestic product, Industry and Trade jubilantly observed that "it was possible to do without the services of the Englishman or of any other kind of foreigner."[115] The triumph, however, was not only premature; the Association nourished no illusions as to the extent of the government's conversion to its own point of view. The same article, while acknowledging that the government had fully recognized in principle the justice of industry's position, pointed out that this recognition had thus far received little practical implementation and cast doubt on the likelihood of obtaining such implementation without the systematic, continuing pressure of organized industrial interests:

> It is impossible to say that our government has not, formally, taken a point of view that is patriotically and economically correct. Our government has, for a long time, assumed this position in principle. Repeatedly, statements have been issued by the Committee and by the Council of Ministers, with Supreme approval, concerning the protection of domestic industry against foreign competition by forbidding all state institutions to place orders abroad whenever there exists the slightest possibility of their being filled by Russian factories. In practice, however, this is of little help. The production of an

> excellent steam turbine in the homeland is not a slight, but an entirely feasible, possibility. But no. A type of turbine is dreamed up that is not particularly remarkable in any way but is not yet produced by domestic factories. And this is enough to justify the failure to order the needed machine in Russia. All of which goes to show that without a benevolent and conscious desire to develop the productive forces of the homeland, no general reminders of any kind can be of help. Reasons of more or less minor importance are always found for placing state orders abroad, to the injury of the welfare of our own country. Obviously, a special agency of control, with the participation of the representatives of native industry, is needed here. Only in this way will it be possible to avoid anxiety about the country's being weakened by superfluous orders abroad.[116]

In later years, the Association's effort to obtain a thorough revision of the procedures governing the issuance of governmental orders and contracts, with provision for the systematic participation of representatives from industry in the making of all such decisions, colored the organization's continuing criticism of the official predilection for things foreign. Revision of the established procedures for deciding on official purchases and awarding contracts was also of vital importance to the Association's efforts to obtain a larger measure of protection for private enterprise against the competition of state-owned factories, mines, and other undertakings. Although the government eventually established a Supreme Commission to draft a new statute governing these activities, practical implementation of a recognized need soon became hopelessly enmeshed in conflicting interests and bureaucratic procrastination, as was often the case in Imperial Russia. The Association continued its campaign throughout the prewar years, but its occasional small successes were in the end lost to view in the general haze of apathy and inaction.

The industrialists' effort to minimize imports and maximize exports while conserving the Empire's gold stocks had much in common with the neomercantilist policies that were then gaining acceptance in the West. In Germany, for example, such ideas had long constituted the theoretical foundation for foreign economic policy. As early as 1905, the Association's future secretary general asserted: "Every country strives, so far as is possible, to manufacture all needed goods at home and to dispose of the surpluses abroad. The universal increase in tariff barriers is the best index of such a striving in the industrial policy of all countries."[117] To the extent that the industrialists sought ideological support for their position on questions of foreign economic policy--and their outlook on these, as on other, issues was primarily pragmatic--they cited Friedrich List and his Russian disciple, Dmitrii I. Mendeleev.[118] Needless to say, "economic liberalism" and "free-trade doctrine" constituted, in the Association's view, dangerous policies of conservative agrarians, liberal intellectuals, "nativist" (samobytnye) economists, and others whom it regarded as hostile to the cause of economic progress.

Although the Association recognized necessity of providing the foreign exchange needed to service an ever-increasing foreign debt, it was by no means the only influence underlying the organizations' economic nationalism. For a variety of reasons, a stringently protectionist program, geared to the reduction of imports, constituted the crux of its commercial policy. During its early years, especially, when persistent economic depression highlighted the inadequacy of the domestic market, the Association vigorously propounded the need for increased governmental protection, by means of the tariff and other measures, for Russia's "infant industries" against the destructive competition of foreign rivals. Only a strongly protectionist policy, moreover, could build up foreign confidence in Russia as a safe and profitable field for investment, and stimulate the inflow of funds from abroad into industry. Although the Association's advocacy of large-scale capital imports brought it into sharp and continuing conflict with influential elements in the governmental bureaucracy and among the articulate public, its resistance to the "isolationist" thinking of its opponents remained unequivocal. Not to export dividends abroad, it protested, "means not to admit foreigners; it means fencing ourselves off from them by a Chinese wall."[119]

Ironically, the words of the German economist, Friedrich List, appeared most relevant not only to Russia's general needs but also to the gnawing problem of the country's relations with a powerful and ambitious Germany. Quoting its mentor, Industry and Trade wrote:

> But, certainly, to introduce tariff protection is a small thing. It is necessary to construct it so that it will actually promote the development of the industry of the homeland, for "a country that is not able, by means of the protectionist system, to convert itself into a manufacturing country is doomed to material and political death." The danger is increased if neighboring nations follow another course, if they move forward in all respects while we go backward, if among those nations the thought of a better future stimulates the courage and the spirit of enterprise of their citizens while in our country a lack of hope increasingly destroys courage and ability.[120]

Repeatedly attacking what it considered to be the inadequacy of most of Russia's existing import duties, the Association set as its goal the increase, in some cases to virtually prohibitive levels, of duties on all industrial goods that were produced, or could be produced, within the Empire. Although this elusive objective was sometimes couched in relatively moderate terms of an "equalization of the conditions of competition" between Russian and foreign industry, and although the organization repeatedly denied any interest in constructing a "Chinese wall" against imports,[121] its objective remained clear: to force industrial expansion by excluding, or severely restricting, the importation of all goods, both manufactures and raw materials, for which some productive capacity, real or potential, might be found in Russia. For example, although Russia possessed virtually no automobile industry, the Association hoped to stimulate the growth of one by placing a duty on imported cars.[122]

In practice, however, the protective principle could not be applied with perfect consistency, if only because of the conflicting interests of the organization's own members. For example, it advocated reductions in protection for certain types of machinery and other producers' goods needed by Russian industrialists. The bitter opposition of Russian manufacturers notwithstanding, the Association supported the duty-free importation of dredges and other excavating equipment needed by the gold and platinum mining industries of Siberia and the Urals. (It should be noted that Avdakov chaired the Consultative Board of Gold and Platinum Producers for many years.) The list of manufactures for which duty-free importation was advocated included such specialized equipment as brakes for streetcars, flax-spinning machinery, dyes, and certain types of cotton thread used in lacemaking.

Duty-free admission was generally advocated only for "exotic" products, such as cocoa beans and tea. As Russia's industrial expansion gathered force, however, the Association sought reductions in duties not only for industrial raw materials of specialized types not commonly produced in Russia, such as certain hides and skins and materials needed by the ceramics industry, but even for more easily obtainable raw materials. When relations with the United States became strained late in 1911 as a result of the latter's abrogation of its tariff agreement with Russia, the Association displayed a strong distaste for the demands raised in some circles for the imposition of a "fighting tariff" on American cotton. Although the fiscal benefits of a low tariff policy received scant attention from the Association, it did acknowledge that reductions in duties did not invariably reduce governmental revenues, inasmuch as

> every cheapening of the raw material, and consequently of the finished product as well, must call forth an increase in the consumption and

production of this commodity, and along with this, the importation of the raw material taxed with a reduced duty will automatically be increased.[123]

Despite a growing sentiment for the reduction of duties on industrial raw materials in the interest of the manufacturers who processed them,[124] the Association generally supported the maintenance of duties at a relatively high level in order to protect and stimulate domestic output. In the case of sugar, for example, the Association supported a virtually prohibitive duty, and it consistently demanded a high level of protection against foreign coal, oil, pig iron, cement, and wool. In the face of critical shortages of coal and iron during the final prewar years, the organization continued to call for more effective protection for Donets coal against English coal in the Baltic region and acceded only with great reluctance to a temporary reduction in the duty on pig iron.[125]

From the early 1890s onward, tariff protection remained a well-established feature of official economic policy. The statements of high officials in the years before World War I seemed to confirm the government's continuing interest in protecting the country's infant industries against the competition of more advanced economies. To a dispassionate observer, it might seem that the business community found few grounds for complaints against governmental policies in the field of foreign trade. Yet such was not the case. True, the Association's resentment of the government's position in this area probably never equaled the bitterness with which it viewed taxation and "state socialism," and, on rare occasions, the Association was even moved to a grudging admission that governmental policy had in fact been one of relatively consistent protection for industry. Nevertheless, the organization expressed sharp and steadily mounting irritation with what it regarded as growing official indifference toward industrial protection and favoritism toward agrarian, free-trade interests. By 1914, the Association's grievances had degenerated into a total disillusionment with governmental intentions.

The Association's early efforts to obtain increased tariff protection for industry had not, however, been without hope of ultimate success. Early in 1908, a delegation to the minister of trade and industry was welcomed with the assurance that he himself was likewise "a convinced protectionist."[126] The organization received similar assurances a year later, when its demands for a broad tariff revision appeared in the official economic program outlined by the minister in an address before the State Duma.[127] Soon thereafter, a special conference undertook a broad review of the tariff with a view to its thorough revision. During the succeeding months, the ministerial conference, headed by Nikolai P.

Langovoi, carried on its work parallel to, and in close cooperation with, a similar conference established by the Association in the summer of 1909 and chaired by Zhukovskii.[128]

The encouragement that the Association derived from these events was tempered, however, by its realization of the limited degree of influence exerted by the Ministry of Trade and Industry within the highest councils of the government, and by its belief that the close personal ties of the minister, Vasilii I. Timiriazev, with the Association and with the commercial-industrial class as a whole diminished his effectiveness in official circles.[129] Underlying and reinforcing these suspicions was the profound resentment with which the Association viewed what it considered to be the predominant influence on governmental policies of agrarian and other "free-trade" interests. Its suspicions were apparently confirmed as the years passed without any concrete action toward tariff reform.

This generally discouraging outlook was briefly relieved, however, during the short-lived period of rapprochement in the relations between government and industry that occurred after the assassination of Prime Minister Petr A. Stolypin in September 1911. The "New Era," in fact, was heralded by a statement in support of tariff protection by Kokovtsov in his new capacity as chairman of the Council of Ministers. Industry and Trade commented:

> This system of protection is firmly approved by V. N. Kokovtsov as the foundation of our commercial-industrial policy. "Since the time when I began to occupy myself with industrial and economic questions," declares the chairman of the Council of Ministers, "I was, am, and will remain a convinced supporter of the protective system. This I have never concealed, and I consider that a state that is fifty years behind on the path of protection for its industry must not interrupt this policy but must carry it still further." This most highly valuable recognition gives us hope that in the immediate future, at least, our tariff policy, firmly established only since 1891 and still at the present time suffering some inconsistency, will not be overturned by any risky experiments.[130]

However, the Association soon became disillusioned with the government's intentions. By the late summer of 1912 it raised its old complaints of official favoritism toward agriculture.

> Any small Rumania, where more is being done toward encouragement and protection than in our country, clearly testifies to the feasibility of developing industry in a country which, it would seem, is predestined by fate to produce only agricultural raw materials. There, they do not weep about

> "sacrifices" for the sake of industrial development but reap the fruits of a far-sighted policy.[131]

At the end of the year, when Kokovtsov declared before the Duma the government's intention of "adhering, with respect to international trade, to the principles of the protective system, which alone is appropriate to the conditions of a country with a developing industry," the journal reacted with polite but scarcely restrained skepticism.[132]

During the final eighteen months before the war, the tariff again became a major issue in the growing antagonism between government and industry. Not only had the government failed to accede to industry's wishes for increased tariff protection; new demands arose for tariff reduction and even for the duty-free importation of scarce commodities. Although the Association grudgingly accepted the necessity of some emergency measures, its general attitude remained one of alarm and apprehension lest the proponents of "free trade" broaden these concessions into a general attack on the protective system. The government's procrastination in undertaking a review of the tariff in preparation for the renegotiation of the trade agreement with Germany suggested official indifference to industry's needs.

The issue was exacerbated by other conflicts between the government and organized industry. Most noteworthy, perhaps, was the issue of industrial syndicates and other allegedly monopolistic organizations. In the spring of 1913, Minister of Trade and Industry Sergei I. Timashev sent to the Council of Ministers the draft of a bill designed to advance the government's campaign against syndicates by empowering it to retaliate against price rises attributable to monopolistic practices. Retaliatory actions included raising or lowering railroad rates; raising, lowering, or abolishing import duties; and introducing export duties or prohibiting exports altogether. Industry and Trade protested:

> This measure is a concession to home-bred doctrinairism, nourished in free-trade prejudices. Until now, our ruling circles have clearly recognized that tariff protection in our country is not a product of harmful caprice but a grim economic necessity. As recently as a year ago, the Chairman of the Council of Ministers, in his well-known speech of April 3 at the meeting of the delegates of the Moscow Exchange Committee, said: "The state, having embarked fifty years ago on the course of protection for our industry, must not interrupt this policy but must carry it still further." Now, to gratify demagogues and doctrinaires, one of the foundations of our economic life can at any time be pulled down. Complete uncertainty, lack of confidence in the most immediate future, is being created, not only for branches of

> industry where syndicates are to be found but for others which are entirely unconnected with them.[133]

A year later, when the bill became law, the Association expressed unbounded alarm and despair. The Ministry of Trade and Industry had commonly been regarded, both within and outside official circles, as the protector of business interests within the government. Now, however, the Ministry emerged as primarily the agent of "the authorities" in their dealings with the business community.

Timashev couched his address to the Eighth Congress in moderate terms, assuring the gathering of his own devotion to the principle of protection while also warning against the industrialists' excessive reliance on the tariff as an instrument of economic expansion and as "a panacea for all ailments."[134] Any hint that his words might have portended a more conciliatory policy toward industry soon evaporated, however. The calculated rebuff administered by the Chairman of the Council of Ministers himself to the delegation that sought to explain the Association's concern over the deteriorating balance of trade and the urgent need for prompt and vigorous measures to reduce the volume of imports seemed, on the eve of World War I, to mark the organization's final and irreversible failure to achieve what had been, since its founding, one of its most cherished objectives.[135]

While the Association's efforts to obtain greater tariff protection for industry focused primarily on the executive bureaucracy, the organization never lost sight of the fact that a revised general tariff, or, indeed, any permanent changes in individual tariff duties, would have to be enacted into law by the legislature. Hence its pressure on the administrative organs of the government was paralleled by a continuing effort to influence legislative thinking. The Association found little to commend, however, in the "free-trade" proclivities of the State Duma's agrarian majority, supported by such oddly assorted groups as liberal intellectuals and "self-styled nationalists" who, it was said, were unable to comprehend the case for "true economic patriotism." With the exception of a small number of individuals, it charged, the Duma remained not only indifferent but openly hostile toward the protection of industry.[136]

The Association's long and vigorous campaign for more stringent tariff protection of Russian industry can hardly be considered successful. Little had been achieved, by 1914, toward the ultimate goal despite occasional, limited victories, such as the abolition of the free port in the Far East, some reductions in orders placed abroad, and isolated instances of increased customs duties. The trend during the prewar period, at least as it appeared to the Association, was clearly toward reduced protection, either in response to goods shortages or as a punitive device wielded by the authorities in their ever-widening conflict with organized industry on other fronts. Ahead loomed the greatest hurdle of all: renegotiation of the trade agreement with Germany. Confronted on these issues, as never before, with an adamantly united front of hostile bureaucrats, conservative agrarians, and liberal intellectuals, the organization found little cause for cheer as it looked to the future.

Toward a Commercial Policy for Russia

The reduction of imports and the attainment of economic independence of other countries were not the Association's only objectives in the field of foreign trade. In addition to promoting the idea of national self-sufficiency, it demonstrated mounting interest in the projection of the Empire's economic influence into the outside world.

Only a program of increased exports could improve Russia's favorable balance of trade and reduce its adverse balance of payments. An increase in exports of every type--agricultural commodities, raw materials, and manufactured goods--appeared essential for the financing of Russia's imports of goods, services, and capital necessary for industrial expansion. Clearly, however, the value of exports could be increased most effectively by raising the proportion of the more valuable goods, namely manufactures and processed raw materials, in the total. In the process, Russia would undergo a transformation from a "backward" into a "cultured" country.

> While not reviving the fallacies of the mercantilists, who dreamed of producing in their own countries everything that was produced elsewhere, we can and should strive to utilize the diversity of Russia's economic condition and to develop not only the grain economy but also more valuable types of production and thereby raise the country to a height consistent with its colossal size.[137]

Other objectives underlay the Association's advocacy of an aggressive commercial policy. Demands for expanding markets abroad reflected the organization's mounting interest in promoting Russia's position as a world power. Not only was the cultivation of foreign markets viewed as a farsighted measure in preparation for the day when a developed Russian industry would participate on equal terms in the bitter commercial rivalries of the already advanced countries; it was also seen as the means by which the homeland might one day achieve the position of glory and power that was its inherent destiny. In this respect, the German Empire appeared as the model for Russian emulation. Only a strong economy could provide the foundation necessary for successful competition in international trade and for the defense of a country's "world position" in international politics.

Clearly, the Association's commercial demands, like other parts of its program, lacked consistency. Although it proclaimed on the one hand the goal of national economic self-sufficiency, albeit untainted by "isolationism," it simultaneously asserted the necessity of a large-scale expansion in exports, the better to project Russia's voice in world affairs. One searches the organization's publications in vain, moreover, for a recognition of the fact that a high volume of exports must be attended, in part at least, by a correspondingly high level of imports.

Russia's ultimate conversion into a country exporting mainly manufactured goods appeared all the more urgent because of the growth of competition in the world market for grain. The "exotic" countries of the Southern hemisphere, which not only produced agricultural and raw materials cheaply and in large quantities but also benefited from inexpensive maritime transport, had already created for many European countries the necessity of choosing between the depletion of their populations through emigration and the development of manufacturing industry with a corresponding increase in industrial exports. "Russia," Industry and Trade warned, "which exports almost exclusively (more than 90 percent) raw materials and semimanufactures, will also have to enter this new path in the very near future."[138]

As early as 1906, Vasilii I. Timiriazev defined as the most important task of the new Association "assistance to the conquest of export markets, to active trade, without which the development of domestic industry cannot proceed successfully."[139] A year and a half later, the Third Congress instructed the Council to organize a special conference on measures to promote exports in both industrial and agricultural products and to petition the Ministry of Trade and Industry to convene an official conference for the same purpose.[140]

During later years, adverse developments in Russia's balance of trade--substantially increasing imports and declining exports--prompted interest in exports not only within the business community but also in official circles and among the articulate public.[141] Adding to this concern, in the industrialists' outlook, was the failure of the popular market for consumers' goods to keep pace with the expanding capacity of manufacturing industry. During 1910, the Association helped to organize two special congresses to consider means of promoting an increase in the export of manufactures.[142] At its Fifth Congress, in March 1911, foreign trade occupied a conspicuous place on the agenda, as it did at all subsequent congresses prior to the outbreak of the war.[143]

From its long-range point of view, the Association called into question the very foundations of the Russian government's commercial and financial policies, which relied almost exclusively on substantial grain exports to pay for imports. Although the organization viewed with satisfaction the increase in total exports that occurred briefly after 1903, it regretted that the rise had been accomplished mainly through increased sales of grain and therefore "at the expense of the progressive malnutrition of the masses of the people and the weakening of future generations."[144]

Only through industrial development and an increased reliance on the export of industrial products could Russia capitalize on the surplus population of its countryside, add labor value to its wealth of natural resources, and thereby obtain the foreign capital that was necessary for the full realization of its inherent economic potentialities.

> For a country with a weakly developed industry, for a country which pays for its foreign indebtedness with grain squeezed from a hungry populace, there remains no other way than to pay for this foreign indebtedness not with the plundered gifts of nature but with the products of the labor of its own people. Is it not time for us to apply ourselves most seriously to a more intelligent exploitation of our wealth? Is it not time for us to enter decisively on the path of industrial development in order, ultimately, to increase our exports not at the expense of hungry peasants but for the benefit of the factory population, which itself is a consumer of our grain and thereby gives support to an agriculture that is growing ever more sickly? The exotic countries, which are now competitors for our agricultural raw materials, will, perhaps, serve us as markets for the sale of our manufactures.[145]

Volskii's report to the Third Congress made the point even more forcefully:

> In accordance with the example of other countries that have begun to develop their productive forces, it is obvious to us that it is necessary to turn abroad for money, and to pay the interest on it by exporting goods. For this reason, our external trade, both in terms of quantity and in the nature of the goods exported and imported, has preeminent importance. . . . We export food products, taking them away from our half-starved population, and import mainly the results of the work of foreign countries.

> Obviously, not only must foreign labor in the satisfaction of our needs be replaced by native [labor], but the latter must replace in our exports a major part of our exportation of food products, which must remain at home for the normal nourishment of the people.[146]

Although the Association thus deprecated the government's excessive reliance on grain as an item of export and held out as its ultimate goal the conversion of Russia into an industrialized country exporting mainly manufactured goods, it recognized that the Empire must continue for many years to rely mainly on grain, and to a lesser extent on other agricultural and raw materials, in order to remain commercially and financially viable. Despite its opposition in principle to any further forcing of grain exports at the expense of Russia's "starving millions," the Association's program made no immediate provision for reducing food exports in order to increase consumption at home. On the contrary, it sought to increase such exports, while presumably minimizing their impact on the population and maximizing their value by intensifying and diversifying agricultural production and by exporting as large a proportion of agricultural commodities and natural resources as possible in processed or semi-processed form. As Industry and Trade observed, "correct economic policy undoubtedly requires that exports take the most highly processed form possible, in order that foreign industry and the foreign worker should not obtain earnings from what could have been produced by Russian labor."[147] Hence the Association urged the need to export a larger proportion of the wheat and rye harvest in the form of flour and also in the form of meat, poultry, butter, and eggs. In addition, it stressed the need to facilitate the marketing abroad of both flour and unprocessed grain at higher prices and with lower costs by reorganizing and rationalizing Russia's still primitive grain trade and by improving the quality of the product.

Toward the end of the prewar period, declining grain exports, combined with the growing inroads of Germany into the Finnish market for flour, and even into the Empire proper, caused the Association to look with keener interest than ever before on the need to increase the output and export of grain.[148] In contrast with the earlier years, moreover, world market conditions now appeared favorable for the sale of Russian grain abroad. No doubt it was this combination of developments that provoked commentary in the press and in public circles generally concerning prospects of Russia's becoming the "granary" of Europe. To these aspirations, the Association gave only cautious encouragement. Late in 1911, its journal observed that "the main role of world supplier of grain is passing to us, and we must take advantage of the future rise in prices. The worldwide high cost of living is profitable for us."[149] Although the organization subsequently favored attaining "predominance on the world agricultural market," it generally opposed any effort to convert Russia into the world's "granary."[150]

The development of industrial exports lay closer to the Association's own interests. Throughout the prewar period, it proclaimed the need to cultivate foreign markets, both in order to dispose of current "overproduction" and to permit the further expansion of productive capacity. In the depression years, much of the Association's insistence on larger foreign markets centered on the needs of the textile industry, in which production consistently exceeded domestic demand. Yet, industry's deep-rooted fears of facing inadequate markets for its products encompassed heavy industry as well. Despite critical shortages in basic industrial commodities during the last years before the war, the Association continued to call for the development of markets abroad in order to forestall the danger that mounting industrial capacity might eventually surpass the absorptive capacities of the domestic market. In the case of the textile and other consumers' goods industries, the danger was considered to be an already established reality. As one of the Council's staff observed in 1913:

> Russian industry will . . . inevitably, in the near future, have to interest itself greatly in the export of its products abroad, that is, mainly to the markets of the Middle and Near East. And if, at the present time, under the influence of the extraordinarily strong increase in demand on the domestic market, such branches of industry as the coal and ironworking industries cannot interest themselves particularly in the export of their products abroad, there is no doubt that any decline in demand within the country will again raise the question of exports as a necessary supplement to production for the domestic market.[151]

The danger of overproduction presented the industrialists, the Association maintained, with only two choices: to reduce production or to export, even at prices well below the domestic level. The organization's own preference was unequivocal. Systematic, unconcealed "dumping" of surplus output offered the only means by which industry might maintain its current level of production and avoid the economically, socially, and politically disruptive consequences of mass unemployment. Such, moreover, was said to be a normal procedure.

> World industry has so developed that the export of manufactures, as a

> general rule, amounts to throwing outside the frontiers of a country the surpluses of production at abnormally low prices. Obviously, we must do likewise if we do not wish to bring our industry into disorder and throw tens and perhaps hundreds of thousands of workers onto the street.[152]

In the Association's candid view, dumping also constituted a legitimate offensive device for advancing a country's position in the international scramble for markets. Hence, the organization pointed out that Russian textile manufacturers, for example, buttressed by their secure if inadequate domestic market, would enjoy a distinct advantage in their rivalry with foreign "dumpers" who must depend upon exports for their very survival.

Dumping, indeed, appeared as the universal panacea for a multitude of economic ills. It was the preferred form of treatment in time of depression; and in better times its use promised continued industrial growth uninhibited by the limitations of the domestic market. In addition, it held out the alluring prospect of economic stability, providing the means of avoiding the accumulation of surpluses and thereby forestalling crises of overproduction.[153]

Far from being immediately advantageous, however, dumping was a sacrifice to be undertaken by the government, the public, and industry itself for the sake of economic development. The government must mobilize all the means of assistance at its disposal for the promotion of exports. The public must accept "the fact, unavoidable in connection with dumping, that the prices of products on the domestic market are necessarily higher than corresponding prices on the external market." As for the industrialists, they must accept sacrifices both in the form of lower prices for exported goods and a loss of freedom for the individual entrepreneur, who must join forces with competitors at home in syndicates for the organization and advancement of sales abroad.

> Industrialists, for their part, must clearly recognize that exports will not bring them a profit, and, on the contrary, will often be attended by losses. Prices on world markets are, as we have said above, always much lower than on the domestic market. . . . But this is not the only sacrifice. Exports must, without fail, be organized, since in foreign markets it is necessary to struggle with a united industry. Our enterprises must, therefore, for the sake of success in export, renounce individual ventures, sacrifice many aspects of their "Ego," and, unified in production, subordinate themselves to common directives. In this connection, it will be necessary to make large expenditures in order to acquaint producers with the market and the market with our products.[154]

Whether the intent behind this call for sacrifices on the part of industry was genuine or specious--as was widely charged in the press--remains unclear. Nevertheless, it is perhaps pertinent to point out that the emphasis on selling without a profit, and even at a loss, contradicted the Association's continuing stress, in other connections, on the necessity of maintaining a high level of profits in order to attract capital into industry. Furthermore, the description of syndicates as a sacrifice of freedom on the part of the individual producer appears unique in the Association's voluminous defense of monopolistic organizations.

In surveying potential markets for the expanded volume of exports that allegedly lay in the future, the Association left unconsidered hardly a spot on the globe except Africa south of the Sahara. Certain areas stood out in clear relief. For grain and other agricultural commodities, as well as raw and semi-processed industrial materials, Central and Western Europe, Russia's traditional markets, still seemed to offer the most likely prospects. Europe, it was hoped, might also become the purchaser of Russian flour, meat, dairy products, and industrial commodities: lumber, coal, kerosene and other petroleum products, manganese, and other ores. Because Russian rails and rail fastenings had once found sales in England, the organization even entertained the hope that some Russian metallurgical products might find their way to European markets.

Although the Association readily conceded the need for a greater measure of "self-help" on the part of businessmen in the quest for exports, it by no means accepted the charges of inertness of which they were so often the target. In its efforts to counter such accusations, the Association sometimes adopted an unusually defensive tone, citing poor conditions of transportation and communication, "unfair" foreign competition, and--on at least one occasion--Russia's lack of appropriate surpluses.[155]

Much more commonly, the Association resorted to the old tactic of the offensive as the best defense. Not surprisingly, its main target was the government, which had provided neither support nor encouragement for the ambitious businessman. In one of its first issues, Industry and Trade complained that

> the current effort of Russian industry and trade to find new markets for the sale of its goods, to open the way for Russian exports on international markets, and thus to compensate for the deficiencies of domestic consumption, is being carried out through their own forces alone, without any particular support on the part of the state.[156]

Other governments vigorously supported the efforts of their businessmen. For example, the President of the French Republic had not considered it beneath his dignity to preside at the annual gala assembly of the Paris Chamber of Commerce in 1913.[157] Even more striking was the diplomatic and military support regularly accorded to foreign trade by the governments of England and Germany:

> In our country, people love to refer to the personal initiative of the Western European, particularly German, industrialist and merchant in exports. No one, certainly, will try to deny the importance of this initiative. But, in this connection, people too often forget the firm support that the same German or English industrialist or merchant finds in his country's diplomatic representatives abroad, who are closely acquainted with the export needs of their own country; who do not disdain the defense of the interests of this export, however insignificant it may be; and who are thoroughly imbued, through a complete system of governmental measures, with a consciousness of the importance of extending the economic influence of their country abroad, not only as such, but also as a support for political influence.[158]

The Russian government's responsibility for the Empire's commercial failures extended beyond its indifference and inaction. By a wide range of domestic and foreign policies injurious to industry and trade, it had actually hampered the businessmen's efforts to expand exports. The loss of markets in Manchuria, Mongolia, and Persia, far from being attributable to the failings of Russian merchants, must in fact be ascribed to the ineptitude of the bureaucracy in St. Petersburg and to the lazy, inefficient, corrupt, and often hostile officials whom it stationed abroad. So unfavorable, indeed, had been the impact of official actions upon Russian commercial interests abroad that the mere cessation of directly injurious activity sufficed to spark an immediate improvement in the business outlook.[159] In its more polemical moments, the Association charged that the Russian government had, in some of its policies, deliberately obstructed the cause of expanded exports.[160]

In moments of less excitement, the Association acknowledged that the government's record with respect to exports had not been entirely negative. Early in 1909, for example, the Council conceded that such governmental assistance had actually been forthcoming "in large measure" and over an extended period of time.[161] More than a year later, its journal again acknowledged the aid that the government had long rendered to Russian exports through its manipulation of the import tariff and railroad export rates, diplomatic action, and other initiatives. In the same breath, however, it also demanded the "full mobilization" of governmental and legislative assistance for the most effective promotion of exports[162] and cited the lack of "proper state measures for the development of the export of the products of domestic factories and mills" as one of the principal causes of business instability in Russia.[163] The Association's complaints of the government's lack of interest in exports mounted from mid-1910 on and reached a peak on the eve of the war.

The Association also placed part of the blame on the public and its official representative body, the State Duma. (As was usual in questions concerning economic policy, the State Council was credited with a far greater measure of understanding than was the Duma.) Itself faced with conflicting charges of indifference and overzealousness in the promotion of exports, the Association found in the public only a profound disinterest and even hostility toward the cause of expanding sales abroad. Whatever the attitude of the Russian public toward exports, it appeared to share the universal distaste of consumers everywhere for the practice of dumping, which inflated domestic price levels. To counter this problem, the Association--with little success--urged the need for a concerted educational campaign among the populace at large and also for the organization of sympathetic members of the public for the purpose of lending group support to a national drive for increased exports. (Whoever these might be was not disclosed.)

Late in 1909, Grigorii A. Krestovnikov professed to see a decline in the popular conviction "that only merchants and manufacturers and not the entire people, not the entire country, are interested in the export trade."[164] His optimistic forecast remained unfulfilled, however. The approach of World War I found Russian interest in exports strangely obscured by conflicting attributions of responsibility for current failures. The Association's mounting discouragement was mirrored in the words of a report of the Council in 1913.

> In the intellectual atmosphere of Russian society, everything has remained as of old; and recognition of the "Rule of Business" [gosudarstvo dela] in commerce and industry, in which Muscovite Rus was so strong, is just as alien to us as is the economic patriotism and imperialism of the contemporary European.[165]

In proposing the limitation of imports and the expansion of exports as the dual objectives of an ideal national commercial policy, the Association remained acutely conscious of numerous obstacles. Among these obstacles none loomed greater in its complexity than the vexed issue of Russia's relations with the German Empire.

The Association expressed ambivalent attitudes toward Germany, the focal point of its deepest admiration and the object of its most profound resentment, suspicion, and apprehension. Although the organization looked with some mistrust upon all the great powers, including the United States, as potential imperialist exploiters of less developed countries, Germany excited its most acute concern. In part, this stemmed naturally from the increasingly predominant position that Germany occupied in Russia's foreign trade, as both the principal market for exports and the primary source of imports.[166] The impact of this disturbing development was immensely magnified, however, by Germany's geographical proximity and the mounting evidence of its expansionist ambitions, political as well as economic, in Eastern Europe generally and in the Russian Empire in particular. In the Association's view, nothing less than the national independence of Russia was at stake.

At the root of the Association's concern lay the trade agreement that had governed Russia's commercial relations with Germany since the beginning of the reign of Nicholas II. When the original agreement was concluded in 1894, Russia's bargaining power had been weakened by a prolonged and unsuccessful tariff war with Germany and by the fact that domestic economic problems urgently required the stabilization of external commercial relations. The supplementary convention of 1904 was signed under considerable German pressure at a time when Russia's domestic political and economic condition and her position in international politics had become weak. The treaty had tended, in the Association's view, to fix Russia in its traditional colonial role as a backward country providing German industry with cheap food, fodder, and raw materials as well as a market for its products. Although the validity of this assessment may be questioned, inasmuch as the agreement discriminated against Russian agriculture as well as industry, its most serious consequence, according to the industrialists, was greatly to reduce, if not to nullify altogether, the protective duties against manufactured imports established in the general tariff of 1891.[167]

Even more seriously, the treaty promoted Germany's alleged goal of hegemony over the Russian economy by restricting Russia's freedom to promote its own industrialization and by contributing substantially to Germany's increasingly profitable position both as middleman in Russia's trade with the outside world and as exporter--to Russia itself, as well as to other countries--of finished and semifinished goods fashioned by German labor from Russian raw materials. For example, by forbidding

Russian export duties on raw timber while leaving Germany free to place high import duties on processed lumber, the treaty allegedly prevented the development of the Russian sawmilling and woodworking industries. Again, the treaty's restriction on Russia's freedom to establish competitive railroad rates on goods intended for export through ports on the Baltic Sea had not only strengthened Germany's role as an intermediary in Russian foreign trade but had prevented Russia from building up its own ports of Riga and Petersburg in competition with the German ports of Königsberg and Danzig.[168] Krestovnikov expressed the Association's position in 1912 when he asserted that Russia's efforts to reduce imports by developing industrial output remained hampered by the fact that

> we meet with obligations assumed by the state in the conclusion of trade agreements with other countries that have deliberately directed their efforts toward restricting the industrial development of Russia, having pronounced to their own advantage tariff rates under which Russia is a secure market for them and, along with this, is restricted in its freedom to make secure the labor and earnings of its own population.[169]

During the last years before the outbreak of World War I, the Association's fear and suspicion of Germany burned with a new intensity. The blaze of injured feeling that flared up late in 1911 as a result of a relatively trivial incident involving the grain trade demonstrated the importance of national pride as well as economics. Wishing to protest against certain alleged abuses on the part of Russian grain exporters, the German Handelstag, as the representative of organized German trade, had chosen, in apparent defiance of established procedures, to lodge its complaints directly with the Russian government rather than with the Russian courts or commercial organizations. While conceding the possible validity of the German grievances, the Association bitterly denounced the methods used by the Handelstag as both an affront to national pride and a humiliating blow to the Russian business community's aspirations for freedom from the tutelage of its own government. Industry and Trade warned that "Russia is not China, where consular courts are to be found"; the Germans were dealing "not with the natives of Patagonia but with the citizens of the Russian Empire"; and the episode did nothing to "assist the growth of our sympathies toward our German customers."[170]

Some two years later, another reignited the flames of Russian industrialists' antipathy toward Germany. German merchants reacted with hostility to Russia's effort to reduce German competition in the Finnish market by imposing an Empire-wide import duty on grain and by extending its application, along with that of the existing imperial duty on flour, to Finland. To threats of reprisals in the German press, Industry and Trade replied with a restraint that bespoke anger and determination:

> As for the favorite German system of intimidation and threats of a virtual tariff war and diplomatic complications, that should not prevent our turning their attention once and for all to the fact that Russia has long since emerged from the infantile age, economically speaking, when it was possible to intimidate it. At the present time, Russia has grown strong enough politically, as well as economically, to be able to defend her just economic rights and interests.[171]

Against German charges that changes in the Finnish import duties would constitute a violation of the Empire's obligation under the 1904 convention not to establish a tariff union with Finland without giving Germany two years' advance notice, the Association contended, rather speciously, that this obligation did not apply to the gradual introduction of a tariff union. Russia, it was said, was defending her own economic interests by legal and peaceful means. At the same time, Industry and Trade gleefully reported observations in the German economic press on the importance of Russia's action in enhancing its bargaining power in the approaching trade negotiation between the two countries.

Because the Association regarded the German trade agreement as a major obstacle to Russia's industrial and commercial progress, it looked forward hopefully to the scheduled date of expiration: 1917. The necessity of negotiating a new agreement with Germany--as well as with Italy and Austria-Hungary, whose trade agreements with Russia were also due to expire in 1917--would provide an opportunity for a thorough review of Russia's economic goals and procedures. At stake was nothing less than the entire course of Russia's economic development in the ten or fifteen years after 1917. The treaty would spell the difference between further progress toward industrialization and a lapse into still greater backwardness and dependence on other countries. Hence, from as early as 1908 to the outbreak of the war, a steadily increasing proportion of the organization's attention focused on preparations for the successful conduct of the all-important negotiations.

If, in the year and a half preceding the outbreak of the World War, the Association seemed to look increasingly to the legislature not only for support for industry's views but also for an effective initiative in the formulation and advancement of a commercial program for Russia, the explanation can be found in the organization's growing distrust of governmental intentions. Increasingly, moreover, the Association seemed to show a lack of confidence in the ability of the business community itself to produce a unified program and to marshal the support necessary to win general acceptance for it.

True, the Timiriazev Commission made steady, if unspectacular, progress in 1913. The main focus of its work had at first been the gathering of statistical and other material on the development and needs of Russian foreign trade. The results of this activity began to appear in a series of reports entitled Materials on the Revision of Trade Agreements.[172] In the autumn, the establishment of ten subcommissions significantly expanded the range of the Commission's work. Organized along industrial lines, the subcommissions intensified the Commission's investigation of industry's needs and, more importantly, sought to harmonize the activity of the central organization with that of local commercial-industrial organizations. In addition, the Commission held conferences with local businessmen to discuss tariff needs. Early in 1914, it began publishing News of the Commission on Revision of Trade Agreements (Izvestiia Komissii po peresmotru torgovykh dogovorov) to acquaint the public, both at home and abroad, with the nature of Russia's commercial problem and the progress that was being made toward its resolution.[173] Surveying its achievements during 1913, the Council reported hopefully that

> the question has already passed out of the stage of preparing statistical and commercial-industrial materials into the stage of elaborating desires, the realization of which must convert our tariff into a reliable weapon in the forthcoming struggle with Germany for the defense of productive work in Russia.[174]

This apparent progress notwithstanding, the first months of 1914 saw the virtual dashing of the Association's earlier aspirations. The optimism that had welled within the organization following the establishment within the Ministry of Trade and Industry of the Langovoi Tariff Commission proved to be ill-founded, as were its hopes for cooperation between the official organ and its own Timiriazev Commission. When the Eighth Congress convened in May, the Association appeared disillusioned.

> The considerable delay in the publication of statistical and informational materials by the departments, on the one hand, and the extraordinary hastiness of the work of the governmental Commission on the revision of the existing tariff, on the other, have reflected unfavorably on the work of the subcommissions of the Timiriazev Commission.[175]

Clearly, the Langovoi Commission's headlong rush toward the completion of its long-delayed program confirmed the Association's suspicion of the government's intentions toward industry in connection with tariff revision and the German trade agreement.

But if the government's activity yielded disappointing results, so too did that of the business community itself. In a memorandum circulated among members of the Association in advance of the Eighth Congress, the Council defensively made known its further complaint that the hastiness and "certain technical shortcomings" in the work of the official commission had

> made it impossible to attain, at the present stage of affairs, a proper harmonizing of the work of the [Timiriazev] Commission on revision of trade agreements with the work being conducted by commercial-industrial organizations in the localities.

The record of the Timiriazev Commission was a profound disappointment, but its failures were deeply rooted in widespread apathy and discord within the business community. The Council declared:

> The first and main condition for the existence of an organ that properly represents and defends the interests of Russian industry in the revision of the trade agreements is unanimous personal and material support on the part of the representatives of industry and trade. Only on the basis of such a relationship can the central organ acquire proper authority before the government and the legislative institutions and have the opportunity to organize the execution of its varied and very serious tasks.[176]

When the Eighth Congress convened, the poor progress of the Commission became the subject of acrimonious discussion. Although Timiriazev pleaded for more generous financial support of its work, the debate revealed the full depth of the cleavages that divided the various groups within the Association. It was evident that not only the business community as a whole, but industry itself, faced a paralyzing inability to reach an accord on the complex issues of commercial policy. Whether "united industry" would have been able, had the war not intervened, to resolve its differences and present the government with its own program must remain a subject for speculation. The evidence suggests, however, that even if the Association had succeeded in unifying the conflicting interests within its own membership--and between its membership and that of the Association of Trade and Agriculture--its proposals would have exerted only limited influence on official policies.

4

Politics, War, and Revolution

The Intrusion of Politics

The Association's founders appeared thoroughly aware in 1906 of the critical nature of the times through which they were living. However, the rigidly nonpolitical posture that marked the organization's first years and its reluctance, throughout the prewar period, to declare itself on political issues seemed hardly consistent with its initial alertness to the dangers, present and future, that confronted Russia. Its attitude, moreover, made it peculiarly vulnerable to charges, both then and later, of collaboration with the tsarist autocracy. In fact, the Association's publications provide little support for early Marxist allegations of a bourgeois "alliance" with the government, and even with the agrarian conservatives, for the purpose of forestalling a popular revolution.

The liberals' accusations of the Association's political inaction in the face of mounting threats to the achievements of 1905 rested on more solid foundations, although the organization deserved credit for its consistent support for the principle of the rule of law in all aspects of national life and for equality in civil rights for all the diverse classes, nationalities, and religions within the Empire. To what extent did political considerations, however defined, played a part in the Association's concept of its ultimate objectives? In particular, to what extent did the industrialists perceive a connection between the unsatisfactory rate of Russia's economic progress and the archaic political system that held the country in its grasp?

Whether the Association's effort to remain aloof from political issues reflected officially imposed necessity, fear of governmental retribution, apathy, coldly calculated economic self-interest, or the difficulty of reconciling widely ranging views within its own membership, is difficult to say. No doubt all these considerations entered into its position. Certainly there was much truth in the contention that the wide diversity of political views held by Russian businessmen made a nonpolitical stance unavoidable if organizational unity were to be maintained. Also plausible was the assertion of the Association's left-wing critics that disillusionment following the business leaders' unsuccessful venture into politics in 1905 and 1906 had convinced them that only through strict nonpartisanship could they hope to cultivate their traditional, direct channels for influencing governmental economic policies. Unquestionably, the Association operated under a constant and direct official surveillance. Under these circumstances it is perhaps doubly significant that the organization abandoned its initial rejection of political commentary during the last prewar years. Indeed, by July 1914, the Association's mounting disillusionment with governmental economic policies and its distrust of official intentions toward the business community found ever more frequent expression in barely camouflaged demands for political change.

Although the Association's publications rarely raised the possibility of a second outbreak of revolutionary violence in Russia, Soviet historians appear correct in their assertion that revolution remained a subject of fear and abhorrence to the businessmen of the Empire. The Association's habitual reference to the events of 1905 as a "time of troubles" (smuta) suggested a repugnance to the methods, if not to the achievements, of that period. This repudiation of radical methods in economic affairs no doubt reflected a general preference for an evolutionary approach to the country's problems.[1]

There seems little reason to doubt, moreover, that the Association's apparent political indifference during its early and middle years revealed a readiness to accept the political order that had emerged from the events of 1905-7 and to work within it for the advancement of industry's interests. In Volskii's practical view, for example, national economic policy should be directed toward "promoting the economic glorification of Russia" and indicating "the paths to a better future, which can be realized under the present cultural, living, and political conditions of Russia."[2] This philosophy rested on a vigorous assertion of the primary importance of economic questions in national life and an insistence on relegating politics to an inferior status. The Association's position found frequent expression both in firmly positive statements and in bitter complaints against the government's alleged tendency to place political above economic considerations, even with respect to issues that were mainly economic in nature. For example, the government was accused of giving primacy to political considerations in its decisions concerning railroad construction, in its conduct of foreign trade, and, above all, in diplomatic affairs. In contrast, Soviet scholarship has contended that

Russian foreign policy was conducted in subordination to the interests of the "bourgeoisie."[3] The economic problem, Industry and Trade characteristically declared, remained "the most urgent state question," to the interests of which all governmental policy must ultimately adapt.[4]

Discreetly veiled though it was, the Association's concern with the possibility of renewed political and social strife was always prominent. Its answer to the potential danger consisted less in political action and social reform, however, than in a broad development of the national economy. "Without an economic rise from below," the Council bluntly told the Fourth Congress, "there can be no talk either of popular well-being or of the hoped-for preservation of that which the propertied classes now possess in Russia."[5] To these words Volskii added his own warning:

> The center of the attention of the state authority must be concentrated . . . on those economic and financial decrees of life itself, without the satisfaction of which the most serious danger (political and economic) threatens all the provinces of the Russian Empire.[6]

The Congress itself voted a resolution designed "clearly and categorically to underline the primary importance of economic questions at the present time."[7]

Despite the firmness with which the Association assigned priority to economic issues, it recognized the inescapable interdependence of economic progress, under Russian conditions at least, and the broad condition of political and cultural life. For example, in the spring of 1908 a delegation from the Council told the minister of trade and industry that

> domestic industry and trade, together with the entire state, are living through a very difficult time. Their improvement will commence only when the life of the state becomes stronger in all its aspects; and therefore the Council of the Association expects the full strengthening of Russian industry and trade only when the entire state system of Russia is restored.[8]

A year later, the issue was raised more clearly in Industry and Trade's comment on the budgetary debates in the State Duma.

> The state must seek a way out of its present position of budgetary imbalance, and this basic striving will, without doubt, impose its special imprint on state life, profoundly taking hold of it. In the name of the struggle with the deficit, in the name of the economic program of raising the national and state economy, changes will be carried out in the persons who govern and in the policies that predominate.[9]

Public speculation, sparked by these words, that the Association might soon forsake its self-imposed abstention from political commentary, prompted a vituperative denial from the journal's editor.[10] Still, some of the Association's leaders refused to share its general emphasis on the primacy of economic over political issues. Reporting on an economic program presented by Zhukovskii to the Commercial-Industrial Group of Members of the Duma and State Council, Industry and Trade observed: "In general, the rapporteur Zhukovskii thinks that major financial reforms are unthinkable at the present time without a radical transformation of our political system."[11]

Nevertheless, Timiriazev, in his capacity as minister of trade and industry, defended, a few days later, his silence respecting politics in a speech that he had recently made to the Moscow Exchange Society.

> It has also been pointed out to me that I was silent about the internal political situation in Russia, that I said nothing about the fact that, however much work is done in the field of economic development, there will be no success so long as political conditions are not changed in the sense of removing restrictions. It seems to me, gentlemen, that it is necessary to appraise this question thoroughly. Certainly, we are now living through a transitional period. To many it seems that the past was better than the present, that innovations in the development of our state are to be feared, that therefore it is better to turn back. On the other hand, there are very many people who are--if you will permit me to express myself thus--too impatient. They wish to move forward very rapidly on the path of reform and progress that all of us desire. But in reality such a demand for an impetuous forward course is completely impossible. The doubts that many hold as to whether we are being restrained on the path to reform and progress, whether the government itself is going backward, are groundless. The actions of the government should give no grounds for such doubt. Surely we must not forget, gentlemen, that a total of fifty years separates us from the time of serfdom and that a quarter-century divides us from the first, very modest attempts to move toward social legislation.[12]

More than two years later, on the occasion of Vladimir N. Kokovtsov's appointment to succeed the murdered Stolypin as chairman of the Council of Ministers, the Association reiterated its belief in the primary importance of economic over political issues. Quoting its own article of March 1909, in which it had predicted that "all internal and external policy will be adapted, to a certain degree, to the economic program,"[13] Industry and Trade cautiously suggested that this goal might even be within sight.

> Our readers know that we are not inclined toward too hasty conclusions. We do not think that the time has yet come for Russia when an economic program can give direction to the whole of political life, but we should like to believe that the appointment of V. N. Kokovtsov to the post of premier is, in fact, a step in that direction.[14]

Ironically, however, the Association itself was about to embark on a new phase of political activity. As the prewar period drew to a close, industry became disillusioned with the government's failure to promote economic development and its adherence to policies considered inimicable to industry. The Association sought to strengthen the representation and influence of industry and trade within the legislature--a cause to which it had never been indifferent--and expressed a new and growing, although still cautious, interest in political liberalization. Symptomatic of this shifting emphasis was Zhukovskii's unchallenged assertion before the Fifth Congress, in 1911, that in the work of the legislature political questions must take precedence and "economic legislation . . . must stand on a secondary plane."[15]

Well before World War I, then, the Association's leadership had become convinced that major political changes might be essential to obtain the kind of governmental economic policies that the organization deemed necessary for the implementation of its program for national economic development. At the Sixth Congress, in 1912, the conservative Avdakov, the archetype of the "petitioning" industrialist, unequivocally declared the business community's opposition to any retrogressive changes in the political order that had been established in 1906. Welcoming Kokovtsov's recent assurances with respect to both economic and political policies, Avdakov nonetheless reminded him that future economic and cultural development "depends entirely on the firm establishment of the new state system."[16] A year later, the liberal Moscow industrialist, Konovalov, carried the point still further in a speech before the State Duma that was warmly approved by <u>Industry and Trade</u>:

> I must express my conviction that the coming tasks of our economic flowering, of the development of the productive forces of the country, of the development of its trade and industry, and, in connection with that, of the external, international power of the state as well, imperatively and persistently require the rapid renovation of our state and public life.[17]

By the spring of 1913, the Association's disillusionment was complete. Far from promoting industrial development, it once again complained, the government actually impeded economic progress. The government's campaign against industrial syndicates, it charged, reflected its ingrained hostility toward industry and the commercial-industrial class. In its most pernicious and pervasive aspect it took the form of "state socialism," characterized by increasingly stringent and unreasonable controls over private industry and the deliberate extension of the state-owned and controlled sector of the economy at the expense of private enterprise.[18] The government's actions not only obstructed industrial expansion in the future; they also threatened to push the economy into a state of renewed depression.

Despite the strife that increasingly marked industry's relationship with the government, the Seventh Congress, meeting in May 1913, contented itself with reiterating its familiar demands for the introduction of economic "planning," particularly in the building of railroads; the improvement of roads, ports, and waterways; and firmness in the commercial negotiations with Germany that were soon to begin.[19] The storm of protest, recrimination, and exhortation reached a crescendo of aggrieved dissonance a year later, on the eve of the war.

Throughout this stormy period, the Association, speaking both as an organization and through its individual leaders, continued to assert the government's obligation "to direct all its energy toward strengthening the economic power of the country."[20] The Ministry of Trade and Industry, Konovalov told the State Duma, must draw up "a broad economic program" for national development. Only by approaching its tasks "systematically and in accordance with a plan" could the Ministry avoid the inconsistencies and contradictions which must result from a piecemeal approach to reform.[21] Likewise, Industry and Trade identified "the lack of a consistent and planned policy directed toward raising the productive forces of the country" as the basic cause of Russia's continued lagging behind "the advanced countries" in economic development.[22] The Council reiterated these opinions in a formal "address" to the minister of trade and industry at the end of the year.[23]

The Association failed, however, to prod Russia's heavy-handed bureaucracy into action. The brief flurry of hopeful speculation that followed the Emperor's issuance of a Rescript on January 30, 1914, proclaiming industrial development to be the goal of official policy, could not offset the discouraging impact of Kokovtsov's nearly simultaneous dismissal and his replacement by the aged and reactionary Ivan L. Goremykin. During the remaining months before the outbreak of war, the conflict between the government and organized industry swelled to a peak of unprecedented acrimony. Although high government officials continued to pay lip service to Russia's need for economic expansion, the

Association openly expressed its lack of faith in the government's good intentions. Even the appointment of a former member of its own Council, Petr L. Bark, as minister of finance did not overcome the Association's disillusionment and despair. Although Bark, in his budgetary speech to the State Duma, admitted that "the further intensive development of our industrial forces is necessary in order to free ourselves from dependence on foreign countries," Industry and Trade observed with dismay that he offered no specific recommendations for promoting this development and had even revealed a disconcerting tendency to favor state over private enterprise.[24]

At the Eighth Congress, in May 1914, the antagonism between the government and industry dominated the proceedings. On the official side, the minister of trade and industry himself, who, of all government officials, presumably stood closest to industrial interests, reiterated the charge that the industrialists themselves bore primary responsibility for the disappointing rate of industrial growth. The industrialists, for their part, condemned the alleged "anti-industrial orientation of governmental policy."[25] In addition to their earlier grounds for complaint, new and alarming grievances had recently arisen in the form of threats to reduce, or even eliminate altogether, tariff protection of industrial products; measures to limit industry's right to own land; restrictions on private enterprise according to religion and nationality; and the open persecution of individual businessmen on allegedly specious legal grounds. Despite generally favorable economic conditions, the Council reported, governmental policies had brought the country to the brink of economic crisis, and, perhaps, to political disaster as well. The near panic that gripped the St. Petersburg stock exchange during May forced its temporary closing.

It was left to Pavel P. Riabushinskii to proclaim the industrialists' conviction that political conditions now constituted the primary obstacle to economic development. In an impassioned speech that met with "prolonged applause," he declared, in a thinly veiled allusion to Grigorii E. Rasputin and his clique, that nothing less than a change in the self-serving group around the Emperor could save Russia.

> We who are working in the field of commercial-industrial affairs, being in closer contact than anyone else with the economic problems of the nation, clearly recognize that it is impossible to continue further in this way. For all other states are developing with such speed, accumulating funds and resources with such rapidity, that we, if only to avoid lagging behind them, must act with extreme decisiveness and must strain all the forces of the intellect. Otherwise we shall be driven out of the stream of world life, where the weak are not tolerated. . . . If the Russian people possess the

exceptional gifts that our minister of finance points out, the question unavoidably arises: how is it to be explained that our talented people lag behind in many ways? In fact, only one conclusion can be drawn. If our gifted nation is not progressing, obviously the persons who are called upon to direct the steps of this nation are themselves not up to their jobs; our government is untalented. . . . You laugh; but if one thinks more deeply about this, grief fills one's heart. I say further: if things continue as they are, even the masses of the people will lose respect and confidence in the government. That will be sad; that will be intolerable; that can lead to grievous consequences. Therefore, the efforts of all of us who value the interests of our native land and of the Russian state above all else, regardless of how they [the authorities] reproach us, must be directed toward creative work and, perhaps, even toward healing the wounds that are being inflicted by our government. . . . Gentlemen, you who are gathered together here, tell me: is there honesty [pravda] among us in Rus? I do not await your reply. . . . But in the past there were men among us, high officials and holy men, not crafty servants of the state, who were not afraid, and who spoke the truth to the tsars. But what are words but leaves, driven by the wind in autumn; both vanish in the darkness of night. The government [vlast'] is blind. The nation is orphaned. The only hope is that our great country will be able to survive its petty government.[26]

Beside Riabushinskii's condemnation, the Congress's complaints of the government's failure to produce an economic program seemed trivial. Yet its discouragement, even on this score, was profound.[27] Summarizing the results of the Eighth Congress, Industry and Trade observed:

At the congresses of our representative organization, questions concerning the mutual relations of the government and industry have certainly predominated before, as well. Those questions have by no means always been decided at the congresses in accordance with governmental proposals. But never, until now, has there been such a significant divergence in the evaluation of those measures which are necessary for the further development of industry. This profound divergence has extended like a red thread through almost the entire congress.[28]

If, the journal warned, the government

persists in the direction it has adopted, it will increasingly diverge from that which the representatives of industry and trade, inspired by an ardent striving to contribute their strength for the sake of a rise in the productive forces of the country, consider useful.[29]

The Congress itself declared its conviction that "the stability of the new representative system is a necessary guarantee of the successful development of the national economy, and of trade and industry in particular."[30] Even Avdakov, who welcomed the "extraordinary growth and development of the productive forces" during the past three years, pointed out that "in the recent period industry has begun to look at the future partly with alarm, partly with mistrust, as if expecting each day new measures of a kind that must constrain the development of this industry."[31]

On the eve of the war, economic growth no longer appeared attainable independently of the general conditions prevailing in Russian life. Russia's industrialists now considered political change, or, at the very least, the full retention of political victories already won, essential to economic progress. Industry and Trade continued to accuse the government of the most transparent hypocrisy in pretending to favor industrial growth while simultaneously strewing its path with obstacles.

> It is impossible simultaneously to pursue mutually contradictory objectives. We are waiting for the government, not only in theory and principle, but also in a series of concrete measures, to give Russian industry the opportunity to realize all the economic potential that is lodged in the natural riches of the country and, thereby, to provide the state treasury in the future with the funds necessary for the satisfaction of all the cultural and great-power needs of an unbounded Russia.[32]

Thus, as the prewar period came to an end, the lines were sharply drawn between the government and industry. Each held the other responsible for the country's disappointing economic progress. With respect to the future, however, the Association considered a change in governmental policies an indispensable condition of further national economic growth.

The Catastrophe of War

In this bleak situation, war and revolution imposed strains that elevated the Association to its highest peak of public activity. In the end, these proved to be almost beyond its capacity to maintain. The immediate effect of the war was to weld together the ranks of large-scale industry behind the Association's leadership in recognizing "its own importance and responsibility and its willingness to sacrifice profits temporarily for the sake of victory and the interests of the country."[33] During the first months of the war, the Association organized an Information Bureau to assist in the continuing conduct of trade and industrial production; a second Bureau assisted Russian subjects stranded abroad; a fund was set up to provide clothing and small luxuries to the troops at the front; and the organization found employment for disabled military men. The Council's delegates sat in the official Central Committee on Fuel, in a commission devoted to problems in foreign trade, and in other bodies concerned with the economic prosecution of the war. At the same time, the Council continued work on a national economic program.

The "truce" between the Association and the government was brief, however.[34] The collapse of the military supply system in the spring of 1915 precipitated a crisis in industry's relations with the government in May, when the Ninth (and last) Congress of the Association met in Petrograd. In an atmosphere of intense excitement, the Council put aside its long-awaited economic program and delayed its major political attack on the government. The Congress proceeded to call into being the Central War Industries Committee as an instrument for the effective prosecution of the war effort. In the following year, the Association experienced its finest moment, as the War Industries Committees, at first under the direction and later with the continuing assistance of the Committee of the Council, assumed much of the burden of restoring Russia's nearly shattered economy.[35]

On the economic level, the Association cooperated with the government even more closely than before. In the spring of 1916, its representatives joined the newly formed Special Supreme Financial-Economic Commission. Politically, however, its relationship with the government steadily deteriorated. By January 1917, the gulf that separated industry and the government would seem to have become unbridgeable.[36]

The Association's growing embroilment with the government resulted not only from the latter's steadily rightward course but also from the Association's own increasingly liberal outlook. This development undoubtedly reflected the death of Avdakov in September 1915 and the rise to unchallenged leadership of the energetic and enterprising Zhukovskii.

During the war, Zhukovskii demonstrated his devotion to Russia's cause by working with Avdakov to create the Central War Industries Committee. Yet political considerations apparently made impossible his appointment as chairman, despite his unanimously acknowledged leadership of the Council. In the short period between Avdakov's death and Zhukovskii's own demise in August 1916, the Association formed a clear rapprochement with both liberals in the Duma and the intelligentsia. Professors contributed articles to <u>Industry and Trade</u> and figured prominently in the meetings held by the Council. An apparently uninhibited exchange of controversial points of view became an accepted part of the scene, although not without some resistance from the more conservative members of the organization. As the Central War Industries Committee grew in strength and independence, the Association, while continuing its cooperation in the prosecution of the war effort, turned once again to the problems of the future and particularly to those of Russia's postwar recovery and economic expansion. At the same time, it continued its efforts to improve the organization of Russian trade and industry and to expand its own membership and activities.[37]

Zhukovskii's death came as a climax to a long series of major losses that left the old leadership of the Association decimated.[38] Zhukovskii's work fell to Nikolai N. Iznar, a representative of the Baku oil industry. It was not until early 1917 that the post of chairman, vacant since Avdakov's death, was filled by the appointment of Nikolai N. Kutler, the Association's last chairman. Well before his appointment, however, demoralization had spread within the organization. To some extent this no doubt reflected the deterioration of conditions in Russia generally and industry's growing political disaffection. In any event, the unity of the industrialists, superficial though it undoubtedly was, quickly evaporated. By the end of 1916, little remained of the former vitality of the Council.[39] Internecine quarrels, which the new leadership seemed powerless to reconcile, also tore at the fabric of the organization.[40]

The full extent of the disunity that had come to prevail within the Russian business community became evident in December 1916, when the exchange committees of central Russia and the Volga region called a commercial-industrial congress in Moscow to discuss questions of economic policy, food supply, and "problems in the correct organization of representative institutions for trade and industry."[41] Although all private conferences of industrialists were forbidden by law, the congress met in January at the home of Pavel P. Riabushinskii, president of the Moscow Exchange Committee. It created a Presidium, chaired by Riabushinskii and dominated by the Moscow Committee, for the purpose of "coordinating all the public forces of the commercial-industrial organizations and institutions of a commercial-industrial character."[42] Meanwhile, the Council of the Association, which had given its delegates to the Moscow Congress complete freedom to attend and to take their positions on issues raised at the meetings, called a congress of its own organization, "or, if for any reason this is unrealizable," a meeting of the Council of the Association "with the broadest participation of the representatives of industry and trade."[43] Nothing came of this, however. The government rejected an almost simultaneous petition of the Association of Trade and Agriculture for permission to call a Special Congress to discuss the food question and "the renewal of the normal activity of the Russian commercial class."[44]

The Association joyfully welcomed the collapse of the tsarist government in February 1917. Its enthusiasm revealed something of the difficulties it had experienced with the old regime. In words of unaccustomed liberalism, the Council included the industrialists among Russia's "fighters for truth, legality, and freedom."

> A part was also taken in this struggle by the commercial-industrial class, which traditionally, ever since the great French Revolution, has been a partisan of civic freedom and a bulwark and vanguard of active liberalism. All the associations, all the organizations of the commercial-industrial class, whatever their objectives in a technical sense, were obliged in practice to turn away from their "business-like" course and enter the path of politics. And justice must be rendered to Protopopov and his myrmidons: they were, from their own point of view, correct when they feared our Association and when they resisted our every attempt at unification. Not for nothing did they ruthlessly paralyze every effort of the commercial-industrial class to organize itself. Our organization was directed against them. Our organization was a powerful detachment in the camp of their enemies.[45]

Yet, as we have seen, the business community entered the period of revolutionary upheaval in a state of marked disunity. Despite the establishment of a felicitous relationship with the Provisional Government and the rise of some of its members to positions of unprecedented importance within it, no unified commercial-industrial "bourgeoisie" existed to hinder the Bolsheviks' seizure of power.

One direct consequence of the collapse of the tsarist regime was the convening in Moscow, March 19 to 23, of the forbidden Commercial-Industrial Congress. Despite short notice in the issuance of invitations and difficult traveling conditions, participants in the Congress numbered more than one thousand. The Association interpreted this fact as evidence of the need for unification throughout the commercial-industrial class.[46] Three tasks confronted the Congress, chaired by Pavel P. Riabushinskii: to prepare for elections to the forthcoming constituent assembly; "to lay the foundations" for the creation of a new, "nonpolitical and exclusively businesslike" organization of the commercial-industrial class, for the purpose of considering "the task of the socioeconomic construction of Russia"; and to assist in resolving the crisis in food supply.[47]

The Congress declared its political support for the Provisional Government, for the convening of a constituent assembly, and for the establishment of a republic that would uphold "the principles of political and civic freedom." Both for the purpose of political action and for the unification of the commercial-industrial class, it created a new organization, the All-Russian Union of Trade and Industry (Vserossiiskii soiuz torgovli i promyshlennosti). Headed by Riabushinskii, with Sergei N. Tretiakov, his colleague in the Moscow Exchange Committee, as his deputy, it was to have its headquarters in Moscow. Its organizational structure followed a familiar pattern. Supervision over its affairs rested with a Council consisting of thirty persons elected by congresses; provincial commercial-industrial committees would elect one delegate each; and five delegates each would represent the Association of Industry and Trade and the Association of Trade and Agriculture. The Council would elect from among its membership a Main Committee (Glavnyi komitet) of twelve to carry out the Union's day-to-day work. At least six of the Committee's members must be chosen from among persons having their residence in Moscow, and one must come from each of the two national associations. The Union's organizers sought to draw its membership not only from existing commercial-industrial organizations, including those representing small-scale industry and handicrafts, but also from unorganized businessmen and the clerical, professional, and administrative employees of industry and trade. Organizationally, the Union was to rest on a network of local and provincial committees of trade and industry.[48]

In practice, the rise of the Union, far from unifying Russian industry and trade, simply added one more national organization to the two existing associations. The long-smoldering rivalry between Moscow and Petrograd came to a head at last, as the new Union challenged to the preeminence of the northern capital.[49] Accordingly, the Association's reaction to the establishment of the new organization was less than cordial. On the one hand, it welcomed the idea of creating local commercial-industrial committees as "completely correct" and called upon the commercial-industrial class to "come forward as a unified, organized collective" in order to "fulfill the great role that history was placed upon it." On the other hand, the Association pointed out that the Union had no plan for "welding" the commercial-industrial class together. Even its organization appeared to have "a primitive character, unstable and inadequate for its needs."[50]

Perhaps in response to Moscow's challenge, the Association began in April to consider the possibility of a merger with the Association of Trade and Agriculture.[51] Although nothing came of this idea, the Association's leaders took a prominent part in the Third Special All-Russian Congress of Trade and Agriculture in Petrograd at the end of the month. This congress revised the organization's charter and instituted a new network of chambers of commerce and industry. To this end, it called for the reform of all existing representative institutions; an expansion in the function of the exchange committees, in which membership by "the whole commercial-industrial class" would be compulsory; and their unification in a system of local councils and congresses.[52]

In May, the Association of Industry and Trade once again assumed the initiative, calling a "Conference" of its own organization (in lieu of a congress), which convened in Petrograd behind closed doors on June 1 and 2.[53] The presidium of the Conference consisted of Nikolai N. Kutler, as chairman, and six vice-chairmen, among whom were S. Ia. Tretiakov and Iulian I. Poplavskii from Moscow, Nikolai F. Ditmar, Nikolai N. Iznar, and Aleksandr A. Bublikov. The Conference disavowed profit-seeking as a goal "in the present difficult period for the native land" and dedicated the Association to "the salvation of industry and trade itself --essential, vital factors of a healthy statehood." To this end, it advocated "the creation of a single, powerful, and authoritative all-Russian commercial-industrial organ."[54]

The representatives of Russia's two capitals failed, however, to agree on the means to achieve this goal. In the end, the Conference proposed two major and parallel steps toward unity. First, it suggested the convening of a commission, composed of four representatives from each of the three national organizations, to bring about their "immediate unification."[55] In addition, evidently on the initiative of the Petrograd men, the Conference established a Main Committee of United Industry (Glavnyi komitet ob"edinennoi promyshlennosti) in Petrograd, composed of thirteen commercial-industrial organizations, "for the defense of industry" in its increasingly serious conflict with organized labor.[56] Only the latter organization actually materialized, following its organizing meeting in early August. Significantly, the Committee announced its intention to work "in close unity with the Moscow commercial-industrial committee,"[57] a group that had effectively united all the business organizations of Moscow at the beginning of the revolution.[58]

Meanwhile, despite the unsettled economic conditions in the country, much of the Association's day-to-day business, including its contacts with governmental agencies, seems to have continued as usual. Members of its Council, moreover, now occupied high places in the Provisional Government. Prior to the May crisis, Aleksandr I. Guchkov served as minister of war, and after the crisis the sugar manufacturer and financier Mikhail I. Tereshchenko replaced Pavel N. Miliukov as foreign minister. In April, the Council[59] began publication of a semi-weekly newspaper,

News (Izvestiia), with the announced purpose of expressing the point of view of the commercial-industrial class.[60] Early that month, a reorganization of the Secretariat came under consideration, and, perhaps in connection with it, the work of the Legal Section expanded considerably to assist members with legal and tax questions.[61] Although the Council decided against participating in trade fairs in England and France, it did undertake the formation, under its own aegis, of a Russo-American Committee for the purpose of promoting an economic rapprochement with the United States.[62]

After the June Conference, however, leaders of the Association gave serious thought to a reevaluation of its role in the new Russia. Late in June, the results appeared in Industry and Trade. Apparently the Council decided to abandon the quest for class unity, under its own or any other auspices, and to steer an independent course. The times, it declared, were of such extraordinary complexity that only a greater division of labor could meet the needs of the moment.

> In the present grave moment in the life of Russian industry, the danger arises for our commercial-industrial organizations, and for the Council of our Association in particular, that we shall not succeed in coping with our tasks if each one does not distinguish for itself . . . its own narrow sphere in which it can concentrate and work most productively. Therefore, it is necessary for the Council of our Association, with absolute definiteness, to keep clear of other commercial-industrial organizations, decisively taking the path of the deliberate restriction of its own area of competence.[63]

Political affairs, it decided, lay outside its proper field of competence. Responsibility for waging the "class struggle" between management and labor rested, it said, with the new Committee for the Defense of Industry, formed as a result of the June Conference, rather than with the Council itself. Moreover, because current problems of production and supply no longer properly concerned the Association, the Council had withdrawn from the Central War Industries Committee.[64] The Council, it concluded, must turn its attention to "working out the problems of our future economic development," specifically the elaboration of "a plan for the return of industry to peaceful work" that could "lead the country out of the impasse into which the tornado of revolution has turned it." Basic decisions respecting future economic policies would soon confront the country. These issues which would not be decided without a "stubborn struggle" of conflicting interests.[65]

Whether the Association had abandoned its commitment to class unity may well be doubted, however. With unaccustomed introspection,

Industry and Trade found the cause of Russia's difficulties to lie partly with the persistent failure of the businessmen themselves to achieve genuine unity. Once more, the old slogan of "strength through unity," which had underlain the founding congresses of 1906, seemed to provide the answer for the future.

> We ourselves are partly to blame that the destructive forces of this tornado have been so great. The revolution caught us unprepared, atomized, unaccustomed to act at a common command. Now, when bitter experience has forced us to realize that in unity there is strength, the basic psychological prerequisite for our ultimate victory has been created in the same way. The Russian revolution has not yet ended; it will take many turns, and the sooner the conscious will of the commercial-industrial class flows into the spontaneous course of the revolution, the greater will be the role secured for us in the future state organization of Russia.[66]

Significantly, the organization expressed no desire for an open break with Moscow, and its delegates attended the Second Congress of the All-Russian Union of Trade and Industry in Moscow early in August. That same month witnessed both the formal organization of the Main Committee of United Industry and the establishment of a fifth nation-wide organization, the Russian Union of Manufacturers' Societies (Vserossiiskii soiuz obshchestv zavodchikov i fabrikantov).[67] After the Kornilov affair, according to the Soviet historian Reikhardt, the Association once again raised the question of the unification of the three principal organizations of businessmen, which it had first broached at its June Conference. The project was rejected by Moscow, however, on the grounds that "two-thirds of the votes in it the proposed committee would belong to Petrograd and only one-third would remain as the share of Moscow and all the rest of Russia."[68]

The last weeks before the Bolshevik seizure of power were relatively quiet ones for the Association. Industry and Trade continued to appear in its usual size and format. After Aleksandr F. Kerenskii's reorganization of the government early in October, two members of the Association, Sergei N. Tretiakov and Aleksandr I. Konovalov, held ministerial posts. On November 7, at the height of the crisis, the latter briefly held the reins of "power" after Kerenskii fled Petrograd. Ironically, only a few days before, the leaders of the Association had declared that the likelihood of a Bolshevik seizure of power appeared to be diminishing.[69] In their complacency, they continued to debate whether the commercial-industrial class needed more effective organization or whether the existing organizations were adequate to the tasks that confronted it.

The results of Bolshevik rule were immediately apparent. Industry and Trade appeared several days late, apologizing to its readers for the delay caused by "the extraordinary circumstances of the times through which we are living."[70] Publication continued until the end of the year, although the size of the newspaper dwindled noticeably, partly because of the disappearance of advertisements, which had previously added to its bulk. Ironically, the last issue, dated December 23, was actually fuller than usual. Nothing indicated that its end was at hand. The business class had received, however, an unmistakable warning of its approaching fate in the arrest of Kutler in November. The Council's protest, issued "in the name of the entire commercial-industrial class," stressed his role as the sole delegate of the business class to the forthcoming Constituent Assembly.

> In the Constituent Assembly, called to create the foundations of the future state and economic life of Russia, the voice of trade and industry must be heard. N. N. Kutler is at the present time the only representative of industry and trade in the Constituent Assembly and his forceful removal, manifestly, deprives the entire commercial-industrial class of the possibility of sharing in the building of a new Russia.[71]

Curiously, however, the Association seemed not to understand the full import of this event. Indeed, on the eve of their own disappearance from the public scene, the Association's leaders, evidently ignorant of the nature of Bolshevik power, looked forward hopefully to the establishment of "businesslike relations" with the new Soviet government. In a joint meeting of the Association of Industry and Trade and the Association of Trade and Agriculture, the two Councils voted in favor of such relations and offered to participate, through their representatives, in Soviet governmental institutions.[72] In a conference held by the Council of the Association of Industry and Trade on January 18, 1918 (probably the last such meeting to be held), Timiriazev raised this possibility once again. With what, in the light of hindsight, must appear as extraordinary naïveté, he declared:

> It is necessary in the interests of the native land, while in no way giving up their own political platform, [for business leaders] to be in contact with the current authority [vlast'] and by their knowledge and experience to influence it in the direction of a correct resolution of state affairs. It was necessary, without assuming any responsibility for the decisions of the authority, to point out to it the error of its intended decisions and to propose to it necessary correctives.[73]

Thus, the leadership of the Association remained optimistic to the last. "Strength through unity" had indeed eluded them. In the years that followed, in exile in Paris and London, they were to continue their vain quest.

5

Conclusion

Did the Association of Industry and Trade succeed in producing a program for Russia's economic development? Certainly, if it is a question of a comprehensive program providing for the scheduled and coordinated growth of all sectors of the economy according to a preconceived system of priorities over a period of years, the answer must be no. In the eight years from 1906 to the outbreak of World War I, the organization's so-called "program" consisted of a number of rather sketchily drawn recommendations for the advancement of various sectors of the Empire's economy. Although these proposals, taken together, embraced every aspect of economic life, however insignificant, they did not constitute parts of an integral whole. The essence of each could be discovered only by a painstaking search through the voluminously detailed statements of the Association on the entire range of economic problems, large and small, current and prospective, that confronted the Empire during its final decade. As the record starkly reveals, few of the industrialists' contemporaries possessed the patience, or the interest, to carry out such a project.

To the historian who has undertaken this task, it is evident, moreover, that the Association, although consciously groping toward a definition of economic priorities, remained deeply enmeshed in the dilemmas of national economic backwardness. These dilemmas were by no means peculiar to Russia, despite the variants introduced by its own national idiosyncracies. However, as the industrialists could only dimly discern, their economic difficulties mirrored, and in large measure foreshadowed, the problems that have since been more widely recognized in recent studies of underdeveloped countries aspiring to rapid modernization. The dilemmas were clearly reflected in the conflicts and ambiguities that characterized the Association's own proposals: the conflict, for example, between industry's desire for a domestic market based on increased popular purchasing power and its quest for greater profits and savings in order to expand productive capacity; between its recognition of the central importance of agriculture as a foundation for national economic growth and its unwillingness to accept, in the interest of agriculture, any infringement on its own immediate financial interests; between industry's desire for the security that could be offered by a benevolent and paternalistic government and its resentment of the "tutelage" that often accompanied such assistance; between its quest for national self-sufficiency and its ambitions for Russia to play the role of a truly great power in the international economy; and, finally, between the admiration with which it viewed the West and its fear of economic "enslavement" by the advanced industrial countries, particularly Germany. Conditions peculiar to Russia--its deep-rooted heritage of communalism and the long tradition of governmental direction of the economy--fed the Association's ambivalence toward individual initiative and economic competition, on the one hand, and "cooperation" on the other, both in economic life generally and in economic "planning" for future development.

These difficulties notwithstanding, the Association perceived Russia's economic needs with remarkable clarity. If the question of means remained unresolved, the organization at least understood that the problems of capital and the market posed the greatest economic challenge for those who sought greater national growth and prosperity. It also articulated the need for an orderly approach to the problems of economic development, particularly the desirability of "planning," both for economic growth and for the moderation of the business cycle. In most of these respects, the industrialists were well in advance of their contemporaries. Pragmatists though they were, they unquestionably acted as harbingers of many of the elements of the Keynesian school of economic thought, which later gained ascendancy in the West. They certainly anticipated some of the more sophisticated thinking on the development of backward areas that absorbed much of the world's attention in the mid-twentieth century.

As we have seen, the political inertness of the Russian middle class has been a frequent theme of historians, both Russian and western, who commonly, although in varying degree and according to their own lights, have held its failings responsible for the subsequent course of Russia's history. The few Soviet historians who considered the question in depth suggested that the failure of the businessmen to see a connection between the economic and the political issues of the day inevitably vitiated any effort they may have made to assume positions of leadership in propelling Russia onto the high road of economic development. Yet, the present study has revealed the extent to which the industrialists' efforts to take the initiative in fostering national economic growth were frustrated by a lethargic, despotic, and often hostile government. Reluctant as the businessmen unquestionably were to take a stand in opposition to the tsarist regime, events forced their hands. Although many details of their political outlook remain unclear, on the eve of World War I the businessmen stood close to an open break with the government. Thus, they shared the general restlessness of Russian society during the immediate prewar period. We may only speculate as to the course that Russia might have followed, and the role which the businessmen might have undertaken, had the war not intervened and briefly smoothed the troubled waters of national life with the oil of patriotism.

The scant attention that the Russian business class has thus far received from historians may, perhaps, be attributed to a general reluctance to engage in the often thankless labor of chronicling a lost cause. Yet the validity of this latter judgment is indeed questionable. True, this class met an abrupt end in the Russian Civil War, and few of its members remained in Russia to participate in the work of industrialization under the Soviet regime. Nevertheless, in their common belief in the inevitability of industrial development and the desirability of planning; in their emphasis on the prime importance of developing heavy industry at the expense of consumers' goods and current living standards; in their stress on the need to achieve a "cult of work" that would create the new economic man of the future; and also in many of the specific projects that were advocated for the improvement of the vast country, the line of continuity uniting prerevolutionary Russian businessmen and their Soviet successors is unmistakable.

No doubt the political views of the industrialists would not have permitted the enforcement of such a rigorous regimen as that which prevailed during the Stalin period. But the forms of socioeconomic organization that the Association advocated, in the interest of promoting its narrow economic objectives, were not entirely consistent with the avowed "westernism" of its outlook. Russian society under the auspices of its business class in the twentieth century might well have had more in common with the moderate socialism of Scandinavia, the syndicalism of Italy in the 1920s, the authoritarian rule of Poland and the Baltic states between the wars, or the pattern of industrial organization that emerged in postwar Germany than with the open and competitive society that has been the American ideal.

Appendix I

The Charter of the Association
(Approved August 24, 1906)

(Reprinted from Sovet S"ezdov gornopromyshlennikov Iuga Rossii, Spravochnaia kniga dlia gornopromyshlennikov Iuga Rossii [Kharkov: Sovet . . . Rossii, 1916], 73-80.)

I. General Provisions

1. The Association of Industry and Trade is established for the purpose of the examination and discussion of questions concerning the general needs of industry and trade, for the elaboration of measures directed toward their advancement, and, equally, for the unification of the representation of the common interests of industry and trade.

2. The Association of Industry and Trade is under the jurisdiction of the Ministry of Trade and Industry.

3. The Congresses [of the Association] may be:

a. general--on questions concerning all branches of industry and trade, and

b. group congresses--on questions concerning particular branches of industry and trade.

II. Objectives and Rights of the Association

4. Objectives of the Association:

a. to unify the representation of the interests of industry and trade in general, and of their individual branches, before governmental and public institutions;

b. to make possible the rise of local public and professional institutions for industry and trade;

c. to make possible the regulation of the relationship between capital and labor;

d. to organize competitions, exhibitions, experimental stations, laboratories, museums, schools, courses for workers, and similar institutions;

e. to collect statistical information; to publish research, periodical organs and such [materials] on questions of industry and trade.

5. The Association may, in its own name, acquire rights to property, including the right of ownership and other rights in real estate, the right to assume obligations, to bring suit and defend itself in court, and to have its own press.

III. The Membership of the Association

6. The Association is composed of full and consultative members.

7. Full members of the Association are those that are based on statutes and charters approved under the established procedure:

a. public institutions for trade and industry, such as: exchanges, committees of trade and manufacturing, associations and consultative boards industrialists, and so forth.

b. industrial and commercial organizations, made up of the owners of commercial-industrial enterprises or their representatives and having as their purpose the unification of their members on the basis of economic interests.

Note. The organizations referred to in paragraph b also include institutions that unite credit, insurance, railroad, steamship, and transport enterprises.

8. Consultative members are joint-stock enterprises having a basic capital of no less than 300,000 rubles, and also enterprises having no obligation of public accountability with an annual turnover of no less than the same sum.

9. Institutions, organizations, and enterprises that wish to become members of the Association should declare their desire in writing to the Council of the Association, which will admit them to membership if they satisfy the requirements of paragraphs 7 and 8 of the Charter.

10. Full members (paragraph 7) participate in the meetings of the Congresses through representatives appointed by them, the number of whom from each member may not exceed twice the number of votes that it has in accordance with paragraph 12. The representatives collectively cast the number of votes belonging to each full member. Each consultative member (paragraph 8) may send no more than two representatives to

a Congress. One and the same person may not serve as representative of more than three full members at a Congress and may not have at his disposition more than ten votes altogether.

11. Only the representatives of full members have the right to cast deciding votes in the meetings of the Congresses. The representatives of consultative members have only advisory votes.

12. For the purpose of exercising their voting rights at the Congresses on all questions other than elections to the Council of the Association and to the Audit Commission, the full members are divided into five classes depending on the importance and volume of activity of their institutions and organizations: the first class has five votes; the second, four; the third, three; the fourth, two; and the fifth, one vote. In the election of members of the Council of the Association and of the Audit Commission, each full member, through its representatives, has only one vote. Institutions and organizations are assigned to classes by the Council of the Association, in which connection each institution and each organization has the right to ask to be placed in a class lower than that to which it was assigned by the Council without losing the right freely to transfer in the future into the higher class to which it was originally assigned by the Council.

IV. The Administration of the Association

13. The Council, and the Committee constituted under it, are charged with the administration of the Association.

14. The Council of the Association consists of:

a. no more than thirty-six elected members, who are chosen at the regular, general Congresses by the full members of the Association from among the representatives of the institutions and organizations that comprise the membership of the Association, and

b. member-delegates, appointed at the rate of one each from those institutions and organizations that pay no less than 500 rubles in membership dues.

The elected members of the Council are chosen for terms of two years, insofar as is possible from among representatives of all districts and all branches of industry and trade. Half of the elected members of the Council leave office every year, according to lot in the first year and according to the sequence of their election thereafter. Outgoing members may be reelected. Delegates appointed to the Council by institutions and organizations that cease to be representatives of those institutions and organizations are considered to have left the membership of the Council of the Association. Similarly, they leave the membership of the Council when the institutions or organizations that appointed them withdraw their membership in the Association. Institutions and organizations that appoint delegates to the Council have the right to appoint one or more alternates to them.

15. The Council of the Association has its permanent headquarters in Petrograd.

16. The Council of the Association annually elects from among its own members a chairman and three vice-chairmen.

17. The duties of the Council include:

a. the composition of the programs of questions to be discussed by the Congresses, the preliminary investigation of these questions and the presentation to the Congresses of reports on them, and also the presentation of lists of candidates proposed by the Council for election as members of the Council (paragraph 14);

b. the convening of the Congresses;

c. the implementation and fulfillment of the decisions of the Congresses;

d. the representation of the congresses before governmental and public institutions;

e. relations with appropriate institutions and persons on subjects that enter into the sphere of the Council's activity;

f. the general conduct of the affairs of the Association;

g. the acceptance of new members into the Association and their assignment to classes in accordance with paragraph 12;

h. the receiving of funds, their custody, and their expenditure within the limits of the budgets approved by the Congresses or in accordance with their special instructions;

i. the presentation to the Congresses of reports on its activity and also estimates and reports on the income and expenditure of funds;

j. the investigation of measures for the development of the activity of the Association, for the fullest possible unification of commercial-industrial representation, and for the growth of local institutions on industry and trade.

Note 1. The Council is obligated to report to the next general Congress on all special measures taken by the Council without instructions to that effect by the Congresses.

Note 2. The lists of candidates for membership in the Council that are presented to the Congresses include: all persons named for such membership by institutions and organizations; and persons nominated by the Council itself with a view to assuring that all branches of industry and trade and all districts have their own representatives in the Council.

18. The Council meets as necessary. A quorum of the Council consists of no less than twelve persons, including the chairman or one of the vice-chairmen. Questions are decided in the Council by a simple majority vote of those present; in the case of a tie, the chairman casts the deciding vote.

19. In the Council's consideration of questions that closely concern a particular branch of industry or trade, or a particular district, it is obligatory to invite to the Council's meeting the representatives (paragraph 10) of the public institutions for trade and industry and the commercial-industrial organizations that have an interest in the resolution of the given question. The decision of the Council on such a question is valid only if the majority of the said representatives participating in the meeting of the Council are in agreement with the opinion of the majority of the members of the Council. If they side with the minority, the question is presented by the Council for consideration by the next Congress. Questions considered in the above-mentioned conferences are decided by a simple majority vote of the representatives present at the meeting; in case of a tie, the chairman casts the deciding vote.

20. The Council is authorized to invite to its meetings, with the right to cast advisory votes, the representatives of industrial and commercial organizations and institutions and of individual enterprises that are not members of the Association, and, in general, all persons whose participation will be useful in the discussion of questions to be decided by the Council.

21. All correspondence regarding the affairs of the Association is conducted in the name of the Council by the Committee constituted under it, over the signature of the Chairman of the Council or one of his vice-chairmen.

22. The Committee of the Council, which consists of the Chairman of the Council, his three vice-chairmen, and three members elected by the Council from among its own membership, is charged with the direct management of the affairs of the Association within the limits of the instructions given to it.

Note. By decision of the general Congresses, members of the Committee may be compensated [for their services].

23. The Chairman of the Council or one of his vice chairmen presides over the meetings of the Committee, for which no less than three persons in addition to the presiding officer constitute a quorum.

24. The director of the affairs of the Association and his assistants

are appointed and removed by the Council, which determines their compensation within the limits of the budget. The appointment of other employees is left to the Committee.

V. The Procedure in the Convening and in the Work of the Congresses

25. The general Congresses are either regular or special. The regular Congresses are convened annually, at dates named by the preceding Congress. Special Congresses are called according to need, at the discretion of the Council or on the demand of full members having a total of no less than one-tenth of the votes that belong to all members. In this case, the Congress must be convened by the Council with the least possible delay.

26. Group Congresses are convened by the Council according to need, on the request of the representatives of the respective groups of industry and trade. All institutions and organizations for industry and trade that are members of the Association are informed of the convening of a Group Congress.

27. The General and Group Congresses are convened in Petrograd, Moscow, and other cities, according to the decision of the preceding Congress or of the Council. The local administration is informed well in advance of the convening of the Congresses.

> Note. All administrative actions in connection with the convening of the First Regular Congress of Representatives of Industry and Trade are the responsibility of the Provisional Council of the Association, which was elected by the Commercial-Industrial Congress in St. Petersburg on April 14, 1906, and which, following the election of the members of a Council on the basis of this Charter, will transfer its powers to the said Council.

28. Information concerning the calling of Congresses must be sent to members by registered mail at least one month before the appointed date, or by telegram no later than two weeks in advance.

29. The Congresses are opened by the Chairman of the Council or one of his vice-chairmen. Before beginning its work, the Congress elects a commission for the verification of the credentials of those present, after which it elects the Chairman of the Congress, a vice-chairman, and its secretary.

30. The order in which questions are considered is determined by the agenda, which is distributed at the time the Congress is convened. Deviations from the agenda are permitted only by decision of the Congress.

31. In the event that the representatives of particular branches of industry and trade (paragraph 10) should declare the necessity of discussing in advance, among themselves, questions that directly concern the said branches and are subject to consideration by the Congress, the Congress must separate these questions for preliminary consideration by a conference of the representatives of the particular groups or districts. In this connection, decisions concerning the group or district to which a given question pertains and the membership of the given group or district are left to the Council.

32. All questions on the agenda, mentioned in paragraph 30, must be introduced to the Congress with a presentation by the Council of the Association. Questions introduced by members for discussion by the Congress no later than four weeks before the congress must be included on the agenda, except that in the case of Special Congresses this period is reduced to three weeks. Questions presented later may be placed on the agenda at the discretion of the Council.

33. The membership of a Congress is considered to consist of the entire number of the representatives present.

34. Questions included on the agendas of the Congresses (paragraphs 30 and 32), with the exception of questions concerning changes in the Charter of the Association and the liquidation of its affairs, are decided by a simple majority vote of the full members present; in case of a tie, the Chairman casts the deciding vote. Questions that are not on the agenda or arise at the Congress itself can be decided only if the full members who are present possess a total of no less than one-third of the votes of all members. Questions concerning changes or additions to the Charter of the Association and concerning the liquidation of the affairs of the Association may be discussed only if they were included on the agenda distributed in advance of the Congress. Decisions on questions concerning changes in the Charter of the Association require the presence of no less than half the total number of votes of all members of the Association and the concurrence of no less than two-thirds of the votes of the members present; and decisions on liquidation require the presence of no less than three-fourths of the total number of votes of all members of the Association and the concurrence of no less than two-thirds of the votes of the members present. In all cases, only members that have paid their membership dues have the right to take part in the voting.

35. Questions that are not decided at a General Congress because an insufficient number of members is present are carried over to the following Congress, at which they are decided by a simple majority vote of the full members present, excepting questions concerning liquidation,

for which a majority of two-thirds is again required.

36. In connection with the resolution by a General Congress of issues that directly concern a particular group of industry or trade, or a particular district, in the event that the conference of the representatives of this group or district does not concur with the decision of the majority of general Congress, this decision does not have the force of an enactment of the Association.

VI. The Resources of the Association

37. The resources of the Association consist of members' dues, contributions, proceeds from the sale of publications, and other receipts.

38. The amount of the annual dues of full members is determined by the General Congress for each forthcoming year depending on the class to which a given institution or a given organization belongs, the amount of the above-mentioned dues for 1906 being: for the first class, 5,000 rubles; for the second, 3,000 rubles; for the third, 1,500; for the fourth, 500; and for the fifth, 200. The amount of the annual dues of consultative members is determined, for publicly accountable enterprises, according to the amount of their basic or share capital, and for enterprises that are not publicly accountable, according to their annual turnover. In this connection, for 1906, enterprises with a capital or annual turnover of from 300,000 to 1,000,000 rubles pay 100 rubles; those having a capital or turnover of more than 1,000,000 rubles pay at the rate of 100 rubles for each 1,000,000 rubles or part thereof above 1,000,000 rubles.

39. Membership dues must be paid for each calendar year in advance, no later than in December of the preceding year.

Note. During 1906 membership dues are to be paid no later than a month from the time of admission as a member of the Association.

40. For the purpose of inspecting the substantive activity of the Council and for the auditing of books, budgets, and reports and the verification of funds, the regular Congress annually elects an Audit Commission of five persons, which presents a report to the next regular Congress.

VII. Resignation from the Association, the Cessation of Its Activity, and the Liquidation of Its Affairs

41. Institutions, organizations or enterprises that belong to the Association and wish to resign their membership send a statement to that effect to the Council of the Association. They are thereby considered to

have left the membership of the Association, in which connection the dues paid by them for the current year are not returned.

42. Institutions, organizations or enterprises that have not paid the dues owned by them during the first three months of a calendar year are considered to have left the membership of the Association. The readmission of such members is permitted only upon the reception of the arrears charged to them, in accordance with the general procedure adopted for the acceptance of new members.

43. Institutions, organizations or enterprises that leave the membership of the Association have no rights to the property of the Association.

44. In the event of the liquidation of the affairs of the Association, the Ministry and Trade and Industry is informed, and the property of the discontinued Association must be used for generally useful purposes connected with the tasks of the Association (paragraph 4). Most directly, the disposition of the property is determined by the last General Congress, and, if that is impossible, at the discretion of the Council of the Association.

Appendix II

The Structure of the Association

The rules governing the Association's membership and organizational structure clearly reflected its primary concern with the representation of large-scale capital. Membership was available in two categories, full (deistvitel'nyi) and consultative (soveshchatel'nyi). Eligibility for admission as full members was limited to "public" and representative organizations uniting commercial-industrial, banking, insurance, and transportation enterprises.[1] For purposes of voting in the annual congresses on both substantive and procedural issues and for payment of dues, full members fell into five classes. Those in the first class paid 5,000 rubles annually and had five votes; those in the second paid 3,000 and had four; the third, 1,500 and three; the fourth, 500 and two; and the last, 200 and one.[2] Only in the election of the Council and the Audit Commission did the full members vote on a basis of equality. Consultative membership in the Association, with an advisory vote only, was open to individual enterprises having either a basic capital of 300,000 rubles, in the case of corporations, or an annual business turnover of the same amount, in the case of unincorporated firms, typically partnerships.[3] Dues amounted to 100 rubles annually for those with a capital or turnover of up to 1,000,000 rubles, plus an additional 100 rubles for each additional 1,000,000 or part thereof.[4]

Under its charter, the ultimate authority within the Association lay with the general congresses of the membership, which were to be convened annually. Provision was also made for the holding of special congresses and "group" congresses concerned with particular branches of the economy. The actual conduct of the organization's affairs was entrusted to an executive Council, which was to meet "as necessary." Among its specific duties were the convening and drawing up of agendas of the congresses; the preparation of reports for submission to the congresses; the implementation of the congresses' decisions; the representation of the organization in governmental and public institutions; and the investigation of "measures for the development of the Association's activity, for the fullest possible unification of commercial-industrial representation and for the expansion of local institutions of industry and trade." (See full text in Appendix I.)

It was within the Council that the concentration of power over the affairs of the Association in the hands of a relatively small group of men was most clearly to be seen. This concentration was only slightly affected by the expansion that took place in both the size and the functions of the organization after 1906. Within the Council, membership was, again, in two categories, elected and appointed. As originally constituted, the Council was to include no more than thirty-six elected members, elected for terms of two years by the regular congresses from among the organization's full membership with a view to assuring representation for all geographic districts and branches of industry and trade. Half the members of this group were to leave office, or, more commonly in practice, to be reelected each year. In addition, one delegate was to be appointed by each of the full members that paid at least 500 rubles in dues and therefore had at least two votes.[5] In 1910, the charter was revised to provide for forty-eight elected members in the Council.[6] By 1914, the size of the Council had increased to include fifty-nine elected members and thirty-five "member-delegates."[7]

Large and unwieldy (although only twelve members were needed to constitute a quorum), the Council was primarily a policy-making and supervisory organ. In practice, responsibility for the day-to-day conduct of the Association's activities was entrusted to the Council's much smaller Committee and Presidium, the members of which were entitled, at the discretion of the Congresses, to receive compensation for their services. The Presidium consisted of the Chairman of the Council and the Vice-Chairmen, of whom there were three until 1910 and four thereafter, all chosen by the Council. The Committee, originally composed of three members, also chosen by the Council from among its own membership, was expanded to eight in 1907 and to ten in 1910. The Presidium, in particular, worked closely with the Association's permanent staff. The latter, despite the important place that it occupied in the affairs of the organization, received only the briefest attention in the charter, which noted almost incidentally that its director and his assistants were to be appointed, dismissed, and compensated at the discretion of the Council.

As early as the First Congress in 1906, the tendency toward the concentration of power in a few of the largest organizations elicited strong protests among the less influential groups. Consequently, the charter, as it was finally approved, included provisions designed to meet those objections and to protect the autonomy of individual organizations against a majority that might have "contrary interests."[8] Dissatisfaction with high membership dues and the inequality in voting rights led to some flexibility in admitting enterprises as consultative members and an increase in the number of full members that were permitted to appoint delegates to the Council.[9] When debating questions directly affecting particular industries or geographic regions, the Council was required to invite the full members most closely concerned to attend its sessions; and its decisions were valid only if a majority of those representatives were in agreement. In the case of the general congresses, such special interests had the right to assemble in preliminary conferences organized by the Council in order to discuss issues affecting their common interests. In any case, decisions of the congresses affecting particular industries or districts would be valid only if endorsed by the latters' representatives. Full members were also entitled to have reports and memoranda of their own included on the agendas of the congresses.

Despite these provisions, however, the trend toward the centralization of power within the Association caused dissatisfaction, and some of the revisions introduced in the charter in 1910 were designed to meet this criticism. Most important was the decision empowering the Council to appoint "correspondent members" to its own membership, with the right to a consultative vote, for terms of one year. This provision was deemed necessary not only because of the increase in the Association's membership and the growing diversity of its work, but also because of the desirability of establishing closer ties with the provinces.

> The number of elected members of the Council is generally not great; among them the number of members from the provinces is quite limited. In order to popularize the activity of the Council in the localities, to attract new members into it, and to enliven the relations of the Council with the provinces, it would be useful to introduce into the Council correspondent members, who should be appointed from among persons well known in local commercial-industrial circles and closely acquainted with the questions that interest them.[10]

In addition, the method of determining the dues of consultative members was changed to encourage the lagging admission of unincorporated enterprises. (It was pointed out that of the Association's 211 consultative members, no more than 20 were unincorporated.)

Under the charter, the Council had the right to invite to its meetings, with a consultative vote, organizations and enterprises not belonging to the

Association and "in general, all persons whose participation will be useful in the discussion of questions to be decided by the Council" (Article 20). This provision was utilized often. Study groups included persons drawn from governmental and "public" institutions, from the learned professions, and from such rival economic interests as agriculture and the railroads.

The growth of the Association of Industry and Trade and the changes that occurred in its membership are mirrored in the following figures.[11]

Year	Full Members	Consultative Members
1906 (October)	40	82
1907	48	100
1908 (March)	43	142
1909 (October)	44	211
1910	47	252
1911	51	256
1912	54	266
1913	59	277
1914 (December)	63	315
1917 (mid-year)	67	588
1917 (November)	65	- -

The forty full members enrolled at the time of the First Regular Congress included thirteen exchange committees (including the Moscow and Baku Committees and the Kharkov Coal and Iron Exchange Committee, but not the Petersburg Exchange Committee) and four committees of trade and manufacturing. Of the remaining twenty-three, all but two (Russian Insurance Association and the Association of Ship-Owners) were entirely or predominantly industrial.[12] All Russia's major industries and industrial regions were represented, although the cotton textile industry had representation only through the Moscow Exchange Committee and the Ivanovo-Voznesensk Committee of Trade and Manufacturing, while the southern coal mining industry was dependent for its representation on the Kharkov Exchange Committee, the Association of Southern Coal and Steel Producers having lagged in assuming membership. Since the leadership of the two latter organizations rested mainly in the same individual, Nikolai S. Avdakov, a vice-chairman of the new Association, the mine owners' delay was hardly a serious handicap. (Avdakov, chairman of the Kharkov Exchange Committee, had only recently resigned as chairman of the Southern Association in order to become its permanent representative in St. Petersburg.) After becoming a member, shortly after the First Congress, the Southern Association rapidly became perhaps the most influential organization within the Association.[13]

The decline in the number of the Association's full members in 1908 no doubt reflected uncertainty on the part of those that represented primarily commercial interests, particularly in view of the organization's increasingly clear tendency to develop as an organization representative mainly of industry, rather than of trade.[14] Of the Association's sixty-three full members in 1914, twenty-eight represented trade or finance as well as of industry.[15] The remaining thirty-five, entirely industrial in function, included the dominant groups within the Association: the Southern Association of Coal and Steel Producers, the Baku Petroleum Association, the Russian Society of Sugar Producers, and the Polish Coal and Iron Association. To the list of leading organizations should also be added the Moscow Exchange Committee, the Petersburg Society of Mill and Factory Owners, and, probably, the Russian Insurance Association. In 1910, these were the only organizations enrolled in the first three categories of the Association's membership.[16] Other primarily industrial members were the Kharkov Coal and Iron Exchange Committee; the associations of the mine owners of the Urals and of Poland; the metal-working factories of the northern and Baltic provinces; the iron, manganese, and gold and platinum producers; and the agricultural machinery, glass, flour, paper, lumber, brewing, distilling, and textile manufacturers. The latter group was represented in 1914 not only by the Moscow Exchange Committee and the Ivanovo-Voznesensk Committee of Trade and Manufacturing but also by the Russian Society of Linen Manufacturers, the Russian Society of Woolen Manufacturers, and the Russian Society of Cotton Textile Manufacturers.[17]

The extent to which the Association was dominated by large-scale industry (and, in some measure, perhaps, by the financial interests with which industry was closely associated) is revealed even more clearly in the data concerning its consultative membership. Its 315 consultative members in 1914 included 64 commercial and financial enterprises: 17 banks, including all the largest banks of Petersburg and Moscow; 17 insurance companies; 11 enterprises engaged in shipping and grain storage; and 19 miscellaneous, mainly unincorporated, commercial houses. The remaining 251 members were industrial, of which the largest groups were in mining and metallurgy (68), textiles (52), beer production (24), and sugar and other food products (20).[18] Several syndicates held consultative membership, among them Prodameta (iron and steel), Produgol (coal), Krovlia (roofing iron), and Truboprodazha (iron pipes). Also included were a few organizations for the defense of special group interests, such as the Russian Mutual Credit Union and the Association of

Russo-French Factories. Membership was overwhelmingly composed of incorporated enterprises, the unincorporated amounting to no more than twenty in 1909.[19]

Despite their lack of full voting powers, the influence of the consultative members of the Association would seem to have been considerable. Many of their delegates at the congresses also represented full members and hence possessed full voting rights. Financially, the consultative members were indispensable, since their dues provided some 60 percent of the income of the organization, which was almost entirely dependent on members' dues for its support.[20] Although the Association never claimed to represent financial interests, the substantial dues paid by the consultative members in banking and finance raise a question as to their role within the organization. It seems doubtful, however, that they exercised a truly independent influence. Among full members, finance was represented solely by the Russian Insurance Association. Moreover, the connection between banking and large-scale industry was so close that in numerous instances the same individuals occupied leading positions in both. While much has been made in the Soviet historical literature of the alleged domination of industry by financial interests, the relationship was not always clear. In Moscow at least, the predominant influence lay with industry.[21]

In contrast, the influence of trade within the Association was greater, but it was clearly diminishing. By 1911, it had become accepted practice, on the part of both the Association itself and outside observers, to refer to it as "the organ of united industry," or even as the "general staff" of industrial interests. By the beginning of the war, references to trade as an object of the Association's concern had become perfunctory indeed.[22] The few studies of Russian business organizations that appeared before 1914 confirmed its position as the representative of almost exclusively industrial interests.[23] This judgment has been generally accepted by historians, who have stressed not only the Association's role as "the central representative organ of industry"[24] but also its ties with monopolistic industrial and financial enterprises. Hence its appellation as "the central laboratory of syndicates" and "the true general staff of Russian industrial and banking monopolies."[25]

Yet there can also be no doubt that control over the Association's work rested with its executive organs. The Council itself, which counted among its membership nearly all the leading figures in the Russian business community as well as men prominent in public affairs,[26] held seventy or more plenary sessions during the twelve years of the Association's existence, fifty-two of them prior to the outbreak of the World War.

The number of its actual meetings was somewhat larger, but these occurred erratically. In general, it seems to have been most active during the first and last years, while the years immediately preceding the war were marked by a notable decline in activity. The Council met four times during the two and one half months in 1906 following the First Congress, twelve times in 1907, sixteen times in 1908, and thirteen times in 1909. In contrast, during the year between the Seventh and Eighth Congresses, it met only twice. The seventieth session of the council met in April 1917, so that its wartime meetings averaged six per year.

In many cases, Council meetings were poorly attended, often bringing together only a dozen or so of its members. Nevertheless, the Council, or the group that acted in its name, was unquestionably the principal authority in charge of the organization's affairs. It regularly reviewed the work of its permanent staff and of the commissions and conferences that met under its aegis; it managed the finances of the organization; and it maintained relations with the government and with other business organizations. The appointment of the Association's delegates to governmental and other meetings was also the Council's responsibility, as was the approval of the agendas for the annual congresses. In its consideration of reports to be submitted to the congresses, its concern was thorough and substantive. It also regularly heard and acted upon communications from members of the organization.[27]

Immediate supervision over the daily conduct of the Association's affairs rested not with the Council, however, but with its far more active Committee. Throughout the prewar years, the Committee met on an average of once a week, in theory at least, although with rather frequent lapses in practice. Its importance increased steadily during the first half of the Association's existence, as shown by the growing frequency of its meetings, which rose from an average of about two and one-half times per month during the first six months of the organization's existence to a peak of four and one-half times during the middle years, 1909-12. A decline to an average of three and one-half times a month during the last year before the war no doubt reflected the growing tendency of the Presidium or Bureau of the Council (consisting of its chairman and vice-chairmen) to assume some of the Committee's functions. After the outbreak of the war, however, the Committee met regularly three times a week.[28]

Of crucial importance, clearly, is the question of the composition of the Committee and Presidium of the Council. Together, they constituted a small and closely knit group. During the nine most active of the Association's twelve years, the chairmanship of the Council was occupied by one man, Avdakov, who assumed the office in March 1907, after the brief term of Timiriazev, and remained in the post until his death in September 1915. The roster of the vice-chairmen of the Council was also limited, consisting of only six men between 1908 and 1914. Two of these, Nobel (Baku oil and the Petersburg Society of Mill and Factory Owners) and Iasiukovich (chairman of the board of the largest firm in the southern iron and steel industry, and the principal founder of the syndicate Prodameta), served throughout the period. Belotsvetov, an insurance representative and one of the most active founders of the Association, resigned in 1908 because of the pressure of personal affairs and was replaced by Count Bobrinskii, leader of the sugar refiners, who served throughout the remainder of the period. Nikolai A. Iasiuninskii, representing the Moscow Exchange Committee and the Ivanovo-Voznesensk Committee of Trade and Manufacturing, served from 1910 until his death in 1912, when he was replaced by Zhukovskii. In addition, it should be noted that both the Kharkov Coal and Iron Exchange Committee and the Association of Southern Coal and Steel Producers had an additional delegate in Avdakov.

Between 1908 and 1914, a total of fourteen men served on the Committee of the Council. Of these, six served throughout the entire period, while a seventh, Zhukovskii, left the Committee only because of his election as one of the vice-chairmen of the Council. The interests represented by these "permanent" members were Baku oil (Nikolai N. Iznar); sugar refining (Nikolai V. Monakhov); Petersburg manufacturing (Boris A. Efron); Polish mining and metallurgy (Vladislav V. Zhukovskii); the Lodz Committee of Trade and Manufacturing (Faddei A. Novoveiskii); and the industry and trade of Riga (Konstantin A. fon-Giubbenet). Other organizations represented on the Committee were the Kharkov Coal and Iron Exchange Committee (Vladimir I. Arandarenko); the Association of Southern Coal and Steel Producers (Sergei A. Auerbakh); the metal industry of the northern and Baltic districts (Sergei A. Erdeli); manganese (Aleksandr A. Bublikov); the Consultative Bureau of Iron Producers (Magnus F. Norpe); the Kalashnikov Grain Exchange Committee in St. Petersburg (Vorobiev); the Ivanovo-Voznesensk Committee of Trade and Manufacturing (Genrikh G. Vissendorf); the Moscow Merchant Society; and the Kostroma Committee of Trade and Manufacturing (Sergei S. Novoselov).

During its early years (1907-9), when the Association was plagued with financial difficulties, its operating deficits were overcome only through generous contributions by its principal members. It is probably no exaggeration to say that the organization owed, if not its survival, at least its ability to function on a broad and steadily expanding basis to the assistance that it received, in particular, from the southern mine owners, the Baku oil industrialists, and the sugar refiners.[29]

The initial budget of 100,000 rubles drawn up by the Provisional Council was early recognized as unrealistic, and expenditures during 1907 were held at 81,200 rubles. The expansion of both membership and the activity of the Association during the following years was reflected in the increase of its budget to 100,000 in 1908 and 129,000 in 1909. Despite its difficulties, the Council in its annual reports to the congresses justified its operating losses on the grounds that "the intensive work of the Council of the Association on all questions, without exception, that concern the industry and trade of the country is sufficient to explain our deficits." The Council warned the Fourth Congress that the organization "cannot be restricted to the exact limits of budgetary estimates."[30] Subject to these qualifications, it submitted a budget of 110,000, with an anticipated surplus of 10,000, for 1910. The year proved to be the turning point in the Association's financial affairs, as its revenues rose to 124,150 rubles from dues alone, plus an additional 14,700 from gifts and other sources, leaving for the first time a surplus of 12,458 rubles.[31] In view of its new financial solvency and prospects for increasing revenues in the future, the Fifth Congress voted to incorporate the budget of the Council's journal, Industry and Trade, which had also been operating with a sizable deficit, into the Council's budget for 1911, which estimated an income of 172,550 rubles and expenditures of 169,830.[32] Early in 1912, Industry and Trade reported that "the Association is now securely established on a sound financial basis; in fact, its budget has more than tripled since 1906."[33]

From the beginning, the Association pursued three principal objectives; to influence governmental economic policies through direct contact with official agencies and with the legislature; to educate public opinion toward a more sympathetic understanding both of the national economy and of the specific problems confronting industry and trade; and to promote the organization of business interests. In attempting to carry out these tasks, the Council worked through numerous representative commissions and conferences, organized under the Council, and through its permanent professional staff or Secretariat. Although the commissions undoubtedly played a crucial role in the formation and elaboration of the Association's policies, a substantial amount of initiative in the development of policy also emanated from the staff, or "third element."

The Association's commissions and conferences customarily were headed by a member of the Council or its Committee or Presidium and occasionally by the chief of one of the sections into which the Secretariat was divided. Their membership, depending on the nature of the questions under consideration, consisted of delegates from interested members of the Association, from economic interests outside the Association, and from governmental ministries, local government agencies, and the legislature. Technical specialists and persons drawn from academic and political circles were also often invited to participate. An indication of the vigor with which the new Association began its work is to be found in the fact that a total of sixty-eight such meetings were held during the first six months of its activity. From then until the outbreak of the war, an average of twelve or more such meetings were held each month, and an average of fifteen were held during the final year.[34] About one-third of this number consisted of meetings of the Council's three standing commissions, on railroads, railroad rates, and legal and tax questions. In addition, thirty-five or more special conferences and commissions, some of which met year after year, were usually active at any one time. Their work encompassed a wide variety of substantive problems, ranging from the most technical (the use of spirits in perfume production, for example) to broad issues of governmental economic policy; business, labor, and social legislation; and the development of the economy as a whole.

Although much, and probably most, of the work of the Council's study groups originated in instructions issued by the congresses or by the Council itself, often acting on requests by members of the Association, a substantial proportion of their projects arose out of governmental initiatives, in response either to an official request for information and opinions or to a governmental decision to undertake an investigation of its own on a given question. In the latter case, the Association was normally invited, with other business organizations, to send delegates to participate in governmental meetings. The Council would then establish a parallel conference of its own in order to enable the business community to develop a unified position in the official body. Customarily, the Council's conference would canvas the opinion of all the Association's members before arriving at its conclusions. In this way, the Association developed a close working relationship with certain governmental agencies, especially the ministries of trade and industry, finance, and communication.[35] As a result, Avdakov was able to assure the Eighth Congress that "not a single question was raised within the Ministry of Trade and Industry on which the opinion of our organization was not asked," although he also noted that the Association was "sometimes not in agreement with the opinion of the Ministry."[36] Inasmuch as these procedures included a review of all prospective legislation submitted by the ministries to the legislature, the Association had, in some measure at least, realized its ambition to serve as a "pre-parliament" on the German pattern.[37]

Such procedures did not, however, tell the whole story of the Association's relationship with the government. From its commissions, conferences, and staff emanated a stream of reports, notes, and memoranda, copies of which were dispatched to appropriate governmental agencies and to the legislature. Ministers, including the Chairman of the Council of Ministers, and other high officials were also frequent recipients of the Association's petitions. In urgent cases, these petitions were presented in person by delegations composed of the Council's most prominent members. In critical moments, petitions from the Association reached the Emperor himself through the intermediation of government officials. In addition, the Association, along with other business organizations, enjoyed permanent representation on the governing boards of a number of official and semiofficial agencies concerned with transportation, taxation, and finance. In particular, its representatives regularly attended the General Rate Congresses of the Russian Railroads, the congresses on the regulation of freight shipments, the Council of the All-Russian Export Chamber, the Council of the Volunteer Fleet, and the Council on Commercial Navigation.

Reference has already been made to the presence of ministers and other high officials at the regular congresses of the Association. The Association also benefited from the close personal ties that existed between the governmental bureaucracy and some of its own leaders. Two members of its Council, for example, Timiriazev and Fedorov, served as ministers of trade and industry, while a third, Bark, succeeded Kokovtsov as minister of finance. Arandarenko resigned from the Committee of the Council in 1912 to take the post of director of the Mining Department in the Ministry of Trade and Industry; and Kutler, the last chairman of the Association, had once been deputy chief of the Main Administration of Land Tenure and Agriculture.

In addition, the Association maintained its own direct ties with the legislature, although the observation of Sir Bernard Pares that its annual congresses "worked hand in hand" with the State Duma would seem to be greatly exaggerated.[38] In its relations with the legislature the Association operated as a pressure group, submitting materials to its committees and inviting legislators to attend its own meetings. Its main avenue of influence lay, however, through those of its members who sat in either the Duma or the State Council. From 1906 to 1914, at least a dozen of the most prominent members of the Association's Council were also members of the State Council, usually as elected representatives of industry or trade. Among them were Avdakov, Timiriazev, Krestovnikov, Iasiuninskii, P. O. and L. O. Gukasov, Glezmer, M. N. Tripolitov, Rotvand, fon-

Ditmar, Prince Aleksandr D. Obolenskii, and Count Bobrinskii (who represented agriculture). Members of the Council who sat in the Third and Fourth Dumas included Kutler, Zhukovskii, Count Bobrinskii, Bublikov, Konovalov, G. G. Lerkhe (chairman of the Finance Committee of the Third Duma), and Aleksandr I. Guchkov (leader of the Octobrists and President of the Third Duma). The activity of the Association's legislative representatives was coordinated through its Commercial-Industrial Group of Members of the State Duma and State Council, which met regularly, probably weekly, in its building when the legislature was in session.

Behind the Association's commissions and conferences, and to some extent paralleling and supplementing them, stood the Secretariat, or permanent staff of the Council, which consisted of perhaps one hundred clerical and professional employees, including economists, statisticians, and lawyers.[39] Its work was organized under four basic sections--railroad, commercial-industrial, legal, and statistical; in 1912 a fifth section on the work of the legislature was added.[40] The Secretariat's library, one of the best in St. Petersburg as early as 1909, served not only the staff and members of the Association but also governmental institutions and private persons.[41]

The Secretariat had multiple functions. It bore primary responsibility for providing the Council and its study groups with the information that they required. It also assisted them in drawing up their reports, petitions, and other documents. Its other duties included answering queries not only from members but also from the government, private persons, foreign consulates, and business interests in other countries. It assisted the government and business groups in holding industrial exhibitions, both in Russia and abroad. It organized group congresses of smaller industries to consider their special problems and to promote their organization. On occasion, it dispatched members of its staff to provincial industrial centers to win support for the Association's policies. The Secretariat also assisted the Council in maintaining contacts with an impressive number of other business organizations, both in Russia and in other countries, and it frequently sent delegations to their meetings. It maintained particularly close ties with the Association of Trade and Agriculture. Greeting the Second Congress of that organization on behalf of his own Association, Volskii decried the current tendency to view the two groups as competitors. In Russia, he pointed out, there was more than enough work for both organizations.[42] In subsequent years, they developed common policies toward the railroads and foreign trade.

The Secretariat also furthered the Council's policy of promoting foreign trade and a cooperative relationship with related organizations in other countries.[43] It helped to found and develop the work of the Anglo-Russian and Italo-Russian Chambers of Commerce, placing its auditorium and other facilities at their disposal. The Association joined the International Association of Chambers of Commerce and Commercial-Industrial Organizations and sent its delegates to its congresses. Its accredited representatives also attended the international conference in The Hague in 1908 on the establishment of uniform standards of currency law, international congresses on refrigeration, and an international congress for combatting the adulteration of food products. Highly unusual, given its efforts to remain apolitical, was its decision to send a delegation, consisting of Avdakov and Count Bobrinskii, to an assembly held in Prague in 1908 on the question of Slavic unity.[44]

The most important aspect of the Secretariat's work was substantive, however. Especially during the early years, under the guidance of its energetic, if volatile, director, Volskii, it initiated numerous projects and channels of inquiry. Undoubtedly Gushka exaggerated in asserting that the Association and the Association of Trade and Agriculture "consider the entire sphere of economic and socio-political life as their own domain."[45] The Association, as we have seen, was created as a strictly nonpolitical organization, and it frequently reiterated its refusal to discuss political issues. Yet the passing of the years did, in fact, reveal a tendency on its part to recognize the inescapable connection, under Russian conditions at least, of economics and politics and to consider the former from what was increasingly a semipolitical point of view.

Because of the Association's preoccupation with the broad issues of Russia's national development, the statistical section became the most active group in the Secretariat. Abundant evidence testifies to the Council's urgent and continuing interest in expanding and improving the limited data that were available on the state of the Russian economy. Although its use of these data was motivated at times by partisan concerns, such as the desire to demonstrate the inadequacy of corporate profits or the excessive tax burden borne by industry, the Council also recognized the fruitlessness of any effort to regulate and develop the economy in the absence of a solid factual foundation.[46]

Appendix III

Congresses of the Association

Superficially, it might seem that the Association bequeathed to historians an abundance of material concerning its development and activities. These include its membership rolls, the reports of its congresses and its Council, records of its finances, to say nothing of its fortnightly journal and its many other publications. Nevertheless, precisely how the Association functioned as an organization remains elusive. Whose were actually the dominant voices in this "leviathan of industrial organizations"?[1] Even among the best informed contemporary observers and persons who were once active in the Association, there is little agreement on the answers to these questions.[2] According to a critical representative of Odessa industry at the Fourth Congress, power within the Association remained centered within a small, stable oligarchy of individual leaders who controlled both the Council of the Association and its most important member organizations.[3] Gushka went still further, suggesting that the dominant voice within the Association belonged not to the industrialists themselves but to the "third element," the "organization men" who dominated its Council as well as its permanent professional staff.[4]

Unfortunately, the validity of these various assessments is only dimly illuminated by the Association's published records. During the twelve years of its existence, nine regular congresses were convened, the last in May 1915. In addition, one Special Congress was held, in November 1911, and in June 1917 a large-scale Conference virtually amounted to a congress. The Association's charter provided also for the convening of "group" congresses of particular industries or economic interests, and several of these met under its auspices. From the organization's founding until 1915, with the notable exception of 1910, regular congresses met for three or four days each year. Both the circumstances surrounding the repeated postponement of the Fifth Congress, which was originally scheduled for late October 1910 but finally met in March 1911, and other evidence suggest that the Association faced at that time a crisis in its internal affairs and, perhaps, in its relationship with the government.[5]

Although the Association's charter provided that its congresses should meet in Petersburg, Moscow or other cities, all were held in Petersburg except the second, which met in Moscow. In general, they were rather large and lively occasions,[6] although the lack of variety in their presiding officers and in some of their procedures might seem to belie this impression. The chairmanship of the ten congresses that took place between 1906 and 1915 was shared (with one partial exception) by only two men: Grigorii A. Krestovnikov, president of the Moscow Exchange Committee, and Nikolai S. Avdakov, chairman of the Council of the Association from 1907 until his death in 1915 and a delegate from both the southern mine owners and the Kharkov Coal and Iron Exchange Committee. Both were unfailingly elected by a unanimous vote.[7] Only slightly more diversity was shown in the lists of vice-chairmen, who also normally received the unanimous vote of the congresses. Among them certain names appeared with astonishing regularity, notably those of Count A. A. Bobrinskii, chairman of the sugar refiners' organization; Emanuil L. Nobel, representing the Petersburg Society of Mill and Factory Owners and the Baku oil industrialists; and Ignatii I. Iasiukovich of the southern mine owners. During the last years before the war, vice-chairmen included Vladislav V. Zhukovskii of the Polish Coal and Iron Association; Nikolai N. Iznar of the Baku oil producers; and Pavel P. Riabushinskii, Krestovnikov's successor in 1914 as president of the Moscow Exchange Committee and a prominent textile manufacturer, financier, publisher, and political liberal.

The growth in the size and activities of the Association was clearly mirrored in the changing character of its congresses. The Second Congress, actually the first working congress, met in May 1907. This relatively small and quiet affair was attended by 143 persons, including five representatives of three government agencies (the ministries of communication and of trade and industry and the Chief Administration of Land Tenure and Agriculture); seventy-seven representatives of thirty-six full members; twenty-nine delegates from twenty consultative members; seven members of the Council of the Association; and twenty-five guests. Among the full members, the Moscow Exchange Society was most heavily represented, with eight delegates. The Baku oil industrialists followed, with six; and the sugar refiners, the southern mine owners, the Kostroma and Ivanovo-Voznesensk Committees of Trade and Manufacturing, and the Moscow Branch of the Council of Trade and Manufacturing sent four each.

The Third Congress, which met in March 1908, was significantly larger and livelier. Its participants numbered more than 400, including fourteen representatives of five governmental agencies (the ministries of finance, trade and industry, internal affairs, agriculture, and state control); 125 representatives of thirty-five full members; ninety delegates from fifty-three consultative members; and fifty-one guests. The number of full members sending delegates actually declined, despite an increase in the total membership in this category, but their own evaluation of the importance of the occasion, as indicated by the size of their delegations, shifted notably. The Moscow Exchange Society remained in the front rank but shared its position with the southern mine owners and the Russian Insurance Association, all of which sent ten delegates each. Next in size was the six-man delegation of the Petersburg Society of Mill and Factory Owners.

Twenty months later, in November 1909, the Fourth Congress reportedly attracted more than 500 persons. Twenty-nine government officials attended, including the ministers of finance and trade and industry and three deputy ministers. The ministries represented included communication, agriculture, internal affairs, war, navy, justice, and state control. In addition, twenty members of the State Council and State Duma, mostly businessmen active in the Association, were present. Thirty-seven full members were represented by 129 men, while 93 consultative members sent 144 delegates. At the Special and Sixth Congresses, held in November 1911 and May 1912, respectively, full members sending delegates numbered forty-five and forty-two, respectively The Seventh and Eighth Congresses, in May 1913 and May 1914, respectively, included representatives from fifty-three full members. Representation among full members thus fluctuated between 81 and 90 percent of the total full membership and showed some increase with the advancing years. If the Fourth Congress may be taken as typical, it appears that only the smallest or least industrial of the member organizations failed to send delegates.[8] In contrast, representation among the consultative members rose from about 20 percent in 1907 to a high of 44 percent in 1909, declining thereafter to 29 percent in 1912 and 33 percent in 1914.

Participation in the congresses of the Association was not limited to its own members and high government officials. The guest lists included a broad sampling of economic interests.[9] Officers of the Association of Trade and Agriculture were regularly included, as were delegates from other economic organizations not belonging to the Association of Industry and Trade. Lesser governmental officials, engineers, technical specialists, members of the State Duma and State Council concerned with industry and trade, and occasionally members of local governmental institutions received invitations. Among the guests figured representatives of economic interests that were traditionally less than amicable toward industry, such as agriculture and the railroads. As the years passed, a noteworthy diversity in political and intellectual outlook appeared at the congresses.

During the later years, especially, the Congresses attracted members of the academic community and the State Duma who were rarely sympathetic toward the Association's activities. Such critics of organized industry, for example, as the distinguished Legal Marxist economist, Professor Mikhail I. Tugan-Baranovskii, and the Kadet leaders, A. I. Shingarev and Petr B. Struve, participated at the last congresses. Far more sympathetic, but nonetheless often outspokenly critical, was Count Sergei Iu. Witte, also a perennial guest. The presence of such frequently dissident but respected voices contributed to the growing interest of the debates and, no doubt, to the importance with which the congresses were viewed in the press. Undoubtedly, they reflected a broadening both of the Association's outlook and of its influence among the educated public during the second half of its organizational lifetime.

The proceedings of the congresses followed an established sequence. After the unanimous election of the chairman and vice-chairmen (the latter being the nominees of the newly elected chairman) came speeches of welcome by the new chairman, by Avdakov (if he were not presiding over the gathering), by the highest ranking representatives of the government, and, perhaps, by prominent members of the Association's Council. A reading of congratulatory telegrams from still more government officials and prominent persons outside the Association concluded the formalities. The congresses, with the outstanding exception of the Ninth, adhered strictly to the agendas prepared by the Council and its staff. (The Ninth Congress, meeting in May 1915 under the strain imposed by the increasingly precarious military position, set the agenda completely aside in order to devote itself entirely to issues of current politics and the prosecution of the war effort.) Major items on the agenda included the presentation and discussion of a number of reports on both administrative and substantive questions. Some reports were presented in the name of the Council itself, while others were submitted by study groups working under the Council, by the director or a member of the Council's staff, or by member organizations.[10] The Congresses generally concluded after the election of members to the Council and to the Audit Commission and the offering of a brief farewell address by the chairman. In the case of the Fourth and Fifth congresses, at least, the working sessions were followed by "gala" banquets in one of the restaurants of St. Petersburg.[11]

In their methods of voting, the congresses followed procedures that lent substance to charges of oligarchic control. The complement of full members was often not in attendance, and sometimes votes could not be taken for lack of a quorum. Moreover, unanimous votes occurred in an astonishing percentage of cases, not only in the election of officers but also in the adoption of substantive resolutions establishing the Association's position on questions of policy. Yet the emphasis on unanimity may have been evidence not so much of an absence of divergent opinions as of traditional Russian patterns of behavior, in which the initial airing of differences was followed, whenever possible, by a unanimous decision. In fact, disagreements, sometimes sharp and bitter, often punctuated the sessions. The rejection, in whole or in part, of the recommendations submitted by the Council or by such prominent leaders as Volskii and Zhukovskii was not unusual.[12] In the election of members of the Council, moreover, the leadership made no attempt to arrange a unanimous vote. In fact, there seems little doubt that, despite the strong and generally predominant leadership exercised by the Council and its staff, the congresses retained an effective and often decisive voice in the determination of the Association's policies.

Appendix IV

Sources for the Study of the Association

I. Publications of the Association

The Bibliography includes only those publications of the Association of Industry and Trade that the author located and used. A complete list of the publications of the Association prior to January 15, 1912 appears in the issue of Industry and Trade for that date.[1]

The statistical section's major continuing projects, many of which were published in the Council's journal, Industry and Trade, contained data on current market conditions; foreign trade; freight shipments; the money, stock, and bond markets; the financial position of banks and other business and financial corporations; and the cost of industrial accidents. Toward the end of the prewar period, it undertook an investigation of the business cycle in Russia in cooperation with the editors of the Ministry of Finance's journal, The Herald of Finance. In 1912, 1913, and 1914, it published its Statistical Annual (Statisticheskii ezhegodnik) on the economy of the Empire. Unfortunately, the implementation of these useful projects was severely handicapped by budgetary limitations.[2]

The Council's many publications, remarkable for both their number and diversity, disseminated its views among governmental circles and the public at large.[3] When the Second Congress convened in May 1907, the Council already listed fifty-nine substantial reports and other publications, including two series of Materials (Materialy) on the labor and railroad questions.[4] By January 1912, the list of the Council's publications had grown to 221 items.[5] Among the many separate reports published by the Association, one stood out as representing the culmination of its long-standing effort to produce a comprehensive economic program for Russia: the impressive report to the Ninth Congress, On Measures for the Development of the Productive Forces of Russia.[6]

Particularly noteworthy among the Council's serial publications were, in addition to its Statistical Annual, its directory of Manufacturing Enterprises of the Russian Empire (Fabrichno-zavodskie predpriiatiia Rossiiskoi Imperii), issued in 1909 and 1914; its surveys of the work of the legislature during the period of the Third Duma[7] and in 1913; and its Materials on the Revision of Trade Agreements (Materialy po peresmotru torgovykh dogovorov), issued jointly with the Association of Trade and Agriculture.[8] In April 1917, the Council began publication of a semi-weekly newspaper, the News of the Council of the Association of Industry and Trade (Izvestiia Soveta S"ezdov predstavitelei promyshlennosti i torgovli), which was to be sent free to members of the organization and to subscribers to Industry and Trade. It appeared to have come out less often, however, and to have been a rather short-lived venture.

By far the most important of the Council's continuing publications was its journal, Industry and Trade (Promyshlennost' i torgovlia), which made its first appearance on January 1, 1908, under the editorship of Adolf A. Volskii. Although its function, as defined by the Second Congress in May 1907, was limited, for financial reasons, to acquainting the Association's members and other interested persons with the work of the organization,[9] it quickly assumed a broader role under Volskii's energetic direction. Indeed, in its first issue, the new journal assured its readers:

> Our young organization is beginning the publication of its own printed organ. The year's activity of the Association of Industry and Trade has shown that without the printed word it is impossible to conduct a proper defense of the interests of domestic industry and trade. Our journal, consequently, is called to serve for the good of Russian industrial-commercial work. . . . We shall strive to obtain for our industry and trade that honorable position in the eyes of Russian society that this branch of the people's work occupies in the eyes of cultured humanity everywhere else in the world. Let us permit ourselves to hope that both our contemporary press and, with its cultured mediation, our public at large, will assist us. We begin our new task with faith in the creativeness of our efforts.[10]

Within a year, the journal had shifted its sights well beyond the defense of class interests and presented itself to the public as

> a publication devoted to questions of industry and trade, of practical economics, of economic and financial policy, and also to the defense of the interests not only of the commercial-industrial class but of the entire economic development of Russia.[11]

Industry and Trade suffered from serious financial difficulties during the early years, which necessitated repeated appeals to the Association's membership for assistance and encountered frequent criticism from both the right and left wings of Russian politics. Lenin, for example, held the journal up to ridicule, stressing its weighty and allegedly ungrammatical articles. Still, the journal prospered.[12] Its circulation of about 3,000 copies was not limited to the Russian Empire but included business groups in other countries, and, on the request of the Ministry of Foreign Affairs, all Russian consulates abroad.[13] Recognized as "the official voice of the united bourgeoisie," it was regularly read by high government officials and members of the legislature.[14] Early in 1912, the Association saw fit to announce that "in the comparatively short time" since its first appearance, Industry and Trade had won recognition as "Russia's leading economic and commercial review."[15] Originally a semimonthly publication, the journal became a weekly on August 1, 1915. Its last issue appeared on December 23, 1917.

During the decade of its publication, Industry and Trade underwent a significant expansion and some change in its character. From the beginning, each issue included a lead editorial article; several factual articles; and a variety of statistical and informational surveys on such questions as the activities of other business organizations, the State Duma, the State Council, the Council of Ministers, and other governmental agencies; and overviews of economic and business legislation, administrative regulations, and international economic trends.[16] Beginning in August 1915, Industry and Trade served for a time as the organ of the Central War Industries Committee, regularly publishing information on the work both of the central and local committees. It also added to its regular contents a section on the mobilization of industry and an Information Section. The Association's increasing embroilment with the government during the war years was evident, however, in the mounting number of censored blank spaces that marred its pages.

Well before the outbreak of the war, occasional controversial articles, by persons within and outside the business community, began to appear in Industry and Trade. Usually such articles bore appended footnotes in which the editor disclaimed all responsibility for the views expressed. Toward the end of 1915, the range, the liveliness, and the liberalism of the journal's contents increased notably in response, no doubt, to changes in the leadership of the organization at that time. During the last two years of the publication's existence, contributions by persons active in both academic and political circles frequently appeared in its pages without editorial disclaimers. Among these contributors were such well-known figures as Petr B. Struve, A. I. Rafalovich, and A. V. Rodionov, as well as Professors Mikhail V. Bernatskii, Iosif M. Kulisher, Mikhail I. Fridman, and Mikhail I. Tugan-Baranovskii.[17] On the eve of the February Revolution of 1917, the Association's new liberalism was also evident in its decision to publish, over the protests of one of its most powerful members, a collection of articles on financial and economic questions (Finansovo-ekonomicheskii sbornik) with complete "freedom of opinion" for its wide range of authors.[18]

II. Other Publications and Materials

The literature, both Soviet and prerevolutionary, on the economic development of Russia during the later nineteenth and early twentieth centuries is quantitatively substantial. Its usefulness, however, is limited both by the inadequacies of its factual data and by the heavy imprint of the political and ideological pressures. An outstanding exception, in the latter respect especially, is the still valuable work of Margaret Miller, The Economic Development of Russia, 1905-1914, first published in 1926 and reissued in a second edition in 1967. More recently, Haumann (with an exhaustive bibliography of the secondary literature to 1980), Gregory, Gatrell, and Davies have added useful new data and interpretations. Unfortunately, the analyses of economic cycles from 1870 onward by the early Soviet statistician Sergei A. Pervushin[19] have been ignored.

The contributions made to this general literature by Soviet historians have tended to concentrate on a relatively small number of topics, in particular industrial monopoly, banking, and the role of foreign capital in Russian industry. Those of Ananich, Bovykin, Bokhanov, Shepelev, and Solovieva are especially valuable. However, Soviet scholars tended to neglect other aspects of the Russian economy and the impact of governmental policies on economic conditions.

In contrast to the large number of works devoted to the broad subject of Russian economic development, the literature concerning business organizations for "representative" purposes--as distinct from syndicates, trusts, and other organizations having primarily economic functions--has been remarkable for its paucity. Although a large number of such organizations existed and many of them published journals and other materials,[20] their reluctance to disclose information concerning their own activities limited the usefulness of their publications and was a serious handicap to those few prerevolutionary investigators who sought to compile data about their work. The effect was apparent, for example, in the studies based on surveys undertaken in 1910 by the Imperial Russian

Technical Society, compiled by A. Gushka, and by the Ministry of Trade and Industry at about the same time.[21] Evidently, moreover, only a relatively small portion of the published material survived the upheaval of 1917 and found its way into the state archives of the Soviet Union.[22]

Until recently, prerevolutionary businessmen in Russia attracted little attention from western historians, with the noteworthy exception of Professor Roger Portal in France. Carl A. Goldberg's dissertation on the Association (1974) remains unpublished. Organized topically, it contains separate chapters devoted to the Association's efforts to influence state policy on the labor question, monopolies, tax reform, zemstvos, tariff protection, railroads, the Jewish question, anti-pollution legislation, and chambers of commerce and industry. The most ambitious studies of the Russian commercial-industrial elite, such as those of Haumann, Hogan, Joffe, Kirchner, McCaffray, McDaniel, McKay, Owen, Pietrzak-Pawłowska, Rieber, and Ruckman, did not analyze the activities of the Association of Industry and Trade in detail.

Perhaps even more heavily than in the case of Russia's general economic development, the historical investigation of its business organizations in Russian and Soviet scholarship has been influenced by political considerations. Much of the output of Russian historians directly reflected ideological preconceptions. Before 1917, the work of Spasskii, Lure and, in some measure, Tugan-Baranovskii, was relatively free of tendentiousness. Lure offered particularly useful information, a result, no doubt, of the advantages that he enjoyed as a member of the staff of the Association of Industry and Trade. The principal Marxist contributor to the prerevolutionary literature was the Menshevik historian Osip A. Kogan, who wrote under the pseudonyms A. Ermanskii, Osip A. Ermanskii, and A. Gushka. His work was bitterly denounced by Lenin in an article that set the guidelines for the subsequent treatment of the subject by Soviet historians.[23]

Two major studies by Pavel A. Berlin and S. E. Sef in the 1920s were followed only in 1939 by Evgenii D. Chermenskii's work on the bourgeoisie during the revolution of 1905. (Chermenskii's second edition appeared in 1970.) A still longer interval preceded the appearance in 1959 of an article by Ia. I. Livshin, who called attention to the neglect of the industrial middle class in Soviet scholarship.[24] This article initiated a period of more active interest among historians in the Soviet Union. Although Livshin's book, which appeared two years later and included his earlier article, dealt primarily with the question of monopolies, it also offered much useful information on the representative organizations of the prerevolutionary business community. Valuable contributions were also made by the prolific historian of prerevolutionary banking, Iosif F. Gindin, and by Pavel V. Volobuev, who specialized in the period of the Provisional Government. It is regrettable, however, that their frequent references to archival materials were invariably cited in terms of the archive's numerical system of classification, a practice that, unless supported by additional explanatory material, left both the date and the title of the source to the imagination of the reader.

Soviet scholarly studies of business organizations tended to be short and uninformative. Major exceptions were the meticulous books and articles by the St. Petersburg archivist and historian Leonid E. Shepelev, whose wife, Galina A. Ippolitova, also worked as an archivist at the Central State Historical Archive. Shepelev's book on corporations provided the best Soviet account of corporate law and statistics, and his two volumes on business-government relations, published in 1981 and 1987, reviewed of a wide variety of issues and contained many verbatim quotations from archival documents.

Curiously enough, the business elite of one of the least developed regions of the Russian Empire, Siberia, received unusually competent analysis at the hands of assiduous historians there, especially the late G. Kh. Rabinovich and his students at the University of Tomsk, notably Iia G. Mosina.[25] The historiography of the business elite in Poland is also relatively rich. For example, until the era of perestroika there existed in the USSR no counterpart of the irregular Polish periodical Dzieje burżuazii w Polsce: Studia i materiały, edited by Ryszard Kołodziejczyk, or the fine study of the Polish Coal and Iron Association by Irena Pietrzak-Pawłowska. A leader of Polish industry after World War I, Andrzej Wierzbicki, left an informative memoir that described his early career as a technical expert in the Association of Industry and Trade, but its publication was delayed until the Khrushchev era.[26]

Among the most important memoirs by members of the Association are those of Aleksandr A. Bublikov, who represented railroad companies and manganese producers; Sergei I. Chetverikov, the liberal Moscow manufacturer; and V. A. Auerbakh, who analyzed the social composition of competing groups in the Russian Revolution. Unfortunately, the obscurity of these sources, published in exile in New York, Berlin, and Prague, respectively, has prevented historians from using them to full advantage.[27] Except for Charles A. Ruud's biography of the publisher Ivan D. Sytin, who expressed hostility to the Association of Industry and Trade, and Robert W. Tolf's monograph on the Nobel family, in which Emanuil L. Nobel figured prominently, there exists no biographical literature on the prerevolutionary Russian business elite in the form of published books. The memoir of the mining engineer Aleksandr I. Fenin, admirably edited by Susan P. McCaffray, offers much valuable material, but like all memoirs it is necessarily subjective. Without comprehensive biographies of Russian business leaders, questions of motivation and political orientation remain obscure, even for such major figures as Avdakov, Krestovnikov, Volskii, and Zhukovskii.

In 1970, Nauka press in Leningrad advertised a forthcoming monograph by Iakov S. Rozenfeld, The Big Bourgeoisie of Russia and its Political Development (Krupnaia burzhuaziia Rossii i ee politicheskoe razvitie), which examined the political activities of the Association of Industry and Trade, characterized by the press as "the central 'general staff' of the Russian monopolies." The book was scheduled for publication in 5,000 copies just before the fifth international congress on economic history, held in Leningrad in August 1970. However, the book was not published and no reference to it has since appeared in the scholarly literature. As an employee of the Association from 1908 to 1917, Rozenfeld had an intimate knowledge of the organization and its leaders. On the basis of interviews with Rozenfeld in 1971-2, Goldberg included in his dissertation many useful observations by the eyewitness. All in all, however, the disappearance of Rozenfeld's manuscript represented a serious loss to historical scholarship.[28]

The activities of the leaders of the Association in emigration after the Russian Revolution yet to receive scholarly attention.[29]

Among the works of a general nature listed in the Bibliography are selections from the heterogeneous literature that is available. Included are only those works that pertained directly to this study.

Notes

These notes contain abbreviations for the names of two newspapers: P i T for Promyshlennost' i Torgovlia and T-p G for Torgovo-promyshlennaia gazeta.

Foreword

1. See the recent monographs and collections of articles by Davies (ed.), Gatrell, and Gregory.

2. See studies by Amburger, Ananich, Carstensen, Fursenko, Girault, Diakin, Diakonova, Henriksson, Kirchner, McKay, Owen, Ruckman, Ruud, Shepelev, and Tolf. Three important collections of essays are those edited by Guroff and Carstensen; Clowes, Kassow, and West; and Balzer.

3. See works by Buranov, Diakin, Hartl, Haumann, Hogan, Joffe, King, McCaffray, McKay, Owen, Pietrzak-Pawłowska, Rieber, Ruckman, Shepelev, Siegelbaum, and West.

4. See the remarks on Goldberg's dissertation and the manuscript of Iakov S. Rozenfeld in Appendix IV.

Chapter 1

1. See the works discussed in Appendix IV.

2. Seton-Watson, Decline, 118-19.

3. Lure, Organizatsiia, 104; Chermenskii, Burzhuaziia, 18. (All references to Chermenskii, Burzhuaziia, are to the first edition.)

4. Berlin, Burzhuaziia, 134-5, 164-6; Von Laue, "Count Witte," 25-46.

5. Quoted in Berlin, Burzhuaziia, 167.

6. Quoted in Berlin, Burzhuaziia, 134-45, 165.

7. With much justification the Menshevik historian Dan, "Ocherk," 102, described the activities of industry's representative organizations as follows:

> Unconnected among themselves, not having succeeded in developing a single, "central" line of conduct which, by smoothing the sharp corners of the particular

> interests of the separate groups, would harmonize their economic interests, these organizations load the government with contradictory petitions, predominantly in the field of economic policy--questions of the tariff, taxation, credit, and railroad rates. Questions of general policy enter into their outlook only spasmodically and almost exclusively to the extent that they touch directly on the "needs" that command their attention.

See also Owen, "Impediments."

8. See, for example, Volskii, Sily, 1-2.

9. Quoted in Ermanskii, "Do 1905," 59, and in Berlin, Burzhuaziia, 167. On tutelage (opeka) in tsarist corporate law, see Owen, Corporation, ch. 4.

10. Ermanskii, "Do 1905," 317-18; also Berlin, Burzhuaziia, 166-7.

11. Quoted in Chermenskii, Burzhuaziia, 90. Significantly, the industrialists who were involved in this discussion voted to retain the existing procedures, whereby special governmental permission was required for the convening of congresses, and the chairmen were appointed by the appropriate ministry. For different reasons than those advanced by Kovalevskii, no doubt, a report of the Ministry of Finance issued in 1905 declared that the representative organizations of industry and trade were poorly adapted to the needs of their members and were not viable. Chermenskii, Burzhuaziia, 18.

12. Quoted in Reikhardt, "Gruppirovki," 35.

13. Volskii, Predstavitel'stvo, 14. This position was supported by the Soviet historian Gindin: "Before the revolution of 1905-7, stable forms of influence of the bourgeoisie on governmental policy had not yet been developed. The tsarist bureaucracy clearly preferred non-official communication with prominent representatives of big capital." Gindin, "Burzhuaziia," 74. Shepelev, Tsarizm . . . XIX veka, 216, reached the same conclusion: that at the end of the nineteenth century, Russian business leaders generally resented the lack of vigorous representative organs, such as chambers of commerce and industry, that existed in the West.

14. Von Laue, Sergei Witte, 177, 222.

15. "Graf Sergei Iul'evich Vitte," P i T, 5 (173), Mar. 1, 1915, 232. The reference to political ideas, evidently Witte's defense of the autocracy, no doubt related to the period after 1905. See Von Laue, Sergei Witte, 121, 160-3.

16. Volskii, Sily. Berlin, Burzhuaziia, 150, observed:

> All these diverse facts show that if our government with one hand cultivated big industry and the big bourgeoisie, then with the other hand it destroyed the conditions necessary for the broad and stable development of this very industry and this very bourgeoisie.
>
> The absence of any firm and consistent economic course; the abrupt, capricious break in economic policy with each new reign; the archaic nature of legislation; the completely unsuitable personnel in the administration--such were the conditions, not to mention the general political and cultural environment, in which our bourgeoisie developed and formulated its attitudes toward the government.

17. Against the protests of the manufacturers, the government in 1903 passed two laws, providing for the establishment of workers' elders and for workers' accident compensation. See: Petrov, Partiia, 15-16; Finn-Enotaevskii, Khoziaistvo, 497-8; and Schneiderman, Zubatov, 45.

18. According to Alexander Kerensky, however, the government's sponsorship of the Zubatov movement was itself partially inspired by the increasing political discontent of the industrialists:

> These unions offered the additional advantage, not outwardly apparent, of helping the authorities to restrain the industrialists, who were becoming more and more progressive to the extent that they had come to share with the zemstva the aim of replacing absolutism with a constitutional monarchy.

Kerensky, Russia, 46. In any event, the extent of the industrialists' bitterness is well illustrated by Sir Bernard Pares' recollection that when he appeared at a large factory near Moscow bearing letters of introduction from Plehve, the minister of internal affairs who had originated the Zubatov system, he was virtually refused admission. Pares, Memoirs, 60. See also Schneiderman, Zubatov; Owen, Capitalism and Politics, 163-5; Rieber, Merchants, 261-3; and McDaniel, Autocracy, 64-89.

19. Even generally like-minded historians have found it difficult to agree concerning the extent of the business class's political consciousness on the eve of 1905. Ermanskii, "Do 1905," 347-8, asserted that the industrial bourgeoisie retained its political unawareness "right up to the events of 1905." There were, he says, only a few small indications of political discontent on their part and a general failure to recognize the impact of political affairs on economic conditions. Berlin generally followed Ermanskii but offered no consistent appraisal. On the one hand, Berlin, Burzhuaziia, 141, noted as early as the 1890s "an awakening of both a political awareness of the necessity of the reconstruction of Russian life and a striving to take part in this reconstruction." However, he also referred (167) to the "apparent political indifference of the big bourgeoisie" and the "politically lulling effect" on it of the government's alleged willingness to accede to all its demands. At least under Witte, "not one question of any importance from the field of socio-political life was decided without the direct participation of the representatives of the bourgeoisie. Between the government and the bourgeoisie there existed a stable and reliable political wire [provod]." Berlin, 165. Gindin, "Burzhuaziia," no. 2, 80, followed Ermanskii in stressing the political inertness of the large-scale industrialists on the very eve of 1905.

20. On the March congress, see Sef, Burzhuaziia, 24-35; Reikhardt, "Gruppirovki," 11; Ermanskii, "1905-7," 50-1; Lure, Organizatsiia, 90; Petrov, Partiia, 30-1; and Owen, Capitalism and Politics, 180-3.

21. Reikhardt, "Gruppirovki," 13-14. Although Russian business leaders later blamed the Ministry of Finance for the failure to create a permanent organization, it is also possible that, under the circumstances of the moment, direct political action offered a greater attraction to businessmen than did the more tedious prospect of advancing industrial organization. Reikhardt, "Gruppirovki," 12. Unquestionably, the untimely death of the Congress's leading spirit, Savva T. Morozov, dealt the business community a blow from which it was slow to recover. Morozov, a scion of one of Moscow's great textile families, committed suicide in France on May 13, 1905, after having been removed as head of his family's enterprises. Politically, he had stood far to the left of most Russian industrialists, having been a patron of Gorkii, the Moscow Art Theater, and the Social Democratic Party. See Bill, Forgotten Class, 27-32; Buryshkin, Moskva, 114-18; and Owen, Capitalism and Politics, 121-4. Nearly three years later, the journal of the Association of Industry and Trade attributed the failure to achieve a union of commercial and industrial organizations in the spring of 1905 to

Morozov's death. "Vozniknovenie i deiatelnost' nashei organizatsii," P i T, no. 1, Jan. 1, 1908, 23.

22. The reforms proposed by the commission but rejected by the industrialists included the establishment of a ten-hour workday, the abolition of overtime work, and the participation of the employers on an equal basis with the workers in a system of limited social insurance. The uncompromising attitude of the industrialists, led by Grigorii A. Krestovnikov, caused the suspension of the commission after its first meeting on March 15. When it attempted to resume work in mid-May, the industrialists, taking advantage of recent military defeats in the war with Japan and of growing popular disturbances throughout the Empire, walked out of the commission, declaring that the discussion of labor problems must await more favorable circumstances. According to Sef, Burzhuaziia, 27-32, Kokovtsov, while urging the industrialists to cooperate with the commission, revealed his own understanding that "the government's last serious ally had gone over the revolution." See also Ermanskii, "1905-7," 46-9; Petrov, Partiia, 31-4; Chermenskii, Burzhuaziia, 83-9; Owen, Capitalism and Politics, 180-2; Rieber, Merchants, 345-8; McDaniel, Autocracy, ch. 5; and Roosa, "Labor Reform."

23. The memorandum, dated May 30, was signed by Vladimir Kovalevskii, Vladislav Zhukovskii, Fedor Enakiev, Pavel Gukasov, and Stanislav Glezmer, all of whom later participated in the Association of Industry and Trade. Sef, Burzhuaziia, 33-4, 118-19; and Chermenskii, Burzhuaziia, 70-1.

24. Sef, Burzhuaziia, 119; see also Chermenskii, Burzhuaziia, 70-1.

25. Sef, Burzhuaziia, 119.

26. Quoted in Sef, Burzhuaziia, 121.

27. Quoted in Sef, Burzhuaziia, 119.

28. Quoted in Sef, Burzhuaziia, 120.

29. Ermanskii, "1905-7," 52. Pavel P. Riabushinskii and Ivan A. Morozov, successor to Savva as head of the family enterprises, were among the leaders of the minority favoring a legislative duma. See also Owen, Capitalism and Politics, 185-6, and Rieber, Merchants, 310.

30. The program advocated an assembly with full legislative powers and two chambers, one to be elected by universal suffrage and two stages in voting, the other to be elected by "districts and institutions." It called for full civil liberties, the liberation of the economy from the many "constraints" that hampered its functioning, and protection "in accordance with a plan" for all branches of work. Reikhardt, "Gruppirovki," 17. See also Rieber, Merchants, 333-7.

31. The institutional membership included nine exchange committees, four specialized exchange committees, two committees of trade and manufacturing, and eight industrial organizations. Of those invited, only the exchange committees of St. Petersburg, Warsaw, and Odessa refused to send delegates. Chermenskii, Burzhuaziia, 96. See also Sef, Burzhuaziia, 55.

32. Quoted in Reikhardt, "Gruppirovki," 18.

33. Quoted in Sef, Burzhuaziia, 56.

34. Lure, Organizatsiia, 90. See also Ermanskii, "1905-7," 53-4; Berlin, Burzhuaziia, 243; and Livshin, "Organizatsii," 110-11. Among the members of the Bureau figured such prominent members of the future Association of Industry and Trade as Magnus F. Norpe, Adolf A. Volskii, Aleksandr I. Konovalov, Emanuil I.

Nobel, Pavel P. Riabushinskii, Iulii P. Guzhon, Count Aleksei A. Bobrinskii, Aleksandr A. Auerbakh, Aleksandr F. Volkov, Fedor E. Enakiev, Vladimir I. Kovalevskii, M. G. Pappe, and Sergei I. Chetverikov. Reikhardt, "Gruppirovki," 20. See also Owen, Capitalism and Politics, 186-7.

35. The contention of Livshin, "Organizatsii," 111, that the gathering at the Riabushinskii residence had "as its main aim the struggle with the revolution" is undocumented. On tensions with the Zemstvo-City Congress, see Owen, Capitalism and Politics, 187.

36. Quoted in Sef, Burzhuaziia, 124.

37. Sef, Burzhuaziia, 124; Reikhardt, "Gruppirovki," 19. It remains unclear whether the congress also advocated equal votes for all. Sef repeatedly alleged that it did, but the text of the resolution contained no reference to equality in voting. The extension of the suffrage to women, while rejected as currently impractical, was recognized as desirable in principle and as an objective to be attained as soon as circumstances permitted.

38. Sef, Burzhuaziia, 124.

39. Sef, Burzhuaziia, 87. A less precise account of these events appeared in Akademiia nauk SSSR, Istoriia Moskvy, 127-9.

40. Sef, Burzhuaziia, 125-6; Akademiia Nauk SSSR, Istoriia Moskvy, 128-9.

41. There is, however, a conspicuous divergence among the various Menshevik and Soviet historians in their assessment of the impact of the Manifesto on the industrialists. Chermenskii, Burzhuaziia, 121-2, asserted that the Bulygin Duma represented the "capitalists' ideal" and that their outlook shifted from the broadly liberal position that they had taken during July toward an increasing preoccupation with narrow class interests. Another Soviet work of the Stalin period went beyond Chermenskii to assert that

> the opposition of the "group of young men" of the industrial bourgeoisie disappeared quickly when, on August 6, 1905, the manifesto on the State Duma was published. . . . Disquieted by the growth of the revolution, the liberal bourgeoisie accepted with joy the Tsar's sop of August 6, 1905.

Akademiia Nauk SSSR, Istoriia Moskvy, 129. In contrast, Sef, Burzhuaziia, 7, 77, maintained that the liberal movement of the industrialists continued unabated until after the October Manifesto. Ermanskii, "1905-7," 53-4, contended that their constitutional demands actually increased during the period immediately preceding the publication of the October Manifesto.

42. Volskii, Sily, 4.

43. Volskii, Sily, 8.

44. Volskii, Sily, 2.

45. Volskii, Sily, 4. Volskii's propensity for interlarding his statements with foreign words and phrases was an occasionally amusing by-product of his westernizing inclinations. The Latin sentence came from Cicero, De Officis.

46. Chermenskii, Burzhuaziia, 123. See also Owen, Capitalism and Politics, 188-9.

47. Chermenskii, Burzhuaziia, 136. See also Owen, Capitalism and Politics, 191.

48. T-p G, 221, Sep. 30 (Oct. 13), 1906, 2. Krestovnikov himself was not a liberal in his political views, and he preserved much of his patriarchal heritage.

However, as one of the biggest industrialists and bankers in Moscow, he participated in the trend toward modernizing and westernizing Moscow industry. As chairman of the Exchange Committee, he undoubtedly represented a compromise between the old and the new. See Owen, Capitalism and Politics, 187-91.

49. Quoted in Sef, Burzhuaziia, 126-7. Interpretation of the Moscow industrialists' statement has varied widely among historians. Ermanskii, "1905-7," 53, viewed it as an indication that the political demands of the industrialists were increasing on the eve of the Manifesto. Berlin, Burzhuaziia, 235, likewise contended that the industrialists received the general strike "with full sympathy," gladly "paying the workers for striking time" and for time spent in political demonstrations. Sef, however, found in the statement evidence of waning liberalism on the part of the industrialists and characterized their attitude toward the revolutionary movement between October 1 and 17 as one of "hostile neutrality." Burzhuaziia, 71, 77 (quoted). The Soviet Academy of Sciences viewed the industrialists' statement as an expression of alarm, an effort to prod the government into making concessions before it was too late. Akademiia Nauk SSSR, Istoriia Moskvy, 142.

50. For example, Chermenskii, Burzhuaziia, 149, maintained that "after October 17, the commercial-industrial bourgeoisie took the path of active and unqualified support of the government."

51. Chermenskii, Burzhuaziia, 179-80.

52. Ermanskii, "1905-7," 39, 53-4. See also Dan, "Ocherk," 122; Sef, Burzhuaziia, 76; and Chermenskii, Burzhuaziia, 150.

53. The liberalism of the iron producers did not, however, extend to toleration of the rights of non-Russian peoples of the Empire. For their part, the Petersburg Society of Mill and Factory Owners asserted the necessity of maintaining a united and indivisible Russia unimpaired by concessions to national self-determination or even to national cultural autonomy. Chermenskii, Burzhuaziia, 179-80.

54. Quoted in Dan, "Ocherk," 123.

55. Sef, Burzhuaziia, 79-80.

56. Ermanskii, "1905-7," 51. Various exchange committees demanded that the reformed State Council contain twenty-four seats, to be filled by delegates elected by commercial-industrial organizations; the Moscow Exchange Committee proposed thirty. The most prominent industrial organizations objected that exchange committees (as institutions devoted primarily to trade) must not be allowed to elect all the commercial-industrial delegates. In the end, the various exchange committees and committees of trade and manufacturing received the right to elect six delegates from trade and six from industry, for a total of twelve. Diakin and others, eds., Krizis, 276-7.

57. Sef, Burzhuaziia, 99, noted that the bloc of commercial-industrial parties and the Union of October 17 placed fourteen men in the State Duma, or 3.1 percent of the total. On the elections, see Emmons, Formation.

58. Genrikh G. Vissendorf, one of the leaders of the Commercial-Industrial Union and later a prominent member of the Association of Industry and Trade, bluntly stated the priority of economic over political interests that remained basic to the outlook of virtually all large-scale businessmen at this time. Discussing the collapse of industry's political aspirations, he remarked: "Do not forget that political activity was always, for the Union, only a superstructure, a means; our real base was and will

continue to be professional economic interests." T-p G, 109, May 14 (27), 1906, 2. This article also reported that, before their final demise, all the parties representing industry and trade, with the possible exception of the Progressive Economic Party, attempted to convert themselves into nonpolitical organizations for the promotion of their economic interests. See also the following issues of the T-p G: 85, Apr. 14 (27), 1906, 3; 181, Aug. 10 (23), 1906, 2; and 209, Sep. 16 (29), 1906, 2.

59. This has been the universal contention of both Soviet and Menshevik historians. See, for example, Ermanskii, "1905-7," 55; Berlin, Burzhuaziia, 240; and Sef, Burzhuaziia, 7.

60. Published materials offer little substantiation, certainly with respect to the first ten months of 1905, for the contention of Soviet historians (e.g. Livshin, "Organizatsii," 110) that throughout the revolution the activities of the "big bourgeoisie" were primarily directed toward the conclusion of "a compromise deal with tsarism for the suppression of the revolution."

61. T-p G, 180, Aug. 9 (22), 1906, 2.

62. This success resulted largely from a governmental initiative, begun in 1902, that culminated in the approval of the charter in May 1905 and the convening of the first congress in November 1906. Membership in the Association consisted of the exchange committees and a few other business organizations. Although structurally it resembled the Association of Industry and Trade, it remained a much smaller and less influential organization. Its interests lay mainly in wholesale and foreign trade, especially the grain trade. Apart from the trade in agricultural commodities, it ignored agriculture. The first chairman of its Council, Aleksei Ia. Prozorov, president of the Petersburg Exchange Committee, was succeeded by Vasilii I. Timiriazev, who had earlier served briefly as the first chairman of the Association of Industry and Trade. The two organizations had a largely overlapping membership and cooperated closely on matters of common interest, most notably those concerned with the tariff and the development of exports. See Livshin, "Organizatsii," 110; Ermanskii, "1905-7," 97; Lure, Organizatsiia, 96; Sobolev, Ocherki, 26; Ministerstvo Finansov, Pravitel'stvennye uchrezhdeniia, 16, 19-20; Shepelev, Tsarizm . . . 1914, 76-9, 91-5; and Shepelev, "Business Organizations," 46-53.

63. Volskii referred specifically to the tariff, labor policy, and the government's failure to grant petitions for increased representation for industry and trade in the reformed State Council. Volskii, Predstavitel'stvo, 14ff. In addition, the following reports were heard: Volkov, Blizhaishie zadachi; Ivaniukov, Promyshlenno-torgovye organizatsii; and Nemirovskii, Perspektivy.

64. The most outspoken opposition to the proposed charter came from a group of twenty-five Moscow firms led by Konstantin A. Iasiuninskii; the Polish industrialists, led by Karl F. Chaikovskii; the metal working industry of the Baltic and Northern districts, led by Sergei A. Erdeli; and the mining industrialists of the Urals, led by A. E. Bogdanovich. First Congress, Zhurnal pervogo zasedaniia, 6-9.

65. In addition to delegates appointed by the forty organizations, the Bureau's membership included twelve persons elected by the Congress. Among the organizations represented were twenty-four exchange committees, not including that of St. Petersburg, and one committee of trade and manufacturing. The other organizations represented both heavy and light metallurgical industries (although the mine-owners of the South were absent), the Baku petroleum industry, the sugar refiners, and the

Petersburg Society of Manufacturers. First Congress, Zhurnal zasedanii Organizatsionnogo Biuro, 16; First Congress, Spisok, 17-19.

66. First Congress, Zhurnal tret'ego zasedaniia, 17-18. See also the accounts in Lure, Organizatsiia, 90-1; Ermanskii, "1905-7," 86; Livshin, "Organizatsii," 111; Reikhardt, "Gruppirovki," 37; T-p G, 180, Aug, 9 (22) 1906, 2; and Shepelev, Tsarizm . . . 1914, 84-90.

67. First Congress, Zhurnal zasedaniia Organizatsionnogo Biuro, 1-3.

68. These included eleven exchange committees; two committees of trade and manufacturing and their central Council; the Consultative Board of Iron Producers and of the gold and platinum industry; the coal and steel producers of the South, Urals and Central Russia; the Petersburg Society of Manufacturers; the Russian Society of Sugar Producers; the Baku Petroleum Association; the metal producers of the Baltic and North; and the Russian Insurance Association. Conspicuously absent was the Petersburg Exchange Society. Among those sending delegates, some, such as the Association of Southern Coal and Steel Producers, had not yet decided to join the new organization. First Congress, Spisok, 23-31. See also Livshin, "Organizatsii," 112, and T-p G, 84, Apr. 13 (26), 1906, 2.

69. The congress rebuffed a last-minute attempt, sponsored by the Moscow Exchange Society, to convert the new organization into an employers' union primarily concerned with conducting management's conflict with labor. T-p G, 83, Apr. 12 (25) 1906, 2. See Lure, Organizatsiia, 86, 92, 164. Conversely, the congress also rejected a proposal that labor unions be admitted to membership in the new association, although "the assembly took this statement under advisement and expressed the view in principle that concern about improving the working and living conditions of the workers is already accepted as part of the idea of promoting the regularization of relations between labor and capital." First Congress, Zhurnal pervogo zasedaniia, 2.

70. I. I. Iasiukovich, quoted in T-p G, 86, Apr, 15 (28), 1906, 2.

71. This sum, roughly equivalent to $75,000, represented an increase of 25,000 rubles over the amount proposed by the Bureau of the July Congress.

72. Membership was divided as follows: the Consultative Board of Iron Producers, with five representatives, of whom the most prominent were Ignatii I. Iasiukovich, Iulii P. Guzhon, and Magnus F. Norpe; the Moscow Exchange Committee, three (Grigorii A. Krestovnikov, Konstantin A. Iasiuninskii, and Baron Andrei F. Knoop); the Petersburg Society of Manufacturers, three (Emanuil L. Nobel, Stanislav P. Glezmer, and Boris A. Efron); the Russian Insurance Association, three (including Nikolai A. Belotsvetov and Vladimir V. Maksimov); the Warsaw Exchange Committee, two (Stanislav M. Rotvand and Karl F. Chaikovskii); the Ural mine-owners, two; the Baku Exchange Committee, two; the Russian Railroad Association, two; the Russian Society of Sugar Producers, two (including Count Andrei A. Bobrinskii); the Moscow Section of the Council of Trade and Manufacturing, one (Vasilii I. Timiriazev); the Polish Coal and Iron Association, one (Zhukovskii); the Association of Southern Coal and Steel Producers, one; the Baku Petroleum Association, one (Pavel O. Gukasov); the Kostroma Committee of Trade and Manufacturing, one (Aleksandr I. Konovalov); the Consultative Board of Gold and Platinum Producers, one; the mine-owners of central Russia, one; the metal producers of the Baltic and North, one; the Samara Union of Trade and Industry, one; and the exchange committees of Rostov-on-Don, Astrakhan, and Rybinsk, one each. First

Congress, Zhurnal chetvertogo zasedaniia, 13-14; see also Sovet S"ezdov, Polozhenie ob obshcheimperskikh s"ezdakh, 2-3; T-p G, no. 82-86, Apr. 11-15 (24-28), 1906; and Lure, Organizatsiia, 91.

73. T-p G, 86, Apr. 15 (28), 1906, 1.

74. T-p G, Apr. 20 (May 3), 1906, 1.

75. T-p G, 180, Aug. 9 (22), 1906, 2. Among the organizations already committed to entering the Association were the Moscow Exchange Society, the Baku Petroleum Association, the Russian Society of Sugar Producers, the Petersburg Society of Mill and Factory Owners, and the Russian Insurance Association. Others had agreed "in principle": the Association of Southern Coal and Steel Producers, the Polish Coal and Iron Association, the Union of Warsaw Factory Owners, and the Paper Mill Owners. See also T-p G, 195, Aug. 27 (Sep. 9), 1906, 2.

76. T-p G, 218, Sep. 27 (Oct. 10), 1906, 2.

77. T-p G, 229, Oct. 10 (23), 1906, 2. See also Lure, Organizatsiia, 92.

78. Under the charter, full members were defined as "industrial and commercial organizations composed of the owners of commercial-industrial enterprises or their representatives, which have as their purpose the unification of their members on the basis of economic interest." (On the distinction between full and consultative members, see Appendix II.) This paragraph appeared to many, both within and outside the Association, to apply to syndicates, and it was on the basis of this clause that the Provisional Council voted in October 1906 to admit syndicates to full membership. Curiously, the status of syndicates within the Association has confused historians who have described the organization. Even one so intimately connected with its operations as Lure asserted that syndicates enjoyed active membership in the organization. Lure, Organizatsiia, 93. Livshin, one of the few who recognized that the syndicates could join only as consultative (soveshchatel'nye) members, maintained with much justification that this fact did not limit their influence within the Association, since their delegates simultaneously represented full members. Livshin, "Organizatsii," 113.

79. T-p G, 90, April 20 (May 3), 1906, 1 (quoted). See also First Congress, Zhurnal pervogo zasedaniia, 2; and T-p G, 84, Apr. 13 (26), 1906, 2. These assurances appeared all the more impressive in view of the fact that the proposed Association, as a "union of unions," was technically illegal under the temporary rules enacted on March 4, 1906, governing organizations for representative purposes, and required special governmental authorization to acquire legality. Belotsvetov quoted in T-p G, 180, Aug. 9 (22), 1906, 2. In later years, the Association singled out Mikhail M. Fedorov, director of the Division of Trade in the Ministry of Trade and Industry, for his role as one of its "founding fathers." On Fedorov's career, see Owen, Russian Corporate Capitalism, 56-7. On "strength through unity," T-p G, 90, April 20 (May 3), 1906, 1.

80. T-p G, 90, Apr. (May 3), 1906, 1.

81. Volskii, Programma blizhaishei deiatel'nosti, quoted in Ermanskii, "1905-7," 88-9.

82. At the last of these, Volskii was the sole representative of "public" organizations. Lure, Organizatsiia, 91. See also T-p G, 180, Aug. 9 (22), 1906, 2, and 226, Oct. 6 (19), 1906, 2.

83. First Congress, Zhurnal zasedanii Organizatsionnogo biuro, 1-2. The

Organizational Bureau also heard a lengthy and detailed report on the organization and functioning of the Handelstag: Organizatsionnoe biuro s"ezda, Germanskii torgovyi s"ezd, 34.

84. Fourth Congress, Zhelatel'naia organizatsiia; Ermanskii, "1905-7," 90-1; Spasskii, ed., Ocherk, 59-60. In reference to the Association, Genrikh G. Vissendorf, head of the All-Russian Commercial-Industrial Union, declared that "the idea of the renowned German commercial parliament, the so-called Handelstag, which has brought so much benefit to industry and trade, has at last found application in Russia also." Quoted in T-p G, 109, May 14 (27), 1906, 2.

85. The Petersburg and the Moscow Exchange Committees led this opposition. See T-p G, 93, Apr. 23 (May 6), 1906, 1; 98, Apr. 29 (May 12), 1906, 4; 108, May 13 (26), 1906, 4; 123, June 1 (14), 1906, 1; and 227, Oct. 7 (20), 1906, 4.

86. T-p G, 85, Apr. 14 (27), 1906, 2.

87. T-p G, 90, Apr. 20 (May 3), 1906, 1.

88. According to Livshin, "Organizatsii," 111, this action of the government indicated a desire "to narrow the scope of activity" of the Association.

89. T-p G, 232, Oct. 13 (26), 1906, 1. The speaker, Mikhail M. Fedorov, had consistently promoted the organization of industrial and commercial interests. In his address to the Congress, he also stressed the weakness of local organizations in Russia. The new Association's first task, he said, must be to strengthen its base by creating "a correct local representation of the commercial-industrial class." Not long afterward, the project for chambers of commerce was revived and actively promoted by the Association itself. See Shumilov, "Proekty reformy."

90. Lure, Organizatsiia, 91-2; Finn-Enotaevskii, Khoziaistvo, 498-9.

91. These rules, which greatly facilitated the rise of "representative" organizations, stipulated that all new organizations must belong to only one of two categories, political or professional. T-p G, 84, Apr. 13 (26), 1906, 2.

92. Chto do sikh por sdelano dlia ob"edineniia otechestvennoi promyshlennosti i torgovli na ekonomicheskoi pochve?, quoted in Ermanskii, "1905-7," 59-60.

93. See, for example, T-p G, 101, May 4 (17), 1906, 4, and 109, May 14 (27), 1906, 2.

94. This action allegedly showed deference to the views of member organizations on the eve of the congress. The extremely technical nature of most of the topics proposed for discussion might have had some bearing on this last-minute decision. See T-p G for August-October 1906: 195, Aug. 27 (Sep. 9), 2; 210, Sep. 17 (30), 2; 213, Sep. 21 (Oct. 4), 2; 221, Sep. 30 (Oct. 13), 3; 222, Oct. 1 (14), 3; 224, Oct. 4 (17), 3; 229, Oct. 10 (23), 2; and 231, Oct. 23 (Nov. 5), 2.

95. T-p G, 232, Oct. 13 (26), 1906, 1.

96. Ironically, the Association of Southern Coal and Steel Producers had not yet joined the new Association. However, Avdakov assured the Congress that it would not delay further in assuming membership. T-p G, 232, Oct. 13 (26), 1906, 1.

97. "The Association of Industry and Commerce of Russia," English Supplement, P i T, no. 2 (98), Jan. 15, 1912, 7.

98. T-p G, 232, Oct. 13 (26), 1906, 1.

99. Ermanskii, "1905-7," 89.

100. Ermanskii, "1905-7," 89; see also T-p G, 232, October 13 (26), 1906, 1.

101. A second dispute focused on the status of industrial syndicates in the

Association. In a decision taken after "a prolonged and lively debate," the Congress reversed a decision of the Provisional Council admitting syndicates to the organization as full members (see note 78). T-p G, 233, Oct. 14 (27), 1906, 1 (quoted).

102. Spasskii, ed., Ocherk, 63; and T-p G, 234, Oct. 15 (28), 1906, 1. Other prominent members of the new Council who had also belonged to the Provisional Council were Count Andrei A. Bobrinskii, Nikolai A. Belotsvetov, Iulii P. Guzhon, Pavel O. Gukasov, Nikolai F. fon-Ditmar, Vladislav V. Zhukovskii, Aleksandr I. Konovalov, Grigorii A. Krestovnikov, Baron Andrei L. Knoop, Mikhail I. Lazarev, Magnus F. Norpe, Stanislav M. Rotvand, Boris A. Efron, and Konstantin A. Iasiuninskii. New members of the Council included Pavel P. Riabushinskii and Fedor E. Enakiev, a mining engineer active in the Association of Southern Coal and Steel Producers.

103. Timiriazev was an outstanding representative of that small but influential group of men who, under the close relationship that had traditionally prevailed in Russia between business and the government, had their roots in both branches of activity. A former deputy minister of finance, he twice headed the Ministry of Trade and Industry and served several terms as the elected representative of either industry or trade in the State Council. The versatility of his business interests, to which he devoted much of his attention after 1909, was illustrated in the fact that after a brief term as chairman of the Association of Industry and Trade he served as chairman of the Association of Trade and Agriculture for many years. He also chaired the association of the lumber industry and the Anglo-Russian Chamber of Commerce. See Shepelev, Tzarizm . . . 1914, 97-8, and Shepelev, "Business Organizations," 53-4.

104. See notes 9 and 11.

105. T-p G, 234, Oct. 15 (28), 1. There is no evidence that the special congress ever met.

106. See T-p G, 213, Sep. 21 (Oct. 4), 1906, 3; 231, Oct. 12 (25), 1906, 2; and 234, Oct. 15 (28), 1906, 1.

107. In practice, however, the preliminary meetings failed to attain the unity that their privacy was undoubtedly designed to promote. The first meeting of the official Conference witnessed a sharp exchange of views between the representatives of the oil industry, Emanuil L. Nobel and Pavel O. Gukasov, who insisted on the need to raise oil prices in Moscow, and the spokesman for the industry of the central district, Iulii P. Guzhon, who not only complained that "the arbitrary, immoderate prices dictated by the oil industrialists are beyond its strength" but also demanded a reduction in railroad freight rates on the shipment of foreign coal from St. Petersburg to Moscow. T-p G, 234, Oct. 17 (30), 1906, 4.

108. Volskii, Predstavitel'stvo, 15-18.

109. In part, this apparently stems from the failure of many of the organizations to keep adequate records of their work. According to a report to the Fourth Congress of the Association of Industry and Trade in 1909, half of the 143 organizations known to the Council published no reports on their activities and kept no statistics in the fields of their interests. Fourth Congress, Organizatsiia, 1-2. In addition, studies undertaken by contemporary observers in this area were severely hampered by the reluctance of the business organizations to divulge information concerning their activities. In the major study conducted by the Imperial Russian Technical Society in 1911, for example, only 62 out of 143 organizations answered the questionnaires that were sent

to them, and then, often, only partially and in response to repeated queries. The Association of Industry and Trade was one of the least cooperative. Gushka, Organizatsii, 38. Ironically, when the Association later attempted to carry out a survey of the textile industry, it encountered the same recalcitrance. Fourth Congress, Doklad . . . dela Imperii. Finally, much of the documentary evidence apparently failed to survive the revolutionary upheaval of 1917. Liashchenko, Istoriia, 293-4; Shepelev, Tsarizm . . . 1914, 9-11.

110. Livshin, "Organizatsii," 99, 108-9. According to a list published by the Ministry of Trade and Industry in 1914, Russia had 93 exchange committees, 13 committees of trade and manufacture, 7 chambers of commerce, and 34 "consultative" organizations, of which 19 were associations ("councils of congresses"). Ministerstvo Torgovli i Promyshlennosti, Otdel Torgovli, Dopolnenie. Lure, Organizatsiia, 185-91, listed 199 organizations as of January 1911, not including exchange committees, committees of trade and manufacturing, and boards of the merchant estate. The usefulness of his compendium is limited, however, by its lack of a systematic classification of the organizations listed and by its inclusion of numerous organizations of only local, or of doubtful, commercial and industrial importance. Gushka, using materials collected by the Imperial Russian Technical Society in 1910, listed 143 organizations, including 71 exchange societies, 31 associations, 2 "consultative bureaus," and 22 miscellaneous organizations, in addition to the 14 largely moribund committees of trade and manufacturing and the 3 boards of the merchant estate in existence before 1905. Gushka, Organizatsii, 32-8. A still shorter listing, also for 1910-11, appears in Spasskii, ed., Ocherk, 60-1. For a concise overview of local representative bodies, see Shepelev, Tsarizm . . . 1914, 108-17.

111. Lure, Organizatsiia, 130-1.

112. Sovet s"ezdov, Polozhenie ob obshcheimperskikh s"ezdakh, 1. The charter, approved by the Council of Ministers on August 24, 1906 and amended on October 23, 1907, appears in the Code of Laws of the Empire for 1908: Svod zakonov Rossiiskoi imperii . . . 1908 goda, vol. XI, part 2, Ustav torgovyi, 832-75. The charter was further amended on October 3, 1910. Its final form is presented in Appendix I.

This statement of objectives is quoted from the charter as revised in October 1907. According to the original text, the Association was established "for the examination and elaboration of questions raised by the industrial life of Russia in the fields of legislation, commercial-industrial policy, public-economic relationships, and the relations between labor and capital, and equally for the unification and representation of the common interests of industry and trade, and the carrying out of common measures." Sovet s"ezdov, Polozhenie ob obshcheimperskikh s"ezdakh, 1.

113. Gushka, Organizatsii, 135-6.

114. Lenin, "Anketa," 43-4, considered Gushka's conclusions exaggerated. However, Berlin, Burzhuaziia, 299-300, regarded the growing influence of the "third element" as a measure both of the "Europeanization" of the big bourgeoisie and of the penetration of the intelligentsia itself by capitalism. He went beyond Gushka in attributing "the formation and strengthening of the political movement within the bourgeoisie" in part to the influence of the "third element." Although Livshin, "Organizatsii," 114, remained noncommittal on the extent of the influence exercised by the "third element," he stressed the large numbers of its members employed in

responsible posts in organized industry.

115. At least half of these 143 organizations published no reports on their activities, kept no statistics in the fields of their interests, and "seldom manifest life of any kind at all." He concluded: "The reality is clear for everyone and without any statistics: we are not organized." Fourth Congress, Organizatsiia, 1-2. (The author of this report was probably the Odessa merchant and canned-food manufacturer Saul Isaakovich Sokolovskii.)

116. Fourth Congress, Organizatsiia, 3-4. It was hardly reasonable to complain that the leadership of the two associations consisted of men who were leaders in member organizations. Sokolovskii's conclusions were widely cited by Soviet historians to refute the claim of Gushka and other Mensheviks that organized industry exerted influence on governmental policies.

117. "Nikolai Stepanovich Avdakov," P i T, 22 (189), Sep. 19, 1915, 305-6.

118. See N. I., "Kratkii ocherk istorii s"ezdov gornopromyshlennikov iuga Rossii," P i T, 23, Dec. 1, 1908, 629-30; "Sorokoletnyi iubilei Nikolaia Stepanovicha Avdakova," P i T, 12 (132), June 15, 1913, 541-2; "Chestvovanie N. S. Avdakova," P i T, 12 (132), June 15, 1913, 545-6; G. Mertsalov, "N. S. Avdakov i iuzhnaia gornopromyshlennost'," P i T, 22 (189), Sep. 19, 1915, 307-9; A. M. Ossendovskii, "Trudy Nikolaia Stepanovicha Avdakova v oblasti zolotopromyshlennosti," P i T, 23 (190), Sep. 26, 1915, 345-6; Shepelev, Tsarizm . . . 1914, 98-9; and Shepelev, "Business Organizations," 54-6.

119. Pares, Memoirs, 139, 173.

120. V. Sharyi, "Pamiati V. V. Zhukovskogo," P i T, 36-37 (231), Sep. 17, 1916, 195-6.

121. Odin iz sluzhashchikh, "V. V. Zhukovskii i sluzhashchie," P i T, 36-37 (231), Sep. 17, 1916, 204.

122. Baron G. Maidel, "V. V. Zhukovskii, kak ideinyi rukovoditel' Soveta s"ezdov predstavitelei promyshlennosti i torgovli," P i T, 36-37 (231), Sep. 17, 1916, 192-3. See also P i T, 36-37 (231), Sep. 17, 1916, the entire issue of which was devoted to Zhukovskii; and Ip. Glivits, "Politiko-ekonomicheskie vzgliady V. V. Zhukovskogo," P i T, 42 (235), Oct. 22, 1916, 306-9.

123. See, for example, A. Volskii, "Byt'-by i predely," P i T, 19, Oct. 1, 1909, 384. On Volskii, see Shepelev, Tsarizm . . . 1914, 102, and Shepelev, "Business Organizations," 58-9.

124. See "Pravitel'stvo i zheleznaia promyshlennost'," P i T, 18, Sep. 15, 1908, 323-4; and Fourth Congress, Zhurnaly, 48.

125. Moscow was strongly represented on the Council by Krestovnikov, Konovalov, Morozov, Riabushinskii, Knoop, Chetverikov, and others. On the roles of Krestovnikov and Konovalov in the Association, see Shepelev, Tsarizm . . . 1914, 99-100, and Shepelev, "Business Organizations," 56-7.

126. In 1908, two of the three vice-chairman of the Council represented Petersburg, and the third was from Kharkov. Of the seven members of the Committee in addition to Vissendorf, two represented Petersburg, two Poland, one Kiev, one Baku, and one Riga.

127. Gindin, "Burzhuaziia," no. 3, 15-46. Moscow's relative indifference to the Association is corroborated in the testimony of former Moscow businessmen. See, for example, Buryshkin, Moskva, 266-72.

128. Two of the four delegates from Petersburg in the leadership in 1908 were members of the Society. One of these, Emanuil L. Nobel, also figured prominently in the Baku oil industry. On Nobel's role in the Association, see Shepelev, Tsarizm . . . 1914, 100, and "Business Organizations," 57.

129. See, for example, "Dnevnik Soveta," P i T, 7 (251), Feb. 18, 1917, 175.

130. See Gushka, Organizatsiia, 15.

131. Seventh Congress, Zhurnal, 67-83, esp. 76.

132. A., "75-letie Moskovskoi birzhi," P i T, 22 (166), Nov. 15, 1914, 501-2.

133. "Dnevnik Soveta," P i T, 9, May 1, 1908, 572-9.

134. Third Congress, Zhurnaly, 15-16.

135. Fourth Congress, Zhurnaly, 47-8; emphasis in original.

136. Other members were V. Monakhov, who, along with Guzhon, represented Moscow, and Matvei B. Pappe. Pavel P. Riabushinskii was elected but declined to serve. Fifth Congress, Zhurnaly, 45, and Otchet po izdaniiu, 2.

137. "Tozhe priemy!" P i T, 12, June 15, 1908, 770-2.

138. "Dnevnik Soveta," P i T, 23, Dec. 1, 1908, 612, 614.

139. "Tretii ocherednoi s"ezd predstavitelei promyshlennosti i torgovli," P i T, 8, Apr. 15, 1908, 524; Fourth Congress, Zhurnaly, 41; "Ekonomichesko-finansovaia politika Rossii," P i T, 22, Nov. 15, 1909, 521.

140. During the eleven months between the Seventh and Eighth Congresses, for example, the Commission met twenty-three times. Eighth Congress, Otchet, 2.

141. Fourth Congress, Zhurnaly, 2.

142. Fourth Congress, Doklad . . . izmeneniia, 2.

143. Fifth Congress, Zhurnaly, 12.

144. "O deiatel'nosti Zakonodatel'nykh Uchrezhdenii po voprosam, kasaiushchimsia promyshlennosti i torgovli," P i T, 7 (79), Apr. 1, 1911, 305.

145. "Piatyi s"ezd," P i T, 6 (78), Mar. 15, 1911, 248.

146. "Dnevnik Soveta," P i T, 3 (99), Feb. 1, 1912, 160-1.

147. Eighth Congress, Zhurnaly, 132-61.

148. See, for example, "Obzor pechati," P i T: 22 (94), Nov. 15, 1911, 439; 2 (122), Jan. 15, 1913, 72: 6 (150), Mar. 15, 1914, 322; and Baron G. Kh. Maidel, "Graf S. Iu. Vitte i chastnoe zheleznodorozhnoe khoziaistvo," P i T, 1 (145), Jan. 1, 1914, 4.

Chapter 2

1. K., "Vserossiiski torgovo-promyshlennyi soiuz. Beseda s G. G. Vissendorfom," T-p G, 190, May 14 (21), 1906, 2. Belotsvetov, a vice-chairman of the Association's Provisional Council, described the task of the new organization more modestly as that of "renovating the almost patriarchal system of our industry and trade as they now exist and bringing them out onto new paths." Vl. S., "Osushchestvlenie s"ezdov predstavitelei promyshlennosti i torgovli. Beseda s N. A. Belotsvetovym," T-p G, 190, Aug. 9 (22), 1906, 2.

2. "V kakikh usloviiakh razvivaetsia promyshlennost' Rossii," P i T, 13 (133), July 1, 1913, 1.

3. "Adres Soveta S"ezdov predstavitelei promyshlennosti i torgovli Gospodinu Ministru Torgovli i Promyshlennosti," P i T, 24 (144), Dec. 15, 1913, 567.

4. V. Sh--skii, "Zadachi torgovo-promyshlennoi gruppy. Beseda s K. A. Iasiuninskim," T-p G, 101, May 4 (17), 1906, 4.

5. "Pervyi ocherednoi s"ezd predstavitelei promyshlennosti i torgovli," I, T-p G, 232, Oct. 13 (26), 1906, 1. A few days earlier, Minister of Trade and Industry Dmitrii A. Filosofov had similarly declared that "the raising of the general productivity of the country must constitute the most important task of the state." "Rech' Ministra torgovli i promyshlennosti Moskovskomu birzhevomu obshchestvu," T-p G, 227, Oct. 7 (20), 1906, 4.

6. Fourth Congress, Zhurnaly, 52.

7. Fifth Congress, Zhurnaly, 1.

8. In 1907, the Association declared with premature optimism: "In our country people are beginning to become acquainted with the idea that questions of pure politics, with which society has been so captivated, necessarily must yield primacy to economic questions." Sovet S"ezdov, Zapiska . . . mashinostroeniia, 58.

9. "Vybory v Gosudarstvennyi Sovet," P i T, 13, July 1, 1909, 3.

10. Fourth Congress, Zhurnaly, 43; see also 42.

11. "Rezoliutsiia S"ezda," P i T, 22 (94), Nov. 15, 1911, 407.

12. "Novyi premer," P i T, 18 (90), Sep. 15, 1911, 200, and "Simptomaticheskoe naznachenie," P i T, 17 (89), Sep. 1, 1911, 162.

13. Sovet S"ezdov, Promyshlennost' . . . 1907-1912 gg., i.

14. "Rechi na VI S"ezde," P i T, 10 (106), May 15, 1912, 509.

15. "Obzor pechati," P i T, 4 (100), Feb. 15, 1912, 210.

16. "Gosudarstvennaia oborona i promyshlennost'," P i T, 18 (114), Sep. 15, 1912, 196.

17. "Dve rechi N. S. Avdakova v Gosudarstvennom Sovete," P i T, 18 (138), Sep. 15, 1913, 233.

18. Noting that Russia's rate of economic growth lagged behind that of "the advanced industrial countries," Industry and Trade increasingly attributed the situation to unfavorable governmental policies. "Ekonomicheskoe polozhenie strany i dumskie preniia," P i T, 11 (131), June 1, 1913, 491. In January 1914, a Rescript issued by the Emperor himself apparently gave full recognition to the necessity of promoting national economic development as rapidly as possible. "Smena rukovoditelei finansovogo vedomstva," P i T, 4 (148), Feb. 15, 1914, 178. Such assurances were offered by the new minister of finance, Petr L. Bark, a member of the Association's Council; see "Novyi kurs", P i T, 9 (153), May 1, 1914, 458. However, Kokovtsov's abrupt dismissal in January 1914 signalled a sharp deterioration in the relationship between the government and industry.

19. "Rechi na VI S"ezde," P i T, 10 (106), May 15, 1912, 509.

20. Iz rechi A. I. Konovalova v Gosudarstvennoi Dume," P i T, 11 (131), June 1, 1913, 499.

21. "Dve rechi N. S. Avdakova," 232. See also "Ob"iasnitel'naia zapiska k proektu gosudarstvennoi rospisi na 1914 god i sovremennoe polozhenie promyshlennosti," P i T, 23 (143), Dec. 1, 1913, 513.

22. "Rech' N. S. Avdakova v Gosudarstvennom Sovete," P i T, 13 (157), July 1, 1914, 7.

23. "Rech' N. S. Avdakova v Gosudarstvennom Sovete v zasedanii 9 iunia," P i T, 14 (158), July 15, 1914, 61-2.

24. "Pravitel'stvo i promyshlennost'," P i T, 13 (157), July 1, 1914, 3.

25. "Chto nuzhno v nastoiashchii moment Rossii?" P i T, 14 (158), July 15, 1914, 58.

26. Volskii, Sily, 3-4.

27. "Politika torgovogo moreplavaniia," P i T, 5, Mar. 15, 1908, 292.

28. B. Ashov, "Dokhodnost' russko-bel'giiskikh predpriiatii v 1910 i 1910-1911 gg," P i T, 7 (103), Apr. 1, 1912, 358.

29. "Dve rechi N. S. Avdakova," 232.

30. "Chto nuzhno?" 58.

31. Sovet S"ezdov, Promyshlennost' . . . 1912-1913 gg., xii-xiii.

32. "Torgovo-promyshlennye problemy i obshchestvennoe mnenie," P i T, 10 (106), May 15, 1912, 506.

33. "Pervye lastochki," P i T, 24, Dec. 15, 1908, 638.

34. Baron G. Maidel, "Teoriia i praktika," P i T, 10 (154), May 15, 1914, 517.

35. "Obsledovanie promyshlennosti," P i T, 15 (111), Aug. 1, 1912, 84.

36. The quotation, cited from Mendeleev's Tolkovyi tarif, appeared, for example, on the title page of a major report of the Council: Eighth Congress, Peresmotr, 1.

37. "Blagoi pochin," P i T, 7 (103), Apr. 1, 1912, 350.

38. "Promyshlennost' i pechat'," P i T, 1, Jan. 1, 1910, 2.

39. The Association's leaders no doubt would have endorsed the words of the merchant Taras Maiakin, in one of Gorkii's novels, perhaps replacing "British" with "German":

> Bear in mind that there are no people as hard working as the British, and this explains their extraordinary success in trade and industry. Labour for them is almost a cult. The cultural level of a nation is always in direct proportion to their love of work. The more cultured a people and the more completely their demands are satisfied, the fewer the barriers to the further satisfying of their demands. Happiness lies in the fullest satisfaction of a man's demands. And so, you see, a man's happiness depends upon his attitude to work.

Gorky, Foma Gordeyev, 232. On attitudes toward labor in Russian culture after 1905, see Rosenthal, "Orthodox Work Ethic," and Rosenberg, "Representing Workers."

40. The term "state socialism" in the Association's usage referred to the peculiar compound of bureaucratic tutelage (opeka) over private enterprise and state ownership and operation of industry and trade that characterized the Russian economic system. See Roosa, "Russian Industrialists and 'State Socialism.'"

41. "Dvigateli russkogo sel'skogo khoziaistva" P i T, 7, Apr. 1, 1908, 398.

42. On Witte's death, Industry and Trade expressed the ambivalent attitude of the business class toward him:

> But the commercial-industrial class, in spite of many disagreements, both personal and in the field of ideas, has benevolent and kind memories of him. For his powerful creative activity not only left great marks on the economic life of the country; he also provided the impetus for the development of its internal self-consciousness and for the elucidation of the state views and the state program of the commercial-industrial class.

"Graf Sergei Iul'evich Vitte," P i T, 5 (173), Mar. 1, 1915, 232. See also P i T, 6 (174), Mar. 15, 1915, which was entirely devoted to Witte.

According to Von Laue, Witte himself entertained similarly mixed views of the businessmen and their place in Russian life:

> Like a Russian Colbert, Witte criticized the business community for its lack of initiative and its habit of relying on government orders and taking subsidies. On the other hand, he left no doubt that in a modern economy this class, emancipated from the narrow traditions of the kupechestvo [merchant estate], occupied the most important position, socially as well as politically.

Sergei Witte, 190-1.

43. "Obzor pechati," P i T, 22 (94), Nov. 15, 1911, 439.

44. "Obzor pechati, P i T, 10 (106), May 15, 1912, 531.

45. Livshin, Monopolii, 261-2. In 1915, Volskii could hardly be considered a spokesman for the Association, having left it in 1911.

46. Livshin, Monopolii, 446.

47. Many Soviet historians asserted that Russia's prerevolutionary businessmen enjoyed extremely high profits. This judgment finds some support in the enormous fortunes that many of them amassed. According to Livshin, Monopolii, 31, the railroad car syndicate, Prodvagon, paid dividends of 17 to 22.5 percent on its basic capital. However, Lyashchenko, History, 676, pointed out that commercial profits substantially exceeded industrial profits. For example, machine-building factories paid dividends of only 2.0 and 2.7 percent, while commercial firms paid 6 and 7.9 percent in 1906-8. Solovieva, "Pribyli," gave an intelligent commentary on the problem but accepted published profit rates and resorted to typical Soviet verbiage: "By plundering [za schet grabezha] the working masses, the Russian bourgeoisie extracted enormous sums of 'superprofits.'" (40). Writing in the era of perestroika, Sorokin, "Izuchenie," admitted that Soviet historical scholarship had not rendered a clear verdict on this question. Thus, a thorough study of the profits of Russian industrial enterprises during the inter-revolutionary period is needed. The available evidence remains inconsistent and incomplete.

The Association, for its part, repeatedly attributed the dearth of foreign capital to the low level of industrial profits in Russia. In 1909, Volskii set the general profitability of Russian corporations at 4.45 percent, in contrast with 7.01 percent for Germany. In trade, credit, and agriculture, however, Russia was said to exceed the German rate of profits. Fourth Congress, Ekonomichesko-finansovaia politika, 19-21. See also Third Congress, Osnovy, 10-12. As a result of contemporary criticism of allegedly high industrial profits by members of the State Council, the Sixth Congress instructed the Council of the Association to revise its method of calculating financial data on corporations and to compare the profitability of Russian and foreign enterprises. "Shestoi ocherednoi s"ezd predstavitelei promyshlennosti i torgovli," P i T, 10 (106), May 15, 1912, 522.

48. "Anketa o sindikatakh," P i T, 13 (61), July 1, 1910, 2.

49. "Promyshlennost' i pechat'," P i T, 1, Jan. 1, 1910, 2.

50. "Inostrannyi kapital," P i T, 15 (63), Aug. 1, 1910, 116. In its further defense of foreign capital, the article, 115, with no apparent sense of inconsistency, stressed "its tremendous cultural work" in Russia and cited its role in the growth of towns and railroads in the empty steppe and in the creation of schools and hospitals

connected with factories and mines.

51. Sily, 2, 4, 8, 34.

52. A. Volskii, "Dve besedy," P i T, 13, July 1, 1909, 55.

53. "Odin poluvekovoi iubilei," P i T, 21, Nov. 1, 1908, 460. See also "Pervye lastochki," P i T, 24, Dec. 15, 1908, 639.

54. Fourth Congress, Organizatsiia, 3, 6-7, 8. On his criticisms, see ch. 1, note 116.

55. Fourth Congress, Organizatsiia, 52-3.

56. Fifth Congress, Zhurnaly, 40.

57. Fifth Congress, Zhurnaly, 2.

58. "O deiatel'nosti zakonodatel'nykh uchrezhdenii po voprosam, kasaiushchimsia promyshlennosti i torgovli," P i T, 7 (79), Apr. 1, 1911, 304-5.

59. Sovet S"ezdov, Promyshlennost' . . . 1907-1912 gg., xxii-xxiii.

60. Sixth Congress, Zhurnal, 41-2.

61. Sovet S"ezdov, Promyshlennost' . . . 1907-1912 gg., xxii.

62. "Vo imia chego torgovo-promyshlennomu klassu nado idti v Dumu?" P i T, 12 (108), June 15, 1912, 632-3.

63. Vladimir I. Arandarenko, in Sixth Congress, Zhurnal, 33.

64. Aleksandr A. Bublikov, in Sixth Congress, Zhurnal, 34.

65. "Torgovo-promyshlennye problemy i obshchestvennoe mnenie," P i T, 19 (106), May 15, 1912, 507. (Emphasis in original.)

66. "Chestvovanie stoletnego iubileia Tovarishchestva manufaktur Ivana Konovalova s synom 2 sentiabria 1912 g. v Moskve," P i T, 18 (114), Sep. 15, 1912, 199-200.

67. "Chestvovanie," 201.

68. "Chestvovanie," 201.

69. "Obzor pechati," P i T, 1 (121), Jan. 1, 1913, 23.

70. Seventh Congress, Zhurnal, 14.

71. Seventh Congress, Zhurnal, 457.

72. Quotations from "Obzor pechati," P i T, 11 (131), June 1, 1913, 512. The publisher of The Russian Word, Ivan D. Sytin, enjoyed one of the most spectacular entrepreneurial careers in late imperial Russia, but even after 1917, when he continued to operate his presses under Soviet supervision, he never lost his original peasant orientation. See Ruud, Entrepreneur.

73. "Obzor pechati," P i T, 10 (154), May 15, 1914, 534-5.

74. "Obzor pechati," P i T, 10 (154), May 15, 1914, 533.

75. "Pravitel'stvo i promyshlennost'," P i T, 13 (157), July 1, 1914, 1.

76. "Chto nuzhno v nastoiashchii moment Rossii? P i T, 14 (158), July 15, 1914, 57-8.

77. Gerschenkron, Economic Backwardness, 181.

78. Witte's views on this question are admirably set forth in Professor Von Laue's study, Sergei Witte, esp. 77, 179, 182-3, 186-7, and 237-8.

79. Something much closer to a comprehensive economic program, although lacking official approval, appeared in a book published in 1908 by the director of the Division of Industry in the Ministry of Trade and Industry: Litvinov-Falinskii, Nashe ekonomicheskoe polozhenie. The author had worked closely with the Association and other business groups. With only a few qualifications, the Association enthusiastically

praised it. P i T, 6, Mar. 15, 1908, 396.

80. Fainsod, Russia, 24, for example, observed that "The 'protecting' hand of the government guided industrial development." Similarly, Carr, "'Russia and Europe,'", 383, stated:

> Industry was "planned" in the sense that it depended primarily on Government orders, not on spontaneous market demand, and was financed by loans accorded for political reasons rather than for the traditional "capitalist" motive of earning commercial profits; in these respects it anticipated much that was to happen under the Five Year Plans thirty years later.

At the opposite extreme, Berlin, Burzhuaziia, 149-50, contended that governmental policies not only failed to assist but actually hampered industrial development.

> The lack of a governmental authority that would develop and change in accordance with the economic evolution of the country, the naive mixing at the top of the bureaucracy of economic laws with laws and administrative decrees that it prescribed, caused the course of Russian economic policy to veer from side to side in response to political tides. And from this the bourgeoisie suffered acutely, being deprived of the possibility of accurate calculation and prediction, without which large-scale industrial activity is impossible.

Berlin's position, in its denial of effective governmental assistance to industry, its emphasis on the subordination of economic policy to political objectives, and its stress on the instability of official policies as a handicap to private enterprise, accurately reflected the views of the Association itself.

Between these extremes, Gerschenkron occupied a moderate position. While recognizing the predominant role of the state in economic affairs, he inclined to give greater weight to the element of accident in official policy, viewing it as "partly the result of impersonal economic forces, partly an almost accidental by-product of government decisions pursuing other goals, and partly the result of deliberate governmental policies." Gerschenkron, Economic Backwardness, 186.

Recent scholarship has tended to confirm Kahan's interpretation that, on balance, bureaucratic tutelage hindered the development of capitalist institutions in Russia. See his collected articles: Russian Economic History.

81. The Fifth Congress of Delegates of the Nobility, in February 1909, applauded a report by Vladimir I. Gurko, which presented a fairly comprehensive economic program for Russia similar to the Association's own principal recommendations: Gurko, Nashe . . . khoziaistvo. Volskii declared that it presented "in masterly fashion the ideas which our journal has been advocating for two years." A. Volskii, "Zamechatel'naia i znamenatel'naia kniga," P i T, 11, June 1, 1909, 706.

82. Quoted in Sef, Burzhuaziia, 121.

83. Volskii, Sily.

84. Ninth Congress, Doklad . . . o merakh. A preliminary memorandum on the same subject appeared in the autumn of 1914: Sovet S"ezdov, Dokladnaia zapiska . . . torgovogo balansa. Goldberg, "Association," 469, cited this document in the Central State Historical Archive in Petersburg (TsGIA f. 32, op. 1, d. 422, l. 10) in its unpublished form, dated June 12, 1914.

85. Third Congress, Zhurnaly, 7.

86. "Pervye lastochki," P i T, 24, Dec. 15, 1908, 638.

87. Fourth Congress, Zhurnaly, 41.

88. Fourth Congress, Zhurnaly, 9-10.

89. See, for example, Third Congress, Zhurnaly, 9, and Fourth Congress, Zhurnaly, 37ff.

90. The Third Congress formally approved Volskii's report, which stressed the domestic market, industrial profits, taxation, the supply of capital, and the needs of agriculture. His specific proposals for the development of industry appeared in the following order of importance: transportation and communication; organization of credit, particularly municipal credit; small industry and cooperatives; foreign trade; exploitation of state property; reform of commercial-industrial law; and labor policy. Nearly a year later, Industry and Trade reconfirmed this order of priority for the first three categories: "Korni ekonomicheskogo pod"ema Rossii," P i T, 4, Feb. 15, 1909, 213. Three months later still, he reiterated these priorities as part of the Association's "plan" in A. Volskii, "Mozhno basnei poiasnit'," P i T, 8, Apr. 15, 1909, 524. His report to the Fourth Congress placed greater emphasis improvements in education, the wider introduction of legality into Russian life, the more effective organization of economic interests, and the growth of private initiative. The Congress, it should be noted, did not approve this report.

91. "Eshche o finansovoi i ekonomicheskoi politike," P i T, 17, Sep. 1, 1908, 225.

92. Fourth Congress, Zhurnaly, 38-9.

93. "Piatyi s"ezd," P i T, 6 (78), Mar. 15, 1911, 248.

94. "Proekt gosudarstvennogo biudzheta za 1911 g.," P i T, 20 (68), Oct. 15, 1910, 393-4.

95. "Vtoroi bezdefitsitnyi biudzhet," P i T, 8 (80), Apr. 15, 1911, 344. Simultaneously, Timiriazev, no longer minister of trade and industry but an elected representative of industry in the State Council, called on the government to create "a definite program for securing the correct and broad development of trade and industry." "Biudzhetnye preniia v Gosudarstvennom Sovete," P i T, 8 (80), Apr. 15, 1911, 340.

96. "Biudzhetnye preniia," 350. See also "Bezdefitsitnyi biudzhet," P i T, 9, May 1, 1910, 587-8, and Iakov S. Rozenfeld, "Nekotorye itogi sessii Gosudarstvennogo Soveta 1910-1911 gg.," P i T, 13 (85), July 1, 1911, 35.

97. "Itogi III sessii Gosudarstvennoi Dumy," P i T, 14 (62), July 15, 1910, 102.

98. The text of this report was never published. Outlines of its contents appeared, however, in "Dnevnik Soveta," P i T, 12, June 15, 1910, 808-9, and in the journal of the thirty-fifth session of the Council: Sovet S"ezdov, Zhurnal . . . 18 iiunia 1910 goda, 2-4.

99. "O deiatel'nosti zakonodatel'nykh uchrezhdenii po voprosam, kasaiushchimsia promyshlennosti i torgovli," P i T, 7 (79), Apr. 1, 1922, 295-6, 304-5. The Duma's formally declared "economic wishes," he encouragingly observed, 296, were assuming "a more concrete character," indicative of "the undoubted process of the maturing of state thinking, which is proceeding from commonplaces to the more concrete."

100. "Ekonomicheskaia nezrelost'," P i T, 5 (101), Mar. 1, 1912, 241; see also Eighth Congress, Zhurnaly, 26-7.

101. Eighth Congress, Zhurnaly, 28.

102. Eighth Congress, Zhurnaly, 28; see also Baron G. Maidel, "Teoriia i

praktika," P i T, 10 (154), May 15, 1914, 518.

103. "Vos'moi ocherednoi s"ezd predstavitelei promyshlennosti i torgovli," P i T, 10 (154), May 15, 1914, 526.

104. Baron G. Maidel, "Zavisit-li v Rossii promyshlennyi pod"em ot urozhaev?" P i T, 21 (93), Nov. 1, 1911, 354.

105. Maidel, "Teoriia i praktika," 518.

106. Maidel, "Teoriia i praktika," 518-19.

107. Eighth Congress, Zhurnaly, 33. In his comprehensive study of economic cycles in the Russian Empire, Sergei A. Pervushin utilized a variety of complex statistical tests to measure the interaction of trends in agriculture and industry. See Pervushin, Khoziaistvennaia kon"iunktura and "Cyclical Fluctuations."

108. Maidel, "Teoriia i praktika," 519. Only a year earlier, Industry and Trade had taken issue with an article in The Russian Word that had advocated the Treasury's regulation of orders so as to alleviate economic crisis. The state, it had declared, should not time its orders, which related to basic military and capital requirements, to meet the needs of the market. "Obzor pechati," P i T, 11 (131), June 1, 1913, 513.

109. "Vos'moi ocherednoi s"ezd," 525-6. According to Livshin, Monopolii, 20, 159, the Russian government during Witte's regime had tried to ease the impact of economic crises by offering direct financial aid to industry. The Association, however, neither credited the government with such help in the past nor requested it in the future.

110. "Vos'moi ocherednoi s"ezd," 526.

111. Eighth Congress, Zhurnaly, 33.

112. Caustically denouncing "the dubious calculations of the 'Central Statistical Committee' of the government as having nothing in common with reality," the Seventh Congress had called for a second national population census; periodic population censuses in the future at least every ten years at about the same time as in other countries; and a special business and professional census. Seventh Congress, Zhurnal, 3-12; "Sed'moi ocherednoi s"ezd predstavitelei promyshlennosti i torgovli," P i T, 10 (130), May 15, 1913, 450; "Dnevnik Soveta" P i T, 17 (137) Sep. 1, 1913, 213, and 19 (139), Oct. 1, 1913, 314; and "Vtoraia vserossiiskaia perepis' i perepis' profes-sional'no-promyslovaia," P i T, 19 (139), Oct. 1, 1913, 279-80.

113. Fourth Congress, Doklad . . . dela Imperii, 1.

114. The number of economic indicators to be studied must be greater than those investigated by western economists, partly, it was explained, because Russian statistical data did not permit a review of conditions as far back in the past as did those in the West, and partly because some influences, such as the harvest, were peculiar in some degree to Russia. Although a lack of funds prevented completion of the project, much of the material collected appeared in the Council's report on Russia's economic position. Eighth Congress, Otchet, 42-4. See also "Deiatel'nosti Soveta S"ezdov . . . v 1913 g.," P i T, 1 (145), Jan. 1, 1914, 15; "Dnevnik Soveta" P i T, 12 (132), June 15, 1913, 571; 13 (133), July 1, 1913, 38; and 19 (139), Oct. 1, 1913, 313; and V. Sharyi, "Pamiati V. V. Zhukovskogo," P i T, 36-37 (231), Sep. 17, 1916, 195.

115. Vl. Kiuntsel, "Vozmozhno li nauchnoe predskazanie ekonomicheskikh krizisov?" P i T, 11 (131), June 1, 1913, 508; see also "Obzor pechati," P i T, 14 (134), July 15, 1913, 74. To refute those in Russia who denied the feasibility of this objective, Kiuntsel pointed to the work of the German economist R. Kalver and,

especially, to the indices of economic conditions established by the American, Roger Babson.

116. Maidel, "Teoriia i praktika," 519.

117. Eighth Congress, Otchet, 19-21.

118. Eighth Congress, Zhurnaly, 32. A year earlier, the Seventh Congress had called on the government to render "planned assistance" to private enterprise. "Sed'moi ocherednoi s"ezd," 451.

119. Maidel, "Teoriia i praktika," 517.

120. Maidel, "Teoriia i praktika," 519. The term "syndicate," the most common form of monopolistic organization in Russia, is here used loosely to include trusts, cartels, and other forms of monopoly. According to Livshin, Monopolii, 47-9, on the eve of the war the large-scale industrialists were becoming convinced that syndicates proper had outlived their ability to maintain a high level of profits and to prevent crisis, and that they must be replaced by trusts.

121. Iv. Bragin, "Opasnyi opyt pooshchreniia zheleznodorozhnogo dela," P i T, 12 (132), June 15, 1913, 551.

122. Seventh Congress, Zhurnal, 110; also 17-18.

123. Historians generally agree that technological level of the iron and steel industry of the South and, in somewhat less degree, of the cotton industry, compared favorably with that of western Europe. According to Liashchenko, Istoriia, 286-7, the productivity of the former exceeded that of the German iron and steel industry and was surpassed only by that of the United States; see also Gerschenkron, Economic Backwardness, 128. Livshin, Monopolii, 314, took strong exception to this conclusion, maintaining that Russia's pig-iron output per furnace remained well below that of both Germany and the United States. It would appear, however, that his figures refer to the Empire as a whole, rather than to the South alone. McKay, Pioneers, in a chapter entitled "Advanced Technology in Steel and Coal," demonstrated that foreign entrepreneurs succeeded in applying the latest technology in South Russia. Impressive levels of output resulted partly from the extremely high iron content of ore in the Krivoi Rog region. "All equipment being equal, it seems that the greater richness of iron ore gave southern Russian blast furnaces about 40 percent more output in a given time span" than in western Europe. Pioneers, 122.

124. "Ministr torgovli i promyshlennosti v Moskovskom birzhevom komitete," P i T, 8, Apr. 15, 1908, 485.

125. Eighth Congress, Zhurnaly, 115.

126. M. Selikhov, "Mirovaia zhelenodorozhnaia set'," P i T, 22 (94), Nov. 15, 1911, 429. See also the sources cited in note 39.

Chapter 3

1. "Emkost' mirovogo denezhnogo rynka," P i T, 1, Jan. 1, 1908, 7.

2. The suspicion of foreign capital that united these ill-assorted groups before 1917 figured prominently in Soviet historical scholarship as well. The exploitative character of foreign capital constituted the cardinal theme of Lenin's doctrine of imperialism. As such, it became a feature of Soviet political propaganda and historical

writing. Foreign capital allegedly "enslaved" Russia, hampered economic development, and impoverished the people because it preferred to reap its tremendous profits through the exploitation of cheap labor rather than expend its earnings on technological improvements in industrial methods. For examples of this reasoning, see Akademiia Nauk SSSR, Istoriia Moskvy, vol. 5, 28, 38, 39, and 278; and Akademiia nauk SSSR, Ocherki istorii Leningrada, vol. 3, 240.

It is significant, however, that Soviet works occasionally conceded some benefits to foreign capital. Ocherk istorii Leningrada, 101, for example, admitted that

> the influence of foreign finance capital on the biggest banking monopolies of Russia was not decisive. . . . Moreover, the very principle of "participation," on which all the mutual relationships between the Russian and foreign banks was built, consisted not in the subordination of the Russian banks to the foreign, especially the French banks, but in joint activity on equal terms for the sake of obtaining maximum profits.

Likewise, Lyashchenko, History, 641, recognized that "with the aid of foreign capital, Russian capitalism during the first decade of the twentieth century attained substantial success in the technological reconstruction and concentration of its industry, particularly with regard to its major branches." Some western non-Marxist historians have also perceived in Russia's reliance on foreign capital a deterrent to popular initiative and national independence. See, for example, Fainsod, Russia, 25.

3. "Inostrannyi kapital," P i T, 15 (63), Aug. 1, 1910, 113. See also M. P., "Inostrannyi kapital i russkii natsionalizm," P i T, 24 (72), Dec. 15, 1910, 672.

4. "Inostrannyi kapital," 114.

5. "Boiazn' inostrantsev," P i T, 3 (123), Feb. 1, 1913, 97.

6. "Inostrannyi kapital," 115.

7. "Inostrannyi kapital," 115. See also "Obzor pechati," P i T, 14 (110), July 15, 1912, 60; "V kakikh usloviiakh razvivaetsia promyshlennost' Rossii," P i T, 13 (133), July 1, 1913, 3; and "Chto daiut Rossii inostrannye kapitaly?" P i T, 17 (137), Sep. 1 1913, 175-7. In the autumn of 1913, the twenty-fifth anniversary of I. I. Iasiukovich as director of the South Russian Dnieper Metallurgical Company, founded on Belgian capital and one of the largest of Russia's iron and steel mills, provided an appropriate occasion to emphasize once again the beneficent influence of foreign money. During the course of the celebrations, Iasiukovich received the Belgian decoration of "Grand Officer of the Order of King Leopold II," an honor that must have added fuel to the fire of Russia's opponents of imported capital. "Chestvovanie I. I. Iasiukovicha na Kamenskom zavode," P i T, 19 (139), Oct. 1, 1913, 325-6. On Belgian capital in the Russian economy, see McKay, Pioneers, 31-8.

8. This apparent contradiction is readily explained by the antagonism that prevailed among different departments within the Russian government. In particular, the policies advocated by the ministries of finance and trade and industry were frequently opposed by the ministries of internal affairs and foreign affairs, as well as by the Ministry of Communication and the Department of Agriculture. See Shepelev, Tsarizm . . . 1914, 192-214.

9. In addition to a growing apprehension over Germany's predominant role in Russia's foreign trade, there was also a widely expressed fear lest military secrets be lost to Germany through German ownership of shipyards, armaments factories, machine shops, and chemical works, all areas attractive to German investors.

"Natsionalizatsiia kapitalov," P i T, 8 (152), Apr. 15, 1914, 422-4; and "Obzor pechati," P i T, 2 (146), Jan. 15, 1914, 92-3, and 3 (147), Feb. 1, 1914, 142.

10. For example, the protests of the lumber industry against the awarding of long-term lumbering concessions to foreign capitalists elicited from Industry and Trade the comment that "with such a fear of foreign capital even on the part of industrialists, it is clear that the natural riches of Russia will continue to lie waste for a long time to come." "Obzor pechati," P i T, 17 (113), Sep. 1, 1912, 171. See also Iv. Bragin, "Ispol'zovanie lesnykh bogatstv v Norvegii i Kanade," P i T, 23 (119), Dec. 1, 1912, 474-7.

11. "Boiazn' inostrantsev," 97.

12. This movement, it should be noted, was directed not only against foreign nationals and their capital, but also against the Empire's own Jewish and non-Russian population. "Natsionalizatsiia kapitalov," 422. See also Shepelev, Tsarizm . . . 1914, 204-14, and Owen, Corporation, 175-80.

13. "Obzor pechati," P i T, 4 (148), Feb. 15, 1914, 197-8.

14. See, for example: "Boiazn' inostrantsev," P i T, 100; "Chto daiut Rossii," 177; and "Obzor pechati," P i T, 14 (110), July 15, 1912, 60. On the gradual transition of managerial control to Russians, see McKay, Pioneers, ch. 5. The degree of foreign control of industrial corporations in Russia, whether registered domestically or abroad, inspired a huge polemical literature but no conclusive statistical proofs. A major problem is that it is difficult to ascertain the proportion of shares held in a given company, whether Russian or foreign, by Russians and foreigners.

15. "Boiazn' inostrantsev," 97-8.

16. In this connection, a member of the Council's staff quoted Witte's observation that

> nothing in the world is given free and in order to create its own industry a country must bear certain sacrifices. But these sacrifices are temporary and in any case less than the advantages which are obtained by the broad application of popular labor and by the exploitation of the natural riches of the country by means of foreign capital.

Quoted in Bragin, "Ispol'zovanie," 476-7.

17. "Boiazn' inostrantsev," 99-100.

18. "Natsionalizatsiia kapitalov," 424.

19. Ip. Glivits, "Otnositel'naia stoimost' deneg," P i T, 3, Feb. 1, 1909, 159.

20. S. K., "Novyi zaem," P i T, 2, Jan. 15, 1909, 78-9. See also Glivits, "Otnositel'naia stoimost'," 159.

21. Glivits, "Otnositel'naia stoimost'," 159.

22. Glivits, "Otnositel'naia stoimost'," 158. Even Russia's capital, it was pointed out, lacked sewers and rivalled Peking as "almost the most unsanitary city in the world."

23. "Ukhodit vremia," P i T, 6, Mar. 15, 1910, 368.

24. T--n, "Kosnost' i predpriimchivost'," P i T, 7 (151), April 1, 1914, 376-7. See also "Ugol'nyi 'golod' i Ministerstvo putei soobshcheniia," P i T, 22 (118), Nov. 15, 1912, 339-404; and D. Karnitskii, "Bezpochvennost' mechtanii ob oroshenii Turkestana," P i T, 22 (118), Nov. 15, 1912, 405-9.

25. Second Congress, Po povodu. See also Sovet S"ezdov, Zapiska . . . naloge.

26. Third Congress, Osnovy, 9. See also Fourth Congress, Ekonomichesko-finansovaia politika, 21, 27-8; "Pribyl'nost' russkikh aktsionernykh predpriatii," P i T, 3, Feb. 1, 1908, 139-42; "Finansy russkikh aktsionernykh predpriatii v piatiletie 1901-1905 gg.," P i T, 7, Apr. 1, 1908, 412-19; "Promyshlenno-torgovaia gruppa chlenov Gosudarstvennogo Soveta i Gosudarstvennoi Dumy," P i T, 7, Apr. 1, 1909, 451, and Apr. 15, 1909, 506. The extent to which personal self-interest underlay the Association's concern with maximizing profits occasioned frequent and heated public discussion. The Association's argument that profits must be increased in order to stimulate the investment of capital in industry struck its critics, both of the left and of the right, as a mere rationalization designed to camouflage its true objective: the enrichment of its members. In the absence of clear statistical evidence, the actual level of industrial profits in pre-revolutionary Russia has remained a subject for debate among historians. The general assumption has been that the level was high. Soviet historical writing, especially, has stressed the "enormous" profits of industrial enterprise. Akademiia Nauk SSSR Istoriia Moskvy, 46, for example, cited profits ranging from 12 to 50 percent of basic capital in the textile industry of Moscow. Lyashchenko, History, 641, 676, attributed to "excessive" profits the industrialists' alleged lack of interest in improving techniques of production and in seeking out new markets for their products.

27. "Zakoldovannyi krug," P i T, 22 (94), Nov. 15, 1911, 406.

28. "Shestoi ocherednoi s"ezd predstavitelei promyshlennosti i torgovli," P i T, 10 (106), May 15, 1912, 522. See also N. Iznar, "Dividendnost' nashikh aktsionernykh predpriiatii," P i T, 2 (98), Jan. 15, 1912, 74. "Accountable" enterprises were required to publish their financial accounts. Non-accountable enterprises included relatively few large enterprises. The largest of these published their accounts voluntarily and were therefore included in the Council's study. See Baron G. Maidel, "'Finansovaia eres'," P i T, 9 (105), May 1, 1912, 405. Although it is impossible to settle here the question of the reliability of the Council's data, a certain looseness in terminology, particularly the tendency to equate "dividends" with "profits," should be noted.

29. Maidel, "'Finansovaia eres'," 448.

30. Maidel, "'Finansovaia eres'," 448. See also Baron G. Maidel, "Finansovoe polozhenie aktsionernykh predpriiatii na desiatiletie 1901-1909 gg.," P i T, 23, (119), Dec. 1, 1912, 457-462. The great impact of Witte's remarks on the press and public opinion prompted the Sixth Congress, meeting in May, to instruct the Council to revise its procedures in the publication of statistics on joint-stock enterprise in order to present a clear comparison of the profitability of Russian enterprise and that of other countries. "Shestoi," 522.

31. Third Congress, Osnovy, 9.

32. Fourth Congress, Ekonomichesko-finansovaia politika, 13.

33. Because of high production costs, industrial prices in Russia considerably surpassed those in western Europe, and agricultural prices were about 30 percent lower. Seton-Watson, Decline, 276.

34. K. Adamskii, "Angliiskii kapital v Argentine," P i T, 21, Nov. 1, 1908, 460.

35. Adamskii, "Angliiskii kapital," 461-2. See also "Promyshlenno-torgovaia gruppa," Apr. 1, 1909, 451, and Apr. 15, 1909, 506.

36. Confirmation of the validity of the Association's complaint may be found in several works by Russian economists of the period. For example, Ozeroff, Problèmes, 126, observed that, because of the many expensive and time-consuming legal hurdles that had to be passed before a joint-stock enterprise could be established in Russia, Russian-owned enterprises operating in Russia were sometimes legally instituted in Germany, France or England. This raises an interesting question of the extent to which the data on foreign enterprise in Russia may have been inflated. (See note 14.)

37. "Nashi protivorechiia," P i T, 19 (67), Oct. 1, 1910, 339.

38. Quoted in "Novyi prem'er," P i T, 18 (90), Sep. 15, 1911, 200.

39. "Kazennaia promyshlennost'," P i T, 20 (140), Oct. 15, 1913, 332.

40. Baron G. Maidel, "V kakikh usloviiakh rabotaet russkaia promyshlennost'," P i T, 5 (101), Mar. 1, 1912, 244-5. The quotation was from Witte's Konspekt lektsii o narodnom i gosudarstvennom khoziaistve. See also: "Udobnyi moment," P i T, 6 (102), Mar. 15, 1912, 29.

41. "Ushlo vremia," P i T, 18 (138), Sep. 15, 1913, 227. See also "Razvitie promyshlennosti za poslednie gody i 'ochevidnye fakty'," P i T, 2 (122), Jan. 15, 1913, 51; "Boiazn' inostrantsev," 100; "V kakikh usloviiakh razvivaetsia promyshlennost' Rossii," P i T, 13 (133), July 1, 1913, 1-3; "Iz rechi A. I. Konovalova v Gosudarstvennoi Dume," P i T, 13 (133), July 1, 1913, 4, 5, 11; "Dve rechi N. S. Avdakova v Gosudarstvennom Sovete," P i T, 18 (138), Sep. 15, 1913, 227-34. On the controversy over corporate ownership of land in 1913-14, see Owen, Corporation, 171-80.

42. "Iz rechi A. I. Konovalova," 12.

43. "Kredit v Rossii," P i T, 18, Sep. 15, 1908, 271. See also "Nasha zolotaia valiuta i Komitet Finansov," P i T, 15, Aug. 1, 1909, 113.

44. See, for example, A. Ia. B., "Nashi sberezheniia," P i T, 24, Dec. 15, 659; and A. Babkov, "O finansovoi ustoichivosti nashikh gosudarstvennykh sberegatel'nykh kass," P i T, 8, Apr. 15, 1909, 477-80. Russia's banking system, although inadequate in many respects for the Empire's needs, nevertheless underwent great expansion during the years 1905-14. On the eve of World War I, it encompassed some 50 joint-stock commercial banks (of which five in St. Petersburg held half of all the resources of Russia's joint-stock commercial banks), more than 8,000 state savings banks, over 1,100 mutual credit societies, 319 municipal banks, and numerous small credit institutions of strictly local importance, including savings-and-loan and credit associations, both cooperative and those organized under the aegis of the zemstvos. For a concise summary, see Florinsky, Russia, 1226-7. See also Akademiia nauk SSSR, Ocherki Istorii Leningrada, vol. 3, 89-103; Akademiia nauk SSSR, Istoriia Moskvy, vol. 5, 53-6; Gindin, Russkie kommercheskie banki; and, for a post-Soviet interpretation, Bovykin and Petrov, Kommercheskie banki.

45. "Bankovyi vopros v Germanii," P i T, 10, May 15, 1908, 594.

46. G. T., "Chemu mogut nas nauchit' germanskie banki?" P i T, 21, Nov. 1, 1909, 470, 472.

47. The sum of deposits and current accounts held by commercial and industrial enterprise in joint-stock commercial banks increased from 818.1 million rubles as of January 1, 1908 to 1,817.3 million on January 1, 1912. "Boiazn' inostrantsev," 98. The savings of the urban and village population, deposited mainly in mutual credit

societies and municipal banks, were said to have increased from 79 to 145 million and from 40 to 115.2, respectively, between 1908 and 1911. St. Zverev, "Nakoplenie kapitalov i trebovaniia na nikh v Rossii," P i T, 1 (145), Jan. 1, 1914, 24. These figures, it should be noted, indicate a rate of saving considerably in excess of the figure of 900 million cited by the Minister of Finance in the late spring of 1914 as the total popular savings during the past ten years. "Rechi na VIII ocherednom s"ezde," P i T, 11 (155), June 1, 1914, 564.

48. See, for example, Tb., "Finansiruiushchie obshchestva," P i T, 15 (63), Aug. 1, 1910, 120; S. Antonov, "Nekotorye osobennosti deiatel'nosti kommercheskikh bankov," P i T, 24 (96), Dec. 15, 1911, 539-41; and G. Tenenbaum, "K piatidesiatiletiiu gosudarstvennykh sberegatel'nykh kass," P i T, 22 (118), Nov. 15, 1912, 409-14.

49. G. Tenenbaum, "Obilie deneg," P i T, 18 (90), Sep. 15, 1911, 212.

50. See F. Kubatskii, "Torgovye neplatezhi v Rossii," P i T, 20 (116), Oct. 15, 1912, 303-7; Seventh Congress, Zhurnal, 67-84; and Sovet S"ezdov, Promyshlennost' . . . 1912-1913 gg., xiii-xiv.

51. The Association contended that certain proposals advanced by the government early in 1914 represented an infringement on the rights of bankers and threatened to make banking operations impossible. These measures included limiting the acceptance of deposits and making bankers responsible for all advice, information, and other statements given out by their employees. D., "K zakonoproektu o bankirskikh predpriiatiiakh," P i T, 12 (156), June 15, 1914, 624-6; "Dnevnik Soveta," P i T, 12 (156), June 15, 1914, 650; and "Dnevnik Soveta," P i T, 13 (157), July 1, 1914, 43.

52. For example, A. Lomeier, "Uchet trebovanii po otkrytym schetam," P i T, 20 (140), Oct. 15, 1913, 345-8.

53. In earlier years, as we have seen, the Association had consistently taken a strong stand against an inflationary monetary policy. In calling for a reduction in the gold backing of the paper ruble at this later date, it stressed the need for "financial preparedness" in the event of war. In fact, the ruble continued to be backed more than 100 percent by gold in the reserves of the State Bank. The Association continued to call for an expansion in gold production as a foundation for an expanded currency. See, for example, the following articles in P i T: O. Geiman, "K uchetnoi politike Gosudarstvennogo Banka," 13 (109), July 1, 1912, 4-8; Vl. Zhukovskii, "Odna iz prichin nedostatka deneg," 13 (133), July 1, 1913, 12-15; A. E., "Nasha finansovaia boevaia gotovnost' i Gosudarstvennyi Bank," 23 (143), Dec. 1, 1913, 513-17; "K voprosu o zolotom zapase za granitsei," 5 (149), Mar. 1, 1914, 225-8; "Novyi kurs," 9 (153) May 1, 1914, 458; and "Vos'moi ocherednoi s"ezd predstavitelei promyshlennosti i torgovli," 10 (154), May 15, 1914, 526.

54. Third Congress, Osnovy, 28; Fourth Congress, Doklad . . . melkoi promyshlennosti, 33; Fourth Congress, Zhurnaly, 29-30; and the following articles in P i T; "Tretii ocherednoi s"ezd predstavitelei promyshlennosti i torgovli," 8, Apr. 15, 1908, 523; A. Sh., "Novoe polozhenie o gorodskikh obshchestvennykh bankakh," 12, June 15, 1909, 725; S. Karpinskii, "Bank kooperativnykh tovarishchestv," 15, Aug. 1, 1909, 121-4; A. Babkov, "Polozhenie nashego melkogo kredita," 21, Nov. 1, 1909, 463-7; and A. Babkov, "Kreditnye tovarishchestva," 23, Dec. 1, 1909, 590-3.

55. Ia. Rozenfeld, "Narodnye sberezheniia i narodnyi kredit," P i T, 14 (62),

July 15, 1910, 60-3; quotation from 61. See also A. Babkov, "Organizatsiia kommunal'nogo kredita v Germanii," P i T, 4, Feb. 5, 1910, 224-8.

56. See "Dnevnik Soveta" P i T, 9, May 1, 1910, 630, and 11, June 1, 1910, 750.

57. "Munitsipal'nyi kredit," P i T, 10, May 15, 1910, 646. See also "Kredit dlia gorodov i zemstv," P i T, 2, Jan. 15, 1910, 73-4; P. E., "Reforma obshchestvennykh bankov," P i T, 11, June 1, 1910, 726-8; G. T--m, "Kredit gorodskogo domovladeniia v Rossii," P i T, 23 (71), Dec. 1, 1910, 571-3; and S.U--, "Nasha gorodskaia zadolzhennost'," P i T, 9 (81), May 1, 1911, 400-3.

58. "Munitsipal'nyi kredit," 646. See also "Dnevnik Soveta," P i T, 9, May 1, 1910, 630, and G. T--m, "Vedomstvennye banki," P i T, 1 (73), Jan. 1, 1911, 6-9.

59. G. Tenenbaum, "K piatidesiatiletiiu, 409-14.

60. S. Antonov, "Deiatel'nost' gorodskikh bankov i ikh reforma," P i T, 4 (100), Feb. 15, 1912, 200-5.

61. Lyashchenko, History, 675.

62. I. G., "Promyshlennost' i narodnoe obrazovanie," P i T, 3, Feb. 1, 1909, 152.

63. "Rech' Ministra torgovli i promyshlennosti Moskovskomu birzhevomu obshchestvu," T-p G, 227, Oct. 7 (20), 1906, 4. The First Congress repeated this admonition. "Pervyi ocherednoi s"ezd predstavitelei promyshlennosti i torgovli," I, T-p G, 232, Oct. 13 (26), 1906, 1. See also Ermanskii, "1905-7," 93.

64. "Tretii ocherednoi s"ezd predstavitelei promyshlennosti i torgovli," P i T, 8, Apr. 15, 1908, 521. See also Third Congress, Zhurnaly, 11, and "Ministr torgovli i promyshlennosti v Moskovskom birzhevom komitete," P i T, 8, Apr. 15, 1908, 485.

65. Third Congress, Doklad . . . telefonnom dele v Rossii, 4.

66. Fourth Congress, Zhurnaly, 40. A decade earlier, according to Rotvand, there were no more than 16,000 families in Russia with annual incomes of more than 5,000 rubles and only 400,000 with incomes of over 1,000 rubles. Other sources tend to support these figures. Sergei N. Prokopovich and Litvinov-Falinskii estimated Russia's per-capita income at 67.3 and 58 rubles, respectively, in 1900. The Statistical Bureau of the Association itself later produced an estimate of 65 rubles for the year 1904. This figure was accepted by Finn-Enotaevskii, Kapitalizm, 189.

67. Fourth Congress, Zhurnaly, 38. See also "Ekonomichesko-finansovaia politika Rossii," P i T, 22, Nov. 15, 1909, 520.

68. A. Volskii, "Vernyi put' k vyvozu russkikh fabrikantov," P i T, 23, Dec. 1, 1908, 587.

69. Sovet S"ezdov, Zapiska . . . mashinostroeniia, 27. See also "Khronika deiatal'nosti pravitel'stva," P i T, 11, June 1, 1908, 693, and I. G., "Mezhduvedomstvennoe Soveshchanie o merakh k uluchsheniiu otechestvennoi metallurgicheskoi i mashinostroitel'noi promyshlennosti," P i T, June 15, 1908, 766-9.

70. Lyashchenko, History, 676. In fact, the industrialists were never so brash as to turn against the helping hand of the government, just as they were never so confident of its reliability or its benevolence as to abandon the hopeful potentialities of the popular market.

71. "Chlen Gos. Soveta, E. A. Voinilovich, o podniatii otechestvennoi proizvoditel'nosti," P i T, 9, May 1, 1909, 540.

72. Fourth Congress, Zhurnaly, 29; and Fourth Congress, Doklad . . . melkoi

promyshlennosti, 22.

73. "Russkii fabrichnyi eksport," P i T, 8, April 15, 1910, 511-12.

74. "Istekshii god," P i T, 1 (97), Jan. 1, 1912, 2. See also K. Komarovskii, "Ekonomicheskaia zhizn' Moskovskoi promyshlennoi polosy," P i T, 3 (99), Feb. 1, 1912, 139.

75. See, for example, "Deklaratsiia Predsedatelia Soveta Ministrov i ekonomicheskoe polozhenie strany," P i T, 24 (120), Dec. 15, 1912, 517-19, and "Itogi 1912 goda," P i T, 1 (121), Jan. 1, 1913, 2.

76. "Iz rechi A. I. Konovalova v Gosudarstvennoi Dume," P i T, 11 (131), June 1, 1913, 496-7 (quoted), 498 (quoted), 499 (quoted). Rather inconsistently, Konovalov noted, 498, that per-capita consumption in Russia had increased by 4.6 percent between 1904 and 1911, as contrasted with a growth of more than 20 percent in Germany.

77. "Moskovskie rechi G. A. Krestovnikova i V. N. Kokovtsova," P i T, 8 (104), Apr. 15, 1912, 392-3.

78. "Urozhai," P i T, 17 (113), Sep. 1, 1912, 156.

79. "Ob"iasnitel'naia zapiska k proektu gosudarstvennoi rospisi na 1914 god i sovremmennoe polozhenie promyshlennosti," P i T, 23 (143), Dec. 1, 1913, 513.

80. Eighth Congress, Otchet, 15. The Council's observations may, however, have been intended less as an expression of confidence in the country's economic strength than as a departure point for its attack on official economic policies, which, it contended, were undermining all hope of continued prosperity. Estimates of conditions in Russia during the decade before the war generally assumed a substantial increase in popular well-being. According to Gerschenkron, "Problem," 14, "improvements in standards of living were clearly discernible." The State Planning Committee of the USSR set per-capita national income in the Russian Empire in 1913 at 102.2 rubles. Lyashchenko, History, 697. The Economic Council of the Provisional Government put the figure at 101.35 rubles. Finn-Enotaevskii, allowing for Prokopovich's estimate of a 29-percent increase in prices during 1900-13, arrived at a net figure of 93.7. Finn-Enotaevskii, Kapitalizm, 189, 191.

81. "Strana potrebitelei" P i T, 5, Mar. 1, 1908, 258-9.

82. "Eksport kazennykh deneg za granitsu," P i T, 24, Dec. 15, 1909, 641.

83. "Promyshlennost' i pechat'," P i T, 1, Jan. 1, 1910, 2.

84. "Russkii fabrichnyi eksport," P i T, 8, Apr. 15, 1910, 513. The reference was to issue no. 5 of 1908.

85. "Edinenie," P i T, 14 (86), July 15, 1911, 41.

86. Ip. Glivits, "Sindikat i tseny," P i T, 23 (95), Dec. 1, 1911, 493. See also "Prichina dorogovizny," P i T, 23 (95), Dec. 1, 1911, 471.

87. "Ekonomicheskaia nezrelost'," P i T, 5 (101), Mar. 1, 1912, 243.

88. "Torgovo-promyshlennye problemy i obshchestvennoe mnenie," P i T, 10 (106), May 15, 1912, 507.

89. Sovet S"ezdov, Promyshlennost' . . . 1907-1912 gg., xviii.

90. "Itogi S"ezda," P i T, 10 (154), May 15, 1914, 511.

91. Seventh Congress, Zhurnal, 115.

92. "Kak uvelichit' razmery dushevogo potrebleniia v Rossii?" P i T, 14 (134), July 15, 1913, 58.

93. "Edinenie," 40.

94. B. Ashov, "Organizatsiia predstavitelei srednei i melkoi promyshlennosti v Bel'gii," P i T, 24 (72), Dec. 15, 1910, 634.

95. I. B--n, "Potreblenie zheleza v Rossii," P i T, 14 (134), July 15, 1913, 71-2. A similar statement with respect to coal appeared in "Potrebiteli tverdogo goriuchego v Rossii i Germanii," P i T, 7, Apr. 1, 1913, 348. A book on the metallurgical industry by a member of the Council's staff demonstrated the Association's interest in comparisons between industrial and consumers' demand; see Glivits, Potreblenie.

96. "Gosudarstvennaia rospis'," P i T, 21 (93), Nov. 1, 1911, 351.

97. "Kak uvelichit' razmery dushevogo potrebleniia v Rossii?" P i T, 14 (134), July 15, 1913, 58.

98. "Obzor pechati," P i T, 24 (120), Dec. 15, 1912, 542.

99. In only two years of the early twentieth century, 1909 and 1910, did the Empire's normally favorable balance of trade make possible a favorable balance of payments, the result of exceptionally large harvests. Baron G. Maidel, "Zavisit-li v Rossii promyshlennyi pod"em ot urozhaev?" P i T, 21 (93), Nov. 1, 1911, 354. Given these circumstances, the unfavorable developments in both the debt and the trade balance were particularly ominous. During the period 1900-13, Russia's payments abroad on its growing public and privately held foreign indebtedness increased steadily. The public debt alone nearly doubled between 1899 and 1914. During those same years, however, the favorable balance of trade, on which Russia mainly relied to counterbalance those expenditures, fluctuated widely. A sharp decline from its high point in 1909 to a near record low in 1913 meant that Russia's foreign trade increasingly fell short of covering payments due to other countries. By the end of the period, payments of 5.4 billion rubles on the debt alone exceeded the favorable balance of trade by 1.3 billion. Pokrovskii, Vneshniaia torgovlia, esp. 348, 384-5.

100. Although the Association devoted much attention to questions of foreign trade during the early years, 1906-9, the Council's reports stressed issues as labor policy, taxation, and railroads. In 1910 and 1911, however, by the Council's own account, foreign trade constituted the most important issue confronting the organization. "The Association of Industry and Commerce of Russia," English Supplement, P i T, 2 (98), Jan. 15, 1912, 8.

101. "Eksport kazennykh deneg za granitsu," P i T, 24, Dec. 15, 1909, 643.

102. This view was not peculiar to the Association but was shared by many thoughtful Russians, who were not only alarmed by the growing danger of war and the mounting evidence of German interest in the East, but were also fearful of the less military but, they insisted, nevertheless aggressive economic and political ambitions of the Western Powers. The Association acknowledged the impossibility of excluding all imports. Thus Maidel spoke in terms of reducing imports "to the minimum possible." Baron G. Maidel, "Zavisit-li," 354. Avdakov conceded that "part of this importation will unavoidably remain under all conditions." Fifth Congress, Zhurnaly, 2. Krestovnikov once declared that barely one-third of Russia's imports consisted of goods which, for climatic reasons, could not be produced at home, a conclusion endorsed, incidentally, by Chairman of the Council of Ministers Kokovtsov. "Moskovskie rechi G. A. Krestovnikova i V. N. Kokovtsova," P i T, 8 (104), Apr. 15, 1912, 393-7.

103. "Tretii ocherednoi s"ezd, P i T, 8, Apr. 15, 1908, 523-4. See also Third

Congress, Osnovy, 33.

104. The Association never gave a completely rational and consistent explanation for its fears, although they were in many respects justified and were widely shared by leaders in the government, the legislature, and the press. On the one hand, the increase in imports resulted from Russian industry's temporary inability to satisfy the unexpectedly rapid increase in industrial demand for capital equipment, metals, fuel, and raw materials in the wake of the new prosperity. Avdakov, in an address before the State Council, described Russia's economic difficulties as characteristic of the initial phase of a period of economic expansion. "Rech' N. S. Avdakova v Gosudarstvennom Sovete v zasedanii 9 iiunia," P i T, 14 (158), July 15, 1914, 61. Professors Struve and Tugan-Baranovskii supported this diagnosis. As the latter told the Eighth Congress, an increase in imports, and even an unfavorable balance of trade, occurred in all periods of rapid industrial expansion. "Vos'moi ocherednoi s"ezd," P i T, 10 (154), May 15, 1914, 532-3. Likewise, the Council saw the decline in exports as in part the consequence of temporarily unfavorable agricultural conditions. On the other hand, the Association persistently viewed Russia's foreign trade position almost as a prelude to disaster. See, for example, the following articles in P i T, "Ushlo vremia," 18 (138), Sep. 15, 1913, 225-7; Baron G. Maidel, "Ugrozhaiushchii rost importa i ponizhenie aktivnosti torgovogo balansa," 19 (139), Oct. 1, 1913, 281-5; "Itogi 1913 goda," 1 (145), Jan. 1, 1914, 1-3; "K voprosu o zolotom zapase za granitsei," 5 (149), Mar. 1, 1914, 225-8; V. Gefding, "Vneshniaia torgovlia Rossii v 1901-1912 gg.," 6 (150), Mar. 15, 1914, 308-12; "Rechi na VIII ocherednom s"ezde," 10 (154), May 15, 1914, 512-15; "Rechi na VIII ocherednom s"ezde," 11 (155), June 1, 1914, 563-4; "Chto nuzhno v nastoiashchii moment Rossii?" 14 (158), July 15, 1914, 57-9; and "Rech' N. S. Avdakova . . . 9 iiunia," 59-62. See also Eighth Congress, Peresmotr.

105. "Dnevnik Soveta," P i T, 4 (148), Feb. 15, 1914, 208. See also "Dnevnik Soveta" in the following issues of P i T: 5 (149), Mar. 1, 1914, 282; 13 (157), July 1, 1914, 42; and 14 (158), July 15, 1914, 84-5.

106. Fifth Congress, Zhurnaly, 2. See also "Privetstvennye rechi na V s"ezde," P i T, 7 (79), Apr. 1, 1911, 293.

107. Sovet S"ezdov, Zapiska . . . zheleznykh dorog, 77.

108. In this connection, the Association took sharp exception to the view, attributed to Count Witte, that customs duties and railroad rates should be independent of each other. Iv. Bragin, "Vneshnii rynok i tarify zheleznykh dorog," P i T, 7 (151), Apr. 1, 1914, 365-6.

109. For example, see "Srast' k zagranitse," P i T, 12, June 15, 1908, 716. According to Industry and Trade, governmental expenditures alone for purchases in other countries amounted to some 390 million rubles during the period 1901-7. "Eksport kazennykh deneg za granitsu," P i T, 24, Dec. 15, 1909, 642. During the five-year period 1900-4, the journal asserted in "Srast'," 716, Russia had provided employment for at least three and a half million foreigners "at a time when food relief to the hungry population was becoming a normal item in our state budget." The article continued:

> The Council of our Association, standing guard over the interests of domestic work, has already, repeatedly and not ineffectively, come forward before governmental and public institutions against proposals to place orders abroad. In view of the current depression in domestic industry, the Council of the

> Association is advancing in this direction with redoubled energy whenever its active or consultative members announce their intention of placing orders abroad. If an energetic advance in this direction is not always convenient in a practical sense for individual firms, which would thereby break relations with this or that contracting institution, such an advance is nevertheless the basic duty of organizations uniting the common interests of domestic industry and trade.

110. See, for example, "Eksport," 643.

111. See, for example, I. G., "Mezhduvedomstvennoe soveshchanie," P i T, 12, June 15, 1908, 767.

112. "Kazennye zakazy za granitsei," P i T, 2, Jan. 15, 1909, 71.

113. Third Congress, Osnovy, 33.

114. "Eksport," 641. See also "Strana potrebitelei," P i T, 5, Mar. 1, 1908, 258, and "Strast'," 714. As late as 1914, however, the newspaper continued to bemoan the Russian "pathological mania for everything foreign." "Obzor pechati," 6 (150), Mar. 15, 1914, 322.

115. "Kazennye zakazy," 71.

116. "Kazennye zakazy," 72-3. See also "Eksport," 641-4, and Evg. Liubovich, "Kazennyi milliard," P i T, 3, Feb. 1, 1909, 146-7.

117. Volskii, Sily, 43.

118. Maidel considered Mendeleev "one of the greatest Russians, one of the active participants in the creation of our tariff, and one of the greatest scholars in the world." Eighth Congress, Zhurnaly, 121. On Mendeleev and the fate of his protectionist writings at the hands of tsarist and Soviet censors, see Owen, Corporation, 111-15.

119. "Obzor pechati," P i T, 2 (146), Jan. 15, 1914, 93.

120. "Obsledovanie promyshlennosti," P i T, 15 (111), Aug. 1, 1912, 84. The quotation from List was borrowed from the newly published work by Witte, Po povodu natsionalizma. Von Laue, Sergei Witte, 56-62, discusses Witte's use of List's ideas. On List's economic theories and their importance, see Szporluk, Communism and Nationalism.

121. Timiriazev proffered an unusually moderate statement of the outlook of the organized business community, which probably reflected the views of trade more than those of industry, at a joint meeting of the Councils of the Association of Industry and Trade and the Association of Trade and Agriculture in 1913.

> The tariff of 1891 was in the full sense of the word a "systematic" [tolkovyi] tariff, as our famous scholar and thinker Mendeleev happily called it. Under it, duties were established not according to a theoretical concept of protectionism, not with the aim of creating a Chinese wall around Russia against imports from abroad, but according to a careful study of the conditions of production for each type of good, while taking into account the natural peculiarities of Russia, its financial, commercial, and other kinds of relationships.

Quoted in "Torzhestvennoe zasedanie Sovetov S"ezdov predstavitelei promyshlennosti i torgovli i predstavitelei birzhevoi torgovli i sel'skogo khoziaistva," P i T, 5 (125), Mar. 1, 1913, 205.

122. "Gosudarstvennaia oborona i promyshlennost'," P i T, 18 (114), Sep. 15, 1912, 197-8, and Mertsalov, "Avtomobil'noe delo v Rossii," P i T, 19 (115), Oct. 1, 1912, 245-9.

123. Sovet S"ezdov, Promyshlennost' . . . 1912-1913 gg., 42-3.

124. Some tactical difference of opinion existed within the Council itself on the desirability of reducing duties on raw materials. Thus, the report of the Council to the Seventh Congress on the work of the legislature urged the need for immediate reductions, without waiting for a general tariff revision. Sovet S"ezdov, Promyshlennost' . . . 1912-1913 gg. However, the Council suggested to the Eighth Congress that, in the interest of enhancing Russia's bargaining power in the approaching talks with Germany, the revised general tariff should include only suggestions for increases. Any desired reductions could be incorporated later in the guise of concessions during the negotiations! Eighth Congress, Peresmotr, 20.

125. The Association yielded only under sharp pressure from the government, the Duma, and its own members in the machine and metalworking industries. In so doing, it could not refrain from issuing dire warnings that any decline in the domestic price of pig iron might precipitate a crisis in the metallurgical industry. "Parallel," P i T, 7 (79), Apr. 1, 1911, 289-91; and N. S. Avdakov, "O vvoze chuguna iz-za granitsei," P i T, 12 (84), June 15, 1911, 543-7.

126. "Deputatsiia Soveta S"ezdov . . . u Ministra promyshlennosti," P i T, 5, Mar. 1, 1908, 295.

127. "Programnaia rech' Ministra torgovli i promyshlennosti v Gosudarstvennoi Dume," P i T, 17, Sep. 1, 1909, 250.

128. "Dnevnik Soveta," P i T, 17, Sep. 1, 1909, 250. The Association sought thereby to strengthen Russia's hand in preparation of the renegotiation of the trade agreement with Germany, which was to expire in 1917.

129. Timiriazev admitted this at a meeting of the Moscow Exchange Society. "Moskovskie rechi G. A. Krestovnikova i V. I. Timiriazeva," P i T, 7, Apr. 1, 1909, 409.

130. "Novaia era," P i T, 8 (104), Apr. 15, 1912, 390. See also "Moskovskie rechi Krestovnikova i Kokovtsova," P i T, 8 (104), Apr. 15, 1912, 396-8.

131. "Gosudarstvennaia oborona," 198.

132. "Deklaratsiia Predsedatelia Soveta Ministrov i ekonomicheskoe polozhenie strany," P i T, 24 (120), Dec. 15, 1912, 516.

133. "Bor'ba s sindikatami i tamozhennoe pokrovitel'stvo," P i T, 9 (129), May 1, 1913, 394-5.

134. Quoted in "Rechi na VIII ocherednom s"ezde," P i T, 10 (154), May 15, 1914, 516.

135. A year earlier, Russia's businessmen, speaking through a joint meeting of their two Empire-wide organizations, had taken advantage of the opportunity offered by the tercentenary celebrations of the House of Romanov to praise the tariff policies of such diverse rulers as Catherine II, Nicholas I, and Alexander III. The reign of Nicholas II, however, was passed over in pointed silence. "Torzhestvennoe zasedanie," 202-6.

136. Sovet S"ezdov, Promyshlennost' . . . 1907-1912 gg., 66-7.

137. "Sleduet-li Rossiia stremit'sia byt' zhitnitsei mira?" P i T, 6 (150), Mar. 15, 1914, 303-4.

138. "Organizatsiia samopomoshchi v vyvoznoi torgovle," P i T, 9, May 1, 1908, 552.

139. "Pervyi ocherednoi s"ezd predstavitelei promyshlennosti i torgovli," T-p G,

no. 232, Oct. 13 (26), 1906, 1.

140. "Tretii ocherednoi s"ezd predstavitelei promyshlennosti i torgovli," P i T, 8, Apr. 15, 1908, 523-4. See also Third Congress, Osnovy, 33. Shortly afterward, Minister of Trade and Industry Timiriazev again proclaimed Russia's urgent need to increase its exports of manufactured goods, especially, he noted, since domestic purchasing power could be expected, at best, to develop only very slowly. "Moskovskie rechi," 1909, 409.

141. Russia's favorable balance of trade declined from 429.7 million rubles in 1911 to 146.1 million in 1913, as imports increased by about 212.3 million rubles per annum, while exports declined only by 71.3 million. The bulk of the increased imports consisted of metals, coal, and their products, thus reflecting the inability of Russian industry to supply the growing domestic demand for these commodities. Khromov, Ekonomicheskoe razvitie, 470-9.

142. An all-Russian congress of representatives of trade and industry on the development of trade with the Near East was held in Moscow in May; and the First South-Russian Commercial-Industrial Congress, meeting in Odessa later in the year, devoted a major part of its time to the question of exports. Neither gathering had any formal connection with the Association, and the first was convened under semi-official auspices. Personal connections were numerous, however. The membership of the Moscow Congress included delegates from the Council of the Association. It was chaired by Grigorii A. Krestovnikov, and others active in the Association took part in its proceedings. "Iz deiatel'nosti obshchestvennykh uchrezhdenii po promyshlennosti i torgovle," P i T, 10, May 15, 1910, 699-700; and "Dnevnik Soveta," P i T, 15 (63), Aug. 1, 1910, 152.

143. The Association's mounting concern with foreign trade was noted in a contemporary publication of the Ministry of Finance. Statement of Vladislav Iu. Shimanovskii in Ministerstvo finansov, Pravitel'stvennye uchrezhdeniia, 21.

144. Third Congress, Osnovy, 9. See also "Rossiia na mezhdunarodnom rynke," P i T, 2, Jan. 15, 1908, 97-9. The justice of the Association's complaint has been confirmed by historians, both in the West and in the Soviet Union, to whom the peasantry has appeared as the hapless victim of a commercial policy that sought to maintain the Empire's favorable balance of trade mainly by extracting an inordinate proportion of the grain crop from a rural population that was already subsisting at a minimal level of food consumption. See, for example, Miller, Economic Development, 49, 111; and Lyashchenko, History, 737. For recent reassessments based on new statistical research, see Gregory, Before Command, 52-4, and the articles on agriculture in Davies, ed., From Tsarism.

145. "Rossiia na mezhdunarodnom rynke," 98-9 (italics in original).

146. Third Congress, Osnovy, 29-30.

147. "Vytesnenie russkoi muki s inostrannykh rynkov," P i T, 13 (109), July 1, 1912, 4.

148. Grain sales amounted to 52.5 percent of total exports in 1909 but declined to 36.3 and 39.1 percent in 1912 and 1913 respectively. Khromov, Ekonomicheskoe razvitie, 474.

149. "Prichina dorogovizny," P i T, 23 (95), Dec. 1, 1911, 471.

150. In the spring of 1914, the Administration of Agriculture declared its goal of bringing Russia nearer "to predominance on the world agricultural market, to the

great objective of serving as the granary of the world." Quoted in "Sleduet-li Rossiia," 301.

151. V. Gefding, "Perspektivy nashei torgovli s Balkanskimi gosudarstvami," P i T, 7 (127), Apr. 1, 1913, 303. It should be noted that this opinion was not universally accepted in Russia. The semi-official New Times, for example, wrote that "neither Russian industry nor Russian trade needs at the present time or will need, for a long time, foreign markets." Quoted in "Obzor pechati," P i T, 17 (137), Sep. 1, 1913, 199. Even within the Association itself there were evidently some doubters. Maidel conceded that "the export of our manufactures will not become firm until Russian industry becomes the master of the situation on the domestic market, and, as the growth in imports of manufactures shows, this has not yet taken place." Maidel, "Ugrozhaiushchii rost importa i ponizhenie aktivnosti torgovogo balansa," P i T, 19 (139), Oct. 1, 1913, 283.

152. A. Volskii, "Vernyi put' k vyvozu russkikh fabrikantov," P i T, 23, Dec. 1, 1908, 589. See also "Promyshlenno-torgovaia gruppa chlenov Gosudarstvennogo Soveta i Gosudarstvennoi Dumy," P i T, 7, Apr. 1, 1909, 451; and "Russkii fabrichnyi eksport," P i T, 8, Apr. 15, 1910, 512.

153. See, for example, Ip. Glivits, "Mezhdunarodnye promyshlennye soglasheniia," P i T, 16 (64), Aug. 15, 1910, 188.

154. "Russkii fabrichnyi eksport," P i T, 8, Apr. 15, 1910, 513.

155. "Obzor pechati," P i T, 9 (153), May 1, 1914, 475. This statement weakened one of the Association's favorite arguments in defense of dumping, namely that it provided a means of stabilizing production at a constant level and avoiding the accumulation of surpluses on the home market. See Glivits, "Mezhdunarodnye soglasheniia," 188.

156. "Uchasti gosudarstva v vyvoznoi torgovle," P i T, 6, Mar. 15, 1908, 356.

157. "Obzor pechati," P i T, 22 (142), Nov. 15, 1913, 461.

158. V. Gefding, "Polozhenie na Balkanakh i russkii eksport," P i T, 20 (140), Oct. 15, 1913, 339-40.

159. "Obzor pechati," P i T, 9 (153), May 1, 1914, 475-6. Also "Obzor pechati," P i T, 3 (147), Feb. 1, 1914, 142-3.

160. Cited as one example of such obstruction were the restrictions imposed on the activities of Jewish traveling salesmen. "Obzor pechati," P i T, 12 (156), June 15, 1914, 638.

161. "Dnevnik Soveta," P i T, 3, Feb. 1, 1909, 194-6.

162. "Russkii fabrichnyi eksport," 513.

163. "Dnevnik Soveta," P i T, 12, June 15, 1910, 809.

164. Fourth Congress, Zhurnaly, 2. Also "Privetstvennye rechi," P i T, 22, Nov. 15, 1909, 523.

165. Sovet S"ezdov, Promyshlennost' . . . 1907-1912 gg., xxi-xxii.

166. In 1913, 29.8 percent of Russia's total exports, in terms of rubles, went to Germany, but 47.5 percent of imports came from that country. In 1901, the figures were 23.5 and 35.5 percent, respectively. Khromov, Ekonomicheskoe razvitie, 490-3.

167. See "Torgovyi dogovor s Germaniei," P i T, 12 (84), June 15, 1911, 531-2; Eighth Congress, Peresmotr, 18ff.; and Pokrovskii, Vneshniaia torgovlia, 361-6. Contemporary agrarian economists, in contrast, considered the treaty to be discriminatory mainly against agriculture. They emphasized the high German duty on Russian

grain (an effort to appease Germany's own agrarian interests) and the prohibition on the import of Russian livestock, defended by Germany as a health measure. For example, Tugan-Baranovskii, "Torgovyi dogovor s Germaniei," in K luchshemu budushchemu, 219, wrote that "the interests of our agriculture were sacrificed [in 1904], as is usually the case in our country, to the interests of big capital."

168. The importance of Germany's role, both in exporting to Russia and other countries goods produced from Russian raw materials and as a middleman in Russia's foreign trade generally, is attested by significant differences in the statistical data provided by the two countries. According to the Russian figures, which did not distinguish as to the place of origin of imported goods, imports from Germany in 1912 amounted to 45.4 percent of total Russian imports. In the German statistics, however, which did not include goods of non-German origin in the figure for German exports to Russia, the percentage fell to 26.9. Conversely, Russian exports to Germany amounted to 46.5 percent of total Russian exports according to German figures, which included goods imported and subsequently reexported by Germany. If Russian figures, which listed exports according to the country of ultimate destination, were used, the percentage dropped to 29.9. Eighth Congress, Peresmotr, 9-14; and Pokrovskii, Vneshniaia torgovlia, 348-85.

169. "Moskovskie rechi G. A. Krestovnikova i V. N. Kokovtsova," P i T, 8 (104), Apr. 15, 1912, 393. See also Eighth Congress, Peresmotr, 14, 18.

170. "Strannaia missiia," P i T, 21 (93), Nov. 1, 1911, 351-2. The impact of the incident was heightened by certain contemptuous remarks made by the representatives of the Handelstag concerning the slowness of Russian ships, the inefficiency of Russian lawyers, and the "uncultured" quality of the Russian language. Referring, apparently, to one particular member of the mission, Industry and Trade remarked, 151: "It is certainly surprising that the Handelstag could not have found in its midst a delegate with a smaller dose of arrogance and Junker haughtiness and with a greater store of tact and patience."

171. G. Ia. Rokhovich, "Naivnye pretenzii," P i T, 14 (134), July 15, 1913, 63. See also G. Ia. Rokhovich, "Tamozhennaia trevoga," P i T, 8 (152), Apr. 15, 1914, 428-30.

172. Sovet S"ezdov, Materialy po peresmotru torgovykh dogovorov.

173. See Eighth Congress, Otchet, 45-6; and "Deiatel'nost' Soveta s"ezdov predstavitelei promyshlennosti i torgovli v 1913 g.," P i T, 1 (145), Jan. 1, 1914, 16-17.

174. "Deiatel'nost'," 17.

175. Eighth Congress, Otchet, 46. See also V. V., "Peresmotr tamozhennogo tarifa," P i T, 13 (157), July 1, 1914, 12.

176. Quoted from an internal memorandum, no. 30757, in Eighth Congress, Otchet, 2, 5.

Chapter 4

1. In 1912, a prominent member of the Council, Aleksandr A. Bublikov, stated: "The commercial-industrial class knows well that the slogan 'radical needs call for radical treatment' is absolutely unacceptable in the field of economics." Sixth Congress, Zhurnal, 31. Likewise, Volskii defined the task of the Association as "determining the path of our economic evolution, and in forestalling and precluding revolutionary methods in the resolution of socio-economic questions." Quoted in Livshin, Monopolii, 253.

2. Fourth Congress, Ekonomichesko-finansovaia politika, 2 (emphasis added).

3. See, for example, Livshin, Monopolii, 192.

4. "Biudzhetnye preniia v Gosudarstvennoi Dume," P i T, 5, Mar. 1, 1909, 280.

5. Fourth Congress, Doklad . . . melkoi promyshlennosti, 22.

6. Fourth Congress, Ekonomichesko-finansovaia politika, 27-8. In the same spirit, Zhukovskii declared, 28, that "all attention must be concentrated on the solution of preeminently economic questions."

7. Fourth Congress, Zhurnal, 39.

8. "Deputatsiia Soveta nashikh s"ezdov u Ministra torgovli i promyshlennosti," P i T, 5, Mar. 1, 1908, 294.

9. "Biudzhetnye preniia," 280.

10. A. Volskii, "Oni suzhdenie vozliubili," P i T, 9, May 1, 1909, 588.

11. "Promyshlenno-torgovaia gruppa chlenov Gosudarstvennogo Soveta i Gosudarstvennoi Dumy," P i T, 5, Mar. 1, 1909, 325.

12. "Moskovskie rechi G. A. Krestovnikova i V. I. Timiriazeva," P i T, 7, Apr. 1, 1909, 411.

13. "Biudzhetnye preniia," 277, quoted in "Novyi prem'er," P i T, 18 (90), Sep. 15, 1911, 200.

14. "Novyi prem'er," 201.

15. "Deiatel'nosti zakonodatel'nykh uchrezhdenii po voprosam, kasaiushchimsia promyshlennosti i torgovli," P i T, 7 (79), Apr. 1, 1911, 295. Two years later, Zhukovskii reiterated that "although commercial-industrial interests cannot claim priority over all others, nevertheless they have their own great state importance." Seventh Congress, Zhurnal, 14.

16. "Rechi na VI s"ezde," P i T, 10 (106), May 15, 1912, 507.

17. "Iz rechi A. I. Konovalova v Gosudarstvennoi Dume," P i T, 13 (133), July 1, 1913, 12. P i T, July 1, 2 and July 15, 74, warmly approved the speech.

18. In May 1914, the Council asserted the existence of a governmental plan for the expansion of state entrepreneurial activity. Eighth Congress, Zhurnaly, 32.

19. Seventh Congress, Zhurnal, 19, 23.

20. "Iz rechi A. I. Konovalova v Gosudarstvennoi Dume," P i T, 11 (131), June 1, 1913, 499.

21. "Iz rechi A. I. Konovalova," July 1, 1913, 5, 8.

22. "Ekonomicheskoe polozhenie strany i dumskie preniia," P i T, 11 (131), June 1, 1913, 491.

23. "Adres Soveta S"ezdov predstavitelei promyshlennosti i torgovli gospodinu

Ministru torgovli i promyshlennosti," P i T, 24 (144), Dec. 15, 1913, 567.

24. "Novyi kurs," P i T, 9 (153), May 1, 1914, 458-9. Bark's speech sparked the most diverse commentary in the press. The Moscow News hailed it as offering "a real program for the rise of the productive forces of the country," while The Russian News and The Voice of Moscow condemned it as totally lacking in a plan for financial policy. "Obzor pechati," P i T, 9 (153), May 1, 1914, 473.

25. Eighth Congress, Zhurnaly, 3-6, 31.

26. Eighth Congress, Zhurnaly, 100-1.

27. The industrialists' position in this respect found some support outside their own midst. One I. V. Titov, a member of the State Duma who was not an industrialist, assured the Congress that he concurred in its judgment that the government lacked "any definite views, any general plan for the development of productive forces." Eighth Congress, Zhurnaly, 101. The general discouragement was, perhaps, reflected in the extreme, and undoubtedly minority, view of one of the delegates, Mikhail P. Fedorov. Questioning the ability of either the government or the legislature to promote the development of "productive forces," he declared that the task "must naturally be taken on their own shoulders by industrial and agricultural organizations themselves and by local zemstvo and municipal institutions of self-government." Zhurnaly, 108.

28. "Itogi s"ezda," P i T, 10 (154), May 15, 1914, 511-12. See also "Rechi na VIII ocherednom s"ezde," P i T, 11 (155), June 1, 1914, 564.

29. "Itogi s"ezda," 512.

30. "Vos'moi ocherednoi s"ezd predstavitelei promyshlennosti i torgovli," P i T, 10 (154), May 15, 1914, 531. Somewhat more ambiguously, Baron Maidel observed that a change in official economic policies "requires political changes and changes in the conditions of life and will not take place so long as our country fails in its development to approximate the level of cultured industrial countries." Baron G. Maidel, "Teoriia i praktika," P i T, 10 (154), May 15, 1914, 517.

31. "Rechi na VIII ocherednom s"ezde," P i T, 10 (154), May 15, 1914, 512-13.

32. "Strannaia neposledovatel'nost,'" P i T, 12 (156), June 15, 1914, 622-3.

33. "Obzor pechati," P i T, 19 (163), Oct. 1, 1914, 316.

34. For example, see "Imeniny otechestvennoi promyshlennosti," P i T, 4 (172), Feb. 15, 1915, 173-6, and "Krizis ekonomicheskoi politiki," P i T, 7 (175), Apr. 1, 1915, 339-41.

35. On the War Industries Committees, see Siegelbaum, Politics; Roosa, "Russian Industrialists during World War I," 177-9; and Rieber, Merchants, 374-98.

36. "Deiatel'nost' Soveta S"ezdov . . . v 1916 g.," P i T, 1 (245), Jan. 7, 1917, 9. The fact that the Association of Trade and Agriculture was allowed to meet in the spring of 1916, while the Association of Industry and Trade evidently was not, was probably a further symptom of this strained relationship.

37. "Deiatel'nost'," 11; also "O neobkhodimosti razvitiia v strane birzhevykh uchrezhdenii," P i T, 2 (204), Jan. 9, 1916, 48-9; and "Obzor pechati," P i T, 17 (219), Apr. 30, 1916, 490.

38. The last two or three years before the war saw the death of several men active in the Council, among them Nikolai A. Iasiuninskii, Moscow's only representative among its vice-chairmen. Deaths during the war, in addition to those of Avdakov

and Zhukovskii, totalled at least ten of the Council's most influential and active members, including Ignatii I. Iasiukovich, August 1914; Konstantin A. fon-Giubbenet, April 1916; Magnus F. Norpe, July 1916; and Abram O. Gukasov, January 1917. "Deiatel'nost'," 11-12.

39. "Iz deiatel'nosti Soveta nashikh s"ezdov," P i T, 49 (242), Dec. 10, 1916, 491.

40. See, for example, "Dnevnik Soveta," P i T, 51-52 (244), Dec. 24, 1916, 542-3; and 1 (245), Jan. 7, 1917, 24.

41. "Dnevnik Soveta," P i T, 4 (248), Jan. 28, 1917, 94.

42. "Dnevnik Soveta," P i T, 5 (249), Feb. 4, 1917, 118-19.

43. "Dnevnik Soveta," P i T, 5 (249), Feb. 4, 1917, 118-19. See also Roosa, "Russian Industrialists during World War I," 186.

44. "Khronika ekonomicheskoi zhizni," P i T, 6 (250), Feb. 11, 1917, 149.

45. Izvestiia Soveta S"ezdov, no. 1, Apr. 12, 1917, 1. Aleksandr D. Protopopov served as the Empire's last Minister of the Interior. A tool of Rasputin, he was perhaps the most hated symbol of the reaction and repression that characterized the last phase of the old regime.

46. Izvestiia Soveta S"ezdov, no. 1, Apr. 12, 1917, 2.

47. "Vserossiiskii torgovo-promyshlennyi s"ezd v Moskve," P i T, 10-11 (253), Apr. 1, 1917, 238.

48. "Vserossiiskii torgovo-promyshlennyi s"ezd," 239.

49. The Soviet historian Reikhardt interpreted the new Union as symptom of the rise of a new group of "native" holders of stock in Russian joint-stock enterprise in opposition to the "old" stockholders, who were presumably tainted by their ties with foreign capital. Differing attitudes toward the labor question also divided them. Reikhardt, "Russkaia burzhuaziia," 24.

50. Izvestiia Soveta S"ezdov, no. 1; quotations from 2, 1. For a Soviet treatment of this organization, see Laverychev, "Soiuz." The most comprehensive account in English is that of Rieber, Merchants, 385-91, who called it the All-Russian Association of Trade and Industry.

51. "Dnevnik Soveta," P i T, 14-15 (255), Apr. 29, 1917, 290.

52. Timiriazev chaired the congress. At least six of the nine vice-chairmen were active in the Association of Industry and Trade, among them Nikolai N. Kutler, Emanuil L. Nobel, V. I. Vorobiev, Nikolai F. Ditmar (formerly fon-Ditmar), and Leonid F. Davydov. "III Chrezvychainyi Vserossiiskii S"ezd predstavitelei birzhevoi torgovli i sel'skogo khoziaistva," P i T, 16-17 (256), May 13, 1917, 324.

53. According to Reikhardt, "Russkaia burzhuaziia," 24, the conference was "only in a formal sense" not called the Tenth Congress of the Association.

54. "S"ezdy i torgovo-promyshlennye organizatsii," P i T, 20-31 (258), June 10, 1917, 387-8.

55. A rather confused account of how this decision was reached, based on admittedly limited archival materials, is given in Reikhardt, "Russkaia burzhuaziia," 24. According to this account, the Moscow delegates, Tretiakov and Poplavskii, apparently favored the establishment of a committee of five, made up of delegates from Petrograd, Moscow, Baku, South Russia, and the Urals. Its decisions would be binding on all commercial-industrial organizations.

56. "S"ezdy," 388-9; see also Reikhardt, "Russkaia burzhuaziia," 25-6, 29-35.

57. "Glavnyi Komitet ob"edinennoi promyshlennosti," P i T, 28-29 (262), Aug. 5, 1917, 81.

58. Reikhardt, "Russkaia burzhuaziia," 25.

59. The membership of the Committee of the Council now differed markedly from earlier years. Among its members were Baron Maidel, no longer director of the Secretariat; Evgenii L. Liubovich, Maidel's successor as director, and the head of the Legal Section: I. A. Dynin, head of the Council's Information Section; Lazar G. Rabinovich; Matvei B. Pappe; I. P. Bragin; and E. F. Davydov.

60. Izvestiia Soveta S"ezdov, no. 1, 1. News was free to subscribers to Industry and Trade and to members of the Association. It appears to have been quite short-lived.

61. "Dnevnik Soveta," P i T, 14-15 (255), Apr. 29, 1917, 290; and 22-23 (259), June 24, 1917, 410.

62. "Dnevnik Soveta," P i T, 16-17 (256), May 13, 1917, 320-1.

63. "Zadachi Soveta nashikh s"ezdov," P i T, 22-23 (259), June 24, 1917, 393.

64. "Zadachi," 395. In practice, however, the Council's close cooperation with the Committee continued. See "Dnevnik Soveta," P i T, 22-23 (259), June 24, 1917, 410, and Reikhardt, "Russkaia burzhuaziia," 38ff.

65. "Zadachi," 395-6.

66. "Zadachi," 396-7.

67. On the union of employers' societies, see McDaniel, Autocracy, 329, 343.

68. Quoted in Reikhardt, "Russkaia burzhuaziia," 26.

69. This conclusion was presented by Kutler at a meeting of the Petrograd Society of Mill and Factory Owners on October 28. Volobuev, "Predprinimatel'skie organizatsii," 206. Many of the principal participants in the meeting of the Petrograd Society were men prominent in the Association, particularly Kutler, Ditmar, and Arandarenko.

70. P i T, 40-41 (268), Nov. 11, 1917, insert.

71. "Rezoliutsiia po povodu aresta predsedatelia Soveta S"ezdov N. N. Kutlera," P i T, 42-43 (269), Nov. 28, 1917, 271.

72. Reikhardt, "Russkaia burzhuaziia," 44.

73. Quoted from the minutes of the conference, in Reikhardt, "Russkaia burzhuaziia," 43.

Appendix II

1. The interpretation of this provision stirred considerable debate within the Provisional Council and the membership of the Association. The First Congress decided to exclude industrial syndicates from active membership in the Association. See ch. 1, note 78.

2. Fourth Congress, Doklad . . . izmeneniia, 4; Zhurnaly, 45-6; "Dnevnik Soveta," P i T, 20 (68), Oct. 15, 1910, 439.

3. Some founding members sought to limit membership and voting powers in the Association even more narrowly, to the benefit of the largest organizations. The April Congress in 1906 hotly debated the suggestion that consultative membership be

limited to corporations with basic capital of at least one million rubles. First Congress, Zhurnal tret'ego zasedaniia, 9-10; T-p G, 86, Apr. 15 (28), 1906, 2; and T-p G, 85, Apr. 14 (27), 1906, 2.

4. In this connection, Livshin, "Organizatsii," 112, cited a survey by the Soviet historian Strumilin in 1928, which estimated the average amount of basic capital of industrial enterprises in 1912 at only 138,000 rubles. This figure contrasted sharply, however, with those advanced in other studies. Gushka, Organizatsii, 106, found that the lowest amount of turnover in the flour millers' association--an organization composed of relatively small enterprises--was 258,000 rubles in 1910. Shepelev, "Statistika," 167, estimated an average basic capital of 1,817,694 as of January 1, 1914 for all incorporated business enterprises except banks and railroads and an average capital of 1,867,356 rubles for commercial-industrial enterprises. Lyashchenko, History, 714, cited similar conclusions by Kritsman, whose work pointed to an average basic capital for incorporated business establishments of approximately 1.8 million rubles in 1914. Judging from the dues paid to the Association by its consultative members, the estimates of Shepelev and Kritsman appear accurate.

5. Initially, the intention had been to limit the privilege of appointing delegates to members possessing at least four or five votes. T-p G, 85, Apr. 14 (27), 1906, 2.

6. Fourth Congress, Doklad . . . izmeneniia, 1, and Zhurnaly, 46.

7. The actual membership of the Council was apparently only eighty-three, since ten elected members also served as member-delegates, while one prominent member was listed in neither category through some oversight. Sovet s"ezdov, Promyshlennost' i Torgovlia, published as a pamphlet in 1915 and also as a "Supplement" to the Council's journal, P i T, 23 (167), Dec. 1, 1914.

8. Ermanskii, "1905-7," 87-88.

9. T-p G, 218, Sep. 27 (Oct. 10), 2.

10. Fourth Congress, Doklad . . . izmeneniia, 2, and Zhurnaly, 46.

11. The published data on membership in the Association reveal numerous small inconsistencies, most of which no doubt result from the fact that figures were occasionally published more than once during a single year. The figures presented here have been compiled for the most part from annual reports and other publications issued by the Council of the Association. Those for 1906, however, were taken from an account in the semi-official Torgovo-promyshlennaia gazeta, 234, Oct. 15, 28, 1906, 1; 1917 figures are from Livshin, "Organizatsii," 112, and "Rezoliutsiia po povodu aresta predsedatelia Soveta S"ezdov N. N. Kutlera," P i T, 42-43, 269, Nov. 28, 1917, 271. Slightly different figures for 1906 and some other years are to be found in Livshin; in "Deiatel'nost' Soveta S"ezdov predstavitelei promyshlennosti i torgovli v 1913 g.," P i T, 1 (145), Jan. 1, 1914, 8; and in Spasskii, Ocherk, 63.

12. T-p G, 234, Oct. 15 (28), 1906, 1.

13. For a recent review of the relationship between the Association of Southern Coal and Steel Producers, founded in 1874, and the Association of Industry and Trade, see McCaffray, Politics, 196-201.

14. The eight organizations that allowed their membership to lapse between 1907 and March 1908 were four exchange societies, a local merchants' society, the society of book publishers and sellers, the society of Petersburg printing enterprises, and the Central Coal and Iron Association. The latter, the only really industrial organization in the group, appears to have ceased to function. Three new members

joined during this period: two exchange societies and the Moscow Society of Manufacturers of Confectionery Goods. The ten new members added between 1908 and 1911 were four exchange committees, a committee of trade and manufacturing, the merchant boards of Moscow and Petersburg, and three industrial organizations (distilling, chemicals, and cloth); and two exchange societies dropped out. Third Congress, Vznosy; Spisok; and Sixth Congress, Spisok.

15. They included sixteen exchange committees, not including the Kharkov Coal and Iron Exchange Committee; four committees of trade and manufacturing; one local society of trade and industry; two merchant societies; two societies for the inspection of steam boilers; national organizations of insurance companies and ship-owners; and one society of fishermen. Sovet S"ezdov, Promyshlennost' i torgovlia (1915).

16. Of these, four belonged to the first class of full members and paid the maximum of 5,000 rubles in annual dues: the Moscow Exchange Society, the Southern Association, the Baku Petroleum Association, and the Russian Insurance Association. The second class was represented by only one organization, the sugar refiners. The third class was composed of two members: the Polish Coal and Iron Association and the Petersburg Society of Mill and Factory Owners. The fourth class had twenty-seven members; and thirteen were enrolled in the fifth and lowest class. Fifth Congress, Spisok.

17. Of the thirty-five active members empowered to elect member-delegates to the Council in 1914, fifteen represented trade or finance as well as industry; seven, exchange societies; three, committees of trade and manufacturing, including that of Ivanovo-Voznesensk; two, merchant societies; two, employers' unions; and one, the insurance association. The remaining twenty were entirely industrial. Fifth Congress, Spisok.

18. Sovet S"ezdov, Promyshlennost' i torgovlia, 1915. By comparison with 1910, the percentage of primarily commercial for financial enterprises had declined from 23.8 to 20.3. In 1910, textiles had been the largest group, with 55 consultative members, as against 53 in mining and heavy metallurgy. Fifth Congress, Spisok. Additional industries represented among the advisory members included petroleum, paper, cement, lumber and other forest products, rubber, matches, glass, perfume, and miscellaneous mechanical and electrical equipment.

19. Fourth Congress, Doklad . . . izmeneniia, 4.

20. Third Congress, Zhurnaly, 31. In 1907 only 44.2 percent of the Association's income from dues came from consultative members. Third Congress, Finansovyi doklad, appendix 1. The percentage rose steadily thereafter, to 55.9 in 1908 (Fourth Congress, Finansovyi doklad, 7), 62 in 1909, and 66.3 in 1910 (Fifth Congress, Finansovyi doklad, 9, 17). In 1910, the largest amount of dues from a consultative member was 3,000 rubles, paid by the Russian Bank for Foreign Trade. As a group, banking paid more heavily than any other, its average per enterprise being 1,029 rubles. Among industrial enterprises, dues ranging from 1,000 to 1,800 rubles were paid by nine enterprises, of which three were in metallurgy, two in oil, and one in textiles. One shipping firm also paid dues of 1,000 rubles. The average dues were, however, only 354 rubles in textiles and 343 in metallurgy. The lowest dues, of 100 and 200 rubles each, were paid by most of the predominantly commercial enterprises. Of the total dues received from consultative members in 1910, 71.4 percent was paid by industrial enterprise, 21.6 percent by banking and insurance, and 7 percent by

transport and commerce. Of the industries represented, the largest total amount was paid by textiles (23.7 percent) and metallurgy (22.1 percent). The oil industry paid only 4.2 percent of the total, although this averaged 583 rubles per enterprise. Fifth Congress, Spisok.

21. Gindin, "O nekotorykh osobennostiakh," 48, 61, 65. Recent works by Bokhanov, especially Krupnaia burzhuaziia and Delovaia elita, contain much biographical information on this subject, but the issue remains unclear.

22. An editorial footnote to an article in Industry and Trade observed: "Until now the exchanges, with the exception of several of the biggest, have reflected mainly the commercial interests of the country, while the industrial Association and the Society of Mill and Factory Owners represent industry." "O neobkhodimosti razvitiia v strane birzhevykh uchrezhdeniia," P i T, 2 (204), Jan. 9, 1916, 48. See also "Chestvovanie stoletnego iubileia Tovarishchestva manufaktur Ivana Konovalova s synom 2 sentiabria 1912 g. v Moskve," P i T, 18 (114), Sep. 15, 1912, 199; and Baron G. Maidel, "Kak napravit' nashu zheleznodorozhnuiu tarifnuiu politiku?" P i T, 20 (116), Oct. 15, 1912, 295.

23. According to Lure, Organizatsiia, 96, the Association was composed "of industrialists predominantly, if not exclusively." Gushka, Organizatsii, described it as "the central organization of industrialists" (15), the "leviathan of industrial organizations" (27), and the "Industrial Center," (i.e. in contrast with the "Commercial Center," the Association of Trade and Agriculture) (159); see also 74-7. In Lenin's less academic view, "The big-wig millionaires, the clever managers of our big industry, are united in the Council of the Association of Industry and Trade." Lenin, "Kupetskie raschety," 39.

24. Lyashchenko, History, 676.

25. Livshin, "Organizatsii," 110. Liashchenko, Istoriia, vol. 2, 321, 324, referred to "the united industrialists, the Council of the Association, Prodameta" as one and the same thing, and he even described the Association's journal, Industry and Trade, as the "organ" of Prodameta. In propounding this view, Soviet historical writing merely reiterated a common contemporary criticism of the Association, one of which it was well aware. See, for example, P i T, 10, 1913, 441, which Livshin quoted in his reference to the "laboratory of syndicates."

26. From Moscow came the industrialists Iulii P. Guzhon (Jules Goujon), in iron and steel; Baron Andrei L. Knoop, textiles; Aleksandr I. Konovalov, textiles; Grigorii A. Krestovnikov, textiles; Nikolai D. Morozov, textiles; Sergei N. Tretiakov, linen; the Riabushinskii brothers, textiles and a wide variety of other industrial, financial, and public interests; and Aleksandr I. Guchkov, scion of an established textile family, leader of the Octobrist Party, and president of the Third State Duma. St. Petersburg was represented by, among others, Emanuil L. Nobel, a prominent figure in machinery and metalworking, as well as Baku oil; Aleksei I. Putilov, machinery and metal working; and Petr L. Bark, a financier and sometime vice minister of trade and industry who became minister of finance in 1914. Zhukovskii and Stanislav M. Rotvand spoke in the name of Polish heavy industry, while the Baku oil industry was represented by Nobel, Stepan G. Lianozov, and the Gukasov brothers; the southern metallurgical industry by Nikolai S. Avdakov, Nikolai F. fon-Ditmar, Ignatii I. Iasiukovich, and Vladimir I. Arandarenko; the Ural iron industry by Nikolai N. Kutler, former deputy director of the Main Administration of Land Tenure and

Agriculture; sugar by Count Andrei A. Bobrinskii; and glass by Prince Aleksandr D. Obolenskii.

Noteworthy also was the social and ethnic diversity of the leadership of the Association. The Council's membership in 1914 included several titled members: Count Andrei A. Bobrinskii, a member of a highly placed family who chaired the Association of the United Nobility; two princes, Obolenskii and Ch. K. Sviatopolk-Mirskii; and one Baron, Knoop, of an ennobled mercantile family. Among other titled persons active in the Association there were Count Tizengausen (probably Gustav Vasil'evich); Count Mikhail N. Grabbe; Prince S. A. Dolgorukii, of ancient lineage; and Baron A. (probably Aleksandr or Al'fred) G. Gintsburg, a member of the Empire's only titled Jewish family. Although the great majority of the names appeared to be Russian, those of evidently German origin bulked large. Poland provided two of the Association's most vigorous and effective leaders: Zhukovskii and Volskii. A scattering of seemingly Jewish names was also to be found among the Council's members, along with isolated representatives of other nationalities, such as Swedish (Nobel) and French (Guzhon, held Russian and French citizenship). According to Shepelev, Tsarizm . . . 1914, 98, Avdakov's father was an army doctor of Armenian extraction.

27. This assessment of the work of the Council is based largely on the day-to-day chronology of its activities and on the annual reports on its work published in Industry and Trade. Similar reports were presented with equal regularity to the congresses. Unfortunately, very few of the Council's journals have been available for study.

28. "Deiatel'nost' Soveta S"ezdov predstavitelei promyshlennosti i torgovli," P i T, 1 (169), Jan. 1, 1915, 13. Again, the unavailability of the committee's journal, which was distributed to all members of the Association, has been a handicap in assessing its activity. Its work was, however, specifically included in the chronology of the Council's activity, published in Industry and Trade.

29. The first two of these groups, for example, contributed 5,000 rubles each in 1909, over and above their payments in dues. Fourth Congress, Zhurnal, 40; Fifth Congress, Zhurnaly, 46; and Fifth Congress, Finansovyi doklad, 2, 4.

30. Fourth Congress, Finansovyi doklad, 2.

31. In contrast, the budget of the Association of Trade and Agriculture in 1908 amounted to only 8,850 rubles. Ermanskii, "1905-7," 97. Yet the income of the Association of Industry and Trade was not large. At least five of its active members had substantially larger incomes from dues. By far the largest of these was the Baku Petroleum Association, with an income from dues of 1,925,000 rubles. Others were the Association of Southern Coal and Steel Producers, 513,624; the manganese industry, 275,000; and the Petersburg and Moscow merchant boards, 457,104 and 218,485, respectively. The Moscow Exchange Committee, however, received only 46,848 rubles from dues. All figures are for 1910 in Gushka, Organizatsii, 120-3.

32. The budget called for expenditures of 77,500 rubles for the wages and salaries of its staff, as compared with 60,000 in the 1908 budget; 14,000 for the rental and maintenance of the Council's headquarters at 100 Nevskii Prospekt, as against 9,500 in 1908; and 41,180 for the publication of Industry and Trade. Fifth Congress, Finansovyi doklad, 2-4; and Otchet po izdaniiu, 5.

33. "The Association of Industry and Finance," English Supplement, P i T, 2

(98), Jan. 15, 1912, 7.

34. In the spring of 1911, Industry and Trade placed the work of the Council's study groups in a somewhat different perspective. From April 1908 through February 1911, it noted, the Association had held a total of 517 meetings, including those of the Council and its Committee. "In other words, excluding the summer months, there was an average of 21-22 meetings a month; that is, almost no working day passed without a meeting." "Piatyi ocherednoi s"ezd," P i T, 6 (78), Mar. 15, 1911, 248.

35. See, for example, "Dnevnik Soveta," P i T, 4, Feb. 15, 1908, 244, and Fifth Congress, Zhurnaly, 2. Compare Gushka, Organizatsii, 177-99, and Berlin, Burzhuaziia, 248-52.

36. Eighth Congress, Zhurnaly, 2.

37. According to Gushka, Organizatsii, 178, "there was not a single legislative bill, however indirectly touching the interests of the commercial-industrial class, that was not submitted for preliminary discussion to special governmental conferences, with the participation of the commercial-industrial organizations, and to the organizations themselves." This applied, in particular, to the two national Associations, which, with perhaps some exaggeration, he credited with exercising "a greater influence of legislation than the State Duma." See also Berlin, Burzhuaziia, 251.

38. Pares, Memoirs, 223.

39. The Association published almost no information on the size or composition of its staff. According to Livshin, "Organizatsii," 114, its staff exceeded one hundred persons. Gushka, Organizatsii, 135, reported that the Association employed forty-eight members of the "third element" in 1910. Sir Bernard Pares, Memoirs, 223, observed that the Association possessed "a standing office staffed with able and independent young economists."

40. How effectively this organizational structure functioned in practice may be questioned, however, inasmuch as Volskii, director of the Secretariat, admitted in 1909 that because of the organization's limited financial resources "the division into sections exists in fact only on paper" and "one and the same person is obliged to take part in the elaboration of a whole series of the most diverse questions." Fourth Congress, Zhurnaly, 46.

41. "Deiatel'nost' Soveta S"ezdov predstavitelei promyshlennosti i torgovli za 1908 g.," P i T, 1, Jan. 1, 1909, 26. Gushka, Organizatsii, 41, referred to the "generally rich" library of the Association. So great were the demands on the library that Volskii recommended in 1909, apparently unsuccessfully, that borrowing privileges be restricted. He also opposed a suggestion that it be kept open evenings, arguing that this was impractical until such time as the Association's funds permitted the hiring of an assistant librarian. Fourth Congress, Zhurnaly, 47.

42. "Iz deiatel'nosti obshchestvennykh uchrezhdenii po promyshlennosti i torgovle," P i T, 3, Feb. 1, 1908, 190.

43. "Dnevnik Soveta," P i T, 11, June 1, 1908, 688.

44. "Dnevnik Soveta," P i T, 13, July 1, 1908, 43.

45. Gushka, Organizatsii, 177 (emphasis in original); 174-175. See also Berlin, Burzhuaziia, 252, 306. Lenin's criticism of Gushka on this point seems at least partially justified:

> Mr. Gushka looks at "sociopolitical life" from the narrow little window of the merchant's point of view. He is unable to understand that, in fact, the absolute

> excessiveness [of the Association's work] is evidence not of its breadth but of its narrowness. The questions raised by the merchants are distinguished by their narrowness, for they concern only the merchants. The capitalists fail to rise to broad political questions.

Lenin, "Anketa," 45 (emphasis in original).

46. The extent to which the Association was ahead of much of its membership in this respect was demonstrated in the failure of its effort, initiated by the Fourth Congress, to gather statistics on the condition of the textile industry. The Committee of the Council reported in the autumn of 1910 that despite repeated efforts and elaborate provisions for secrecy, 461 questionnaires distributed at the beginning of the year had generated only 60 replies. "Dnevnik Soveta," P i T, 20 (68), Oct. 15, 1910, 438. See also Fourth Congress, Zhurnaly, 21, and Fourth Congress, Doklad . . . dela Imperii. Cf. Gushka, Organizatsii, 42. The Council also failed to persuade the government of the need for a second Empire-wide census of the population.

Appendix III

1. Gushka, Organizatsii, 27.

2. Several persons interviewed listed coal, oil, and heavy metallurgy as the predominant interests within the Association. Others broadened this list to include, variously, the textile industry; the Moscow Exchange Society; the sugar, glass, and lumber industries, in that order; and banking.

3. Fourth Congress, Organizatsiia, 3. This general position is supported by Livshin, "Organizatsii," 113-14.

4. Gushka, Organizatsii, 136.

5. As late as October 4, 1910, the Council set November 11 as the date for the convening of the Fifth Congress, for which preparations in the form of major reports by the Council's staff had long been underway. On October 13 the Committee of the Council, in a special meeting, decided to ask the Council at its next meeting, on October 22, to postpone the Congress until the beginning of December. When the Council met on October 22, however, it postponed the calling of the congress "for an indefinite period." No explanation of these developments was ever offered. Sovet S"ezdov, Zhurnaly tridtsat' sed'mogo zasedaniia, 1, and "Dnevnik Soveta," P i T, 20 (68), Oct. 15, 1910, 438-9, and 21 (69), Nov. 1, 1910, 493.

6. Pares, Memoirs, 233, reported that "these yearly congresses were very interesting. Sometimes they seemed to me almost more important than the Duma."

7. Krestovnikov chaired the First, Fourth, Special, and Sixth Congresses. He was also elected Chairman of the Second Congress, but declined on the ground that it was not proper for a Muscovite to preside over a congress held in Moscow. It was therefore decided to rotate the chairmanship of that congress among Krestovnikov, Avdakov, and Nobel, a representative of the Petersburg Society of Mill and Factory Owners.

8. Of the eight organizations unrepresented at the Fourth Congress were five predominantly commercial ones: two exchange societies, one grain exchange, the Moscow Branch of the Council of Trade and Manufacturing, and the Society of Polish

Merchants. The three industrial organizations were of limited importance: those of producers of lumber in Archangel, petroleum in the Terek region, and paper.

9. In its freedom to invite whomever it wished to attend its congresses, the Association, according to Gushka, Organizatsii, 168-9, enjoyed a privilege that had not been extended to other elements in Russian society.

10. The Fourth Congress, for example, considered seventeen reports, of which eight were submitted by the Council (only two concerned substantive issues), one by the Audit Commission, five by special conferences or permanent commissions operating under the Council, one by Volskii, and two by other individuals. With the passage of time, however, the reports by the Council tended increasingly to dominate the agendas of the congresses. The Eighth Congress, in May 1914, considered nine substantive reports, all presented by the Council. The evidence suggests, moreover, that although members of the Association, both full and consultative, availed themselves of their right to submit reports for inclusion on the agendas of the congresses, only a small number of the total were accepted by the Council for presentation to the congresses.

11. In its report on the Fourth Congress, Industry and Trade, after modestly noting the importance of banquets in "the cultured life of the West" and the impossibility of rivaling their splendor in Russia, pointed out happily that the Association's banquet had turned out to be not only very imposing in the number and importance of its participants but also "a very lively" affair. Those present included the vice-ministers of finance, agriculture, and trade and industry; numerous heads of departments in the ministries and other high government officials; and members of the State Council and Duma. Among the bewildering number of toasts that contributed to the jollity of the occasion were those to the health of the Emperor, "drowned by the strains of the National Anthem and by the loud shouts of 'hurrah' of those present"; to the prosperity of Russia and its legislative institutions; to the ministers of finance, agriculture, and trade and industry; to the happiness of industrial workers and employees; to Avdakov and Volskii, "who carry on their shoulders the whole burden of the daily and varied work of the Council"; to the Fourth Congress; and to the founders of the Association, Nobel and Iasiukovich. After the reading of telegrams of congratulations and "many other speeches, . . . the banquet broke up into groups and conversation continued in the vast halls of the restaurant." "Chetvertyi ocherednoi s"ezd predstavitelei promyshlennosti i torgovli," P i T, 22, Nov. 15, 1909, 540-1.

12. Disagreements emerged clearly in the journals of the congresses, despite the lack of stenographic reports on their meetings. A proposal to have stenographers record the proceedings of the congresses was rejected by the Fourth Congress on the grounds of expense, although this may well have been only a convenient cover for other, more serious, objections. Certainly the preservation of the outward appearance of unity among its membership was a continuing problem for the Association. See Fourth Congress, Zhurnaly, 4.

Appendix IV

1. "Izdaniia Soveta S"ezdov predstavitelei promyshlennosti i torgovli," P i T, 2 (98), Jan. 15, 1912, i-vii. (The editor has included two publications of the Association's Special Congress of November 1911, listed in Goldberg, "Association," 465.)

2. According to the Council, the work on business cycles remained incomplete for lack of funds; an effort to revise and improve its joint stock statistics had to be cut short; and financial considerations prevented the publication of the Statistical Annual in Paris and Berlin. Eighth Congress, Otchet, 42-4. Concerning the quality of the Association's data, no judgment can be offered in the present study, but it is noteworthy that contemporary observers differed widely in assessing it. In 1912, The Russian News purported to express the consensus of Russian economists in asserting that the Association's publications "testify to the 'skillful' elaboration of material." Russian economists, it declared,

> do not accept on faith the materials and data, conclusions, and figures with which the government on the one hand and the industrialists on the other are ready to supply them. Russian economists . . . cannot, and they do not wish to, rely on data presented by interested groups.

"Obzor pechati," P i T, 24 (120), Dec. 15, 1912, 543. On the other hand, Pares, Memoirs, 223, praised the statistical work of the Association: "What the zemstva had done for local government, this standing office now did for trade, and the accessibility for trustworthy statistics of course greatly increased financial confidence abroad."

3. Concerning the publications of the Association and other business organizations, Gushka, Organizatsii, 156, wrote that "without a study of this valuable material it is impossible to compose for oneself a true picture of the balance of the dominant public forces in Russia" (emphasis in original).

4. Sovet S"ezdov, Kratkii ocherk, 11-14.

5. "Izdaniia Soveta S"ezdov predstavitelei promyshlennosti i torgovli," P i T, 2 (98), Jan. 15, 1912, i-vii.

6. Ninth Congress, Doklad . . . o merakh.

7. Sovet S"ezdov, Promyshlennost' . . . 1907-1912 gg.

8. Eighth Congress, Otchet, 45-50.

9. Second Congress, Zhurnaly, 4-5.

10. "Russkaia promyshlennost' i torgovlia," P i T, 1, Jan. 1, 1908, 1-3.

11. Sovet S"ezdov, Rynki, back cover.

12. Fifth Congress, Otchet po izdaniiu, 2.

13. "Dnevnik Soveta," P i T, 15, Aug. 1, 1909, 144.

14. Berlin, Burzhuaziia, 284 (quoted); Fourth Congress, Zhurnaly, 47-8.

15. "The Association of Industry and Commerce," English Supplement, P i T, 2 (98), Jan. 15, 1912, 8.

16. It was reported in 1911 that the seventy-two issues that appeared during the first three years contained 494 lead articles, 408 smaller articles, and 883 surveys. Fifth Congress, Otchet po izdaniiu, 2.

17. For a convenient listing of frequent contributors, see P i T, 2 (246), January 14, 1917, v.

18. "Dnevnik Soveta," P i T, 7 (251), February 18, 1917, 175.

19. Khoziaistvennaia kon"iunktura and "Cyclical Fluctuations."

20. According to Industry and Trade, some 176 periodical publications devoted to industry and trade existed in Russia at the end of 1910. Of these, only 62 were classified as trade journals. F. Shober, "Nasha torgovo-promyshlennaia pechat'," P i T, 1 (73), Jan. 1, 1911, 14-17.

21. Gushka, Organizatsii. The results of this latter study, which was conducted at the request of the State Duma, were published as an appendix to the Explanatory Note (Ob"iasnitel'naia zapiska) to the Ministry's budget for 1912. Ministerstvo Torgovli i Promyshlennosti, Smeta.

22. See Liashchenko, Istoriia, vol. 2, 293-4.

23. Lenin, "Anketa." Kogan's pseudonyms, Ermanskii and Gushka, are specified in Livshin, "Organizatsii," 95. The New York Public Library catalog also identifies Gushka as Osip A. Ermanskii (spelled Yermanskii). Under this pseudonym, Kogan left a memoir, Iz perezhitogo, which contains, 202-3, a list of his publications.

24. Livshin, "Organizatsii," 95.

25. See Govorkov, Mosina, and Rabinovich, "Organizatsii," and Mosina, Formirovanie.

26. Pietrzak-Pawłowska, "Z dziejów monopolizacji"; and Wierzbicki, Wspomnienia i dokumenty.

27. Bublikov, Russkaia revoliutsiia; Chetverikov, Bezvozvratno ushedshaia Rossiia; and Auerbakh, "Revoliutsionnoe obshchestvo." Among the unpublished memoirs of prominent members of the Association still held in Russian archives, those of Nikolai N. Iznar appear especially relevant. According to Shepelev, Tsarizm . . . 1914, 265, this document is held in the central historical archive in St. Petersburg, f. 1101, d. 778.

28. Sovetskie knigi, catalog 1/73, item 46. According to Valerii I. Bovykin, who read the manuscript and recommended publication at that time, the project encountered three obstacles. Although he lived in Leningrad, Rozenfeld had no affiliation with the Leningrad branch of the Soviet Academy of Sciences; Iosif F. Gindin, who had edited the manuscript in Moscow, enjoyed little influence in Leningrad; and in 1970 the leadership of the Institute of History of the USSR in the Academy discouraged further research on this subject on the grounds that the "Russian bourgeoisie was numerically small, economically weak, and historically doomed." Bovykin, letter to Thomas C. Owen dated November 30, 1991. Kornelii F. Shatsillo in Moscow and Boris N. Mironov in St. Petersburg likewise reported to Owen in 1990 and 1991, respectively, that no trace of the manuscript could be found. Apparently it was lost after Gindin's death.

29. In 1921, a congress of Russian commercial-industrial representatives in Paris published thirteen reports on the sorry state of the Russian economy: Obshchii s"ezd predstavitelei russkoi promyshlennosti i torgovli, Doklady. The title of this organization and the names of the authors leave no doubt that it was the direct descendant of the Association of Industry and Trade. Bovykin and Petrov, Kommercheskie banki, 309-11, provided a useful list of Russian bankers in emigration--thirty-one in Paris and fifteen in Berlin--and brief remarks about their main organization, the Russian Financial, Industrial, and Commercial Association, headquartered in Paris. Bovykin and Petrov, 313, citing the organization's charter, published in Paris in 1921,

called it the Rossiiskii torgovo-promyshlennyi i finansovyi soiuz. The French title, L'Association financière, industrielle et commerciale russe, appears in Roosa, "Russian Industrialists during World War I," 187, without reference. In 1922, the Association financière, industrielle et commerciale russe published a pamphlet for submission to the Genoa Conference: La débacle des Soviets et la restauration économique de la Russie. Materials dating from 1922-3 on the Rossiiskii finansovo-promyshlenno-torgovyi soiuz (probably the same organization) are held in the Bakhmeteff Archive at the Columbia University Library in the papers of M. M. Zolotarev, a tsarist official who served as comptroller of the port of Vladivostok in World War I, in part 15, folder 3. Zolotarev's papers also contain, in part 14, folder 3, notes and minutes of the "Russian Financial and Commercial Association in America" for 1922-6.

Bibliography

I. PUBLICATIONS OF THE ASSOCIATION

(Note: All items in section I were published in St. Petersburg or Petrograd.)

A. CONGRESSES (S"ezdy Predstavitelei Promyshlennosti i Torgovli).

The First Congress
(Pervyi Ocherednoi S"ezd Predstavitelei Promyshlennosti i Torgovli)

Zhurnal zasedanii s"ezda Soiuza promyshlennykh i torgovykh predpriiatii Rossiiskoi Imperii 12-14-go ianvaria 1906 g.

Zhurnal zasedanii kommissii [sic] po obsuzhdeniiu zaiavlenii, vyskazannykh o proekte soiuza promyshlennykh i torgovykh predpriiatii Rossiiskoi Imperii na pervom zasedanii s"ezda 12 ianvaria 1906 g.

Zhurnal zasedanii Organizatsionnogo Biuro Soiuza Promyshlennykh i Torgovykh Predpriiatii Rossiiskoi Imperii, sostoiavshikhsia 1-4-go fevralia 1906 g.

Trudy uchreditel'nogo obshcheimperskogo S"ezda predstavitelei promyshlennosti i torgovli, sostoiavshegosia 12 aprelia 1906 g. v S.-Peterburge.

Spisok uchastnikov uchreditel'nogo s"ezda.

Zhurnal 1-4 zasedanii Uchreditel'nogo Obshcheimperskogo S"ezda Predstavitelei Promyshlennosti i Torgovli, sostoiavshegosia 12-14 aprelia 1906 g.

The Second Congress
(Vtoroi Ocherednoi S"ezd Predstavitelei Promyshlennosti i Torgovli)

Zhurnaly zasedanii Vtorogo Ocherednogo S"ezda Predstavitelei Promyshlennosti i Torgovli, sostoiavshegosia 22, 23, i 24 maia 1907 goda v Moskve.

Doklad Soveta S"ezdov Predtavitelei Promyshlennosti i Torgovli Vtoromu Ocherednomu S"ezdu o ego deiatel'nosti so vremeni Pervogo Ocherednogo S"ezda (v oktiabria 1906 g.) po 1 maia 1907 goda.

Kratkii otchet o rabotakh, proizvedennykh Sovetom S"ezdov po zhelezno-dorozhnomu voprosu.

Po povodu vnesennogo v Zakonodatel'nye Uchrezhdeniia proekta podokhodnogo

naloga. Doklad Soveta S"ezdov.
Osnovy zhelatel'noi organizatsii poraionnogo predstavitel'stva promyshlennosti i torgovli.

The Third Congress
(Tretii Ocherednoi S"ezd Predstavitelei Promyshlennosti i Torgovli)

Zhurnaly Tret'ego Ocherednogo S"ezda Predstavitelei Promyshlennosti i Torgovli, sostoiavshegosia 27, 28, 29, 30, i 31 marta 1908 g.
Doklad Soveta Sezdov ob izdanii organa Soveta zhurnala "Promyshlennost' i Torgovlia."
Doklad Soveta S"ezdov o neobkhodimykh uluchsheniiakh v pochtovom, telegrafnom i telefonnom dele v Rossii.
Doklad Soveta S"ezdov Predstavitelei Promyshlennosti i Torgovli tret'emu ocherednomu S"ezdu o deiatel'nosti Soveta so vremeni vtorogo ocherednogo S"ezda (v mae 1907 g.) po 15 marta 1908 g.
Doklad Soveta S"ezdov Predstavitelei Promyshlennosti i Torgovli po rabochemu voprosu.
Finansovyi doklad Soveta S"ezdov Predstavitelei Promyshlennosti i Torgovli i prikhodo-raskhodnaia smeta na 1908 g.
Osnovy torgovo-promyshlennoi politiki Rossii. Doklad A. A. Volskogo.
O kazennykh podriadakh i postavkakh. Zapiska E. L. Liubovicha.
Otchet o deiatel'nosti Soveta S"ezdov Predstavitelei Promyshlennosti i Torgovli po voprosam promyslovogo oblozheniia.
"Dve paralleli." Doklad Pravleniia Tovarishchestva Manufaktury "Emil Tsindel" v Moskve (o torgovykh snosheniiakh Rossii s Persiei).
K voprosu o sovremennom polozhenii tarifnogo dela na russkikh zheleznykh dorogakh. Zapiska Odesskogo Birzhevogo Komiteta.
K voprosu o zashchite torgovogo kredita. Doklad Pravleniia Tovarishchestva Manufaktury "Emil Tsindel" v Moskve.
L'novodstvo i l'nianaia promyshlennost' v Rossii. Doklad Soveta Vserossiiskogo Obshchestva L'nopromyshlennikov.
Spisok Chlenov Predstavitelei Promyshlennosti i Torgovli na 22 marta 1908 goda.
V Sovete S"ezdov Predstavitelei Promyshlennosti i Torgovli. Zaiavlenie Tovarishchestva Manufaktury "Emil Tsindel."
Vznosy Chlenov S"ezdov Predstavitelei Promyshlennosti i Torgovli za 1907 gg.
Zapiska Biuro S"ezdov Steklozavodchikov po voprosu o neobkhodimosti zakonodatel'nym poriadkom ogranichit' perevod i peredachu torgovtsami-dolzhnikami svoikh predpriiatii na chuzhoe imia, s tsel'iu neplatezha dolgov.
Zapiska Moskovskogo Birzhevogo Komiteta o predel'nykh stavkakh zheleznykh dorog i o neobkhodimosti izmeneniia zakona o tarifakh i tarifnykh uchrezhdeniiakh.

The Fourth Congress
(Chetvertyi Ocherednoi S"ezd Predstavitelei Promyshlennosti i Torgovli)

Zhurnaly Chetvertogo Ocherednogo S"ezda Predstavitelei Promyshlennosti i Torgovli, sostoiavshegosia 10, 11, 12, i 13 noiabria 1909 g.

Spisok lits, prinimavshikh uchastie v zaniatiiakh Chetvertogo Ocherednogo S"ezda Predstavitelei Promyshlennosti i Torgovli.
Otchet Soveta S"ezdov o ego deiatel'nosti so vremeni Tret'ego Ocherednogo S"ezda.
Chleny S"ezdov Predstavitelei Promyshlennosti i Torgovli na 10-e oktiabria 1909 goda.
Doklad revisionnoi komissii.
Finansovyi doklad Soveta S"ezdov Predstavitelei Promyshlennosti i Torgovli za 1908 g., prikhodo-raskhodnaia smeta na 1909 god i smeta na 1910 g.
Doklad Soveta S"ezdov ob izdanii organa Soveta Zhurnala "Promyshlennost' i Torgovlia."
Doklad Soveta S"ezdov Chetvertomu Ocherednomu S"ezdu o zhelatel'nosti izmeneniia, 14, 16, 22, i 38 VYSOCHAISHE utverzhdennogo 24 avgusta 1906 g. Polozheniia o S"ezdakh Predstavitelei Promyshlennosti i Torgovli.
Doklad Soveta S"ezdov ob organizatsii pri Sovete statistiki tekstil'nogo dela Imperii.
Doklad Soveta S"ezdov o razvitii v Rossii melkogo kredita i melkoi promyshlennosti.
Zhelatel'naia organizatsiia Torgovo-Promyshlennykh Palat. Doklad obrazovannoi pri Sovete S"ezdov Osoboi Komissii pod predsedatel'stvom Chlena Soveta M. M. Fedorova.
Doklad Soveta S"ezdov Predstavitelei Promyshlennosti i Torgovli o Khode rabot po rabochemu zakonodatel'stvu.
Doklad Soveta S"ezdov "Ob uchrezhdenii pri Sovete ssudosberegatel'noi kassy sluzhashchikh."
K predstoiashchemu peresmotru Obshchego Ustava rossiiskikh zheleznykh dorog. Doklad uchrezhdennoi pro Sovete S"ezdov Postoiannoi Kommissii po Tarifnym Delam.
Doklad Soveta S"ezdov "O zhelatel'nosti sosredotocheniia obiazatel'nykh publikatsii torgovo-promyshlennykh i kreditnykh predpriiatii v kakom-libo odnom periodicheskom organe pechati."
Doklad obrazovannoi pri Sovete S"ezdov pod predsedatel'stvom chlena Soveta A. R. fon-Dezena osoboi komissii "O kazennykh podriadakh i postavkakh."
Doklad obrazovannogo pri Sovete S"ezdov pod predsedatel'stvom Tovarishcha Predsedatelia Soveta, E. L. Nobelia, osobogo soveshchaniia po voprosu ob ustanovlenii edinoobraznykh norm veksel'nogo prava.
Glavnye osnovaniia reformy gosudarstvennogo i mestnogo oblozheniia promyshlennosti i torgovli. Doklad sostoiashchei pri Sovete S"ezdov Postoiannoi Komissii po iuridicheskim i nalogovym voprosam po povodu vnesennogo Ministrom Finansov v Gosudarstvennuiu Dumu Proekta Polozheniia o gosudarstvennom promyslovom naloge.
Ekonomichesko-finansovaia politika Rossii. Doklad A. A. Volskogo.
Doklad P. P. Regira "O poshline na suda inostrannoi postroiki i o pooshchrenii otechestvennogo sudostroeniia."
Doklad Kievskogo Birzhevogo Komiteta o neobkhodimykh meropriiatiiakh v dele usovershenstvovaniia vodnykh putei i uluchsheniia uslovii perevozki po nim gruzov.
Organizatsiia Predstavitel'stva Promyshlennosti i Torgovli na mestakh. Doklad Chlena-Delegata Soveta Obshchestva dlia zashchity interesov i razvitiia Odesskoi promyshlennosti S. I. Sokolovskogo.
Glavneishie polozheniia soobshcheniia P. P. Rudnikova "Vodnyi put' Riga-Kherson."

The Fifth Congress
(Piatyi Ocherednoi S"ezd Predstavitelei Promyshlennosti i Torgovli)

Zhurnaly Piatogo Ocherednogo S"ezda Predstvitelei Promyshlennosti i Torgovli. Otchet Soveta S"ezdov o ego deiatel'nosti so vremeni Chetvertogo Ocherednogo S"ezda.
Finansovyi doklad Soveta S"ezdov Predstavitelei Promyshlennosti i Torgovli za 1909 i 1910 gody i prikhodo-raskhodnaia smeta na 1911 god.
Otchet po izdaniiu organa Soveta S"ezdov Predstavitelei Promyshlennosti i Torgovli zhurnala "Promyshlennost' i Torgovlia."
Spisok Chlenov S"ezdov Predstavitelei Promyshlennosti i Torgovli v 1910 gody.
Zheleznye dorogi v Rossii. Doklad Soveta S"ezdov.
N. F. fon-Ditmar. O zemskom oblozhenii promyshlennykh i torgovykh predpriiatii i o predstavitel'stve torgovopromyshlennogo klassa v zemskikh uchrezhdeniiakh.
Ekonomicheskie interesy Rossii na Blizhnem Vostoke. Doklad Chlena-delegata Soveta ot Obshchestva dlia zashchity interesov i razvitiia Odesskoi promyshlennosti, S. I. Sokolovskogo.

The Special Congress
(Ekstrennyi S"ezd Soveta Predstavitelei Promyshlennosti i Torgovli)

Zhurnaly zasedanii Ekstrennogo S"ezda Soveta Predstavitelei Promyshlennosti i Torgovli, sostoiavshegosia 10, 11, 12 noiabria 1911 g.
Doklad Soveta S"ezdov po proektu uvelicheniia sredstv zemstv i gorodov.

The Sixth Congress
(Shestoi Ocherednoi S"ezd Predstavitelei Promyshelennosti i Torgovli)

Zhurnal zasedanii Shestogo Ocherednogo S"ezda Predstavitelei Promyshlennosti i Torgovli, sostoiavshegosia 7, 8, i 9 maia 1912 g.
Spisok chlenov S"ezdov Predstavitelei Promyshlennosti i Torgovli v 1911 g. Lichnyi Sostav Komiteta i Soveta Sezdov Predstavitelei Promyshlennosti i Torgovli.
Tovarishchestva s ogranichennoi otvetstvennost'iu. Doklad Postoiannoi Iuridicheskoi Komissii pri Sovete S"ezdov.
Osnovaniia zhelatel'noi reformy gerbovogo oblozheniia. Doklad Postoiannoi Iuridicheskoi Komissii pri Sovete S"ezdov.
Polozhenie voprosa o stochnykh vodakh fabrik i zavodov v Rossii. Doklad V. V. Rota.

The Seventh Congress
(Sed'moi Ocherednoi S"ezd Predstavitelei Promyshlennosti i Torgovli)

Zhurnal zasedanii Sed'mogo Ocherednogo S"ezda Predstavitelei Promyshlennosti i Torgovli.
Krizis topliva. Doklad Soveta S"ezdov Predstavitelei Promyshlennosti i Torgovli.
Rost promyshlennosti v Rossii za poslednee desiatiletie i opasnost' zastoia vsledstvie nedostatochnogo razvitiia seti zheleznykh dorog, vodnykh i shosseinykh putei.

O merakh bor'by s neplatezhami. Doklad Postoiannoi Iuridicheskoi Komissii pri Sovete S"ezdov.

The Eighth Congress
(Vos'moi Ocherednoi S"ezd Predstavitelei Promyshlennosti i Torgovli)

Zhurnaly zasedanii Vos'mogo Ocherednogo S"ezda Predstavitelei Promyshlennosti i Torgovli, sostoiavshegosia 2, 3, i 4 maia 1914 g. v Petrograde.
Otchet Soveta S"ezdov o ego deiatel'nosti so vremeni Sed'mogo Ocherednogo S"ezda.
Doklad Soveta S"ezdov "O sovremennom polozhenii promyshlennosti i torgovli v sviazi s predprinimatel'skoi deiatel'nosti kazny."
Doklad Soveta S"ezdov o shosseinom stroitel'stve.
Doklad Soveta S"ezdov o polozhenii voprosa o Kazennykh podriadakh i postavkakh.
Doklad Soveta S"ezdov o tarifnom politki Kitaiskoi Vostochnoi zheleznoi dorogi.
Peresmotr Torgovogo Dogovora s Germaniei. Doklad Soveta S"ezdov.
O merakh pooshchreniia stroitel'stva deshevykh i zdorovykh zhilishch dlia rabochikh. Doklad Postoiannoi Iuridicheskoi Komissii pri Sovete S"ezdov.
Ob ogranicheniiakh aktsionernykh kompanii v prave priobretat' v sobstvennosti i prinimat' v zalog nedvizhimye imushchestva. Doklad Postoiannoi Iuridicheskoi Kommissi pri Sovete S"ezdov.

The Ninth Congress
(Deviatyi Ocherednoi S"ezd Predstavitelei Promyshlennosti i Torgovli)

Doklad Soveta S"ezdov o merakh k razvitiiu proizvoditel'nykh sil Rossii.
Doklad Deviatomu Ocherednomu S"ezdu Predstavitelei Promyshlennosti i Torgovli. Ob uchrezhdenii Vysshei Ekonomicheskoi Komissii.
Russkaia promyshlennost' i fiskal'nye monopolii. Doklad Soveta S"ezdov.
Biuro dlia oblegcheniia polozheniia russkikh poddannykh, nakhodiashchikhsia za granitsei (15 avgusta-15 noiabria 1914 goda).

B. THE COUNCIL (Sovet s"ezdov predstavitelei promyshlennosti i torgovli)

1. Serial Publications.

Fabrichno-zavodskiia predpriiatiia Rossiiskoi Imperii. Pod nabliudeniem Redaktsionnogo komiteta, sostoiashchego iz chlenov Soveta s"ezdov predstavitelei promyshlennosti i torgovli, sostavil inzhener L. K. Ezioranskii. Izdanie Torgovogo doma A. Sroka i Ko., 1909.
Fabrichno-zavodskiia predpriiatiia Rossiiskoi Imperii. 2nd ed. Redaktor F. A. Shober. D. P. Kandaurov, 1914.
Izvestiia Soveta S"ezdov Predstavitelei Promyshlennosti i Torgovli, nos. 1-4 (12 aprelia-3 maia 1917 g.).
Materialy po promyslovomu oblozheniiu.
No. 5. Glavnye osnovaniia proekta izmenenii Polozheniia o gosudarstvennom promyslovom naloge (sostavleno Ministerstvom Finansov k soveshchaniiu 24

marta 1908 g.). 1908.
No. 8. Otvet Soveta S"ezdov Predstavitelei Promyshlennosti i Torgovli na zamechaniia Ministerstva Finansov po povodu prodleniia zakona 2 ianvaria 1906 goda o promyslovom naloge. 1908.
Materialy po rabochemu voprosu.
No. 7. Sravnitel'naia spravka po inostrannomu zakonodatel'stvu otnositel'no pravil o rabochem vremeni. Pravila o rabochem vremeni dlia lits, ne dostigshikh 17-letnego vozrasta, i zhenshchin.
No. 8. Sravnitel'naia spravka po inostrannym zakonodatel'stvam otnositel'no strakhovaniia rabochikh ot neschastnykh sluchaev.
No. 10. Tablichnyi obzor zakonodatel'noi normirovki rabochego vremeni v razlichnykh stranakh.
No. 11. Tablichnyi obzor obespecheniia rabochikh ot posledstvii neschastnykh sluchaev v razlichnykh stranakh.
No. 12. Tablichnyi obzor zakonodatel'stv po dogovoru o naime rabochikh v razlichnykh stranakh.
No. 15. Zapiska ob obshchikh nachalakh upravleniia strakhovymi tovarishchestvami i ob organizatsii strakhovykh sudov. (Inzh.-Tekhn. N. P. Shalkina.)
No. 16. Statisticheskaia spravka o bol'nichnykh kassakh v Germanii.
No. 18. Kratkii otchet ob Osobom Soveshchanii, proiskhodivshem pod predsedatel'-stvom Ministra Torgovli i Promyshlennosti 14-21 dekabria 1906 g., otnositel'no osnovnykh polozhenii izgotovliaemykh Ministerstvom Torgovli i Promyshlennosti proektov po rabochemu zakonodatel'stvu.
No. 20. Statisticheskie dannye otnositel'no strakhovaniia starosti i invalidnosti v Germanii.
No. 29. Proekt polozheniia o strakhovanii rabochikh ot neschastnykh sluchaev v redaktsii, predlagaemoi Sovetom S"ezdov Predstavitelei Promyshlennosti i Torgovli. 1909.
No. 30. Proekt polozheniia ob obespechenii rabochikh na sluchai bolezni v redak-tsiei, predlagaemoi Sovetom S"ezdov Predstavitelei Promyshlennosti i Torgovli. 1909.
No. 31. Proekt polozheniia o Prisutstviiakh po delam strakhovaniia rabochikh v redaktsii, predlagaemoi Sovetom S"ezdov Predstavitelei Promyshlennosti i Torgovli. 1909.
Materialy po strakhovaniiu rabochikh.
No. 1. Raspredelenie fabrichno-zavodskikh predpriiatii i rabochikh po strakhovym okrugam. 1913.
Materialy po zhelezno-dorozhnomu voprosu.
No. 28. K voprosu ob organizatsii chastnogo zheleznodorozhnogo stroitel'stva. Zametki po povodu ustava Obshchestva Severo-Donetskoi zheleznoi dorogi. 1909.
Promyshlennost' i Torgovlia. 1908-1917.
Promyshlennost' i Torgovlia v Zakonodatel'nykh Uchrezhdeniiakh 1907-1912 gg. 1912.
Promyshlennost' i Torgovlia v Zakonodatel'nykh Uchrezhdeniiakh 1912-1913 gg. 1913.
Statisticheskii Ezhegodnik. Pod redaktsiei V. I. Sharogo, Zavedyvaiushchego

Statisticheskim Otdelom Soveta S"ezdov. Vol. 1, 1912, 1912; vol. 2, 1913, 1913; vol. 3, 1914, 1914.

2. Reports, Notes, Memoranda, and Journals.

Dokladnaia Zapiska Soveta S"ezdov Predstavitelei Promyshlennosti i Torgovli Ego Vysokoprevoskhoditel'stvu Gospodinu Predsedateliu Soveta Ministrov.

Dokladnaia zapiska Soveta S"ezdov predstavitelei promyshlennosti i torgovli o merakh k razvitiiu proizvoditel'nykh sil Rossii i k uluchsheniiu torgovogo balansa. 1914.

Kratkie svedeniia o S"ezdakh predatavitelei Promyshlennosti i Torgovli i deiatel'nost' za 1908 i 1909 gg. N. Ia. Stoikova, 1910.

Kratkii ocherk deiatel'nosti Soveta S"ezdov Predstavitelei Promyshlennosti i Torgovli so vremeni Pervogo Ocherednogo S"ezda (s oktiabria 1906 g. po aprel' 1907 g.).

Materialy dlia statistiki topliva v Rossii. M. Ia. Minkov, 1906.

Ot Soveta S"ezdov predstavitelei Promyshlennosti i Torgovli. 1909.

Otchet Soveshchaniia po voprosu o ponizhenii eksportnykh zhelezno-dorozhnykh tarifov na kerosin i smazochnye masla v napravlenii cherez Batum i Novorossiisk, sost. 8 fev., 28 marta, 3 i 6 aprelia 1907 g.

Pamiatnaia Zapiska po voprosu o tamozhennom ob"edinenii Finliandii s ostal'nymi chastiami Imperii, sostavlennaia predstaviteliami finliandskoi promyshlennosti i torgovli.

Perevozki iuzhnykh gornozavodskikh gruzov za vremia voiny. N. Ia. Stoikova, 1917.

Po proektu pravil o predprinimatel'skikh ob"edineniiakh.

Polozhenie ob Obshcheimperskikh S"ezdakh predstavitelei promyshlennosti i torgovli. V. Kirshbaum, 1906.

Polozhenie o S"ezdakh predstavitelei Promyshlennosti i Torgovli. N. Ia. Stoikova, 1911.

Predpolozheniia Ministerstva Finansov otnositel'no stavok novogo proekta pro myslovogo naloga. 1908.

Proekt Ministerstva putei soobshcheniia o postroike kazennogo metallurgicheskogo zavoda v Kerchi. Doklad komissi I. V. Glivitsa Osobomu soveshchaniiu obrazovannomu pri Sovete S"ezdov po voprosu o kazennom predprinimatel'stve. 1917.

Proekt zakona o sdache v razrabotku kazennykh neftenosnykh zemel, vyrabotannyi osobym soveshchaniem pri Sovete S"ezdov Predstavitelei Promyshlennosti i Torgovli; ob"iasnitel'naia zapiska k etomu proektu i zhurnaly zasedanii osobogo soveshchaniia, obrazovannogo pri Sovete S"ezdov Predstavitelei Promyshlennosti i Torgovli dlia rassmotreniia sostavlennogo Gornym Departamentom, Ministerstva Torgovli i Promyshlennosti, zakonoproekta o sdache kazennykh neftenosnykh zemel' v razrabotku chastnym litsam po dogovoram. 1909.

Promyshlennost' i Torgovlia [pamphlet]. 1915.

Rynki glaveneishikh tovarov v 1909 g. Otdel'nyi ottisk iz zhurnala "Promyshlennost' i Torgovlia." 1909.

Stat'i 766-819 ust. torgovli i proekt ikh izmeneniia. [No date.]

Zakliucheniia obrazovannogo pri Sovete S"ezdov Predstavitelei Promyshlennosti i

Torgovli pod predsedatel'stvom Tovarishcha Predsedatelia Soveta E. L. Nobelia Soveshchaniia dlia rassmotreniia proekta izmeneniia zakona i pravil 11 iiunia 1891 g. ob ispytanii, perevozke, khranenii i prodazhi nefti i ee produktov, vyrabotannogo v Ministerstve Torgovli i Promyshlennosti (odobren Komitetom Soveta S"ezdov Predstavitelei Promyshlennosti i Torgovli v zasedanii 6 marta 1909 g.). 1909.

Zakony 15 noiabria 1906 goda ob obespechenii normal'nogo otdykha sluzhashchikh v torgovykh zavedeniiakh, skladakh i kontorakh i v remeslennykh zavedeniiakh. 1906.

Zametka o Moskovsko-Revel'skoi zheleznoi doroge. A. A. Bublikova. 191-.

Zapiska o prave uchastiia gorodov i zemstv v dokhodakh kazny ot ustanovlennogo zakonami 2 ianvaria 1906 g. naloga na lichnye promyslovye zaniatiia i o dopolnitel'nykh sborakh v pol'zu kazny s summe etogo naloga. 1907.

Zapiska o tsenakh russkogo sveklovichnogo sakhara. 1908.

Zapiska Soveta S"ezdov Predstavitelei Promyshlennosti i Torgovli o merakh k pod"emu otechestvennoi zheleznoi promyshlennosti i mashinostroeniia. 1908.

Zapiska Soveta S"ezdov Predstavitelei Promyshlennosti i Torgovli o neobkhodimykh na 1908 g. kreditakh na usilenie propusknoi i provoznoi sposobnosti zheleznykh dorog. 1907.

Zapiska Soveta S"ezdov Predstavitelei Promyshlennosti i Torgovli o Tarifakh na perevozku kamenno-ugol'nykh gruzov po vsei seti Rossiiskikh zheleznykh dorog. 1907.

Zapiska Soveta S"ezdov Predstavitelei Promyshlennosti i Torgovli o vydache iz Gosudarstvennogo Banka ssud pod rechnye i morskie suda. 1909.

Zapiska Soveta S"ezdov Predstavitelei Promyshlennosti i Torogovli po povodu vnesennogo Ministerstvom Finansov v Gosudarstvennuiu Dumu predstavleniia o prodlenii deistviia zakona 2 ianvaria 1906 goda ob izmenenii nekotorykh postanovlenii o gosudarstvennom promyslovom naloge. 1907.

Zapiska Soveta S"ezdov Predstavitelei Promyshlennosti i Torogovli po povodu vnesennogo Ministrom vnutrennykh del v Zakonodatel'nye upravleniia proekta "Pravil o sbore v pol'zu gorodov s gruzov, privozimykh v goroda i otvozimykh iz nikh po zheleznym dorogam." 1909.

Zapiska Soveta S"ezdov Predstavitelei Promyshlennosti i Torgovli po voprosu o pod"ezdnykh putiakh (vetviakh) chastnogo vladeniia i pol'zovaniia. 1910 (?).

Zhurnal tridtsat' piatoi sessii Soveta S"ezdov Predstavitelei Promyshlennosti i Torgovli, sostoiavsheisia 10 i 18 iiunia 1910 goda .

Zhurnal tridtsat' shestogo zasedaniia . . . , sost. 11 sentiabria 1910 g.

Zhurnal tridtsat' sed'mogo zasedaniia . . . , sost. 4 oktiabria 1910 g.

Zhurnaly Soveshchaniia, sozvannogo pri Sovete S"ezdov dlia rassmotreniia predpolozhenii Gornogo Departamenta ob izmeneniiakh i dopolneniiakh v deistvuiushchikh pravilakh zakona o neftianom promysle, pod redaktsiei M. I. Lazareva. 1908.

(Memorandum) 30757. April 28, 1914.

3. Joint Publications with the Association of Trade and Agriculture (Sovet S"ezdov Predstavitelei Birzhevoi Torgovli i Sel'skogo Khoziaistva).

K voprosu ob otdelenii perevozochnoi operatsii zheleznykh dorog ot skladochnoi operatsii. 1911.

Osobaia Komissiia po Peresmotru Torgovykh Dogovorov. Materialy po peresmotru torgovykh dogovorov. Nos. 1-7, 9-11. N. Ia. Stoikova, 1911-15.

Proekt obshchego ustava rossiiskikh zheleznykh dorog, vyrabotannyi po porucheniiu sovetov s"ezdov predstavitelei promyshlennosti i torgovli i s"ezdov predstavitelei birzhevoi torgovli i sel'skogo khoziaistva, komissiei pod predsedatel'stvom chlena oboikh sovetov s"ezdov, F. A. Novoveiskogo i odobrennyi v soedinennom zasedanii sovetov s"ezdov, 4 oktiabria 1911 goda. N. Ia. Stoikova, 1911.

II. Other Publications and Materials.

Akademiia Nauk SSSR. Institut Istorii. Istoriia Moskvy. Vol. 5. Moscow: Akademiia nauk, 1955.

----------. Ocherki Istorii Leningrada. Vol. 3. Moscow and Leningrad: Akademiia nauk, 1956.

Amburger, Erik. Fremde und Einheimische im Wirtschafts- und Kulturleben des neuzeitlichen Russland: Ausgewählte Aufsätze. Ed. Klaus Zernack. Wiesbaden: F. Steiner, 1982.

Ananich, Boris V. Bankirskie doma v Rossii 1860-1914 gg.: ocherki istorii chastnogo predprinimatel'stva. Leningrad: Nauka, 1991.

----------. Rossiia i mezhdunarodnyi kapital, 1897-1914 gg. Leningrad: Nauka, 1970.

Apostol, Paul and Alexandre Michelson. La lutte pour le pétrole et la Russie. Paris: Payot, 1922.

Ascher, Abraham. The Revolution of 1905: Russia in Disarray. Stanford: Stanford University Press, 1988.

Auerbakh, V. A. "Revoliutsionnoe obshchestvo po lichnym vospominaniiam." Arkhiv russkoi revoliutsii, vol. 14 (Berlin: Slovo, 1924), 5-38.

Ball, Alan. Russia's Last Capitalists: The Nepmen, 1921-1929. Berkeley: University of California Press, 1987.

Balzer, Harley. "The Problem of Professions in Imperial Russia." In Between Tsar and People: Educated Society and the Quest for Public Identity in Late Imperial Russia, edited by Edith W. Clowes, Samuel D. Kassow, and James L. West, 184-98. Princeton: Princeton University Press, 1991.

----------. ed. Russia's Missing Middle Class: The Professions in Russian History. Armonk, NY: M. E. Sharpe, 1996.

Bark, Petr L. "Memoirs." Peter L'vovich Bark Papers. Bakhmeteff Archive. Columbia University Library, New York.

Berlin, P.A. Russkaia burzhuaziia v staroe i novoe vremia. Moscow: Kniga, 1922.

Bill, Valentine T. The Forgotten Class. New York: Praeger, 1959.

Blanc, Simone. "Aux origines de la bourgeoisie russe." Cahiers du monde russe et soviétique 5 (1964): 294-301.

Blum, Jerome. Lord and Peasant in Russia from the Ninth to the Nineteenth Century. Princeton: Princeton University Press, 1961.

Bogolepov, M. "Gosudarstvennoe khoziaistvo i finansovaia politika pravitel'stva." In Obshchestvennoe dvizhenie v Rossii v nachale XX-go veka, edited by L. Martov, P. Maslov, and A. Potresov. Vol. 1, 151-80. St. Petersburg: Obshchestvennaia pol'za, 1909.

---------. O putiakh budushchego: K voprosu ob ekonomicheskom plane. Petrograd: Ministerstvo finansov, 1916.

Bokhanov, Aleksandr N. "Rossiiskoe kupechestvo v kontse XIX-nachale XX veka," Istoriia SSSR, 1985, no. 4 (July-Aug.): 106-18.

---------. Krupnaia burzhuaziia Rossii: konets XIX v.-1914 g. Moscow: Nauka, 1992.

---------. Delovaia elita Rossii 1914 g. Moscow: Nauka, 1994.

Bouryshkine, Paul A. [Buryshkin, Pavel A.] "The Internal Trade of Russia during the War." Collection of Ruth A. Roosa.

Bovykin, Valerii I. Zarozhdenie finansovogo kapitala v Rossii. Moscow: Moskovskii universitet, 1967.

---------. Formirovanie finansovogo kapitala v Rossii konets XIX v.-1908 g. Moscow: Mauka, 1984.

Bovykin, Valerii I. and Iurii A. Petrov. Kommercheskie banki Rossiiskoi imperii. Moscow: Perspektiva, 1991.

Bublikov, Aleksandr A. Russkaia revoliutsiia (ee nachalo, arest Tsaria, perspektivy): vpechatleniia i mysli ochevidtsa i uchastnika. New York: n.p., 1918.

Bulletin de la Chambre de Commerce Russe de Paris. 1905-1913.

Buranov, Iurii A. "S"ezdy ural'skikh gornopromyshlennikov v kontse XIX-nachale XX vv." In Voprosy istorii kapitalisticheskoi Rossii: problemy mnogoukladnosti, edited by Vladimir V. Adamov, 268-82. Sverdlovsk: Ural'skii gosudarstvennyi universitet, 1972.

Buryshkin, Pavel A. Moskva kupecheskaia. New York: Chekhov, 1954.

Carr, E.H. "'Russia and Europe' as a Theme of Russian History." In Essays Presented to Sir Lewis Namier, ed. by R. Pares and A. J. P. Taylor, 357-93. New York: St. Martin's Press, 1956.

Carstensen, Fred V. American Enterprise in Foreign Markets: Studies of Singer and International Harvester in Imperial Russia. Chapel Hill: University of North Carolina Press, 1984.

Chermenskii, E. D. Burzhuaziia i tsarizm v revoliutsii 1905-1907 gg. Moscow and Leningrad: Gosudarstvennoe sotsial'no-ekonomicheskoe izdatel'stvo, 1939. 2nd ed., Moscow: Mysl', 1970.

Chetverikov, Sergei I. Bezvozvratno ushedshaia Rossiia: neskol'ko stranits iz knigi moei zhizni. Berlin: Moskva-Logos, 192-.

Clowes, Edith W. "Social Discourse in the Moscow Art Theater," in Between Tsar and People: Educated Society and the Quest for Public Identity in Late Imperial Russia, edited by Edith W. Clowes, Samuel D. Kassow, and James L. West, 271-87. Princeton: Princeton University Press, 1991, 271-87.

Dan, F. "Ocherk politicheskoi evoliutsii burzhuaznykh elementov gorodskogo naseleniia." In L. Martov, P. Maslov, and A. Potresov, eds., Obshchestvennoe dvizhenie v Rossii v nachale XX-go veka. Vol. 2, part 2, 101-45. St. Petersburg: Obshchestvennaia pol'za, 1909.

Dan, Theodore. The Origins of Bolshevism. Ed. and trans. Joel Carmichel. New

York: Harper and Row, 1964.

Davies, R. W., ed. From Tsarism to the New Economic Policy: Continuity and Change in the Economy of the USSR. Ithaca: Cornell University Press, 1991.

Diakin, Valentin S. Germanskie kapitaly v Rossii: elektroindustriia i elektricheskii transport. Leningrad: Nauka, 1971.

---------. Samoderzhavie, burzhuaziia i dvorianstvo v 1907-1911 gg. Leningrad: Nauka, 1978.

---------. Russkaia burzhuaziia i tsarizm v gody pervoi mirovoi voiny (1914-1917 gg.) Leningrad: Nauka, 1967.

Diakin, Valentin S., and others, eds. Krizis samoderzhaviia v Rossii, 1895-1917. Leningrad: Nauka, 1984.

Diakonova, I. A. Nobelevskaia korporatsiia v Rossii. Moscow: Mysl', 1980.

Dobb, Maurice. Soviet Economic Development since 1917. London: Routledge and Kegan Paul, 1948.

Dzieje burżuazii w Polsce: Studia i materiały. Edited by Ryszard Kołodziejczyk. Wroclaw, 1974, 1980, 1983.

Emmons, Terence. The Formation of Political Parties and the First National Elections in Russia. New York: Cambridge University Press, 1983.

Ermanskii, A. [Kogan, Osip A.] "Krupnaia burzhuaziia do 1905 goda." In Obshchestvennoe dvizhenie v Rossii v nachale XX-go veka, edited by L. Martov, P. Maslov, and A. Potresov. Vol. 1, 313-48. St. Petersburg: Obshchestvennaia pol'za, 1909.

---------. "Krupnaia burzhuaziia v 1905-1907 gg." In Obshchestvennoe dvizhenie v Rossii v nachale XX-go veka, edited by L. Martov, P. Maslov, and A. Potresov. Vol. 2, part 2, 30-100. St. Petersburg: Obshchestvennaia pol'za, 1910.

Ermanskii, Osip A. [Kogan, Osip A.] Iz perezhitogo (1887-1921 gg.). Moscow: Gosudarstvennoe izdatel'stvo, 1927.

Fainsod, Merle. How Russia is Ruled. Cambridge: Harvard University Press, 1953.

Fedorov, B. A. "K voprosu o formirovanii russkoi burzhuazii." Voprosy istorii, 1962, no. 7: 197-8.

Fenin, Aleksandr I. Coal and Politics in Late Imperial Russia: Memoirs of a Russian Mining Engineer. Trans. Alexandr Fediaevsky; ed. Susan P. McCaffray. DeKalb: Northern Illinois University Press, 1990.

"Finansovoe polozhenie Rossii pered Oktiabrskoi revoliutsiei." S predisloviem B. A. Romanova. Krasnyi Arkhiv 60 (25) (1927): 3-33.

Finn-Enotaevskii, A. Kapitalizm v Rossii (1890-1917 gg.) Moscow: Narodnoe komissariat finansov, 1925.

---------. Sovremennoe khoziaistvo Rossii (1890-1910 gg.) St. Petersburg: M. I. Semenov, 1911.

Fischer, George. Russian Liberalism from Gentry to Intelligentsia. Cambridge: Harvard University Press, 1958.

Flige, Nicholas. "Vopros o konkurentsii mezhdu obshchestvami i konkurentsiia s neaktsionernykh uchrezhdeniami i priviligirovannom polozhenii v kotorom nakhodilis' krupnye strakhovye obshchestva." Nikolai Nikolaevich Flige Papers. Bakhmeteff Archive. Columbia University Library, New York.

Florinsky, Michael T. Russia: A History and an Interpretation. 2 vols. New York: Macmillan, 1960.

Freeze, Gregory L. "The Soslovie (Estate) Paradigm and Russian Social History." American Historical Review 91 (1986): 11-36.

Fursenko, Aleksandr A. Neftianye tresty i mirovaia politika 1880-e godu-1918 g. Moscow and Leningrad: Nauka, 1965.

---------."Parizhskie rotshildy i russkaia neft'." Voprosy istorii, 1962, no. 8: 29-42.

---------. "Russkii Vanderbil't" [on Karl I. Iaroshinskii (Jaroszyński)]. Voprosy istorii, 1987, no. 10 (Oct.): 183-8.

Gatrell, Peter. The Tsarist Economy, 1850-1917. New York: St. Martin's Press, 1986.

---------. Government, Industry, and Rearmament in Russia, 1900-1914: The Last Argument of Tsarism. Cambridge: Cambridge University Press, 1994.

Gerschenkron, Alexander. "The Rate of Industrial Growth in Russia since 1855." Journal of Economic History, supplement to Vol. 7 (1947): 144-74.

---------. "The Problem of Economic Development in Russian Intellectual History of the Nineteenth Century." In Continuity and Change in Russian and Soviet Thought, edited by Ernest J. Simmons, 11-39. Cambridge: Harvard University Press, 1955.

---------. "Part I Review," in Continuity and Change, 100-9.

---------. Economic Backwardness in Historical Perspective. Cambridge: Harvard University Press, 1962.

Gindin, I. F. Russkie kommercheskie banki. Moscow: Gosfinizdat, 1948.

---------. "Russkaia burzhuaziia v period kapitalizma, ee razvitie i osobennosti." Istoriia SSSR, 1963, no. 2: 57-80; no. 3: 37-60.

---------. "O nekotorykh osobennostiakh ekonomicheskoi i sotsial'noi struktury rossiiskogo kapitalizma v nachale XX v." Istoriia SSSR, 1966, no. 3: 48-66.

Gindin, I. F., and L. E. Shepelev. "Bankovskie monopolii v Rossii nakanune Velikoi Oktiabr'skoi sotsialisticheskoi revoliutsii." Istoricheskie zapiski 66 (1960): 20-95.

Girault, René. "Sur quelques aspects financiers de l'alliance franco-russe," Revue d'histoire moderne et contemporaine 8 (1961): 69-76.

---------. Emprunts russes et investissements français en Russie, 1887-1914: recherches sur l'investissement international. Paris: A. Colin, 1973.

Glasgow International Exhibition. Russia. Its Industries and Trade. Glasgow: Hay Nisbet and Co., Ltd., 190l.

Glivits, Ippolit [Gliwic, Hypolit]. Potreblenie zheleza v Rossii. St. Petersburg, 1913.

Goldberg, Carl A. "The Association of Industry and Trade, 1906-1917: The Successes and Failures of Russia's Organized Businessmen." Doctoral dissertation, University of Michigan, 1974.

Goldsmith, Raymond. "The Economic Growth of Russia, 1860-1913." Economic Development and Cultural Change 9 (1961): 441-75.

Golikov, A. P. "K voprosu o sostave, soderzhanii i sokhrannosti dokumentov aktsionernykh kompanii." In Istochnikovedenie otechestvennoi istorii: sbornik statei, 1979, edited by V. I. Budagov, 134-56. Moscow: Akademiia nauk, 1980.

Golitsyn, Prince A. D. "Vospominaniia kniazia A. D. Golitsyna." Golitsyn Papers. Bakhmeteff Archive. Columbia University Library, New York.

Golman, M. Russkii imperializm. Ocherk razvitiia monopolisticheskogo kapitalizma v Rossii. Leningrad: Rabochee izdatel'stvo, 1927 (?).

Gorky, Maxim. Foma Gordeyev. London: Lawrence and Wishart, 1956.

Govorkov, A. A., Iia G. Mosina, and G. Kh. Rabinovich. "'Predstavitel'nye' organizatsii burzhuazii v Sibiri (konets XIX v.-1914 g.)." Voprosy istorii Sibiri, vyp. 6 = Trudy Tomskogo . . . universiteta 226 (1972): 26-40.

Grave, B. B., ed. 1917 goda v dokumentakh i materialakh. Burzhuaziia nakanune fevral'skoi revoliutsii. Moscow and Leningrad: Gosudarstvennoe izdatel'stvo, 1927.

Gregory, Paul R. Russian National Income, 1885-1913. New York: Cambridge University Press, 1982.

----------. Before Command: An Economic History of Russia from Emancipation to the First Five-Year Plan. Princeton: Princeton University Press, 1994.

Grinevetskii, V. I. Poslevoennye perspektivy russkoi promyshlennosti. 2nd ed. Moscow: Vserossiiskii tsentral'nyi soiuz potrebitel'nykh obshchestv, 1922.

Gurko, Vladimir I. Nashe gosudarstvennoe i narodnoe khoziaistvo. Doklad predstavlennyi Vserossiiskomu s"ezdu upolnomochennykh ob"edinennykh dvorianskikh obshchestv. St. Petersburg, 1909.

Guroff, Greg, and Fred V. Carstensen, eds. Entrepreneurship in Imperial Russia and the Soviet Union. Princeton: Princeton University Press, 1983.

Gushka, A. [Kogan, Osip A.] Predstavitel'nye organizatsii torgovo-promyshlennogo klassa v Rossii. St. Petersburg: Imperatorskoe Russkoe Tekhnicheskoe Obshchestvo, 1912.

Haimson, Leopold. "The Problem of Social Stability in Urban Russia, 1905-1917." Slavic Review 23 (1964): 619-642, and 24 (1965): 1-22.

Hamm, Michael F., ed. The City in Late Imperial Russia. Bloomington: Indiana University Press, 1986.

Hartl, Johann. Die Interessenvertretungen der russischen Industrie in den Jahren 1905-1914. Vienna: Bohlau, 1987.

Haumann, Heiko. Kapitalismus im zaristischen Staat 1906-1917: Organisationsformen, Machtverhältnisse, und Leistungsbilanz im Industrialisierungsprozess. Königstein/Ts.: Hain, 1980.

Henriksson, Anders. The Tsar's Loyal Germans: The Riga German Community, Social Change and the Nationality Question, 1855-1905. Boulder, CO: Westview Press, 1983.

Hildermeier, Manfred. Bürgertum und Stadt in Russland 1760-1870: Rechtliche Lage und soziale Struktur. Cologne: Böhlau, 1986.

Hogan, Heather J. Forging Revolution: Metalworkers, Managers, and the State in St. Petersburg, 1890-1914. Bloomington: Indiana University Press, 1993.

Iswolsky, Alexander. Recollections of a Foreign Minister. Trans. Charles Louis Seeger. New York: Doubleday, Page and Co., 1921.

Ivaniukov, I. I. Promyshlenno-torgovye organizatsii za granitsei. [Report to the First Congress of the Union of Commercial-Industrial Enterprises.] St. Petersburg, 1906.

Joffe, Muriel. "Regional Rivalry and Economic Nationalism: The Central Industrial Region Industrialists' Strategy for the Development of the Russian Economy, 1880's-1914." Russian History 11 (1984): 389-421.

----------. "Autocracy, Capitalism, and Empire: The Politics of Irrigation." Russian Review 54, no. 3 (1995): 365-88.

Kahan, Arcadius. "Notes on Jewish Entrepreneurship." In Entrepreneurship in Imperial Russia and the Soviet Union, edited by Greg Guroff and Fred V.Carstensen, 104-24. Princeton: Princeton University Press, 1983.

---------. Russian Economic History: The Nineteenth Century. Ed. Roger Weiss. Chicago: University of Chicago Press, 1989.

Kennan, George F. "America and the Russian Future." Foreign Affairs 29, no. 3 (1951): 351-70.

Kerensky, Alexander. Russia and History's Turning Point. New York: Duell, Sloan, and Pearce, 1965.

Khromov, P. A. Ekonomicheskoe razvitie Rossii v XIX-XX vekakh, 1800-1917. Moscow: Gosudarstvennoe izdatel'stvo politicheskoi literatury, 1950.

---------. Ocherki ekonomiki Rossii perioda monopolisticheskogo kapitalizma. Moscow: Izdatel'stvo VPSh i AON pri TsK KPSS, 1960.

King, Victoria. "The Emergence of the St. Petersburg Industrialist Community, 1870-1905: The Origins and Early Years of the Petersburg Society of Manufacturers." Doctoral dissertation, University of California, Berkeley, 1982.

Kirchner, Walther. Die deutsche Industrie und die Industrialisierung Russlands 1815-1914. St. Katharinen: Scripta Mercaturae, 1986.

Kovalewsky, Maxime. Le regime économique de la Russie. Paris: V. Girard et E. Brière, 1898.

Kokovtsov, V. N. Iz moego proshlogo: vospominaniia 1903-1919 gg. N.p., 1933.

Labry, Raoul. L'Industrie russe et la Révolution. Paris: Payot, 1919.

Laverychev, Vladimir Ia. "Vserossiiskii soiuz torgovli i promyshlennosti." Istoricheskie zapiski 70 (1961): 35-60.

---------. Po to storonu barrikad. (Iz istorii bor'by Moskovskoi burzhuazii s revoliutsiei). Moscow: Mysl', 1967.

---------. Krupnaia burzhuaziia v poreformennoi Rossii (1861-1900 gg.). Moscow: Mysl', 1974.

Leites, K. Recent Economic Developments in Russia. Oxford: Clarendon Press, 1922.

Lenin, Vladimir I. "Anketa ob organizatsiiakh krupnogo kapitala." Sochineniia. 4th edition. 35 vols. Moscow: Gosudarstvennoe izdatel'stvo politicheskoi literatury, 1941-51. Vol. 18, 46-7. [Following references are to this edition.]

---------. "Burzhuaznye del'tsy-finansisty i politiki." Vol. 19, 211-12.

---------. "Fabrikanty o rabochikh stachkakh." Vol. 19, 101-7.

---------. "Kapitalizm i nalogi." Vol. 19, 171-4.

---------. "Kupets Salazkin i pisatel' F. D." Vol. 19, 305-7.

---------. "Kupetskie raschety." Vol. 19, 39-40.

---------. "Liberaly i svoboda soiuzov." Vol. 19, 54-5.

---------. "O liberal'nom i marksistkom poniatii klassovoi borby." Vol. 19, 95-100.

---------. "O 'neftianom golode.'" Vol. 19, 13-16.

---------. "Politicheskie partii v Rossii." Vol. 18, 28-38.

---------. "Printsipial'nye voprosy politiki." Vol. 19, 314-16.

---------. "Raspushchennaia duma i rasteriannye liberaly." Vol. 19, 228-9.

---------. "Rossiiskaia burzhuaziia i rossiiskii reformizm." Vol. 19, 291-3.

---------. "Vekhovtsy i natsionalizm." Vol. 19, 52-3.

Litvinov-Falinskii, V. P. Nashe ekonomicheskoe polozhenie i zadachi budushchego.

St. Petersburg: V. F. Kirshbaum, 1908.
Livshin, Ia. I., "'Predstavitel'nye' organizatsii krupnoi burzhuazii v Rossii v kontse XIX-nachale XX vv." Istoriia SSSR, 1959, no. 2 (Mar.-Apr.): 95-117.
---------. Monopolii v ekonomike Rossii. Moscow: Izdatel'stvo sotsial'no-ekonomi cheskoi literatury, 1961.
Livshits, R. S. Razmeshchenie promyshlennosti v dorevoliutsionnoi Rossii. Moscow: Akademiia nauk, 1955.
Lure, E. S. Organizatsiia i organizatsii torgovo-promyshlennykh interesov v Rossii. St. Petersburg: S.-Petersburgskii politekhnicheskii institut Imperatora Petra Velikogo, 1913.
Liashchenko, P. I. Istoriia Narodnogo Khoziaistva SSSR. Moscow: Gosudarstvennoe izdatel'stvo politicheskoi literatury, 1956.
Lyashchenko [Liashchenko], Peter I. History of the National Economy of Russia. Trans. L. M. Herman. New York: Macmillan, 1949.
McCaffray, Susan P. "The Association of Southern Coal and Steel Producers and the Problems of Industrial Progress in Tsarist Russia." Slavic Review 47 (1988): 464-82.
---------. The Politics of Industrialization in Tsarist Russia: The Association of Southern Coal and Steel Producers, 1874-1914. DeKalb: Northern Illinois University Press, 1996.
McDaniel, Timothy. Autocracy, Capitalism, and Revolution in Russia. Berkeley: University of California Press, 1988.
---------. The Agony of the Russian Idea. Princeton: Princeton University Press, 1996.
McKay, John P. Pioneers for Profit: Foreign Entrepreneurship and Russian Industrialization, 1885-1913. Chicago: University of Chicago Press, 1970.
---------. "Baku Oil and Transcaucasian Pipelines, 1883-1900: A Study in Tsarist Economic Policy." Slavic Review 43 (1984): 603-23.
Medzykhovskii, K. Iu. O svobodnykh gavaniakh. St. Petersburg: K. I. Lingard, 1910.
Migulin, P. P. "Finansovaia politika i finansovyi krakh Sovetskoi Rossii," 1934. Columbia University Library, New York.
---------. "Kratkii ocherk razvitiia russkogo gosudarstvennogo dolga." Columbia University Library, New York.
---------. "Prichiny russkoi revoliutsii." Columbia University Library, New York.
Milyoukov, Paul. Russia and its Crisis. Chicago: University of Chicago Press, 1906.
Miller, Margaret S. The Economic Development of Russia, 1905-1914. 2nd ed., revised. London and New York: Frank Cass and Augustus M. Kelley, 1967.
Minarik, Liudmila P. Ekonomicheskaia kharakteristika krupneishikh zemel'nykh sobstvennikov Rossii kontsa XIX-nachala XX v. Moscow: Sovetskaia Rossiia, 1971.
Ministerstvo finansov. Pravitel'stvennye uchrezhdeniia i obshchestvennye organizatsii, obsluzhivaiushchie v Rossii i Germanii voprosy eksporta. Vol. 6 of Materialy k peresmotru russko-germanskogo torgovogo dogovora. St. Petersburg: Ministerstvo finansov, 1913.
---------. Otchet Soveshchaniia po voprosu o ponizhenii eksportnykh zheleznodorozhnykh tarifov na kerosin i smazochnye masla v napravlenii cherez Batum i Novo-

rossiisk. Zasedaniia sostoialis' 8 fevralia, 28 marta, 3 i 6 aprelia 1907 goda pri Departmente Zheleznodorozhnykh Del. St. Petersburg, 1907.
Ministerstvo torgovli i promyshlennosti. Voprosy vneshnei torgovoi politiki v russkoi povremennoi pechati. Petrograd: V. F. Kirshbaum, 1916.
---------. Smeta dokhodov i raskhodov i spetsial'nykh sredstv Ministerstva Torgovli i Promyshlennosti po obshchei chasti na 1912 g. St. Petersburg.
---------. Stenogrammy soveshchaniia o polozhenii metallurgicheskoi i mashinostroitel'noi promyshlennosti. St. Petersburg: V. F. Kirshbaum, 1908.
---------. Otdel torgovli. Dopolnenie k spravochnoi knige po torgovo-promyshlennoi chasti dlia imperatorskikh rossiiskikh konsulov. St. Petersburg, 1914.
Mosina, Iia G. Formirovanie burzhuazii v politicheskuiu silu v Sibiri. Tomsk: Tomskii universitet, 1978.
Na pamiat' o dni piatidesiatiletiia Emanuila Liudvigovicha Nobel'. Izdano komissiei sluzhashchikh Tovarishchestva neftianogo proizvodstva brat'ev Nobel'. Stockholm: The Nobel Institute, 1909.
Nemirovskii, A. O. Perspektivy russkoi promyshlennosti i torgovli. [Report to the First Congress of the Union of Commercial-Industrial Enterprises.] St. Petersburg, 1906.
Norman, John O. "Pavel Tretiakov and Merchant Art Patronage, 1850-1900." In Between Tsar and People: Educated Society and the Quest for Public Identity in Late Imperial Russia, edited by Edith W. Clowes, Samuel D. Kassow, and James L. West, 93-107. Princeton: Princeton University Press, 1991.
Obshchii s"ezd predstavitelei russkoi promyshlennosti i torgovli. Doklady. [Thirteen reports, paginated separately] Paris: Rirachovsky, 1921.
Organizatsionnoe Biuro S"ezda Promyshlennykh i Torgovykh Predpriiatii Rossiiskoi Imperii. Germanskii torgovyi S"ezd (Der Deutsche Handelstag). Doklad A. F. Volkova. St. Petersburg, 1906.
Owen, Thomas C. Capitalism and Politics in Russia: A Social History of the Moscow Merchants, 1855-1905. New York: Cambridge University Press, 1981.
---------. "The Russian Industrial Society and Tsarist Economic Policy, 1867-1905." Journal of Economic History 45 (1985): 587-606.
---------. The Corporation under Russian Law, 1800-1917: A Study in Tsarist Economic Policy. New York: Cambridge University Press, 1991.
---------. "Impediments to a Bourgeois Consciousness in Russia, 1880-1905: The Estate Structure, Ethnic Diversity, and Economic Regionalism." In Between Tsar and People: Educated Society and the Quest for Public Identity in Late Imperial Russia, edited by Edith W. Clowes, Samuel D. Kassow, and James L. West, 75-89. Princeton: Princeton University Press, 1991.
---------. Russian Corporate Capitalism from Peter the Great to Perestroika. New York: Oxford University Press, 1995.
Ozeroff [Ozerov], Ivan. Problèmes économiques et financiers de la Russie moderne. Paris: Payot, 1916.
Ozerov, Ivan Khristoforovich. Ekonomicheskaia Rossiia i ee finansovaia politika na iskhode XIX i v nachale XX veka. Moscow: I. N. Kushnerev, 1905.
---------. K voprosu o nashikh severnykh lesakh. Moscow: I. D. Sytin, 1911.
---------. Na temy dnia: K ekonomicheskomu polozheniiu Rossii. Moscow: Khudozhestvennaia pechat', 1912.

Pares, Bernard. My Russian Memoirs. London: J. Cape, 1931.

Pervushin, Sergei A. Khoziaistvennaia kon"iunktura: vvedenie v izuchenie dinamiki russkogo narodnogo khoziaistva za polveka. Moscow: Ekonomicheskaia zhizn', 1925.

----------. "Cyclical Fluctuations in Agriculture and Industry in Russia." Trans. Simon Kuznets. Quarterly Journal of Economics 42 (1928): 563-92.

Petrov, M. Progressivnaia ekonomicheskaia partiia: Organizatsiia i partiia peterburgskikh fabrikantov i zavodchikov. St. Petersburg: Donskaia rech', 1906.

Picheta, Vladimir I. Istoriia narodnogo khoziaistva v Rossii XIX-XX v. Moscow, 1922.

Pietrzak-Pawłowska, Irena. "Z dziejów monopolizacji gornictwa i hutnictwa w Królestwie Polskim (Zjazdy przemyslowców w latach 1883-1914)." Kwartalnik Historyzcny 63, no. 4-5 (1956): 341-67.

Pokrovskii, S. A. Vneshniaia torgovlia i vneshniaia torgovaia politika Rossii. Moscow: Mezhdunarodnaia kniga, 1947.

Polnyi sbornik platform vsekh russkikh politicheskikh partii s prilozheniem Vysochaishego Manifesta 17 oktiabria 1905 g. i vsepoddaneishego doklada grafa Vitte. St. Petersburg: N. N. Sh., 1906.

Portal, Roger. "Aux origines d'une bourgeoisie industrielle en Russie." Revue d'histoire moderne et contemporaine 8 (1961): 35-61.

----------. "Industriels moscovites: le secteur cotonnier," Cahiers du monde russe et soviétique 4, no. 1-2 (1963): 4-46.

Potolov, S. I. "Iz istorii monopolizatsii ugol'noi promyshlennosti Donbassa v kontse XIX v." In Iz istorii imperializma v Rossii, edited by M. P. Viatkin, 5-25. Moscow and Leningrad: Akademiia nauk, 1959.

Raud, V. N. Ekonomicheskie predposylki pervoi russkoi revoliutsii 1905-1907 gg. Leningrad: Leningradskii universitet, 1956.

Reikhardt, V. V. "Russkaia burzhuaziia v bor'be za sokhranenie ekonomicheskogo gospodstva (fevral'-oktiabr' 1917 g.)." Krasnaia letopis' 1 (34) (1930): 5-46.

----------. "Partiinye gruppirovki i 'predstavitel'stvo interesov' krupnogo kapitala v 1905-06 godakh." Krasnaia letopis' 6 (39) (1930): 5-39.

Rieber, Alfred J. Merchants and Entrepreneurs in Imperial Russia. Chapel Hill: University of North Carolina Press, 1982.

Rodzianko, M. V. "Gosudarstvennaia Duma i fevral'skaia revoliutsiia 1917 goda." Arkhiv russkoi revoliutsii vol. 6 (Berlin: Slovo, 1922), 5-80.

----------. "Krushenie Imperii (Zapiski predsedatelia Russkoi Gosudarstvennoi Dumy)." Arkhiv russkoi revoliutsii, vol. 17 (Berlin: Slovo, 1926), 5-169.

Roosa, Ruth AmEnde. "Russian Industrialists Look to the Future: Thoughts on Economic Development, 1906-1917." In Essays in Russian and Soviet History in Honor of Geroid Tanquary Robinson, edited by John S. Curtiss, 198-218. New York: Columbia University Press, 1963.

----------. "The Association of Industry and Trade, 1906-1914: An Examination of the Economic Views of Organized Industrialists in Prerevolutionary Russia." Doctoral dissertation, Columbia University, 1967.

----------. "Russian Industrialists and 'State Socialism', 1906-1917." Soviet Studies 23, no. 3 (1972): 395-417.

----------. "'United' Russian Industry." Soviet Studies 24, no. 3 (1973): 421-5.

----------. "Russian Industrialists, Politics, and the Labor Reform in 1905." Russian History 2 (1975): 124-48.

----------. "Workers' Insurance Legislation and the Role of the Industrialists in the Period of the Third State Duma." The Russian Review 34 (1975): 410-52.

----------. "Russian Industrialists during World War I: The Interaction of Economics and Politics." In Entrepreneurship in Imperial Russia and the Soviet Union, edited by Greg Guroff and Fred V. Carstensen, 159-87. Princeton: Princeton University Press, 1983.

----------. "Russian Industrialists and 'obščestvennost' 1880-1917." In Studier i politik, historia och ekonomi: Festskrift tillagnad Lolo Krusius-Ahrenberg 21.6.1989 / Essays in Politics, History and Economics in Honour of Lolo Krusius-Ahrenberg, edited by M.-L. von Bergmann-Winberg, G. Ahonen, and K. Hellbom, 237-55. Helsinki: Swedish School of Economics and Business Administration, 1989.

----------. "Banking and Financial Relations between Russia and the United States." In International Banking, 1870-1914, edited by Rondo Cameron and Valerii I. Bovykin, 291-318. New York: Oxford University Press, 1991.

Rosenberg, William G. "Representing Workers and the Liberal Narrative of Modernity." Slavic Review 55, no. 2 (1996): 245-69.

Rosenthal, Bernice G. "The Search for a Russian Orthodox Work Ethic." In Between Tsar and People: Educated Society and the Quest for Public Identity in Late Imperial Russia, edited by Edith W. Clowes, Samuel D. Kassow, and James L. West, 57-74. Princeton: Princeton University Press, 1991.

Ruckman, JoAnn S. The Moscow Business Elite: A Social and Cultural Portrait of Two Generations, 1840-1905. DeKalb: Northern Illinois University Press, 1984.

Ruud, Charles A. Russian Entrepreneur: Publisher Ivan Sytin of Moscow, 1851-1934. Montreal: McGill-Queen's University Press, 1990.

Schneiderman, Jeremiah. Sergei Zubatov and Revolutionary Marxism: The Struggle for the Working Class in Tsarist Russia. Ithaca: Cornell University Press, 1976.

Schwarz, Solomon M. "Populism and Early Russian Marxism on Ways of Economic Development in Russia." In Continuity and Change in Russian and Soviet Thought, edited by Ernest J. Simmons, 40-62. Cambridge: Harvard University Press, 1955.

Sef, S. E. Burzhuaziia v 1905 godu po neizdannym arkhivnym materialam. Moscow: Gosudarstvennoe izdatel'stvo, 1926.

Seton-Watson, Hugh. The Decline of Imperial Russia. London: Methuen, 1952.

Shatsillo, Kornelii F. "Formirovanie finansovogo kapitala v sudostroitel'noi promy shlennosti Iuga Rossii." In Iz istorii imperializma v Rossii, edited by M. P. Viatkin, 26-56. Moscow and Leningrad: Akademiia nauk, 1959.

----------. ed. "K voprosu o nalichii v Rossii monopolisticheskikh organizatsii vysshego tipa." Istoricheskii Arkhiv, 1960, no. 3: 126-42.

Shepelev, Leonid E. "K istorii toplivnogo 'goloda' v Rossii nakanune pervoi mirovoi voiny." Istoricheskii arkhiv, 1957, no. 1: 59-78.

----------. "Aktsionernoe uchreditel'stvo v Rossii (istoriko-statisticheskii ocherk)." In Iz istorii imperializma v Rossii, edited by M. P. Viatkin, 134-82. Moscow and Leningrad: Akademiia nauk, 1959.

----------. "Aktsionernaia statistika v dorevoliutsionnoi Rossii." In Monopolii i inostrannyi kapital v Rossii, edited by M. P. Viatkin, 165-207. Moscow and Leningrad: Akademiia nauk, 1962.

---------. Aktsionernye kompanii v Rossii. Leningrad: Nauka, 1973.

---------. Tsarizm i burzhuaziia vo vtoroi polovine XIX veka: problemy torgovo-promyshlennoi politiki. Leningrad: Nauka, 1981.

---------. Tsarizm i burzhuaziia v 1904-1914 gg.: problemy torgovo-promyshlennoi politiki. Leningrad: Nauka, 1987.

---------. "Business Organizations in the Russian Empire, 1906-14." Russian Studies in History 34, no. 1 (1995): 40-88.

Shpolianskii, D. I. Monopolii ugol'no-metallurgicheskoi promyshlennosti Iuga Rossii v nachale XX veka. Moscow: Akademiia nauk, 1953.

Shumilov, M. M. "Proekty reformy predstavitel'nykh torgovo-promyshlennykh organizatsii Rossii v kontse XIX-nachale XX v." Istoricheskie zapiski 118 (1990): 292-312.

Sidorov, A. L. "Nekotorye problemy razvitiia rossiiskogo kapitalizma v sovetskoi istoricheskoi nauke." Voprosy istorii, 1961, no. 12: 26-62.

Siegelbaum, Lewis H. The Politics of Industrial Mobilization in Russia, 1914-1917. New York: Cambridge University Press, 1983.

Sobolev, M. N. Ocherki ekonomicheskoi politiki promyshlennosti i torgovli. Kharkov, 1916.

Solovieva, Aida M. "Pribyli krupnoi promyshlennoi burzhuazii v aktsionernykh obshchestvakh Rossii v kontse XIX-nachale XX veka." Istoriia SSSR, 1984, no. 3 (May-June): 34-49.

Sorokin, A. K. "Izuchenie v otechestvennoi istoriografii pribylei kapitalisticheskikh predpriiatii Rossii." Istoriia SSSR, 1989, no. 6 (Nov.-Dec.): 104-18.

Sovet S"ezda Gornopromyshlennikov Iuga Rossii. Spravochnaia Kniga dlia Gornopromyshlennikov Iuga Rossii. Sostavlena Tekhnícheskom Otdelom Soveta S"ezda. 16 marta 1916 g., No. 623. Kharkov, 1916.

Spasskii, P. Kh. ed. Istoricheskii ocherk razvitiia torgovykh uchrezhdenii v Rossii. St. Petersburg: Imperatorskoe uchrezhdenie glukhonemykh (Alenevoi), 1911.

---------. ed. Istoriia torgovli i promyshlennosti v Rossii. St. Petersburg: Gaevskii, 1910.

Strumilin, S. G. Ocherki ekonomicheskoi istorii Rossii. Moscow: Izdatel'stvo sotsial'no-ekonomicheskoi literatury, 1960.

Struve, Peter. "The Past and Present of Russian Economics." In Russian Realities and Problems, edited by J. D. Duff, 47-82. Cambridge: Cambridge University Press, 1917.

Svedeniia o deiatel'nosti i literaturnykh trudakh izbrannogo Khar'kovskim birzhevym komitetom v vyborshchiki Gosudarstvennogo soveta N. F. fon-Ditmara. Kharkov, 1912.

Szporluk, Roman. Communism and Nationalism: Karl Marx versus Friedrich List. Oxford: Oxford University Press, 1988.

Timberlake, Charles E., ed. Essays in Russian Liberalism. Columbia, Missouri: University of Missouri Press, 1972.

Tolf, Robert W. The Russian Rockefellers: The Saga of the Nobel Family and the Russian Oil Industry. Stanford: Stanford University Press, 1976.

Torgovo-Promyshlennaia Gazeta. Nos. 82-235, 1906.

Treadgold, Donald. "The Constitutional Democrats and the Russian Liberal Tradition." American Slavic and East European Review 10 (1951): 85-94.

Tsykernik, A. L. "Popytki restavratsii sindikata 'Prodamet' na Ukraine v 1918 g." Istoricheskii arkhiv, 1958, no. 3: 144-51.

Tugan-Baranovskii, Mikhail I. K luchshemu budushchemu. St. Petersburg: Energiia, 1912.

Volkov, A. F. Blizhaishie zadachi i tseli proektiruemogo Soiuza Promyshlennykh i Torgovykh Predpriiatii Rossiiskoi Imperii. [Report to the First Congress of the Union of Commercial-Industrial Enterprises.] St. Petersburg, 1906.

Volobuev, P. V., ed. "Predprinimatel'skie organizatsii Russkoi burzhuazii v dni oktiabria." Istoricheskii arkhiv, 1959, no. 3: 205-8.

----------. ed. "Iz istorii bor'by Vremennogo pravitel'tva s revoliutsiei." Istoricheskii arkhiv, 1960, no. 5: 78-86.

----------. "Ekonomicheskaia programma burzhuazii i Vremennogo pravitel'stva." Istoricheskie zapiski 67 (1960): 19-76.

----------. "Monopolisticheskii kapital i ekonomicheskaia politika Vremennogo pravitel'stva." Istoriia SSSR, 1960, no. 1: 34-58.

----------. "Monopolisticheskaia burzhuaziia i Vremennoe Pravitel'stvo." In Monopolii i inostrannyi kapital v Rossii, edited by M. P. Viatkin, 240-73. Moscow and Leningrad: Akademiia nauk, 1962.

----------. Proletariat i burzhuaziia Rossii v 1917 godu. Moscow: Mysl', 1964.

Volskii, Adolf A. Proizvoditel'nye sily i ekonomichesko-finansovaia politika Rossii. 2nd ed., revised. Doklad Soveshchatel'noi Kontore Zhelezozavodchikov. St. Petersburg: V. Kirshbaum, 1905.

----------. Predstavitel'stvo russkoi promyshlennosti i torgovli v nastoiashchee vremia i osnovy predstavitel'stva, neobkhodimogo v blizhaishem budushchem. [Report to the First Congress of the Union of Commercial-Industrial Enterprises.] St. Petersburg, 1906.

Von Laue, Theodore H. "Sergei Witte on the Industrialization of Imperial Russia." Journal of Modern History 26 (1954): 61-74.

----------. "Count Witte and the Russian Revolution of 1905." American Slavic and East European Review 17 (1958): 25-46.

----------. Sergei Witte and the Industrialization of Russia. New York: Columbia University Press, 1963.

Vserossiiskii Soiuz Torgovli i Promyshlennosti. Vtoroi Vserossiiskii Torgovo-Promyshlennyi S"ezd v Moskve 3-5 avgusta 1917 g. Stenograficheskii otchet i rezoliutsii S"ezda. Moscow, 1917.

West, James L. "The Riabushinskii Circle: Burzhuaziia and Obshchestvennost' in Late Imperial Russia." In Between Tsar and People: Educated Society and the Quest for Public Identity in Late Imperial Russia, edited by Edith W. Clowes, Samuel D. Kassow, and James L. West, 41-56. Princeton: Princeton University Press, 1991.

Whitman, J. "Turkestan Cotton in Imperial Russia." American Slavic and East European Review 15 (1956): 190-205.

Wierzbicki, Andrzej. Wspomnienia i dokumenty, 1877-1920. Warsaw: Państwowe Wydawnictwo Naukowe, 1957.

Witte, Sergei Iu. Po povodu natsionalizma: National'naia ekonomika i Fridrikh List.

2nd ed. St. Petersburg: Brokgauz i Efron, 1912.
----------. Vospominaniia. Berlin: Slovo, 1922.
----------. The Memoirs of Count Witte. Trans. and ed. Sidney Harcave. Armonk, NY: M. E. Sharpe, 1990.
Zak, S. Promyshlennyi kapitalizm v Rossii. Moscow: Sotrudnichestvo, 1908.
Żukowski, W. [Zhukovskii, Vladislav V.] "Polish Economic Policy." Russian Review (London) 3, no. 1 (1914): 159-66.

Index

Ruth AmEnde Roosa, professor, scholar, and author, had a long career as a historian specializing in prerevolutionary Russian economic history during the late nineteenth and twentieth centuries. Her academic interests included all of Russian and Soviet history as well as modern problems in international relations and Soviet foreign policy.

Born in 1919, she graduated magna cum laude from Classical High School in Providence, Rhode Island. She received an A.B. from Brown University in 1941, an M.A. in European history from Radcliffe College in 1942, a Certificate of the Russian Institute at Columbia University in 1948, and a Ph.D. in Russian and European history from Columbia University in 1967.

After working as a research analyst for the U.S. Office of Strategic Services in Washington, D.C., and London during World War II and as a special assistant to the U.S. Ambassador in London from 1945 to 1946, she returned to graduate studies, but with a focus on Russian history, and soon began a ten-year period as a lecturer in Russian studies and associate in history at Barnard College. Subsequently, she became a lecturer and adjunct professor at Briarcliff College. She also worked at the Russian Institute (later the Harriman Institute) at Columbia University as a visiting and then resident scholar.

Dr. Roosa authored numerous articles largely focused on Russian industrialists and entrepreneurship in the early twentieth century and she traveled often to the former Soviet Union for conferences and research. She died in 1993.

Thomas C. Owen, who received a Ph.D. in history at Harvard University, is a professor of history at Louisiana State University. He is the author of *Capitalism and Politics in Russia: A Social History of the Moscow Merchants, 1855–1905, The Corporation Under Russian Law, 1800–1917,* and *Russian Corporate Capitalism from Peter the Great to Perestroika.*